Cooking at Home

THE MAGAZINE RECIPE COLLECTION

Pictured on front cover:
Mediterranean Chicken and Bean Casserole, page 139

Nutrition Information Guidelines

Each recipe has been analyzed using the Canadian Nutrient File from Health Canada, which is based upon the United States Department of Agriculture (USDA) Nutrient Database.

• If more than one ingredient is listed (such as "hard margarine or butter"), or if a range is given (1 - 2 tsp., 5 - 10 mL), only the first ingredient or first amount is analyzed.

• The lesser number of servings is used if a range is stated.

• Ingredients indicating "sprinkle," "optional" or "for garnish" are not included in the nutrition information.

• Milk used is 1% M.F. (milkfat), unless otherwise stated.

• Cooking oil is canola oil, unless otherwise stated.

Margaret Ng, B. Sc. (Hon.), M.A.
Registered Dietitian

Cooking at Home
Copyright © Company's Coming Publishing Limited

First Printing October 2007

Library and Archives Canada Cataloguing in Publication
Cooking at home / Roxanne Higuchi, editor.
(Special occasion series)
Includes index.
ISBN 978-1-897069-45-5
1. Cookery. I. Higuchi, Roxanne, 1963- II. Series
TX715.6.H54 2007   641.5   C2006-906710-4

Published by
Company's Coming Publishing Limited
2311 – 96 Street
Edmonton, Alberta, Canada T6N 1G3
Tel: 780-450-6223   Fax: 780-450-1857
www.companyscoming.com

Company's Coming is a registered trademark owned by
Company's Coming Publishing Limited

We acknowledge the financial support of the Government of Canada through the Book Publishing Industry Development Program (BPIDP) for our publishing activities.

Printed in China

Cooking at Home

Editorial Director	Roxanne Higuchi
Editors	Rita Feutl
	Amy Hough
Copyeditor	Laurie Penner
Proofreader	Deborah Lawson
Designer	Jaclyn Draker
Cover Design	Hank Leonhardt

Cooking at Home could not have been put together without the talented teams in the Company's Coming Production Department and Recipe Factory. We appreciate their commitment and professionalism.

Our thanks also go to those whose creativity sparked the original *Cooking at Home* magazine and thus, this book: Jean Paré, Grant Lovig, Roxanne Higuchi, Derrick Sorochan, Eleanor Gasparik, Lovoni Walker, Stephanie Amodio, Patricia Meili-Bullock, Halkier + Dutton Strategic Design and Stephe Tate Photo.

We gratefully acknowledge the following suppliers for their generous support of our Test and Photography Kitchens:

Broil King Barbecues
Corelle®
Hamilton Beach® Canada
Lagostina®
Proctor Silex® Canada
Tupperware®

Our special thanks to the following businesses for providing props for photography:

Barbecue Country	Michael's the Arts and Crafts Store
Bernardin	Mikasa Home Store
Bissett Stained Glass	Out of the Fire Studio
Call the Kettle Black	Pier 1 Imports
CC on Whyte	Rocky Mountain Antique Mall
Cherison Enterprises Inc.	Scona Clayworks
Chintz & Company	Stokes
Danesco Inc.	The Bay
Dansk Gifts	The Paderno Factory Store
Emile Henry	Treasure Barrel
Kitchen Treasures	Wal-Mart Canada Inc.
La Cache	Winners Stores
Le Gnome	Zellers
Linens N' Things	Zenari's

Table of Contents

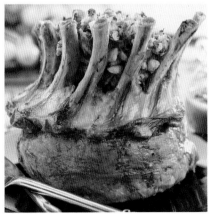

Foreword

During my travels across Canada to talk about my work, I've had the pleasure of meeting many keen cooks who share my passion for good food. I've often come home from these trips with scribbled notes or frayed index cards tucked into my purse, generous gifts from people who want to share their treasured recipes with me.

It was that spirit of generosity that inspired us to create *Cooking at Home* magazine in 2001. Here at Company's Coming, we felt it was time for Canadian food enthusiasts to have a forum where they could exchange stories, tips, and, above all, recipes. If a farmer from a Cape Breton cranberry bog was willing to share her recipe for Cranberry Chutney or Lumber Camp Squares, we would print it. And if a Quebec maple syrup farmer or Okanagan cherry cultivator knew of a great dish to showcase their harvest, what a lovely opportunity to let other Canadians taste this bounty. Try the Quebec Sugar Pie or the Chicken with Sage and Cherries and see if you don't agree.

Of course, we didn't restrict ourselves to food producers. As the issues unfolded, we were delighted to learn about the dishes required for a traditional Ukrainian Christmas Eve dinner, the recipes that a Saskatchewan hockey mom needs to keep her large brood happy, and the fabulous flavour combinations used by a family with roots in northern India. The Ali family's Matchli Soup and Pumpkin Curry will have you dreaming of exotic spice markets!

We sourced the best recipes from Kitchener-Waterloo's Oktoberfest, crashed a dinner group's Tuscan-inspired party, and reported on culinary delights from the Old City Market in Saint John, NB. From everyday cooking to special entertaining, we wanted to show how Canada cooks. Some of our contributors were professionals, but many were your friends and neighbours, regular people who appreciate delicious food.

Naturally, we couldn't resist the fun, and our test kitchen also created recipes for each issue. Whether it was a harvest soup, an elegant New Year's Eve appetizer, a spring luncheon salad or a summer picnic entree, we created dishes to suit nature's changing seasons. And every recipe, whether it was one of ours or from a contributor, was tested and retested until it met our high standards.

By the time *Cooking at Home* magazine stopped publication, we had a collection of over 480 recipes. Now, for the first time, we've gathered every one into this convenient treasury: the *Cooking at Home* cookbook. Devoted fans and contributors to the magazine now have a full-colour, hard-cover compilation to call their own (we've maintained the magazine's style and reprinted the contributor index at the back), while new readers can easily access these wonderful meal suggestions. We've sorted them into chapters ranging from appetizers to treats, and you'll find ideas to take care of breakfast, lunch and dinner. Barbecue buffs, home canners and even pressure cooker fans will find recipes that address their interests.

Scattered through each chapter is helpful information to make your cooking experience successful. We've included many of the magazine's handy tips and illustrated, step-by-step directions. We cover such basics as gravy making and apple coring along with more advanced (but still easy!) instructions for making nori cones or chocolate filigrees. You'll learn how to butterfly a salmon, make a truffle tree and tell the difference between a Belgian endive and a curly endive. Our elaborate Halloween cake can become a wonderful taste-and-learn afternoon for foodies young and old!

In fact, that's the joy, and the point, of *Cooking at Home*. These simple-to-follow dishes from across the country can be created in your own kitchen and shared with family and friends. Try a recipe today—and take part in Canada's enthusiasm for great food.

Jean Paré

Appetizers

Hot Artichoke and Spinach Dip, below.

Hot Artichoke and Spinach Dip

"I love serving this dip with fun summer drinks, like margaritas or slushes, and tostado chips or crackers. A single batch is usually never enough. Add more hot pepper sauce if you like more bite."
— Linda Craig, Edmonton, Alberta

Light cream cheese	8 oz.	250 g
Low-fat salad dressing (or mayonnaise)	1 cup	250 mL
Low-fat sour cream	1 cup	250 mL
Can of artichoke hearts, drained and coarsely chopped	14 oz.	398 mL
Garlic cloves, minced	4	4
Frozen chopped spinach, thawed and squeezed dry	10 oz.	284 g
Grated Parmesan cheese	1/3 cup	75 mL
Hot pepper sauce, dash		
Chopped fresh chives, for garnish		

Mix first 8 ingredients in 1 1/2 quart (1.5 L) casserole. Cover and bake in 350°F (175°C) oven for about 15 minutes until hot.

Sprinkle with chives. Makes 4 2/3 cups (1.15 L).

2 tbsp. (30 mL): 45 Calories; 3.5 g Total Fat; 130 mg Sodium; 1 g Protein; 2 g Carbohydrate; trace Dietary Fibre

Pictured above.

Shrimp and Crab Dip

"My aunt made this for my wedding and I've been making it ever since. It's a terrific Friday night feast—crusty chunks of bread, crackers and fresh veggies all go great with the filling."
— Heather Cunningham, Lashburn, Saskatchewan

Loaf of unsliced French bread	1	1
DIP		
Cream cheese, softened	8 oz.	250 g
Frozen cooked medium shrimp, thawed	4 3/4 oz.	130 g
Can of crabmeat, drained and cartilage removed, flaked	4 1/4 oz.	120 g
Chopped onion (about 1 small)	1/2 cup	125 mL
Salad dressing (or mayonnaise)	3 tbsp.	50 mL
Grated part-skim mozzarella cheese	1 1/2 cups	375 mL

Hollow out loaf. Set aside chunks for dipping.

Dip: Combine all 6 ingredients in medium bowl. Mix well. Turn into bread. Wrap in foil. Bake in 250°F (120°C) oven for 1 1/2 hours. Makes 3 cups (750 mL) dip. Serve with bread chunks.

2 tbsp. (30 mL) dip only: 250 Calories; 13.1 g Total Fat; 446 mg Sodium; 11 g Protein; 22 g Carbohydrate; 1 g Dietary Fibre

Plantain and Yam Crisps with Avocado Dip

"Many people have a bad first experience with plantain. Don't think of them as bananas—plantains are their greener, starchier cousin. They're best when deep-fried, as in this recipe. Enjoy these Caribbean potato chips!" Find plantains in your local Asian grocery store.

— **Jennifer Cockrall-King, Edmonton, Alberta**

Cooking oil, for deep-frying		
Large green plantains, thinly sliced	2	2
Peeled and thinly sliced yam (or sweet potato)	2 cups	500 mL
AVOCADO DIP		
Large ripe avocado, peeled, pitted and sliced	1	1
Lime juice	2 tbsp.	30 mL
Garlic clove, crushed	1	1
Green onions, finely chopped	2	2
Goat cheese, softened	3 oz.	85 g
Coconut milk	1 tsp.	5 mL
Chili powder	1/4 tsp.	1 mL
Salt	1/4 tsp.	1 mL
Freshly ground pepper, to taste		
Green onion, thinly sliced	1	1
Chili powder, sprinkle		

Heat enough cooking oil to deep-fry in large saucepan. Deep-fry plantain and yam, in batches, on medium-high for 2 to 3 minutes until golden. Remove with slotted spoon to paper towel to drain. Makes about 4 cups (1 L) crisps.

Avocado Dip: Combine next 9 ingredients in blender. Process until smooth. Place in serving bowl.

Sprinkle dip with second amounts of green onion and chili powder. Makes 1 1/2 cups (375 mL).

2 tbsp. (30 mL) dip plus 5 yam crisps and 3 plantain crisps: 229 Calories; 14.8 g Total Fat; 187 mg Sodium; 8 g Protein; 18 g Carbohydrate; 2 g Dietary Fibre

Pictured at right.

Seafood Cornmeal Parcels

"In Tobago, these are called 'pastelles.' I first tried them at a beach kitchen at Pigeon Point. Luckily the women from the kitchen shouted to me to 'peel off the ba-na-nah leaf before eatin' it' as they saw me struggling through the tough leaf wrapper." Banana leaves are available at Asian grocery stores.

— **Jennifer Cockrall-King, Edmonton, Alberta**

Medium onion, finely chopped	1	1
Garlic clove, crushed	1	1
Small red chili peppers, finely chopped♦	2	2
Finely grated gingerroot	2 tsp.	10 mL
Cooking oil	2 tbsp.	30 mL
Finely grated lime zest	1/2 tsp.	2 mL
Green onions, finely chopped	2	2
Small red pepper, finely chopped	1	1
Medium tomatoes, chopped	2	2
Uncooked shrimp, peeled and deveined, chopped	8 oz.	225 g
Cans of crabmeat (4 1/4 oz.,120 g, each), drained	2	2
Chopped fresh cilantro leaves	2 tbsp.	30 mL
Salt	1/4 tsp.	1 mL
Cornmeal	1 cup	250 mL
Hard margarine (or butter)	1 tbsp.	15 mL
Cooking oil	2 tsp.	10 mL
Salt	1/4 tsp.	1 mL
Boiling water	3/4 cup	175 mL
Banana leaves	1 lb.	454 g
Cooking oil	4 tsp.	20 mL
Boiling water	4 cups	1 L
Salt	1 tsp.	5 mL

Sauté first 4 ingredients in cooking oil in large frying pan on medium for 5 minutes until onion is soft.

Add next 8 ingredients. Cook for 3 minutes until shrimp starts to change colour. Cool.

Place cornmeal in medium bowl. Cut in margarine until crumbly. Stir in next 3 ingredients. Mix until smooth. Let stand for 5 minutes. Mix into seafood mixture. Makes 6 cups (1.5 L) filling.

Cut banana leaves into 8 x 10 inch (20 x 25 cm) rectangles. Place in large pan of boiling water. Boil for 1 minute. Drain. Pat dry with paper towels.

Brush third amount of cooking oil on banana leaves. Place 1/3 cup (75 mL) filling in centre of 1 leaf. Fold up sides of leaf to enclose filling. Fold ends under to make a parcel. Secure parcel with string. Repeat with remaining banana leaves and filling.

Place parcels in boiling water and salt in large saucepan. Reduce heat. Cover. Simmer for 45 minutes. Drain. Makes 18 parcels.

1 parcel (without banana leaf): 98 Calories; 5.1 g Total Fat; 150 mg Sodium; 5 g Protein; 8 g Carbohydrate; 1 g Dietary Fibre

♦Wear gloves when chopping chili peppers, and avoid touching your eyes.

Plantain and Yam Crisps with Avocado Dip, left

Deep Sea Spread

"This is best when the flavours can blend overnight." Definite crab flavour with a mild onion and pepper undertone. A wonderful spread on a variety of crackers or warm toasted French bread.

— Hannah Irene Hess, Edmonton, Alberta

Cream cheese, softened	8 oz.	250 g
Mayonnaise (not salad dressing)	1/2 cup	125 mL
Sour cream	1/2 cup	125 mL
Imitation crabmeat	1/2 lb.	225 g
Lemon juice	1 tbsp.	15 mL
Finely chopped onion	1/2 tsp.	2 mL
Worcestershire sauce	1 tsp.	5 mL
Salt	1/4 tsp.	1 mL
Freshly ground pepper	1/4 tsp.	1 mL
Finely chopped celery	1/3 cup	75 mL

Process all 10 ingredients in food processor until smooth. Spoon mixture into small bowl. Cover. Chill for 1 hour. Makes 3 1/2 cups (875 mL).

2 tbsp. (30 mL): 74 Calories; 6.9 g Total Fat; 136 mg Sodium; 2 g Protein; 1 g Carbohydrate; trace Dietary Fibre

Pictured below.

Southern-Style Meatballs with Cilantro Yogurt

The combination of pecans and fresh mint reminds us of the South and makes these little meatballs irresistible. They shape up in no time as a perfect barbecue party appetizer.

Lean ground beef	1 lb.	454 g
Small onion, finely chopped	1	1
Garlic cloves, crushed	3	3
Chopped pecans, toasted♦	1/2 cup	125 mL
Sweet chili sauce	3 tbsp.	50 mL
Large egg, fork-beaten	1	1
Dry bread crumbs	1/3 cup	75 mL
Chopped fresh mint leaves	1/3 cup	75 mL
Ground cumin	1 tsp.	5 mL
Salt	1/2 tsp.	2 mL
Freshly ground pepper	1/2 tsp.	2 mL
4 inch (10 cm) bamboo skewers, soaked in water for 10 minutes	18	18

CILANTRO YOGURT

Plain yogurt	1 cup	250 mL
Chopped fresh cilantro	1/3 cup	75 mL
Lemon juice	1 tbsp.	15 mL
Ground cumin	1 tsp.	5 mL

Combine first 11 ingredients in large bowl. Mix well. Chill for 30 minutes. Shape into 36 balls, about 1 1/4 inches (3 cm) in size.

Preheat grill to medium-high. Place 2 meatballs on each skewer. Cook on greased grill for 5 minutes, turning several times. Reduce heat to medium. Cook for 5 to 8 minutes, turning occasionally, until browned and no longer pink inside. Makes 18 appetizer skewers.

Cilantro Yogurt: Combine all 4 ingredients in small bowl. Makes 1 1/3 cups (325 mL) dipping sauce. Serve with appetizer skewers. Serves 6.

1 serving: 271 Calories; 15.6 g Total Fat; 452 mg Sodium; 19 g Protein; 14 g Carbohydrate; 2 g Dietary Fibre

Pictured below.

♦*To toast the pecans, place them in an ungreased frying pan. Heat on medium, stirring often, until golden.*

Friendship

Deep Sea Spread, above

Southern-Style Meatballs with Cilantro Yogurt, above

Billy's Crab Cakes with Cajun Tartar Sauce

Chef Al Barriault, formerly of Billy's Seafood Company, tempted customers with new and different dishes as seasons changed. These zesty crab cakes were just one of his specialties.
— Billy's Seafood Company, Old City Market, Saint John, New Brunswick

Cans of crabmeat (4 1/4 oz., 120 g, each), drained, cartilage removed, flaked	4	4
Dijon mustard	1/4 cup	60 mL
Mayonnaise (not salad dressing)	1/2 cup	125 mL
Cajun seasoning	2 tsp.	10 mL
Large eggs	2	2
Chopped fresh parsley	2 tbsp.	30 mL
Dry bread crumbs	2 1/2 cups	625 mL
Cooking oil, for deep-frying		

CAJUN TARTAR SAUCE

Cajun seasoning	2 tsp.	10 mL
Garlic cloves, crushed	2	2
Freshly ground pepper	1/2 tsp.	2 mL
Lemon juice	1/2 tsp.	2 mL
Sweet pickle relish	1 tsp.	5 mL
Mayonnaise (not salad dressing)	1 1/2 cups	375 mL
Finely chopped hot banana peppers♦	2 tbsp.	30 mL
Hot pepper sauce	1/2 tsp.	2 mL

Combine first 7 ingredients in large bowl. Divide and shape crabmeat mixture into 12 patties, using 1/3 cup (75 mL) each.

Deep-fry patties in cooking oil until golden. Remove with slotted spoon to paper towel to drain.

Cajun Tartar Sauce: Combine all 8 ingredients in medium bowl. Makes 1 2/3 cups (400 mL) sauce. Serve with crab cakes. Makes 12.

1 crab cake: 466 Calories; 38.6 g Total Fat; 772 mg Sodium; 0 g Protein; 19 g Carbohydrate; 1 g Dietary Fibre

Wear rubber gloves when chopping hot peppers, and avoid touching your eyes.

Brie and Pecan in Phyllo with Blueberry Relish, below

Brie and Pecan in Phyllo with Blueberry Relish

"A small, mild onion, the shallot is readily available in most any grocery store. It adds a subtle flavour to recipes without dominating other milder ingredients—like the blueberries in this relish."
— Dean Hossack, Kelowna, British Columbia

Frozen phyllo pastry sheets (12 inch, 30 cm, size), thawed according to package directions	3	3
Butter (not margarine), melted	1/2 cup	125 mL
Pecans, toasted and chopped♦	1/2 cup	125 mL
Brie cheese round, cut into 4 wedges	4 oz.	125 g

BLUEBERRY RELISH

Cooking oil	1 tsp.	5 mL
Shallots, finely chopped	2	2
Fresh (or frozen, thawed) blueberries	2 cups	500 mL
Red (or alcohol-free) wine	1/3 cup	75 mL
Corn syrup	1/3 cup	75 mL
Red wine vinegar	1/4 cup	60 mL
Salt	1 tsp.	5 mL
White pepper, to taste		

Cut each phyllo sheet into 4 squares. Brush 3 squares with melted butter. Stack.

Sprinkle centre of stack with 1/4 of pecans. Place 1 cheese wedge on top. Gather up corners of phyllo. Pinch into pouch. Repeat 3 times with remaining phyllo, pecans and cheese. Bake in 350°F (175°C) oven for about 20 minutes until phyllo is lightly browned and crispy. Makes 4.

Blueberry Relish: Heat cooking oil on medium in frying pan. Sauté shallots for 4 minutes until lightly browned.

Add blueberries. Reduce heat to medium-low. Add red wine and corn syrup. Simmer for 40 minutes, stirring occasionally, until reduced to consistency of jam.

Stir in red wine vinegar. Add salt and pepper. Makes 1 1/3 cups (300 mL) relish. Serve warm with phyllo pouches. Serves 4.

1 serving: 638 Calories; 45.8 g Total Fat; 1135 mg Sodium; 10 g Protein; 49 g Carbohydrate; 3 g Dietary Fibre

Pictured above.

♦To toast the pecans, place them in an ungreased frying pan. Heat on medium, stirring often, until golden.

Oysters with Crunchy Crumb Topping

Lightly seasoned fresh oysters on the half shell, broiled under a blanket of smoky bacon, Parmesan cheese and dilled crumbs, need only a wedge of lemon and a sprig of dill as the finishing touch.

Fresh oysters, in the shell	12	12
Worcestershire sauce	2 tbsp.	30 mL
Bacon slices, cooked crisp and crumbled	2	2
Fresh bread crumbs	2/3 cup	150 mL
Freshly grated Parmesan cheese	1/4 cup	60 mL
Chopped fresh dill	2 tsp.	10 mL
Lemon wedges, for garnish		
Fresh dill sprigs, for garnish		

Scrub oysters under cold running water. Place oyster on counter, flat side up, cup side down. Cover hand well with tea towel for protection from knife. Place covered hand on top of oyster. Hold firmly. Place shucking knife blade between top and bottom shell, near hinge.◆ Insert blade and twist to open oyster (see photo). Cut muscle joining shells together. Remove flat shell. Slip knife under oyster and release from shell. Leave oyster in cup shell, ready to cook. Repeat with remaining oysters.

Place oysters on ungreased baking sheet. Drizzle with Worcestershire sauce.

Combine next 4 ingredients in small bowl. Sprinkle over oysters. Broil 6 inches (15 cm) from heat for 3 to 5 minutes until golden brown. Garnish with lemon wedges and dill. Serves 2.

1 serving: 493 Calories; 16 g Total Fat; 1176 mg Sodium; 41 g Protein; 43 g Carbohydrate; 1 g Dietary Fibre

Pictured below.

◆If you don't have an oyster shucking knife, use a knife with a strong stainless steel blade.

Salt and Pepper Squid

Quick and easy to prepare, squid or calamari provides one of the best values in fresh seafood. It's a great choice when you want to serve a crowd and is also really tasty with tzatziki and fresh lemon or lime wedges. Make sure not to overcook.

Cornstarch	1/2 cup	125 mL
Ground ginger	1 tbsp.	15 mL
Chili powder	2 tsp.	10 mL
Salt	2 tsp.	10 mL
Freshly ground pepper	2 tsp.	10 mL
Squid tubes, cut into 1/2 inch (12 mm) slices	2 lbs.	900 g
Cooking oil, for deep-frying		
Sweet chili sauce, for dipping	1/2 cup	125 mL
Lime wedges, for garnish		

Combine first 5 ingredients in large bowl. Add squid. Mix well.

Cook squid mixture in large saucepan, in 4 batches, in hot 375°F (190°C) cooking oil until golden brown. Remove to paper towel to drain.

Serve with sweet chili sauce and lime wedges. Makes about 50 rings. Serves 6 to 8.

1 serving: 272 Calories; 8.8 g Total Fat; 1190 mg Sodium; 25 g Protein; 23 g Carbohydrate; 2 g Dietary Fibre

Creamy Grilled Scallops, below

Creamy Grilled Scallops

Every bit of tender scallop and sumptuous sauce will be gone when you serve this appealing dish. The sauce also marries well with combinations of shrimp, crab and scallops.

Small onion, finely chopped	1	1
Hard margarine (or butter)	2 tbsp.	30 mL
All-purpose flour	2 tbsp.	30 mL
Milk	1 1/2 cups	375 mL
Salt	1/4 tsp.	1 mL
Ground nutmeg	1/4 tsp.	1 mL
Large fresh (or frozen, thawed) scallops	24	24
Large scallop shells	8	8
Freshly grated Gruyère cheese	1/2 cup	125 mL
Freshly ground pepper, for garnish		
Fresh parsley sprigs, for garnish		

Sauté onion in margarine in small saucepan for about 5 minutes until soft.

Stir in flour until well mixed. Gradually stir in 1/4 cup (60 mL) milk until combined. Stir in remaining milk, salt and nutmeg. Bring to a boil. Reduce heat. Cook, uncovered, stirring frequently, on low for about 5 minutes until sauce is thickened.

Place 3 scallops on each shell. Spoon 3 tbsp. (50 mL) sauce over scallops.

Sprinkle each with 2 tbsp. (30 mL) cheese. Broil 6 inches (15 cm) from heat until scallops reach desired doneness and cheese is golden brown. Do not overcook scallops or they will become tough and rubbery.

Garnish with pepper and parsley. Serves 8.

1 serving: 126 Calories; 6.1 g Total Fat; 229 mg Sodium; 12 g Protein; 6 g Carbohydrate; trace Dietary Fibre

Pictured above.

Bruschetta with Basil

This is the perfect appetizer to make for those who can't eat dairy. When combined with the other ingredients, the chopped tofu provides a similar texture to cheese. (Don't worry, cheese lovers will like this, too!)

Loaf of Italian crusty bread (such as ciabatta), cut into 1/2 inch (12 mm) slices	1	1
Olive oil	1/4 cup	60 mL
Garlic clove, halved	1	1
Medium Roma (plum) tomatoes, quartered, seeded and chopped	6	6
Firm tofu, finely chopped	2/3 cup	150 mL
Finely chopped fresh sweet basil	1/4 cup	60 mL
Olive oil	3 tbsp.	50 mL
Balsamic (or red wine) vinegar	1 tbsp.	15 mL
Garlic clove, minced	1	1
Salt	1/4 tsp.	1 mL
Freshly ground pepper	1/2 tsp.	2 mL

Lightly brush both sides of bread slices with olive oil. Arrange in single layer on ungreased baking sheets. Broil for 2 to 3 minutes on each side until lightly browned. Rub both sides of bread slices with garlic.

Combine next 8 ingredients in medium bowl. Spoon onto bread slices just before serving. Serves 6 to 8 as an appetizer.

1 serving: 352 Calories; 21.2 g Total Fat; 406 mg Sodium; 10 g Protein; 33 g Carbohydrate; 3 g Dietary Fibre

Pictured below.

Pizza Strip Appetizer

This attractive appetizer takes its popular appeal from the pizza. Easy to put together and present, you'll make this often once your family tastes it.
— Patricia Gibb, St. Albert, Alberta

Package of frozen puff pastry, thawed according to package directions	14 oz.	397 g
Tomato paste	2 tbsp.	30 mL
Dried whole oregano	1/2 tsp.	2 mL
Freshly ground pepper, sprinkle		
Finely grated mozzarella cheese	2 cups	500 mL
Can of anchovy fillets, drained and finely chopped♦	1.75 oz.	50 g
Large egg, fork-beaten	1	1

Roll out each pastry block on lightly floured surface to 9 x 11 inch (22 x 28 cm) rectangle. Transfer 1 rectangle onto lightly greased baking sheet. Spread with tomato paste to within 1/4 inch (6 mm) of edges. Sprinkle with next 4 ingredients.

Dampen edges of pastry with egg. Place second rectangle over filling. Press edges together to seal. Cut, through top layer of pastry only, into 1 1/2 x 2 inches (3.8 x 5 cm) strips. Brush with remaining egg. Bake in 425°F (220°C) oven for about 20 minutes until risen and golden. Cut strips all the way through. Serve warm. Makes 20 appetizers.

1 appetizer: 154 Calories; 10.7 g Total Fat; 173 mg Sodium; 5 g Protein; 10 g Carbohydrate; trace Dietary Fibre

♦*Anchovies add a wonderful flavour to this appetizer. You can, however, substitute 2 to 3 tbsp. (30 to 50 mL) finely chopped black or green olives.*

Yogurt, Raisin and Honey Dip

You won't have to coax children to eat fresh fruit when this good-tasting creamy dip is served on the side. Especially good with fresh strawberries, cantaloupe, honeydew melon, pineapple and banana.

Containers of vanilla yogurt (6 oz.,175 g, each)	2	2
Spreadable cream cheese	1 cup	250 mL
Sliced almonds, toasted (optional)♦	1/3 cup	75 mL
Raisins, chopped	1/3 cup	75 mL
Liquid honey	2 tbsp.	30 mL
White grape juice	1/4 cup	60 mL

Combine all 6 ingredients in medium bowl. Cover. Chill until ready to use. Makes 2 3/4 cups (675 mL).

1 tbsp. (15 mL): 31 Calories; 2 g Total Fat; 22 mg Sodium; 1 g Protein; 3 g Carbohydrate; trace Dietary Fibre

♦*To toast the almonds, place them in an ungreased frying pan. Heat on medium, stirring often, until golden.*

Corn Relish Dip

Pack this colourful dip into plastic containers to be enjoyed with carrot, celery, broccoli or cauliflower pieces. Or show the kids how to make a great-tasting wrap by using this dip as a spread on tortillas before adding strips of ham or chicken and shredded lettuce.

Corn relish	1 cup	250 mL
Sour cream	3/4 cup	175 mL
Finely grated Cheddar cheese	1/3 cup	75 mL
Hot pepper sauce (optional)	1/2 tsp.	2 mL

Combine all 4 ingredients in small bowl. Cover. Chill until ready to use. Makes 1 3/4 cups (425 mL).

1 tbsp. (15 mL): 23 Calories; 1.4 g Total Fat; 40 mg Sodium; 1 g Protein; 2 g Carbohydrate; trace Dietary Fibre

Bruschetta with Basil, above

Crispy Fried Tofu with Soy and Sesame Dipping Sauce

Inside the crispy exterior is a soft creamy interior with real taste appeal, especially when combined with the nutty soy dipping sauce.

Packages of soft tofu (10.5 oz., 300 g, each), well drained and cut into 3/4 inch (2 cm) cubes	2	2
Egg yolk (large)	1	1
Ice water	1 cup	250 mL
All-purpose flour	1 cup	250 mL
All-purpose flour	1 cup	250 mL
Salt	1 tsp.	5 mL
Freshly ground pepper	1 tsp.	5 mL
Cooking oil, for deep-frying	5 cups	1.25 L

DIPPING SAUCE

Soy sauce	3 tbsp.	50 mL
Sesame oil	1/2 tsp.	2 mL
Granulated sugar	1 tsp.	5 mL
Sambal oelek (chili paste)	1/2 tsp.	2 mL
Rice (or white wine) vinegar	1 tbsp.	15 mL

Place tofu on paper towels to drain thoroughly.

Combine egg yolk and ice water in large bowl. Whisk in first amount of flour until just combined. Batter should be lumpy. Don't overmix. Makes 1 2/3 cups (400 mL) batter.

Combine next 3 ingredients in shallow bowl. Lightly toss tofu in flour mixture. Dip in batter to coat completely. Deep-fry, in batches, in large saucepan in hot 375°F (190°C) cooking oil for about 7 minutes until golden.♦ Drain on paper towel.

Dipping Sauce: Combine all 5 ingredients in small bowl. Serve with tofu. Serves 8.

1 serving: 322 Calories; 19.2 g Total Fat; 695 mg Sodium; 10 g Protein; 28 g Carbohydrate; 2 g Dietary Fibre

♦Be sure to handle the soft tofu gently when deep-frying. It's quite delicate but works very well in this recipe.

Spicy Jalapeño Tomato Salsa, below

Spicy Jalapeño Tomato Salsa

You may never go back to store-bought salsas! Packed with flavour and colour, this is an inspired accompaniment to everything from nachos and crisp veggies to grilled chicken, sausages and steak.

Medium tomatoes, peeled and chopped (about 4 lbs., 1.8 kg)	14	14
Large red onion, chopped	1	1
Garlic cloves, crushed	6	6
Large green pepper, quartered and chopped	1	1
Large red pepper, quartered and chopped	1	1
Canned jalapeño peppers, drained and chopped♦	5	5
Tomato paste	1/3 cup	75 mL
White vinegar	1/2 cup	125 mL
Brown sugar, packed	3 tbsp.	50 mL
Ground cumin	1 tbsp.	15 mL
Salt	2 tsp.	10 mL

Combine all 11 ingredients in large heavy pot or Dutch oven. Bring to a boil. Reduce heat to medium. Gently boil, uncovered, for 45 to 50 minutes, stirring occasionally, until thickened. Fill hot sterilized pint jars to within 1/2 inch (12 mm) of top. Place sterilized metal lids on jars and screw metal bands on securely. Process in boiling water bath for 5 minutes. Makes about 3 pint (2 cup, 500 mL) jars.

2 tbsp. (30 mL): 17 Calories; 0.2 g Total Fat; 117 mg Sodium; 1 g Protein; 4 g Carbohydrate; 1 g Dietary Fibre

Pictured above and on page 154.

♦Taste near end of cooking time, adding more jalapeños if desired.

Coconut Seafood Cakes with Mango Salsa

Packed with exotic flavours, these crisp little appetizers will disappear in a hurry. Add the hint-of-the-tropics salsa and you've got perfect party food for any summer gathering. Garnish with cilantro.

Can of coconut milk	14 oz.	400 mL
Large egg, fork-beaten	1	1
Fish sauce	1 tbsp.	15 mL
Green curry paste	1 tbsp.	15 mL
Medium fresh (or frozen, thawed) shrimp, peeled and deveined, finely chopped	8 oz.	225 g
Can of crabmeat, drained and cartilage removed, broken up	4 1/4 oz.	120 g
All-purpose flour	1 cup	250 mL
Baking powder	1 tsp.	5 mL
Cooking oil	2 tsp.	10 mL

MANGO SALSA

Small mangoes, pitted, peeled and finely chopped	2	2
Small Roma (plum) tomatoes, seeded and finely chopped	4	4
Green onions, finely chopped	3	3
Sweet chili sauce	2 tbsp.	30 mL
Balsamic (or red wine) vinegar	1 tbsp.	15 mL
Chopped fresh cilantro leaves	3 tbsp.	50 mL

Combine first 4 ingredients in medium bowl. Add shrimp and crabmeat. Mix well. Add flour and baking powder. Mix well.

Heat cooking oil in shallow frying pan on medium. Drop mixture, 2 1/2 tbsp. (37 mL) at a time, onto hot pan. Spread to form 3 inch (7.5 cm) cakes. Cook on medium for about 3 minutes on each side until lightly browned. Makes 24 cakes.

Mango Salsa: Combine all 6 ingredients in medium bowl. Makes 4 cups (1 L) salsa.

Place 3 to 4 cakes on each plate. Spoon salsa over top. Serves 6 to 8.

1 serving: 463 Calories; 30.6 g Total Fat; 528 mg Sodium; 17 g Protein; 34 g Carbohydrate; 3 g Dietary Fibre

Pictured below.

Honey Soy Drumettes

The elevation of the chicken wing! These great-tasting wings can be served hot or cold, as an easy appetizer or a simple meal.

Cooking oil	1 tbsp.	15 mL
Chicken drumettes (about 42)	3 1/2 lbs.	1.6 kg
Soy sauce	1/3 cup	75 mL
Liquid honey	1/3 cup	75 mL
Finely grated gingerroot	2 tsp.	10 mL
Sherry (or alcohol-free sherry)	2 tbsp.	30 mL

Heat 1/3 of cooking oil in non-stick wok or large frying pan. Add 1/3 of chicken. Stir-fry on high for 5 to 7 minutes until lightly browned. Remove chicken to medium bowl. Repeat with remaining cooking oil and chicken. Drain drippings from wok.

Return chicken to wok. Add remaining 4 ingredients. Mix well. Cover. Cook on medium for 15 minutes. Remove cover. Cook for 15 to 20 minutes, stirring occasionally, until chicken is no longer pink and sauce is darkened and syrupy. Serves 6.

1 serving (7 drumettes): 451 Calories; 16.6 g Total Fat; 964 mg Sodium; 52 g Protein; 21 g Carbohydrate; trace Dietary Fibre

Coconut Seafood Cakes with Mango Salsa, above

Coconut Shrimp with Sweet Hot Dipping Sauce

You'll earn rave reviews with these crunchy shrimp appetizers! The dipping sauce is also very good with chicken wings, egg rolls or steamed shrimp.

Large fresh (or frozen, thawed) shrimp (about 40 - 60)	2 1/4 lbs.	1 kg
Large eggs	3	3
Water	1 tbsp.	15 mL
All-purpose flour	1/2 cup	125 mL
Medium unsweetened coconut	3 1/2 cups	875 mL
Cooking oil, for deep-frying		

SWEET HOT DIPPING SAUCE

Cooking oil	1 tbsp.	15 mL
Small red chili peppers, finely chopped♦	3	3
Garlic cloves, crushed	2	2
Sweet chili sauce	1/2 cup	125 mL
Water	1/2 cup	125 mL
Hoisin sauce	1/4 cup	60 mL
Chopped fresh cilantro	1/4 cup	60 mL

Peel and devein shrimp, leaving tails intact. To "butterfly" shrimp, make deep cut along outside spine, almost but not through to other side. Press shrimp out to flatten.

Beat eggs and water together in small bowl with fork. Dredge shrimp in flour. Dip shrimp in egg mixture, then in coconut. Deep-fry shrimp in large saucepan, in batches, in hot 375°F (190°C) cooking oil for 1 to 2 minutes until golden. Remove to paper towel to drain.

Sweet Hot Dipping Sauce: Combine all 7 ingredients in small saucepan. Bring to a boil. Reduce heat to medium. Simmer, uncovered, for 4 to 6 minutes until sauce is thickened. Makes 2/3 cup (150 mL) sauce. Serve with shrimp. Serves 8 to 12.

5 shrimp with 1 tbsp. (15 mL) sauce: 576 Calories; 38.6 g Total Fat; 788 mg Sodium; 33 g Protein; 28 g Carbohydrate; 3.5 g Dietary Fibre

Pictured above.

♦Wear gloves when chopping chili peppers, and avoid touching your eyes.

Deveining Shrimp

To devein shrimp, strip off legs and peel away shell, leaving tail intact, if desired. Using a small, sharp knife, make a shallow cut along the centre of the back. Rinse under cold water to wash out the dark vein. To devein shrimp that you want to cook in the shell, simply slit along back right through the shell to remove the vein. These procedures work for prawns as well.

Hamburger
Cookies, below

Broccoli and Blue Cheese Dip

Even those who don't like blue cheese will love it in this go-with-everything dip. Make this up to two days ahead.

Fresh or frozen broccoli	2 cups	500 mL
Water		
Cooking oil	2 tsp.	10 mL
Small onion, finely chopped	1	1
Garlic cloves, crushed	4	4
Sour cream	2/3 cup	150 mL
Crumbled blue cheese (about 3 oz., 85 g)	1/2 cup	125 mL

Steam broccoli over small amount of boiling water in medium saucepan on high for about 5 minutes until tender. Drain well.

Heat cooking oil in large frying pan on medium-high. Add onion and garlic. Sauté for about 5 minutes until onion is softened.

Combine broccoli, onion mixture, sour cream and blue cheese in food processor. Process until smooth. Makes 2 1/4 cups (550 mL).

2 tbsp. (30 mL): 39 Calories; 2.8 g Total Fat; 62 mg Sodium; 2 g Protein; 2 g Carbohydrate; 1 g Dietary Fibre

Hamburger Cookies

"These are best served fresh out of the oven because they are very tender and flavourful. We enjoy dipping the 'cookies' in ketchup, BBQ sauce or mustard. For a meal, I serve them with a tossed salad, or soup for the kids. They can be frozen, then reheated in the microwave."

— **Shauna Robertson, Unity, Saskatchewan**

BISCUIT BASE		
Biscuit mix	2 cups	500 mL
Onion powder	1 tsp.	5 mL
Water	1/2 cup	125 mL
FILLING		
Lean ground beef	1 lb.	454 g
Large egg	1	1
Salt	1 tsp.	5 mL
Pepper	1/2 tsp.	2 mL
Onion powder	1/2 tsp.	2 mL
Large egg, fork-beaten (optional)	1	1
Sesame (or poppy) seeds (optional)	1 tbsp.	15 mL

Biscuit Base: Combine biscuit mix and onion powder in medium bowl. Gradually add water, mixing with a fork, until soft dough forms. Turn out onto lightly floured surface. Knead 6 to 8 times until smooth. Roll out into 15 x 18 inch (38 x 44 cm) rectangle.

Filling: Combine first 5 ingredients in medium bowl. Mix well. Spread evenly over biscuit base Roll up tightly, jelly roll-style, starting from long side. Cut into 3/8 inch (9 mm) thick slices. Arrange, 1 inch (2.5 cm) apart, on lightly greased baking sheet.

Brush with egg. Sprinkle with sesame seeds. Bake in 450°F (230°C) oven for 15 minutes until biscuit is lightly golden. Makes about 30 pieces.

1 piece: 74 Calories; 3.8 g Total Fat; 206 mg Sodium; 4 g Protein; 6 g Carbohydrate; trace Dietary Fibre

Pictured above.

Hamburger Muffins

"It seems that everyone has their own variation of these appetizers. I wanted to share my version because it's been so well received in my house, yet doesn't require any special or expensive ingredients. The filling can be mixed ahead, refrigerated, then assembled into the toast shells before baking."
— **Shauna Robertson, Unity, Saskatchewan**

TOAST CUPS		
Hard margarine	1 tbsp.	15 mL
Bread slices, crusts removed	16	16
FILLING		
Lean ground beef	1 lb.	454 g
Fine dry bread crumbs	1/2 cup	125 mL
Can of condensed tomato soup	10 oz.	284 mL
Salsa	1/4 cup	60 mL
Large egg, fork-beaten	1	1
Salt	1 tsp.	5 mL
Chili powder (optional)	1/4 tsp.	1 mL
Pepper	1/4 tsp.	1 mL
Grated mozzarella cheese	1/2 cup	125 mL

Toast Cups: Spread margarine on one side of each bread slice. Press each bread slice, margarine side down, into ungreased muffin cups.

Filling: Combine first 8 ingredients in large bowl. Mix well. Spoon 1/4 cup (60 mL) beef mixture into each toast cup.

Sprinkle with cheese. Bake in 350°F (175°C) oven for 45 minutes until beef mixture is firm and browned. Makes 16.

1 filled toast cup: 171 Calories; 7.5 g Total Fat; 488 mg Sodium; 9 g Protein; 17 g Carbohydrate; 1 g Dietary Fibre

Sun-Dried Tomato Dip

This colourful and creamy dip has a zing of spiciness that's delicious with vegetables, toasted pita points and chips. This can be made up to two days ahead.
— **Georgina Robb, Barrie, Ontario**

Sun-dried tomatoes in oil, drained and chopped	1/2 cup	125 mL
Cream cheese, softened	8 oz.	250 g
Sour cream	1/2 cup	125 mL
Mayonnaise	1/2 cup	125 mL
Hot pepper sauce	1/2 tsp.	2 mL
Freshly ground pepper	1/2 tsp.	2 mL

Green onions, thinly sliced	4	4

Process first 6 ingredients in blender or food processor until smooth. Add green onion. Process with on-off motion 2 or 3 times until well combined. Makes 2 1/2 cups (625 mL).

2 tbsp. (30 mL): 98 Calories; 9.9 g Total Fat; 78 mg Sodium; 1 g Protein; 1 g Carbohydrate; trace Dietary Fibre

Tangy Orange Hummus

As good as classic hummus is, the addition of fresh orange juice and a few other non-traditional seasonings makes it even better. *"This is great for potlucks and picnics. I usually serve it with naan, cut into wedges."* Tahini, a thick paste made from ground sesame seeds, is available in the import section of large grocery stores or in health food stores.
— **Kat'e Sidlar, Thunder Bay, Ontario**

Cans of chickpeas (garbanzo beans), 19 oz. (540 mL) each, rinsed and drained	2	2
Freshly squeezed orange juice	3/4 cup	175 mL
Paprika	1 tsp.	5 mL
Chili powder	1/2 tsp.	2 mL
Dry mustard	1/2 tsp.	2 mL
Ground coriander	1/2 tsp.	2 mL
Ground cumin	1/2 tsp.	2 mL
Ground ginger	1/2 tsp.	2 mL
Cayenne pepper	1/8 tsp.	0.5 mL
Garlic cloves	3	3
Tahini	1/3 cup	75 mL
Apple cider (or balsamic) vinegar	3 tbsp.	50 mL
Soy sauce	1 tsp.	5 mL

Process chickpeas, in 2 batches, in food processor until smooth.

Put all chickpea purée into food processor. Add remaining 12 ingredients. Process until well combined. Makes about 4 cups (1 L).

2 tbsp. (30 mL): 43 Calories; 1.8 g Total Fat; 48 mg Sodium; 2 g Protein; 5 g Carbohydrate; 1 g Dietary Fibre

Pictured below.

Tangy Orange Hummus, above

Crab Toasts

These are so attractive no one will believe how easy they are to make. The crab mixture can be made a day ahead and stored in the refrigerator until ready to spread. Toppings can also be prepared in advance.

— Muriel Mayo, Alliston, Ontario

Can of crabmeat, drained, cartilage removed and flaked	4 1/4 oz.	120 g
Mayonnaise	1/4 cup	60 mL
Freshly grated Parmesan cheese	1/4 cup	60 mL
Worcestershire sauce	1/4 tsp.	1 mL
Hot pepper sauce	1/8 tsp.	0.5 mL
Melba toast rounds	24	24
Pimiento strips	24	24
Small fresh parsley leaves	24	24

Combine first 5 ingredients in medium bowl. Mix well.

Spread 2 tsp. (10 mL) crab mixture on toast rounds. Arrange in single layer on ungreased baking sheets. Broil 4 inches (10 cm) from heat for about 2 minutes until heated through.

Top with pimiento and parsley. Can be served warm or at room temperature. Makes 24 appetizers.

1 appetizer: 48 Calories; 2.4 g Total Fat; 143 mg Sodium; 2 g Protein; 4 g Carbohydrate; trace Dietary Fibre

Pictured below.

Variations: Top Crab Toasts with black caviar and tiny cucumber triangles or thinly sliced green onion and sprinkles of paprika.

Curry Phyllo Triangles

Few can resist these crisp, golden packets filled with fragrant ground meat. If made a day ahead, keep well covered in a single layer on baking trays in the refrigerator, then bake when ready to serve (or make and freeze up to two weeks beforehand).

— Kathy Klassen, Winnipeg, Manitoba

Olive oil	1 tbsp.	15 mL
Finely chopped onion	1/2 cup	125 mL
Lean ground beef (or lamb)	8 oz.	225 g
Curry powder	3 tsp.	10 mL
Salt	1 tsp.	5 mL
Finely chopped potato	3/4 cup	175 mL
Finely chopped tomato	1 1/2 cups	375 mL
Chopped fresh parsley	1 cup	250 mL
Olive oil	1/2 cup	125 mL
Curry powder	1 tsp.	10 mL
Frozen phyllo pastry sheets, thawed according to package directions	18	18
Sesame seeds	2 tbsp.	30 mL

Heat first amount of olive oil in large frying pan on medium-high. Add onion. Sauté for about 5 minutes until softened.

Add ground beef. Scramble-fry until no longer pink. Drain.

Add first amount of curry powder and salt. Cook for 1 to 2 minutes until fragrant. Add potato and tomato. Cover. Cook on medium-low for about 8 minutes until potato is tender. Add parsley. Mix well.

Combine second amounts of olive oil and curry powder in small bowl. Lay one pastry sheet on work surface. Cover remaining pastry with damp tea towel. Working quickly, brush sheet lightly with olive oil mixture. Place another phyllo sheet on top. Brush top with olive oil mixture. Cut lengthwise into 4 equal strips. Spoon 1 tbsp. (15 mL) beef mixture

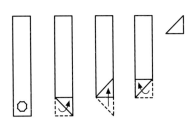

1 inch (2.5 cm) from one end of each strip (see diagram). Fold one corner over to form triangle. Continue folding over in the same fashion to end of strip. Repeat with remaining phyllo sheets, olive oil mixture and beef mixture. Arrange in single layer on 2 lightly greased baking sheets. Brush each triangle lightly with olive oil mixture.

Sprinkle with sesame seeds. Bake in 375°F (190°C) oven for about 15 minutes until golden. Makes 36 appetizers.

1 appetizer: 80 Calories; 5.2 g Total Fat; 117 mg Sodium; 2 g Protein; 6 g Carbohydrate; trace Dietary Fibre

Pictured below.

Curry Phyllo Triangles, above

Crab Toasts, above

Ham and Dijon Pastry Cups

"My mom made these for dinner parties when I was younger and I used to look for leftovers. It's hard to stop at one." You can bake these ahead of time, remove them from the muffin cups, refrigerate, then reheat on baking sheets for 15 minutes in 350°F (175°C) oven.

— Terry Jeyes, Oshawa, Ontario

Package of frozen puff pastry (14 oz., 397 g, size), thawed according to package directions	1	1
Spreadable chive and onion cream cheese	8 oz.	250 g
Ham slices, finely chopped	4	4
Finely chopped red pepper	1/3 cup	75 mL
Grated Swiss cheese	1 cup	250 mL
Large egg, fork-beaten	1	1
Dijon mustard	2 tbsp.	30 mL

Roll out 1/2 of pastry on lightly floured surface to 9 x 12 inch (22 x 30 cm) rectangle. Cut into twelve 3 inch (7.5 cm) squares. Press pastry squares, corners pointing up, into lightly greased muffin cups. Repeat with remaining pastry.

Combine remaining 6 ingredients in medium bowl. Mix well. Spoon 4 tsp. (20 mL) into each pastry cup. Bake in 425°F (220°C) oven for 15 to 18 minutes until golden. Makes 24 appetizers.

1 appetizer: 161 Calories; 12.2 g Total Fat; 182 mg Sodium; 6 g Protein; 8 g Carbohydrate; trace Dietary Fibre

Pictured below.

Chili Lemon Shrimp, below

Ham and Dijon Pastry Cups, above

Chili Lemon Shrimp

A great combination of flavours works its magic on jumbo shrimp. Prepare the shrimp the day before, cover and refrigerate until ready to serve.

Olive oil	2 tbsp.	30 mL
Liquid honey	3 tbsp.	50 mL
Sweet chili sauce	1/4 cup	60 mL
Finely grated lemon zest	1 tsp.	5 mL
Freshly squeezed lemon juice	1/4 cup	60 mL
Chopped fresh parsley	2/3 cup	150 mL
Shallots (or green onions), finely chopped	2	2
Seasoned salt	1 tsp.	5 mL
Dried crushed chilies	2 tsp.	10 mL
White (or alcohol-free) wine	2/3 cup	150 mL
Raw jumbo shrimp, peeled and deveined, tails intact	2 1/4 lbs.	1 kg
Bamboo skewers, 4 inch (10 cm) length, soaked in water for 10 minutes	25 - 30	25 - 30

Combine first 10 ingredients in large bowl.

Add shrimp. Stir to coat. Cover. Marinate in refrigerator for 3 hours, turning several times. Remove shrimp. Pour marinade into small saucepan. Bring to a boil. Boil for 5 minutes.

Thread shrimp lengthwise onto skewers, starting at head end. Grill or broil shrimp for 2 minutes per side, brushing with marinade several times, until shrimp are just pink and tender. Makes 25 to 30 appetizers.

1 appetizer: 72 Calories; 1.9 g Total Fat; 150 mg Sodium; 8 g Protein; 4 g Carbohydrate; trace Dietary Fibre

Pictured above.

Baked Feta, below

Baked Feta

"This is the perfect recipe for a great and elegant starter. It's my favourite dish to make when I'm going to a potluck and running out of time."
— Michelle Law, Nanaimo, British Columbia

Feta cheese	9 oz.	255 g
Olive oil	1/4 cup	60 mL
Paprika	1/4 tsp.	1 mL
Garlic cloves, minced	2	2
Chopped fresh oregano leaves	1 tbsp.	15 mL
Chopped chives	1 tbsp.	15 mL
Salsa, warmed	1/2 cup	125 mL
Baguette slices, 1/2 inch (12 mm) thick	18	18

Place feta on 12 x 16 inch (30 x 40 cm) sheet of foil.

Combine next 3 ingredients in small cup. Drizzle over cheese. Sprinkle with oregano and chives. Secure foil loosely around cheese. Bake in 400°F (205°C) oven for about 20 minutes until cheese is softened.

Serve warm with salsa and baguette slices. Makes 18 appetizers.

1 appetizer: 103 Calories; 6.7 g Total Fat; 254 mg Sodium; 3 g Protein; 8 g Carbohydrate; 1 g Dietary Fibre

Pictured above.

Romano Risotto Balls

These tasty rice balls are well worth the extra effort. They're incredibly delicious and can be prepared and refrigerated up to two days ahead. Serve warm or cold.

Cans of condensed chicken broth (10 oz., 284 mL, each)	3	3
Water	1 1/4 cups	300 mL
Medium onion, finely chopped	1	1
Garlic cloves, crushed	2	2
Butter (or hard margarine)	1 tbsp.	15 mL
Arborio rice	2 cups	500 mL
White (or alcohol-free) wine	1/2 cup	125 mL
Chopped fresh parsley	1/4 cup	60 mL
Chopped fresh oregano leaves	1 tbsp.	15 mL
Freshly grated Romano cheese	1/3 cup	75 mL
Fine dry bread crumbs	3/4 cup	175 mL
Cooking oil, for deep-frying		

Combine broth and water in medium saucepan. Cover. Bring to a boil. Reduce heat to very low to keep warm.

Sauté onion and garlic in butter in large saucepan on medium for about 5 minutes until onion is softened.

Add rice. Stir until coated. Add wine. Heat and stir on medium-low until wine is absorbed. Add 1 cup (250 mL) hot broth mixture, stirring constantly, until broth is absorbed. Repeat with remaining broth mixture, 1 cup (250 mL) at a time, until broth is absorbed and rice is tender. Entire process will take about 30 minutes.

Add next 3 ingredients. Mix well. Turn into large bowl. Cover. Chill.

Place bread crumbs in shallow dish or on waxed paper. Shape rice mixture into 1 1/4 inch (3 cm) balls. Roll balls in bread crumbs to coat completely.

Deep-fry, in batches, in hot (375°F, 190°C) cooking oil for 2 to 3 minutes until golden. Remove to paper towel to drain. Makes about 70 balls.

1 rice ball: 47 Calories; 1.7 g Total Fat; 103 mg Sodium; 1 g Protein; 6 g Carbohydrate; trace Dietary Fibre

Pictured on page 23.

Red Pepper and Goat Cheese Bruschetta

This appetizer tastes as good as it looks. You can prepare the red pepper mixture and refrigerate up to two days ahead.

Medium red peppers	2	2
Olive oil	1 tbsp.	15 mL
Balsamic (or red wine) vinegar	2 tsp.	10 mL
Olive oil	2 tbsp.	30 mL
Baguette slices, 1/2 inch (12 mm) thick	18	18
Garlic clove, halved	1	1
Goat cheese, softened	4 1/2 oz.	127 g
Thinly sliced fresh sweet basil	1/4 cup	60 mL

Cut peppers into quarters. Remove seeds and membranes. Broil, skin-side up, 6 inches (15 cm) from heat for 15 minutes until skins are blackened and blistered. Place in plastic bag or covered bowl for 10 minutes. Peel off and discard skins. Cut into thin slices.

Combine peppers, first amount of olive oil and vinegar in small bowl. Toss until coated. Set aside.

Brush second amount of olive oil on one side of each baguette slice. Place slices, oil-side up, on baking sheets. Bake in 350°F (175°C) oven for 3 to 4 minutes until lightly golden. Turn over. Bake for 2 to 3 minutes further until lightly golden. Rub garlic over oiled side of each slice.

Divide and spread cheese on oil side of baguette slices. Drain pepper slices. Arrange on top of cheese. Sprinkle with basil. Serve immediately. Makes 18 appetizers.

1 appetizer: 72 Calories; 3.6 g Total Fat; 93 mg Sodium; 2 g Protein; 8 g Carbohydrate; 1 g Dietary Fibre

Pictured below.

Date and Blue Cheese Tarts

The savoury taste of blue cheese and the sweetness of dates are a perfect appetizer combination. These are super-quick and easy to make ahead of time. Serve warm or cold.

Pastry for a 2 crust 9 inch (22 cm) pie, your own or a mix		
Large eggs	2	2
Buttermilk (or reconstituted from powder)	1/3 cup	75 mL
Ground nutmeg	1/2 tsp.	2 mL
Finely chopped dates	1/2 cup	125 mL
Blue cheese, crumbled	1 1/2 oz.	43 g

Roll out pastry on lightly floured surface to 1/4 inch (6 mm) thickness. Cut 24 circles with 3 1/4 inch (8.2 cm) fluted cutter. Press circles into ungreased mini-muffin pans.

Whisk next 3 ingredients together in medium bowl. Add dates and blue cheese. Stir. Fill each shell with 2 tsp. (10 mL) date mixture. Bake in 375°F (190°C) oven for about 15 minutes until set. Makes 24 tarts.

1 tart: 79 Calories; 4.5 g Total Fat; 103 mg Sodium; 2 g Protein; 8 g Carbohydrate; trace Dietary Fibre

Pictured below.

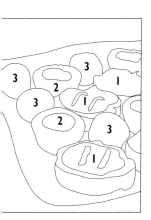

1. Red Pepper and Goat Cheese Bruschetta, above
2. Date and Blue Cheese Tarts, this page
3. Romano Risotto Balls, page 22

Seafood Ravioli with Dill and Caper Butter Sauce

These sumptuous pasta pouches filled with shrimp, scallops, fresh herbs and creamy goat cheese can be assembled beforehand. Place in a single layer on parchment paper-lined baking sheets, dust with a little cornstarch, cover and refrigerate until ready to cook.

Uncooked medium shrimp, peeled and deveined	12 1/3 oz.	350 g
Scallops	6 1/4 oz.	175 g
Chopped fresh chives	2 tbsp.	30 mL
Goat cheese, chopped	1/4 cup	60 mL
Finely grated lemon zest	1/2 tsp.	2 mL
Garlic clove, crushed	1	1
Salt	1/4 tsp.	1 mL
Freshly ground pepper	1/2 tsp.	2 mL
Round dumpling wrappers	40	40
Large egg	1	1
Water	1 tbsp.	15 mL
Boiling water	10 cups	2.5 L
Salt	1 tsp.	5 mL

DILL AND CAPER BUTTER SAUCE

Butter	2/3 cup	150 g
Capers, coarsely chopped	2 tbsp.	30 mL
Chopped fresh dill	2 tbsp.	30 mL
Chopped pecans	2 tbsp.	30 mL
Freshly ground pepper	1/2 tsp.	2 mL
Salt	1/4 tsp.	1 mL

Process first 8 ingredients in food processor until coarsely chopped. Makes 2 cups (500 mL) filling.

Put 1 1/2 tbsp. (25 mL) filling in centre of 1/2 of wrappers. Whisk egg and water in small bowl. Brush edges of wrappers with egg mixture. Place remaining wrappers over filling. Press edges together to seal. Makes 20 ravioli.

Cook ravioli, in 2 batches, in boiling water and salt in large uncovered pot or Dutch oven on medium-high for about 5 minutes until tender but firm. Drain well.

Dill and Caper Butter Sauce: Melt butter in medium frying pan on medium. Add remaining 5 ingredients. Heat and stir for 3 to 5 minutes until butter is lightly browned. Makes about 1/2 cup (125 mL) butter sauce. Arrange 5 ravioli on each individual serving plate. Drizzle with butter sauce. Serves 4.

1 serving: 725 Calories; 40.8 g Total Fat; 1371 mg Sodium; 38 g Protein; 50 g Carbohydrate; trace Dietary Fibre

Pictured below.

Brandied Chicken Livers

A very good choice for a winter cocktail party, these rich chicken livers are irresistible spooned onto rounds of crisp garlic toast. If you have any chicken liver mixture left over, purée until smooth, refrigerate and use as a delicious paté.

GARLIC TOAST ROUNDS

Butter (or hard margarine)	1 tbsp.	15 mL
Crushed garlic	2 tsp.	10 mL
Butter (or hard margarine)	1/2 cup	125 mL
Finely chopped fresh parsley	2 tbsp.	30 mL
Baguette (white or multi-grain)	1	1

BRANDIED CHICKEN LIVERS

Fresh chicken livers	1 lb.	454 g
All-purpose flour	1/2 cup	125 mL
Salt	1/4 tsp.	1 mL
Pepper, just a pinch		
Butter (or hard margarine)	2 tbsp.	30 mL
Chopped shallots	1/2 cup	125 mL
Brandy (or cognac)	1/2 cup	125 mL
Whipping cream	1/2 cup	125 mL

Garlic Toast Rounds: Melt first amount of butter in small saucepan on low. Add garlic. Sauté until garlic just begins to colour.

Add second amount of butter. Heat until melted. Add parsley. Mix well. Remove from heat.

Cut baguette into 1/4 inch (6 mm) slices. Brush both sides lightly with butter mixture. Place on ungreased baking sheet. Bake in 375°F (190°C) oven for 3 to 5 minutes per side until golden. (These can be made a few hours in advance.) Makes about 60 toast rounds.

Brandied Chicken Livers: Trim chicken livers of any fat, veins or green-tinged areas. Cut into 1/2 inch (12 mm) pieces.

Combine next 3 ingredients in shallow bowl. Dredge livers in flour mixture. Shake gently to remove excess.

Melt butter in large frying pan on medium-high. Add shallots. Sauté for about 3 minutes until softened. Add livers. Sauté for about 5 minutes until lightly browned but still slightly pink inside.

Add brandy and whipping cream. Heat and stir until just beginning to boil. Makes about 2 1/2 cups (625 mL) chicken liver mixture. Serve in chafing or heatproof dish with toast rounds on the side. Makes about 60 appetizers.

1 appetizer (with toast): 61 Calories; 3.6 g Total Fat; 72 mg Sodium; 2 g Protein; 4 g Carbohydrate; trace Dietary Fibre

Paté and Apple Tartlets

These savoury, quick-to-make pastries are ideal after a winter outing or when friends gather for casual entertaining—simply cut into quarters and serve warm in front of the fire. Or enjoy them as a sit-down dinner appetizer with a glass of red wine to complement the rich paté.

Package of frozen puff pastry, thawed according to package directions	14 oz.	397 g
Liver paté (cognac or country-style), softened	6 oz.	175 g
Tart medium cooking apples (such as Granny Smith)	1 1/2 - 2	1 1/2 - 2
Large egg, fork-beaten	1	1

Roll out 1/2 of puff pastry on lightly floured surface to 1/8 inch (3 mm) thickness. Cut into quarters. Slightly trim corners of each quarter to make rough circles. Place on lightly greased baking sheet. Repeat with remaining puff pastry.

Remove and discard any gelatin from paté. Divide paté into 8 pieces. Place 1 piece in centre of each pastry circle. Spread paté to within 1/2 inch (12 mm) of edge.

Cut apples into quarters. Remove and discard cores. Cut quarters into very thin slices. Divide and lay slices in fan shape over paté.

Brush apple and pastry with egg. Bake in 400°F (205°C) oven on centre or top rack for 15 to 20 minutes until pastry is golden. Makes 8 tartlets.

1 tartlet: 371 Calories; 25.8 g Total Fat; 284 mg Sodium; 8 g Protein; 28 g Carbohydrate; 1 g Dietary Fibre

Pictured above.

Paté and Apple Tartlets, below

Lobster with Saffron-Scented White Beans

The humble navy bean is transformed in this elegant seafood appetizer that's equally at home on the French Riviera or your dining table.

SAFFRON-SCENTED WHITE BEANS

Dried navy beans	1 cup	250 mL
Water, to cover		
Butter (or hard margarine)	2 tbsp.	30 mL
Chopped shallots	1 cup	250 mL
Garlic cloves, crushed	3	3
Saffron threads, just a pinch (about 15 strands)		
White (or alcohol-free) wine	1 cup	250 mL
Prepared vegetable (or chicken) broth	2 cups	500 mL
Bay leaf	1	1
Ground white pepper	1/4 tsp.	1 mL
Salt, to taste		
Chopped fresh parsley	2 tbsp.	30 mL

LOBSTER

Fresh (or frozen) raw lobster tails (4 oz., 113 g, each, without shell, or 6 oz., 170 g, each, with shell)	8	8
Butter (or hard margarine)	2 tbsp.	30 mL
Salt, to taste		
Pepper, to taste		
Brandy	1/4 cup	60 mL
Chopped fresh parsley, for garnish		

Saffron-Scented White Beans: Soak beans in water in large bowl overnight. Drain.

Heat butter in large saucepan on medium. Add shallots and garlic. Cook for about 5 minutes until shallots are softened.

Add saffron. Cook for 1 minute. Add beans and next 4 ingredients. Stir. Bring to a boil on medium-high. Reduce heat to medium-low. Cover. Simmer for about 2 hours, stirring occasionally, until beans are tender and most of liquid has been absorbed.

Add salt and parsley. Stir. Cover to keep warm.

Lobster: If necessary, remove lobster meat from shell. Cut each tail in half lengthwise. Cut each half into 3 or 4 large chunks.

Heat butter in large frying pan on medium. Add lobster. Sauté for 1 minute.

Add next 3 ingredients. Cook for 1 to 2 minutes until lobster is just opaque and slightly firm.

Place bean mixture in serving dish or on individual plates. Arrange lobster on top. Sprinkle with parsley. Serves 8 as an appetizer or 4 as a main course.

1 appetizer serving: 311 Calories; 7.6 g Total Fat; 608 mg Sodium; 29 g Protein; 22 g Carbohydrate; 5 g Dietary Fibre

Pictured above.

Curried Devilled Eggs

Chutney and curry give these devilled eggs a sweet and spicy flair that's a nice change from the usual version. If you like, add a sprinkle of paprika and a snippet of chive tips to each egg half just before serving.

Hard-boiled eggs, peeled	6	6
Mayonnaise	1/4 cup	60 mL
Mango chutney, any large pieces finely chopped	1 tbsp.	15 mL
Chopped fresh chives	2 tsp.	10 mL
Curry powder	1/4 tsp.	1 mL
Salt, just a pinch		
Freshly ground pepper, just a pinch		

Cut eggs in 1/2 lengthwise. Remove egg yolks to small bowl. Set egg white halves aside. Mash egg yolks until no lumps remain.

Add remaining 6 ingredients to egg yolk. Mix until well combined. Spoon 1 tbsp. (15 mL) into each egg white half. Place in paper towel-lined airtight container. Chill for 2 hours or overnight. Makes 12 devilled eggs.

1 devilled egg: 76 Calories; 6.6 g Total Fat; 56 mg Sodium; 3 g Protein; 1 g Carbohydrate; trace Dietary Fibre

Sticky-Finger Wings

"About once a month, we have 'wing night' and I cook around 25 pounds of chicken wings. After most suppers, the boys line up for the weigh-in. They're all over six feet tall, and it's a real status symbol to weigh more than 200 pounds!" Linda's "hockey sons" board with her while they play for the Weyburn Red Wings.
— **Linda Rudachyk, Weyburn, Saskatchewan**

Brown sugar, packed	1 cup	250 mL
Soy sauce	1/2 cup	125 mL
Finely chopped gingerroot	2 tbsp.	30 mL
Garlic cloves, crushed	6	6
Trimmed chicken wings◆	4 lbs.	1.8 kg

Combine first 4 ingredients in small bowl. Mix well.

Put wings into well-greased 9 x 13 inch (22 x 33 cm) pan. Pour brown sugar mixture over wings. Toss to coat. Bake in 350°F (175°C) oven for 1 3/4 to 2 hours, stirring occasionally, until tender and glazed. Serves 8 as an appetizer.

1 serving: 398 Calories; 19.6 g Total Fat; 1189 mg Sodium; 24 g Protein; 31 g Carbohydrate; trace Dietary Fibre

Pictured below.

◆*If trimmed chicken wings aren't available, buy 4 1/2 lbs. (2 kg) whole chicken wings, remove and discard the tips, then cut the wings apart at the joint.*

Greek Ribs, page 103

Sticky-Finger Wings, above

Beverages

Pineapple Punch

Citrus and tropical fruit flavours blended with tea make an impressive beverage. To ease the last-minute rush before serving, combine all the ingredients except the soda water and soft drink ahead of time.

Prepared strong black tea	2 cups	500 mL
Demerara sugar◆	1/4 cup	60 mL
Prepared orange juice	3/4 cup	175 mL
Sweetened pineapple juice	4 cups	1 L
Can of crushed pineapple	13 1/2 oz.	385 mL
Soda water, chilled	4 cups	1 L
Lemon-lime soft drink, chilled	4 cups	1 L

Combine tea and sugar in punch bowl. Stir until sugar is dissolved.

Add next 3 ingredients. Chill.

To serve, add soda water and soft drink. Makes about 16 cups (4 L).

1 cup (250 mL): 98 Calories; 0.1 g Total Fat; 24 mg Sodium; trace Protein; 25 g Carbohydrate; trace Dietary Fibre

Pictured at right.

◆Demerara sugar is a coarse-textured raw sugar. It has a distinctive caramel flavour. Brown sugar may be substituted.

Pineapple Punch, left

Strawberry and Sparkling Wine Punch, below

Now That's Refreshmint!

Give any fruit beverage or even a jug of water an appealing lift with mint ice cubes. Half-fill an ice cube tray with water, float a mint leaf in each cube and freeze. Top up the tray with water and freeze until set.

Strawberry and Sparkling Wine Punch

Refreshing, pretty and absolutely delicious, this makes brunch extra special.

Bottle of sparkling dry (or alcohol-free) wine, chilled	3 cups	750 mL
Bottle of ginger ale, chilled	4 cups	1 L
Prepared orange juice	4 cups	1 L
Chopped fresh strawberries	1 cup	250 mL

Combine all 4 ingredients in punch bowl just before serving. Makes about 12 cups (3 L).

1 cup (250 mL): 122 Calories; 0.3 g Total Fat; 10 mg Sodium; 1 g Protein; 20 g Carbohydrate; 1 g Dietary Fibre

Pictured above.

Fresh Fruit Smoothie

"This creamy, refreshing drink transports me back to the West Indies. These Caribbean fruits and flavours crept into most island dishes and were the basis for most island drinks."
— Jennifer Cockrall-King, Edmonton, Alberta

Chopped ripe pineapple (about 1 small)	4 cups	1 L
Mango (or guava) nectar	1 cup	250 mL
Peach yogurt	1 cup	250 mL
Ripe medium banana	1	1
Chopped ripe papaya (about 1/2 small), seeds removed	1 cup	250 mL
Ice cubes	6	6

Combine all 6 ingredients in blender. Process until smooth. Makes 6 cups (1.5 L).

2 cups (500 mL): 267 Calories; 2.6 g Total Fat; 47 mg Sodium; 5 g Protein; 61 g Carbohydrate; 5 g Dietary Fibre

Pictured at right.

Banana Yogurt Smoothie

Too many ripe bananas sitting on the counter? Serve everyone in the family this terrific smoothie for breakfast.

Ripe medium bananas	2	2
Milk	2 cups	500 mL
Vanilla yogurt	1/2 cup	125 mL
Ground nutmeg	1/2 tsp.	2 mL
Ground cinnamon	1/2 tsp.	2 mL
Granulated sugar	1 tbsp.	15 mL
Ice cubes, broken up	8	8
Ground nutmeg, sprinkle		

Process first 7 ingredients in blender until smooth.

Pour into tall glasses. Sprinkle with nutmeg. Makes 6 cups (1.5 L).

1 cup (250 mL): 94 Calories; 1.5 g Total Fat; 59 mg Sodium; 4 g Protein; 17 g Carbohydrate; 1 g Dietary Fibre

Mango Maple Smoothie

This is a rich, medium-thick drink with marvelous mango flavour and maple syrup sweetness. Great for a quick breakfast or as a cooling beverage with a spicy dish.

Package of silken tofu (12.3 oz., 349 g)	1/2	1/2

Fresh Fruit Smoothie, left

Chopped mango (about 1 large)	1 1/4 cups	300 mL
Milk♦	1 1/2 cups	375 mL
Maple syrup	3 tbsp.	50 mL
Ice cubes	1/2 cup	125 mL

Process first 3 ingredients in blender until smooth.

Add maple syrup and ice cubes. Process until smooth. To serve, pour into cold glasses. Makes 3 1/2 cups (875 mL). Serves 2.

1 serving: 297 Calories; 6.6 g Total Fat; 108 mg Sodium; 14 g Protein; 50 g Carbohydrate; 3 g Dietary Fibre

♦For a dairy-free alternative, substitute soy milk for regular milk.

Iced Irish Coffee

A dessert in itself, this recipe is perfect after a rich dinner. Top with shavings of bittersweet chocolate.

Granulated sugar	2 tbsp.	30 mL
Water		
Cold prepared strong coffee	2 cups	500 mL
Vanilla ice cream	3/4 cup	175 mL
Irish whisky	1/4 cup	60 mL
Whipping cream	1/2 cup	125 mL
Demerara sugar♦ (or shaved chocolate)	2 tsp.	10 mL

Spread granulated sugar evenly on small plate. Dip rims of 2 large coffee mugs into 1/4 inch (6 mm) of water. Dip into sugar.

Process next 3 ingredients in blender until smooth. Pour into prepared mugs.

Beat cream in small bowl until soft peaks form. Spoon or pipe cream onto coffee mixture. Sprinkle with demerara sugar. Makes 2 3/4 cups (675 mL).

1 cup (250 mL): 316 Calories; 18.9 g Total Fat; 56 mg Sodium; 3 g Protein; 23 g Carbohydrate; 0 g Dietary Fibre

Pictured below.

♦Demerara sugar is a coarse-textured raw sugar. It has a distinctive caramel flavour.

Iced Irish Coffee, left

Melon and Pineapple Slush

The bright tastes of honeydew melon and pineapple make this an especially refreshing drink on a hot summer day. Experiment a little—add some coconut milk to this pretty drink for a taste of the tropics.

Chopped honeydew melon	4 cups	1 L
Sweetened pineapple juice	2 1/3 cups	575 mL
Granulated sugar	1/3 cup	75 mL
Melon liqueur (optional)	1/2 cup	125 mL
Ginger ale	3 1/2 cups	875 mL
Pineapple wedges and melon balls, for garnish		

Process melon in blender until smooth.

Combine next 3 ingredients in large bowl. Cover. Freeze for 12 to 24 hours until frozen but soft enough to remove from bowl and process. Process frozen mixture in blender until coarsely chopped.

Fill tall glasses 2/3 full of slush. Combine melon liqueur and ginger ale in pitcher. Pour over slush mixture.

Garnish with pineapple wedges and melon balls. Makes 8 cups (2 L).

1 cup (250 mL): 147 Calories; 0.2 g Total Fat; 18 mg Sodium; 1 g Protein; 37 g Carbohydrate; 1 g Dietary Fibre

Pictured at right.

Choc-Berry Smoothie, this page

Melon and Pineapple Slush, left

Choc-Berry Smoothie

When fresh raspberries are plentiful, you'll want to try them in place of the strawberries in this rich-tasting variation on a classic malted milk shake.

Chocolate malted milk powder	1/4 cup	60 mL
Milk	1 1/2 cups	375 mL
Fresh strawberries, hulled	10	10
Strawberry ice cream	1 cup	250 mL

Process all 4 ingredients in blender until smooth.

Pour into chilled milkshake glasses. Makes 3 1/2 cups (875 mL).

1 cup (250 mL): 203 Calories; 5.4 g Total Fat; 125 mg Sodium; 6 g Protein; 35 g Carbohydrate; 1 g Dietary Fibre

Pictured on this page.

Spiced Orange Punch

Orange and apple juices go particularly well with spices. Chill thoroughly before serving.

Apple juice	4 cups	1 L
Cinnamon stick	1	1
Whole cloves	1/2 tsp.	2 mL
Prepared orange juice	4 cups	1 L
Lemon-lime soft drink	4 cups	1 L
Ice cubes		
Lime wedges, for garnish		

Combine first 3 ingredients in medium saucepan. Cover. Bring to a boil. Reduce heat. Simmer on medium for 5 minutes. Strain. Cool.

Combine apple juice mixture, orange juice and soft drink in pitcher or punch bowl. Chill until cold.

Place ice cubes in glass. Add punch. Garnish individual servings with lime wedges. Makes 12 cups (3 L).

1 cup (250 mL): 115 Calories; 0.2 g Total Fat; 13 mg Sodium; 1 g Protein; 29 g Carbohydrate; trace Dietary Fibre

Pictured above.

Ginger Cooler

If root beer and cola floats are your summer drinks of choice, you may be surprised at how much you enjoy this gingery change. And be sure to savour it the way it's meant to be savoured—with a long spoon.

Vanilla ice cream	1 cup	250 mL
Bottles of ginger beer (10 oz., 284 mL, each)	3	3

Ginger Cooler,
page 30

Lemon Iced Tea,
this page

Spiced Orange Punch, page 30

Place 1/2 cup (125 mL) ice cream in each of 2 tall glasses. Slowly pour 1 1/2 bottles ginger beer over ice cream. Makes 3 1/2 cups (875 mL).

1 cup (250 mL): 165 Calories; 4.4 g Total Fat; 49 mg Sodium; 1 g Protein; 31 g Carbohydrate; 0 g Dietary Fibre

Pictured above.

Lemon Iced Tea

Nothing refreshes more completely than homemade iced tea. Special blends like Earl Grey or Darjeeling are a nice variation.

Tea bags	8	8
Granulated sugar	1 cup	250 mL
Boiling water	8 cups	2 L
Freshly squeezed lemon juice (about 4 medium)	1 cup	250 mL

Ice cubes
Lemon slices,
for garnish

Combine first 3 ingredients in heat-resistant pitcher. Stir until sugar is dissolved. Let steep for 10 minutes until mixture is dark. Discard tea bags.

Add lemon juice. Stir.

Place ice cubes in tall glasses. Add tea. Garnish with lemon slices. Makes 9 cups (2.25 L).

1 cup (250 mL): 100 Calories; 0 g Total Fat; 7 mg Sodium; trace Protein; 27 g Carbohydrate; trace Dietary Fibre

Pictured above.

Nectarine Sundae Shake

Think of a luxurious ice cream sundae made with ripe nectarines—now put those ingredients in the blender. Voilà—a sundae shake!

Unpeeled ripe nectarines, pitted and chopped	6	6
Milk	3 cups	750 mL
Vanilla ice cream	2 cups	500 mL
Almond flavouring	1/8 tsp.	0.5 mL
Flaked almonds, toasted◆	2 tbsp.	30 mL
Nectarine wedges, for garnish		

Process first 4 ingredients, in 2 batches, in blender until smooth.

Pour into tall glasses. Sprinkle with almonds. Garnish with nectarine wedges. Makes 8 cups (2 L).

1 cup (250 mL): 170 Calories; 6.2 g Total Fat; 76 mg Sodium; 6 g Protein; 25 g Carbohydrate; 2 g Dietary Fibre

◆To toast the almonds, place them in an ungreased frying pan. Heat on medium, stirring often, until golden.

Clockwise from left:
Mulled Wine, right
Apple and Cranberry Cider, below
The Best Mocha Coffee, this page
Rich Hot Chocolate, below

Mulled Wine

Aromatic and wonderfully warming on a cold winter evening, mulled wine can be the perfect accompaniment to many holiday appetizers.

Water	3 cups	750 mL
Granulated sugar	1 1/4 cups	300 mL
Whole cloves	12	12
Cinnamon sticks (4 inch, 10 cm, each)	2	2
Piece of lemon (or orange) peel, 3 inch (7.5 cm) length	1	1
Red wine	3 cups	750 mL
Spiced rum (or brandy)	3 tbsp.	50 mL

Combine first 5 ingredients in large saucepan. Heat and stir on low until sugar is dissolved. Increase heat to medium-high. Boil for 10 minutes.

Reduce heat to medium-low. Add wine. Stir until combined. Heat for 3 minutes. Do not boil. Add rum. Stir. Makes 6 cups (1.5 L).

1 cup (250 mL): 277 Calories; 0 g Total Fat; 7 mg Sodium; trace Protein; 46 g Carbohydrate; 0 g Dietary Fibre

Pictured at left.

Apple and Cranberry Cider

It's easy to give this soothing drink a more grown-up taste with the addition of a little white rum or other spirits, but it tastes so good on its own that you may choose to enjoy it just as is. Float a few fresh cranberries in each glass to make it even more festive.

Apple cider	3 3/4 cups	925 mL
Cranberry juice	2 cups	500 mL
Medium orange, sliced and cut into quarters	1	1
Cinnamon stick (4 inch, 10 cm, length)	1	1
Whole allspice	6	6
Granulated sugar	1/4 cup	60 mL

Combine all 6 ingredients in large saucepan. Heat and stir on medium for 8 to 10 minutes until mixture is hot. Do not boil. Makes about 6 cups (1.5 L).

1 cup (250 mL): 155 Calories; 0.3 g Total Fat; 7 mg Sodium; trace Protein; 40 g Carbohydrate; 2 g Dietary Fibre

Pictured above.

Rich Hot Chocolate

Ultra-rich with mega chocolate flavour, this luxurious drink is even better when stirred with candy canes or whole cinnamon sticks.

Milk	5 1/2 cups	1.4 L
Milk chocolate bars (3 1/2 oz., 100 g, each), chopped	3	3
Hazelnut-flavoured liqueur, optional	1/2 cup	125 mL
Mini marshmallows	20	20
Sifted cocoa, sprinkle		

Heat milk in large saucepan on medium-high until almost boiling. Remove from heat. Add chocolate. Stir until melted. Add liqueur. Stir.

Pour into mugs. Divide marshmallows among mugs. Sprinkle with cocoa. Makes 6 cups (1.5 L).

1 cup (250 mL): 402 Calories; 17.9 g Total Fat; 166 mg Sodium; 11 g Protein; 53 g Carbohydrate; 2 g Dietary Fibre

Pictured above.

The Best Mocha Coffee

Coffee and chocolate must be one of the best flavour couplings ever. Turn your kitchen into your own personal coffee bar with this recipe.

Hot prepared strong coffee	4 1/4 cups	1 L
Hot half-and-half cream	1 1/2 cups	375 mL
Instant hot chocolate powder	1/3 cup	75 mL
Coffee-flavoured liqueur	1/3 cup	75 mL
Whipped cream	1 cup	250 mL
Granulated sugar	2 tsp.	10 mL
Ground cinnamon	1/8 tsp.	0.5 mL

Combine first 4 ingredients in large saucepan. Heat and stir on medium-high until hot. Do not boil. Pour into mugs.

Spoon or pipe whipped cream on top of coffee. Combine sugar and cinnamon in small bowl. Sprinkle on top. Makes about 6 cups (1.5 L).

1 cup (250 mL): 233 Calories; 9.4 g Total Fat; 91 mg Sodium; 3 g Protein; 30 g Carbohydrate; trace Dietary Fibre

Pictured on this page.

Breads & Quick Breads

Kolach
(Braided Bread)

The ring-shaped kolach is the traditional centrepiece of the Ukrainian Christmas Eve table. Three loaves are placed upon each other, and a candle is inserted in the centre. The round shape symbolizes eternity, the three loaves the Holy Trinity, and the candle reminds the family of the Star of Bethlehem and the Light of Christ coming into the world.
— Zonnia Ostopowich, Edmonton, Alberta

Milk	1 1/2 cups	375 mL
Frozen concentrated orange juice	1/4 cup	60 mL
Hard margarine (or butter)	1/4 cup	60 mL
Cooking oil	1/4 cup	60 mL
Freshly grated orange zest	1 1/2 tsp.	7 mL
Vanilla	1 1/2 tsp.	7 mL
Large eggs	4	4
Instant yeast	4 tsp.	20 mL
All-purpose flour	3 cups	750 mL
Granulated sugar	3/4 cup	175 mL
Ground nutmeg	1/2 tsp.	2 mL
Salt	1/2 tsp.	2 mL
All-purpose flour	4 - 5 cups	1 - 1.25 L
Large egg, fork-beaten	1	1

Scald milk in medium saucepan. Add next 5 ingredients. Stir until margarine is melted.

Beat eggs in heavy-duty mixer on low using paddle attachment. Gradually add milk mixture until combined. Switch to dough hook attachment.

Sift next 5 ingredients in medium bowl. Add to milk mixture. Mix until well combined.

Add second amount of flour, 1/2 cup (125 mL) at a time, on low speed, scraping down side of bowl occasionally, until dough is soft and sticky and pulls away from side. Knead with mixer for 5 minutes. Place dough in lightly greased large bowl, turning once to grease top. Cover with tea towel. Let stand in oven with light on and door closed for 20 minutes until dough is slightly risen. Divide dough into 3 equal-sized portions. Divide each portion into 3 equal-sized pieces. Roll pieces into 24 inch (60 cm) lengths, about 3/4 inch (2 cm) thick. Lay 3 lengths side by side. Pinch together at one end. Braid lengths (see photo 1). Pinch ends together. Form circle about 6 inches (15 cm) in diameter around small, empty greased can.◆ Cut 1/2 inch (12 mm) diagonally,

in same direction, off both ends (see photo 2). Brush cut ends lightly with water. Pinch together. Place braid, with can still in the middle, on parchment paper-lined 11 x 17 inch (28 x 43 cm) baking sheet. Cover loosely with tea towel. Repeat with remaining lengths. You will end up with 3 braids on 3 baking sheets.

Let stand for 5 minutes. Brush each braid liberally with egg. Bake in 375°F (190°C) oven for 30 minutes until golden, changing baking sheet positions on rack halfway through. Each kolach cuts into about 6 pieces.

1 piece: 288 Calories; 8.1 g Total Fat; 127 mg Sodium; 7 g Protein; 46 g Carbohydrate; 2 g Dietary Fibre

Pictured above and on page 184.

◆Use empty, clean 5 1/2 oz. (156 mL) tomato paste cans, with labels removed. The 2 inch (5 cm) diameter is just right. Zonnia bakes her kolach in greased tube pans.

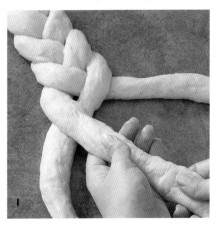

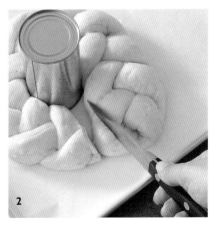

Olive and Thyme Focaccia

Italians love a well-dimpled focaccia for dipping. They'll also split it and fill it with cheese, cold cuts and vegetables to create a sandwich.

All-purpose flour, approximately	2 1/4 cups	550 mL
Instant yeast (1/4 oz., 8 g, envelope)	2 1/4 tsp.	11 mL
Salt	1 tsp.	5 mL
Chopped fresh thyme leaves	1 1/2 tbsp.	25 mL
Sliced pitted ripe olives	1/2 cup	125 mL
Warm water	1 cup	250 mL
Olive oil	2 tbsp.	30 mL
Semolina	1 tbsp.	15 mL
Olive oil	1 tbsp.	15 mL
Small onion, thinly sliced	1	1
Freshly grated Parmesan cheese	1/3 cup	75 mL
Chopped fresh thyme leaves	2 tsp.	10 mL
Coarse sea salt	1/2 tsp.	2 mL

Combine first 5 ingredients in large bowl. Add warm water and first amount of olive oil. Mix until soft dough forms, adding more flour as needed. Turn out onto lightly floured surface. Knead for 5 to 10 minutes until smooth and elastic.

Lightly grease 11 x 17 inch (28 x 43 cm) baking sheet. Sprinkle with semolina. Press or roll dough into 10 inch (25 cm) circle on baking sheet. Cover with waxed paper and tea towel. Let stand in oven with light on and door closed for 45 minutes until doubled in bulk.

Make about 14 indentations randomly over top of dough using your fingertips. Drizzle with second amount of olive oil. Sprinkle with remaining 5 ingredients. Bake in 475°F (240°C) oven for about 25 minutes until golden and bottom is hollow-sounding when tapped. Remove to wire rack to cool. Serve warm or at room temperature. Cuts into 10 wedges.

1 wedge: 175 Calories; 6 g Total Fat; 461 mg Sodium; 5 g Protein; 25 g Carbohydrate; 2 g Dietary Fibre

Pictured at right.

Whole Wheat Pita Bread

You'll find pitas in homes and street markets everywhere in Israel, Syria, Egypt and Greece. The recipe for this round, leavened bread forms the traditional flatbread, instead of the pocket version.

Active dry yeast (1/4 oz., 8 g, envelope)	2 1/4 tsp.	11 mL
Granulated sugar	2 tsp.	10 mL
Warm milk	1 1/4 cups	300 mL
Whole wheat flour	2 1/2 cups	625 mL
All-purpose flour, approximately	1 3/4 cups	425 mL
Salt	1 tsp.	5 mL
Plain yogurt	1/2 cup	125 mL
Water	1/4 cup	60 mL
Olive oil	1 tbsp.	15 mL

Combine first 3 ingredients in small bowl. Cover. Let stand in warm place for 10 minutes. Stir to dissolve yeast.

Sift next 3 ingredients into large bowl. Stir in yeast mixture. Add remaining 3 ingredients. Mix until soft dough forms, adding more all-purpose flour as needed. Turn out onto lightly floured surface. Knead for 5 to 10 minutes until smooth and elastic. Divide dough into 8 equal portions. Knead and shape each portion into ball. Place on lightly greased baking sheet. Cover with waxed paper and tea towel. Let stand in oven with light on and door closed for about 40 minutes until doubled in bulk. Punch dough down. Press or roll each ball into 7 inch (18 cm) circle. Heat 2 ungreased 11 x 17 inch (28 x 43 cm) baking sheets in 500°F (260°C) oven for 5 minutes. Place 2 circles on each hot baking sheet. Bake on 2 racks for about 7 minutes, until golden, switching positions halfway through baking. Repeat with remaining circles. Cover warm bread with foil to keep soft. Makes 8 pitas.

1 pita: 289 Calories; 3.5 g Total Fat; 331 mg Sodium; 11 g Protein; 55 g Carbohydrate; 6 g Dietary Fibre

Pictured on page 200.

Olive and Thyme Focaccia, left

Cumin Seed Turkish Pide, page 37

Flatbread with Sesame
Seeds and Oregano, page 36

Cornmeal Flatbread with Spinach
and Onions, page 36

Cornmeal Flatbread with
Spinach and Onions, below

Cornmeal Flatbread with Spinach and Onions

In the northeastern region of Spain called Catalonia, this rectangular flatbread is called *coca*. Similar to pizza, it can be topped with chorizo sausages and peppers, or simply drizzled with olive oil.

All-purpose flour, approximately	1 1/3 cups	325 mL
Cornmeal	2/3 cup	150 mL
Instant yeast (1/4 oz., 8 g, envelope)	2 1/4 tsp.	11 mL
Salt	1 tsp.	5 mL
Granulated sugar	1 tsp.	5 mL
Hot water	3/4 cup	175 mL
Olive oil	1 tbsp.	15 mL
Olive oil	1 tbsp.	15 mL
Medium onions, thinly sliced	2	2
Garlic cloves, crushed	2	2
Paprika	1 tsp.	5 mL
Salt	1/2 tsp.	2 mL
Dark raisins	1/3 cup	75 mL
Brown sugar, packed	2 tsp.	10 mL
Balsamic (or red wine) vinegar	1 tbsp.	15 mL
Baby spinach leaves	2 cups	500 mL
Slivered almonds	1/3 cup	75 mL
Cornmeal	1 1/2 tsp.	7 mL
Crumbled feta cheese	1/2 cup	125 mL

Combine first 5 ingredients in large bowl. Add hot water and first amount of olive oil. Mix until stiff dough forms, adding more flour as needed. Turn out onto lightly floured surface. Knead for 1 to 2 minutes until well combined. Place dough on greased baking sheet. Cover with another greased baking sheet. Let stand in oven with light on and door closed for 30 minutes until puffy.

Heat second amount of olive oil in large frying pan. Add next 3 ingredients. Cook, stirring occasionally, on medium-low for about 15 minutes until onion is very soft.

Add next 6 ingredients. Heat and stir for about 2 minutes until spinach is wilted. Drain any juices from pan. Set aside.

Roll dough into 10 x 15 inch (25 x 38 cm) rectangle. Sprinkle greased 11 x 17 inch (28 x 43 cm) baking sheet with second amount of cornmeal. Place dough on cornmeal. Fold edges up about 1/2 inch (12 mm) to form rim. Spread spinach mixture evenly over dough. Sprinkle with feta cheese. Bake in 450°F (230°C) oven for about 25 minutes until bottom of crust is crisp and browned. Remove to wire rack to cool. Cuts into 12 pieces.

1 piece: 175 Calories; 6.1 g Total Fat; 383 mg Sodium; 5 g Protein; 26 g Carbohydrate; 2 g Dietary Fibre

Pictured above and on page 35.

Flatbread with Sesame Seeds and Oregano

Moroccans eat flatbread with almost every meal, and each family has its own special variation.

Active dry yeast (1/4 oz., 8 g, envelope)	2 1/4 tsp.	11 mL
Granulated sugar	1 tsp.	5 mL
Warm water	1 cup	250 mL
Whole wheat flour	1 cup	250 mL
All-purpose flour, approximately	2 1/4 cups	550 mL
Salt	1 1/2 tsp.	7 mL
Plain yogurt	3 tbsp.	50 mL
Olive oil	2 tbsp.	30 mL
Semolina	2 tbsp.	30 mL
Olive oil	2 tbsp.	30 mL
Sesame seeds	2 tbsp.	30 mL
Dried whole oregano	2 tsp.	10 mL
Dried sweet basil	2 tsp.	10 mL

Combine first 3 ingredients in small bowl. Cover. Let stand for 10 minutes. Stir to dissolve yeast.

Sift next 3 ingredients into large bowl. Stir in yeast mixture. Add yogurt and first amount of olive oil. Mix until soft dough forms, adding more all-purpose flour as needed. Turn out onto lightly floured surface. Knead for 5 to 10 minutes until smooth and elastic. Place dough in large greased bowl, turning once to grease top. Cover with waxed paper and tea towel. Let stand in oven with light on and door closed for 1 1/4 hours until doubled in bulk.

Punch dough down. Turn out onto lightly floured surface. Knead for about 1 minute until smooth. Divide into 4 equal portions. Press or roll each portion into 6 inch (15 cm) circle, about 1/4 inch (6 mm) thick. Lightly grease two 11 x 17 inch (28 x 43 cm) baking sheets. Sprinkle each baking sheet with semolina. Place 2 circles on each baking sheet.

Drizzle with second amount of olive oil. Sprinkle with remaining 3 ingredients. Bake on two racks in 500°F (260°C) oven for about 15 minutes, until golden, switching positions halfway through baking. Cover warm bread with foil to keep soft. Each flatbread cuts into 4, for a total of 16 pieces.

1 piece: 142 Calories; 4.4 g Total Fat; 226 mg Sodium; 4 g Protein; 22 g Carbohydrate; 2 g Dietary Fibre

Pictured on pages 35 and 201.

Sesame Lavash Bread

A popular Armenian flatbread, lavash (LAH-vohsh) does double duty: when left out at room temperature, its crisp texture makes it a wonderful cracker substitute. Freshly baked, it's pliable enough for wraps.

Instant yeast (1/4 oz., 8 g, envelope)	2 1/4 tsp.	11 mL
Salt	1 tsp.	5 mL
Granulated sugar	2 tbsp.	30 mL
Warm water	1 1/3 cups	325 mL
Olive oil	1/4 cup	60 mL
All-purpose flour	2 cups	500 mL
All-purpose flour	2 cups	500 mL
Milk	1/3 cup	75 mL
Sesame seeds	2 tbsp.	30 mL

Combine first 5 ingredients in large bowl. Beat on high until well combined.

Gradually add first amount of flour. Beat on low until consistency of thick batter.

Gradually stir in second amount of flour. Turn out onto lightly floured surface. Knead for 5 to 10 minutes until smooth and elastic. Place dough in large greased bowl, turning once to grease top. Cover with waxed paper and tea towel. Let stand in oven with light on and door closed for 1 1/2 hours until doubled in bulk.

Punch dough down. Turn out onto lightly floured surface. Divide into 8 equal portions. Roll each portion into 10 x 10 inch (25 x 25 cm) square, about 1/16 inch (1.5 mm) thick. Place 1 square on lightly greased 11 x 17 inch (28 x 43 cm) baking sheet. Brush with milk. Sprinkle with sesame seeds. Pierce with fork randomly over top. Bake on lowest rack in 425°F (220°C) oven for 10 minutes, turning once, until blistered and golden. Repeat with remaining dough. For soft bread, cover with foil while still warm. For crispy bread, remove to wire racks to cool completely. Makes 8 squares.

1 square: 337 Calories; 9.1 g Total Fat; 305 mg Sodium; 9 g Protein; 55 g Carbohydrate; 3 g Dietary Fibre

Pictured on page 198.

Rising to the Occasion

We developed these flatbread recipes using two different types of yeast—active dry and instant. The first takes a bit more time; it must be activated (proofed) in a mixture of sugar and warm water before being added to the dry ingredients. Instant yeast doesn't need dissolving and is simply added directly to the dry ingredients.

Cumin Seed Turkish Pide

Pide (PEE-day) is a long, thin, round or oval flatbread that's a staple of the Turkish diet. Toppings are sometimes added to create *lahmacun* or Turkish pizza.

All-purpose flour, approximately	1 1/4 cups	300 mL
Whole wheat flour	1 cup	250 mL
Instant yeast (1/4 oz., 8 g, envelope)	2 1/4 tsp.	11 mL
Salt	1 1/2 tsp.	7 mL
Granulated sugar	1 tsp.	5 mL
Warm water	1 cup	250 mL
Olive oil	1 tbsp.	15 mL
Olive oil	2 tsp.	10 mL
Cumin seeds	1 tsp.	5 mL

Sift first 5 ingredients into large bowl. Add warm water and first amount of olive oil.

Mix until soft dough forms, adding more all-purpose flour as needed. Turn out onto lightly floured surface. Knead for 1 to 2 minutes until well combined. Place dough in greased bowl, turning once to grease top. Cover with waxed paper and tea towel. Let stand in oven with light on and door closed for about 40 minutes until doubled in bulk.

Punch dough down. Roll dough into 8 x 12 inch (20 x 30 cm) rectangle. Heat ungreased baking sheet in 500°F (260°C) oven for 5 minutes. Place dough on hot baking sheet. Make about 16 indentations randomly over top of dough using your fingertips. Drizzle with second amount of olive oil. Sprinkle with cumin seeds. Bake for 10 to 12 minutes until golden. Remove to wire rack to cool. Serve warm or at room temperature. Serves 6.

1 serving: 213 Calories; 4.6 g Total Fat; 596 mg Sodium; 6 g Protein; 38 g Carbohydrate; 4 g Dietary Fibre

Pictured below and on page 35.

Cumin Seed Turkish Pide, above

Butterhorns, with
Pastry Glaze, below

Photo by: Ian Grant

Butterhorns

"This recipe can be mixed in a bread machine. It can easily be doubled or tripled. My children and grandchildren love these butterhorns, so I need to make more than one batch to freeze. A family favourite!"
— Barbara Pankratz, Edmonton, Alberta

Warm water	1/4 cup	60 mL
Granulated sugar	1 tsp.	5 mL
Active dry yeast (1/4 oz., 8 g, envelope)	2 1/4 tsp.	11 mL
Lukewarm milk	3/4 cup	175 mL
Granulated sugar	1/4 cup	60 mL
Salt	1 tsp.	5 mL
Large egg	1	1
Butter, softened	1/4 cup	60 mL
All-purpose flour	3 - 3 1/2 cups	750 - 875 mL
Butter, softened	1/4 cup	60 mL

Combine first 3 ingredients in large bowl. Let stand in warm place for 10 minutes. Stir to dissolve yeast.

Combine next 5 ingredients in medium bowl. Mix well. Add to yeast mixture.

Add 1 1/2 cups (375 mL) of flour. Stir well with spoon. Slowly work in enough remaining flour to make dough easy to handle. Turn out onto lightly floured surface. Knead for 5 to 10 minutes until smooth and elastic. Place in large greased bowl, turning once to grease top. Cover with waxed paper and tea towel. Let stand in oven with light on and door closed for about 1 1/2 hours until doubled in bulk. Punch dough down. Cover with waxed paper and tea towel. Let stand in oven with light on and door closed for 30 minutes until doubled in bulk. Turn out onto lightly floured surface. Roll out into 16 inch (40 cm) circle.

Spread second amount of butter over dough. Cut into 16 wedges. Roll up each wedge starting from wide end. Arrange 2 inches (5 cm) apart on 2 greased baking sheets. Cover with tea towel. Place in oven with light on and door closed for about 1 hour until doubled in bulk. Bake in 400°F (205°C) oven for 12 to 15 minutes until golden. Makes 16 butterhorns.

1 butterhorn (without glaze): 169 Calories; 6.8 g Total Fat; 222 mg Sodium; 4 g Protein; 23 g Carbohydrate; 1 g Dietary Fibre

Pictured above.

Pastry Glaze

The butterhorns are wonderful the way they are, but we've included a glaze recipe to drizzle on them while they are warm. Toasted sliced almonds are also a lovely addition.

Icing sugar	1 1/2 cups	375 mL
Milk	1 1/2 tbsp.	25 mL
Butter, softened	2 tbsp.	30 mL
Almond flavouring (or vanilla)	1/8 tsp.	0.5 mL

Place all 4 ingredients in small bowl. Mix until smooth. Drizzle over warm Butterhorns. Make about 2/3 cup (150 mL).

1 tbsp. (15 mL): 86 Calories; 2.1 g Total Fat; 26 mg Sodium; trace Protein; 17 g Carbohydrate; 0 g Dietary Fibre

Pictured above.

Doughnuts

Created when maple sugar and syrup were more readily available than granulated sugar, these deep-fried puffs are part of Quebec's annual sugaring ritual. *"We've eaten them as far back as I can remember. They go well with the sugar on snow (a traditional sugaring-off taffy treat)."*
— Anne Jewett-Pagé, Knowlton, Quebec

Large eggs	3	3
Maple syrup	3/4 cup	175 mL
Milk	1 cup	250 mL
Vanilla	1 tsp.	5 mL
All-purpose flour	4 cups	1 L
Baking powder	2 tbsp.	30 mL
Salt	1/2 tsp.	2 mL
Ground nutmeg	1/2 tsp.	2 mL
Butter (or hard margarine), melted	3 tbsp.	50 mL
Cooking oil, for deep-frying	6 cups	1.5 L
Granulated sugar (optional)	1/2 cup	125 mL

Beat eggs in large bowl until light and fluffy.

Add next 3 ingredients. Mix well.

Sift next 4 ingredients together in separate large bowl. Stir into egg mixture.

Add butter. Mix until combined. Cover. Chill for 1 hour. Turn out dough onto floured surface. Press out with lightly floured hands to 1 inch (2.5 cm) thickness. Cover with tea towel. Let stand for 5 minutes. Cut with 2 1/2 inch (6.4 cm) doughnut cutter.♦ Place doughnuts and doughnut holes on lightly floured baking sheet. Repeat until all trimmed pieces of dough are used. (Be sure not to overwork dough or incorporate too much additional flour as this can make doughnuts dense.) Cover with tea towel. Chill.

Deep-fry doughnuts, 2 to 4 at a time, in hot (375°F, 190°C) cooking oil for about 5 minutes, turning once, until golden brown. Deep-fry doughnut holes, 5 to 6 at a time, for about 4 minutes, stirring occasionally, until golden brown. Remove to paper towels to drain.

Roll doughnuts in sugar while still warm. Makes about 20 doughnuts and 20 doughnut holes.

doughnut: 180 Calories; 7.1 g Total Fat; 159 mg Sodium; 3 g Protein; 25 g Carbohydrate; 1 g Dietary Fibre

♦ *You can also use a 2 1/2 inch (6.4 cm) round cutter to make the doughnut, then a 1 1/4 inch (3 cm) cutter to make the hole.*

Cinnamon Rolls

Cinnamon rolls are so popular and so appealing, they've given rise to specialty outlets in malls across the country. But there's nothing like the fragrance of these homemade treats wafting through the house. They're a lot easier to make than you think, especially if you get the kids involved. As always, these are best eaten warm.

Granulated sugar	1/4 cup	60 mL
Warm water	3/4 cup	175 mL
Warm milk	3/4 cup	175 mL
Active dry yeast (1/4 oz., 8 g, envelope)	2 1/4 tsp.	11 mL
Hard margarine (or butter), melted	1/4 cup	60 mL
Large egg, fork-beaten	1	1
All-purpose flour, approximately	4 1/2 cups	1.1 L
Salt	1/2 tsp.	2 mL
CINNAMON FILLING		
Hard margarine (or butter), softened	1/4 cup	60 mL
Brown sugar, packed	2/3 cup	150 mL
Ground cinnamon	1 1/2 tbsp.	25 mL
Hard margarine (or butter), melted	3 tbsp.	50 mL
Brown sugar, packed	2 tbsp.	30 mL

Combine first 4 ingredients in medium bowl. Cover. Let stand in warm place for 10 minutes. Stir to dissolve yeast. Add margarine and egg. Stir.

Sift flour and salt into large bowl. Stir in yeast mixture. Mix until soft dough forms, adding more flour as needed. Turn out onto lightly floured surface. Knead for 5 to 10 minutes until smooth and elastic. Place dough in lightly greased bowl, turning once to grease top. Cover with waxed paper and tea towel. Let stand in oven with light on and door closed for about 1 1/2 hours until doubled in bulk. Turn out onto lightly floured surface. Roll into 12 x 17 inch (30 x 43 cm) rectangle.

Cinnamon Filling: Spread first amount of margarine over dough. Combine first amount of brown sugar and cinnamon in small cup. Sprinkle over dough. Roll up starting from long side. Cut into 1 1/2 inch (3.8 cm) thick slices. Arrange rolls, just touching, in lightly greased 9 x 13 inch (22 x 33 cm) pan. Cover with greased plastic wrap. Let stand in oven with light on and door closed for 45 minutes until doubled in bulk.

Brush with second amount of margarine. Sprinkle with second amount of brown sugar. Bake in 375°F (190°C) oven for about 25 minutes until golden. Best served warm. Makes 12 rolls.

1 roll: 390 Calories; 12.2 g Total Fat; 249 mg Sodium; 7 g Protein; 63 g Carbohydrate; 2 g Dietary Fibre

Pictured below.

Cinnamon Rolls, above

Photo by: Ian Grant

Pampushky
(Filled Sweet Buns)

"Pampushky are a wonderful dessert any time of the year. You can fill them with your favourite fruits like cherries, blueberries or Saskatoon berries. The traditional fillings are poppy seed and prune, but my family also enjoys poppy seed with raisin."
— Zonnia Ostopowich, Edmonton, Alberta

POPPY SEED FILLING

Poppy seeds	1 1/4 cups	300 mL
Boiling water, to cover		
Granulated sugar	2 tbsp.	30 mL
Liquid honey	1 tbsp.	15 mL
Freshly grated lemon zest	1/2 tsp.	2 mL
Egg white (large), fork-beaten	1	1

DOUGH

Large egg	1	1
Granulated sugar	2 tbsp.	30 mL
Salt	1 tsp.	5 mL
Cooking oil	2 tbsp.	30 mL
Hot water	1 cup	250 mL
All-purpose flour	3 cups	750 mL
Instant yeast	1 1/2 tsp.	7 mL
All-purpose flour	3/4 - 1 cup	175-250 mL
Cooking oil, for deep-frying		
Icing sugar, for dusting		

Poppy Seed Filling: Combine poppy seeds and boiling water in medium bowl. Cover. Let stand for at least 8 hours or overnight. Drain. Grind seeds in clean electric coffee grinder, or with mortar and pestle, until finely ground and creamy. Return to same bowl.

Add remaining 4 ingredients. Mix well. Makes 1 1/2 cups (375 mL).

Dough: Combine first 4 ingredients in large bowl. Gradually add water, stirring constantly.

Combine first amount of flour and yeast in small bowl. Add to egg mixture in 2 additions. Stir until dough pulls away from side of bowl and is very sticky.

Turn dough out onto lightly floured surface. Gradually knead in second amount of flour, as needed. Dough should be manageable but still slightly sticky. Place dough in large greased bowl, turning once to grease top. Cover with waxed paper and tea towel. Let stand in oven with light on and door closed for about 1 1/2 hours until doubled in bulk. Divide dough into 2 portions. Place 1 portion in sealed container. Chill until ready to use. Turn out remaining portion onto lightly floured surface. Roll out to 1/8 inch (3 mm) thickness. Cut into 2 1/2 inch (6.4 cm) circles.◆ Place 1 tsp. (5 mL) of filling in centre of each circle, ensuring filling doesn't touch edge so edges stick together when folded. Fold in half. Pinch edges together firmly to seal. (To prevent fingers from getting too sticky, dip them in flour before pinching edges.) Gently roll in palm to form oval shape. Arrange in single layer on lightly floured, tea towel-lined baking sheet. Cover with tea towel. Let stand in oven with light on and door closed for 15 to 20 minutes until slightly risen. Repeat with remaining portion of dough.

Cook, 8 to 12 at a time, in hot (375°F, 190°C) cooking oil in large deep-fryer or pot, stirring occasionally, until golden and puffed. Remove with slotted spoon to paper towel-lined baking sheets. Cool.

Dust lightly with icing sugar just before serving. Makes about 6 dozen.

1 pampushok: 72 Calories; 4.1 g Total Fat; 35 mg Sodium; 1 g Protein; 8 g Carbohydrate; trace Dietary Fibre

Pictured on this page

◆*We used an empty, clean 10 oz. (284 mL) soup can for cutting circles.*

Variations: Substitute one of these fillings for the Poppy Seed Filling.

PRUNE FILLING

Pitted prunes, firmly packed	1 1/2 cups	375 mL
Water, to cover		
Granulated sugar	3 tbsp.	50 mL
Freshly grated lemon (or orange) zest	1/2 tsp.	2 mL
Ground cinnamon, dash		
Ground allspice, dash		
Ground nutmeg, dash		

Combine all 7 ingredients in medium saucepan. Bring to a boil. Reduce heat to medium. Simmer, uncovered, for about 10 minutes until almost all liquid evaporates. Cool slightly. Process in blender until almost smooth. Spoon into medium bowl. Chill well before using. Makes 1 1/2 cups (375 mL).

POPPY SEED WITH RAISIN FILLING

Poppy seeds	1 cup	250 mL
Boiling water, to cover		
Granulated sugar	1/4 cup	60 mL
Raisins	1/3 cup	75 mL
Egg white (large), fork-beaten	1	1

Combine poppy seeds and boiling water in medium bowl. Cover. Let stand at least 8 hours or overnight. Drain. Grind seeds in clean electric coffee grinder, or with mortar and pestle, until finely ground and creamy. Return to same bowl.

Add remaining 3 ingredients. Mix well. Makes about 1 1/2 cups (375 mL).

Overnight Bread,
below

Overnight Bread

This is a great bread to keep on hand in the
freezer. The rich, nutty flavour is terrific with
cheese or cream cheese spreads.
— Barbara Pankratz, Edmonton, Alberta

7-grain cereal	3 cups	750 mL
Whole wheat flour	1 cup	250 mL
Salt	1 tsp.	5 mL
Baking soda	2 tsp.	10 mL
Fancy (mild) molasses	1/4 cup	60 mL
Liquid honey	1/4 cup	60 mL
Hot water	3 cups	750 mL

Combine first 6 ingredients in medium bowl.

Add hot water. Mix well. Pour into fancy or
9 x 5 x 3 inch (22 x 12.5 x 7.5 cm) loaf pan.
Let stand overnight. Bake in 275°F (140°C)
oven for 3 hours. Let stand for 15 minutes.
Turn out onto wire rack to cool completely.
Cuts into 12 slices.

1 slice: 185 Calories; 1.9 g Total Fat; 417 mg Sodium;
5 g Protein; 41 g Carbohydrate; 6 g Dietary Fibre

Pictured above.

Puri
(Deep-Fried Roti)

*"My mum says this versatile Puri (POOR-ee)
dough (can be used for green onion cakes (add
approximately 1/4 cup (60 mL) chopped fresh
green onion at kneading stage) or cumin cakes (add
approximately 1 tbsp. (15 mL) toasted cumin seed).
To use the plain dough as a dessert, sprinkle with
icing sugar."* Ghee is available in South Asian
grocery stores.
— Naazima Ali, Edmonton, Alberta

All-purpose flour	2 cups	500 mL
Baking powder	1 tsp.	5 mL
Salt, just a pinch		
Lukewarm water	1/4-1/2 cup	60-125 mL
Ghee (or butter)	2 tbsp.	30 mL
Cooking oil	2 cups	500 mL

Combine first 3 ingredients in medium bowl.
Add lukewarm water, a little at a time, until
dough is crumbly.

Knead ghee into dough, a little at a time, until
well combined. Dough will be stiff. Roll dough
into 1 1/4 inch (3 cm) balls. Flatten each ball
between palms. Roll out 1/8 inch (3 mm) thick,
to about 4 inches (10 cm) in diameter. Repeat
with remaining dough.

Heat cooking oil in saucepan or frying pan
until small piece of dough dropped in sizzles.
Carefully place 2 dough rounds in oil. Dough
will puff and float to surface. Spoon oil over
top of rounds using long-handled spoon to
increase browning. Cook for 1 to 2 minutes
until crisp and golden. Remove to paper towels
to drain. Repeat with remaining dough rounds.
Makes 12 to 14.

1 puri: 120 Calories; 4.7 g Total Fat; 31 mg Sodium;
2 g Protein; 17 g Carbohydrate; 1 g Dietary Fibre

Pictured on page 150.

Taber Cornfest Cornbread

Molly Cuddeford organizes the cornbread contest for the annual (and famous!) Taber Cornfest. *"This bread is great in the bottom of a bowl topped with hot bean chili."*
— Molly Cuddeford, Taber, Alberta

All-purpose flour	1 1/4 cups	300 mL
Granulated sugar	2 tbsp.	30 mL
Yellow cornmeal	3/4 cup	175 mL
Baking powder	4 tsp.	20 mL
Salt	1/2 tsp.	2 mL
Large egg, fork-beaten	1	1
Can of diced green chilies, with liquid	4 oz.	113 g
Buttermilk (or reconstituted from powder)	2/3 cup	150 mL
Butter (or hard margarine), melted	1/3 cup	75 mL
Fresh corn kernels (about 1 small cob)	1/2 cup	125 mL

Combine first 5 ingredients in large bowl. Mix well.

Combine remaining 5 ingredients in medium bowl. Add to flour mixture. Gently stir until combined. Pour mixture into greased 8 x 8 inch (20 x 20 cm) pan. Bake in 400°F (205°C) oven for about 30 minutes. Wooden pick inserted in centre should come out clean. Cool in pan for 10 minutes. Cuts into 16 pieces.

1 square: 37 Calories; 0.2 g Total Fat; 6 mg Sodium; 1 g Protein; 9 g Carbohydrate; 1 g Dietary Fibre

Pictured below.

Bacon and Cheese Cornbread

Sharon was so excited about finding a good cornbread recipe that she shared it with our readers. *"It was a family hit! I bet you will like it, too."*
— Sharon Radford, Scarborough, Ontario

Cornmeal	1/2 cup	125 mL
Milk	1 1/4 cups	300 mL
Milk	1/4 cup	60 mL
Large eggs, fork-beaten	2	2
Hard margarine (or butter)	1/4 cup	60 mL
Salt	1/4 tsp.	1 mL
Baking powder	1 tbsp.	15 mL
Grated Cheddar cheese	1 cup	250 mL
Bacon slices, cooked crisp and crumbled	5	5

Combine cornmeal and first amount of milk in medium saucepan. Stir on medium for about 5 minutes until thick and dry. Spoon mixture into large bowl.

Add second amount of milk and remaining 6 ingredients. Mix until smooth. Pour mixture into greased 8 x 8 inch (20 x 20 cm) cake pan. Bake in 325°F (160°C) oven for about 45 minutes until wooden pick inserted in centre comes out clean. Cuts into 9 squares.

1 square: 187 Calories; 13.2 g Total Fat; 427 mg Sodium; 8 g Protein; 9 g Carbohydrate; trace Dietary Fibre

Corn Chowder, page 199, with Taber Cornfest Cornbread, above

For no-risk biscuits:

Ingredients

Sift the dry ingredients together and mix well so the **baking powder** is evenly distributed.

Butter should be cold to ensure that it is cut, rather than mashed, into the flour.

Cold milk helps keep the butter hard during mixing.

Utensils

Use a **pastry blender or two knives** to cut the butter into the dry ingredients.

Mix the liquid in with a **fork** and there's less likelihood of overworking the dough.

Technique

For **tender biscuits**, knead the dough gently and quickly after adding the liquid; the more mixing or kneading, the tougher the biscuits.

For **even rising**, don't twist the cutter as you cut the dough cut straight down.

For **soft-sided biscuits**, set them on the baking sheet so they're touching; for **crisp sides**, set the biscuits apart.

Buttermilk Biscuits

These are just the biscuits you need to go with Pearl Hunter's Rhubarb Pineapple Jam, page 151, or any other favourite jam or marmalade.

All-purpose flour	2 cups	500 mL
Baking powder	2 tsp.	10 mL
Salt	1/2 tsp.	2 mL
Hard margarine (or butter)	3 tbsp.	50 mL
Baking soda	1/2 tsp.	2 mL
Buttermilk (or reconstituted from powder)	1 cup	250 mL

Place first 3 ingredients in medium bowl. Cut in margarine until mixture is crumbly.

Stir baking soda into buttermilk in small bowl. Add to flour mixture. Stir until dough forms a ball. Turn out onto lightly floured surface. Knead 8 to 10 times. Roll or pat into circle, 1/2 to 3/4 inches (1.2 to 2 cm) thick. Cut into 2 inch (5 cm) rounds. Place on greased cookie sheet, 1 inch (2.5 cm) apart. Bake in 450°F (230°C) oven for 10 to 12 minutes until lightly golden. Makes 16 biscuits.

1 biscuit: 86 Calories; 2.5 g Total Fat; 200 mg Sodium; 2 g Protein; 14 g Carbohydrate; 1 g Dietary Fibre

Tea Biscuits

The trademark of this quick bread is its texture. Baking powder is the main leavening agent, but layers of butter and flour play an equally important role in creating a light, tender tea biscuit. As the butter melts during baking, it creates tiny spaces that are filled and enlarged into "holes" by the steam created as moisture in the biscuit evaporates.

All-purpose flour	2 cups	500 mL
Baking powder	4 tsp.	20 mL
Granulated sugar	2 tsp.	10 mL
Salt	1/2 tsp.	2 mL
Cold butter (or hard margarine), cut into cubes	1/2 cup	125 mL
Cold milk	3/4 cup	175 mL
Milk	1 tbsp.	15 mL

Sift first 4 ingredients into medium bowl. Mix well. Cut in butter until mixture is texture of coarse crumbs (see photo 1). Make a well in centre.

Tea Biscuits, below

Pour cold milk into well. Use fork or knife to stir until just moistened (see photo 2). Turn out onto lightly floured surface. Gently knead once or twice until smooth. Press out to 3/4 inch (2 cm) thickness. Cut with 2 1/2 inch (6.4 cm) straight-edged round cutter dipped in flour before each cut. Repeat with trimmed pieces of dough, handling gently. Arrange biscuits on lightly greased 8 x 8 inch (20 x 20 cm) baking sheet, just touching each other, for soft sides (see photo 3). For crisp sides, arrange about 1 inch (2.5 cm) apart.

Lightly brush tops of biscuits with second amount of milk. Bake in 450°F (230°C) oven on rack set just above centre position for about 15 minutes until golden and hollow-sounding when tapped on top. Let stand in pan for 5 minutes. Serve warm or turn out onto wire rack to cool. Makes 9 biscuits.

1 biscuit: 217 Calories; 11.3 g Total Fat; 419 mg Sodium; 4 g Protein; 25 g Carbohydrate; 1 g Dietary Fibre

Pictured above.

Bran Muffins

"This is my variation on a recipe received from my mother-in-law. She said they were 'nice and moist and very healthful.' The muffins are also very quick to make, and freeze well!" Unbleached flour gives a nutritional boost.

— Gwen Toole, Saskatoon, Saskatchewan

Hard margarine (or butter)	1/4 cup	60 mL
Demerara sugar♦	1/2 cup	125 mL
Fancy (mild) molasses	1/4 cup	60 mL
Large eggs, fork-beaten	2	2
Milk	1 cup	250 mL
Natural bran	1 cup	250 mL
Wheat germ, toasted♦♦	1/2 cup	125 mL
Unbleached (or bleached) all-purpose flour	1 cup	250 mL
Baking powder	1/2 tsp.	2 mL
Baking soda	1/2 tsp.	2 mL
Golden raisins (or dried cranberries)	1/2 cup	125 mL

Cream margarine and sugar together in large bowl.

Stir in molasses. Add eggs and milk. Mix well.

Combine remaining 6 ingredients in medium bowl. Add to margarine mixture. Stir until just combined. Fill paper-lined muffin cups 3/4 full. Bake in 400°F (205°C) oven for 20 minutes until wooden pick comes out clean. Makes 12 muffins.

1 muffin: 190 Calories; 6.0 g Total Fat; 145 mg Sodium; 5 g Protein; 32 g Carbohydrate; 4 g Dietary Fibre

♦*Demerara sugar is a coarse-textured raw sugar with a distinctive caramel flavour. Brown sugar may be substituted.*

♦♦*To toast the wheat germ, place it in an ungreased frying pan. Heat on medium, stirring often, until golden.*

Morning Glory Muffins

"I used to work at a hospital in Oakville and there was a lady who made muffins every morning for us. When she retired I did some research to find these muffins . . . now I make them myself."

— Karen Hadfield, Long Point, Ontario

All-purpose flour	2 cups	500 mL
Granulated sugar	1 1/4 cups	300 mL
Baking soda	2 tsp.	10 mL
Ground cinnamon	2 tsp.	10 mL
Salt	1/2 tsp.	2 mL
Raisins	1/2 cup	125 mL
Walnuts, chopped	1/2 cup	125 mL
Medium unsweetened coconut	1/2 cup	125 mL
Medium Granny Smith apple, peeled and grated	1	1
Large eggs	3	3
Cooking oil	1/2 cup	125 mL
Vanilla	2 tsp.	10 mL

Combine first 9 ingredients in large bowl.

Whisk remaining 3 ingredients together until just combined. Add to flour mixture. Stir until just moistened. Do not overmix. Fill greased muffin cups 3/4 full. Bake in 350°F (175°C) oven for 20 to 25 minutes. Wooden pick inserted in centre of muffins should come out clean. Makes 12 muffins.

1 muffin: 362 Calories; 17.3 g Total Fat; 332 mg Sodium; 6 g Protein; 48 g Carbohydrate; 2 g Dietary Fibre

Pictured on page 45.

Blueberry Oatmeal Muffins

Moist homemade muffins are great brunch fare. If you have any left over, pack them up with a bit of Cheddar or Monterey Jack cheese for a quick lunch or snack.

Quick-cooking rolled oats (not instant)	1/2 cup	125 mL
All-purpose flour	2 cups	500 mL
Baking powder	2 tsp.	10 mL
Medium coconut	1/3 cup	75 mL
Dried blueberries	2/3 cup	150 mL
Brown sugar, packed	3/4 cup	175 mL
Cooking oil	1/2 cup	125 mL
Buttermilk (or reconstituted from powder)	1 cup	250 mL
Large egg, fork-beaten	1	1
Vanilla	1/2 tsp.	2 mL

Combine first 6 ingredients in large bowl.

Combine remaining 4 ingredients in small bowl. Add to rolled oat mixture. Stir until flour is just moistened. Fill greased muffin cups 3/4 full. Bake in 400°F (205°C) oven for 20 to 25 minutes until wooden pick inserted in centre comes out clean. Makes 12 muffins.

1 muffin: 289 Calories; 12.5 g Total Fat; 99 mg Sodium; 5 g Protein; 41 g Carbohydrate; 2 g Dietary Fibre

Pictured on page 45.

Orange Raisin Muffins

"This is a delicious moist muffin. Dates or nuts can be substituted for raisins." The fresh, sweet orange taste has great kid appeal—and they'll love throwing an unpeeled orange into the blender. We bet mom and dad will be packing these muffins in their lunch bags, too.

— Karen Hadfield, Long Point, Ontario

Small orange	1	1
Prepared orange juice	1/2 cup	125 mL
Large egg	1	1
Hard margarine (or butter), softened	1/2 cup	125 mL
Granulated sugar	2/3 cup	150 mL
Salt (optional)	1/2 tsp.	2 mL
Baking powder	1 tsp.	5 mL
Baking soda	1 tsp.	5 mL
All-purpose flour	1 1/2 cups	375 mL
Raisins	1/2 cup	125 mL

Wash orange. Cut into pieces. Remove seeds. Place orange and orange juice in blender or food processor. Process until peel is finely chopped.

Add egg and margarine. Process for 3 seconds until combined.

Combine remaining 6 ingredients in large bowl. Stir. Make a well in centre. Pour orange mixture into well. Stir until just moistened. Do not overmix. Fill 12 greased muffin cups 2/3 full. Bake in 375°F (190°C) oven for 15 to 20 minutes until wooden pick inserted in centre of muffin comes out clean. Cool in pan for 10 minutes before turning out onto wire rack to cool completely. Makes 12 muffins.

1 muffin: 213 Calories; 8.7 g Total Fat; 239 mg Sodium; 3 g Protein; 33 g Carbohydrate; 2 g Dietary Fibre

Pictured on page 45.

Clockwise from top left:
Morning Glory Muffins, left
Blueberry Oatmeal Muffins, left
Orange Raisin Muffins, above

Date Mini-Muffins

These muffins are perfect for brunch—bite-size and not too filling. Serve them paired with breakfast sausages and warmed applesauce.

Hard margarine (or butter), softened	1/3 cup	75 mL
Brown sugar, packed	1/2 cup	125 mL
Large egg	1	1
Vanilla	1 tsp.	5 mL
Milk	3/4 cup	175 mL
All-purpose flour	1 cup	250 mL
Graham wafer crumbs	1 cup	250 mL
Baking powder	1 tbsp.	15 mL
Salt	1/2 tsp.	2 mL
Chopped dates	3/4 cup	175 mL
Chopped pecans	1/3 cup	75 mL

Beat first 4 ingredients together in large bowl. Stir in milk.

Combine remaining 6 ingredients in medium bowl. Add to milk mixture. Stir until just combined. Fill greased mini-muffin cups 3/4 full. Bake in 375°F (190°C) oven for 15 to 18 minutes. Wooden pick inserted in centre should come out clean. Makes 24 mini-muffins.

1 mini-muffin: 113 Calories; 4.6 g Total Fat; 158 mg Sodium; 2 g Protein; 17 g Carbohydrate; 1 g Dietary Fibre

Mustard, Cheese and Rosemary Muffins, this page

Mustard, Cheese and Rosemary Muffins

Try these muffins as part of a brunch, as an after-school snack or in place of a bread roll with a salad or soup.

All-purpose flour	2 cups	500 mL
Baking powder	1 tbsp.	15 mL
Dry mustard	1 tbsp.	15 mL
Salt	1/2 tsp.	2 mL
Grated medium Cheddar cheese	1 cup	250 mL
Finely chopped fresh rosemary	1 tbsp.	15 mL
Buttermilk	1 cup	250 mL
Cooking oil	1/2 cup	125 mL
Large egg	1	1

Sift first 4 ingredients into large bowl.

Add cheese and rosemary. Stir. Make a well in centre.

Whisk remaining 3 ingredients together in small bowl. Pour into well. Stir until just moistened. Do not overmix. Fill greased muffin cups 2/3 full. Bake in 375°F (190°C) oven for 20 to 25 minutes until wooden pick inserted in centre of muffin comes out clean. Let stand in pan for 5 minutes before turning out onto wire rack. Makes 12 muffins.

1 muffin: 226 Calories; 14 g Total Fat; 282 mg Sodium; 6 g Protein; 19 g Carbohydrate; 1 g Dietary Fibre

Pictured above.

Ham, Zucchini and Cheese Muffins

Hearty muffins like these, featuring chunks of ham and lots of Cheddar, can be used to sandwich together vegetable and cheese fillings, or served as a side for a bowl of soup or chili.

Grated zucchini	3/4 cup	175 mL
Finely chopped ham	3/4 cup	175 mL
Grated sharp Cheddar cheese	1/2 cup	125 mL
All-purpose flour	2 1/4 cups	550 mL
Baking powder	1 tbsp.	15 mL
Milk	1 cup	250 mL
Cooking oil	1/3 cup	75 mL
Large egg	1	1
Finely chopped ham	1/2 cup	125 mL
Grated sharp Cheddar cheese	1/2 cup	125 mL

Combine first 5 ingredients in large bowl. Make a well in centre.

Stir next 3 ingredients together in small bowl. Pour into well. Stir until just moistened. Do not overmix. Fill 12 greased muffin cups 2/3 full.

Sprinkle with second amounts of ham and cheese. Bake in 350°F (175°C) oven for 25 minutes until wooden pick inserted in centre of muffin comes out clean. Cool in pan for 10 minutes before turning out onto wire rack to cool completely. Makes 12 muffins.

1 muffin: 256 Calories; 13.6 g Total Fat; 549 mg Sodium; 11 g Protein; 22 g Carbohydrate; 1 g Dietary Fibre

Cranberry Banana Loaf

Sweet, tart and very moist, this loaf was a winner at the Halifax City Farmer's Market.
— Claire Doyle, Isle Madame, Nova Scotia

Butter (or hard margarine), softened	1/4 cup	60 mL
Granulated sugar	1 cup	250 mL
Large eggs	2	2
Mashed banana (about 2 medium)	3/4 cup	175 mL
Chopped fresh (or frozen) cranberries	1 cup	250 mL
All-purpose flour	1 1/2 cups	375 mL
Baking powder	1 1/2 tsp.	7 mL
Baking soda	1/2 tsp.	2 mL
Salt	1/2 tsp.	2 mL
Ground cinnamon	1/2 tsp.	2 mL

Beat first 3 ingredients together in large bowl until smooth.

Add banana and cranberries. Stir.

Sift remaining 5 ingredients into medium bowl. Add to banana mixture. Stir until just combined. Spread into greased 9 x 5 x 3 inch (22 x 12.5 x 7.5 cm) loaf pan. Bake in 350°F (175°C) oven for about 1 hour until wooden pick inserted in centre comes out clean. Cool in pan 10 minutes. Remove to wire rack to cool completely. Makes 1 loaf. Cuts into 18 slices.

1 slice: 131 Calories; 3.4 g Total Fat; 168 mg Sodium; 2 g Protein; 23 g Carbohydrate; 1 g Dietary Fibre

Pictured below.

Buttermilk Pancakes

"When I was young, my family lived in a small town but my father had a farm nearby. When he got a cow my mother learned to make butter, using the leftover buttermilk for this recipe. These pancakes are a scrumptious favourite of mine for weekend mornings. I prefer to use real buttermilk for thicker texture and better taste, although you can substitute milk mixed with a tablespoon of vinegar or lemon juice."

— **Karen Decoux, Edmonton, Alberta**

All-purpose flour	3 cups	750 mL
Granulated sugar	2 tbsp.	30 mL
Baking soda	2 tsp.	10 mL
Baking powder	2 tsp.	10 mL
Salt	1 tsp.	5 mL
Egg yolks (large)	6	6
Buttermilk	3 1/3 cups	825 mL
Butter (or hard margarine), melted	6 tbsp.	100 mL
Egg whites (large)	6	6

Sift first 5 ingredients together into large bowl. Make a well in centre.

Beat next 3 ingredients together in medium bowl until well combined. Pour into well. Mix until just moistened.

Beat egg whites in separate large bowl until stiff but not dry. Fold into batter. Heat greased frying pan or electric griddle on medium-high until drops of water dance around on surface. For each 4 inch (10 cm) pancake, spoon 1/4 cup (60 mL) batter into frying pan. Cook until bubbles appear on surface and edges are lightly browned. Flip over. Cook until lightly browned. Makes about 40 (4 inch, 10 cm) pancakes.

1 pancake: 72 Calories; 2.7 g Total Fat; 190 mg Sodium; 3 g Protein; 9 g Carbohydrate; trace Dietary Fibre

Pictured above.

Pitcher Pointer

For easy pouring onto the griddle, mix your batter in a juice jug with a spout.

Dad's Griddlecakes

"I grew up on these pancakes. When I was a kid, Dad used to make these for me each day before I went to school. I make them for my grandchildren now, and hopefully they will carry on with their children."

— Adele Zboril, Saskatoon, Saskatchewan

All-purpose flour	2 cups	500 mL
Baking powder	2 tbsp.	30 mL
Granulated sugar	1 tbsp.	15 mL
Salt	3/4 tsp.	4 mL
Butter (or hard margarine), melted	2 tbsp.	30 mL
Large eggs	2	2
Milk	2 cups	500 mL

Sift first 4 ingredients together into large bowl. Make a well in centre.

Beat remaining 3 ingredients in medium bowl until well combined. Pour into well. Mix until just moistened. Batter will be thick and lumpy. Heat greased frying pan or electric griddle on medium-high until drops of water dance around on surface. For each 2 inch (5 cm) pancake, spoon 1 tbsp. (15 mL) batter into frying pan. Cook until bubbles appear on surface and edges are lightly browned. Flip over. Cook until lightly browned. Makes about 65 (2 inch, 5 cm) pancakes.

1 pancake: 24 Calories; 0.6 g Total Fat; 69 mg Sodium; 1 g Protein; 4 g Carbohydrate; trace Dietary Fibre

Muesli Pancakes

Muesli is a Swiss breakfast dish of oats soaked in milk and combined with dried fruits, yogurt and honey. Prepare the batter for these dense, moist pancakes the night before and refrigerate to allow the oats to soften. Pass on the syrup for these hotcakes and enjoy them with yogurt and fresh fruit instead.

Milk	1 3/4 cups	425 mL
Quick-cooking rolled oats (not instant)	1/2 cup	125 mL
Raisins	1/2 cup	125 mL
Plain yogurt	1/4 cup	60 mL
Liquid honey	3 tbsp.	50 mL
Vanilla	1/2 tsp.	2 mL
Large eggs, fork-beaten	2	2
Tart medium cooking apple (such as Granny Smith), with peel, cored and grated	1	1

All-purpose flour	1 cup	250 mL
Baking powder	1 tbsp.	15 mL
Salt	1/4 tsp.	1 mL

Combine first 8 ingredients in large non-reactive bowl.

Sift remaining 3 ingredients together into small bowl. Add to oat mixture. Mix until just moistened. Cover. Chill overnight. Heat greased frying pan or electric griddle on medium-high until drops of water dance around on surface. Stir batter well. For each 4 inch (10 cm) pancake, spoon 1/4 cup (60 mL) batter into frying pan. Cook until bubbles appear on surface and edges are lightly browned. Flip over. Cook until lightly browned. Makes about 15 (4 inch, 10 cm) pancakes.

1 pancake: 92 Calories; 1.3 g Total Fat; 124 mg Sodium; 3 g Protein; 18 g Carbohydrate; 1 g Dietary Fibre

Orange Spice Pancakes

For pancake lovers who can't tolerate gluten or lactose, these low-fat pancakes are great! They have a slightly grainy texture and a lovely orange and spice flavour.

Rice flour	2 cups	500 mL
Granulated sugar	1/4 cup	60 mL
Baking soda	1 tsp.	5 mL
Salt	1/4 tsp.	1 mL
Ground cinnamon	1/4 tsp.	1 mL
Ground nutmeg, just a pinch		
Large eggs	2	2
Orange juice	1 cup	250 mL
Cooking oil	1 tbsp.	15 mL
Vanilla	1/2 tsp.	2 mL

Sift first 6 ingredients together into medium bowl. Make a well in centre.

Beat eggs in separate medium bowl until light and fluffy. Add remaining 3 ingredients. Stir. Pour into well. Stir until thoroughly combined. Heat greased frying pan or electric griddle on medium-high until drops of water dance around on surface. For each 2 inch (5 cm) pancake, spoon 1 tbsp. (15 mL) batter into frying pan. Cook until top appears dry. Flip over. Cook until lightly browned. Makes about 50 (2 inch, 5 cm) pancakes.

1 pancake: 36 Calories; 0.7 g Total Fat; 41 mg Sodium; 1 g Protein; 7 g Carbohydrate; trace Dietary Fibre

Express Yourself

If you find yourself going round and round in circles, try your hand at pouring the batter in animal, fruit or vegetable shapes instead. Add a chocolate chip happy face or a candy sprinkle starburst. Or personalize each pancake with an initial.

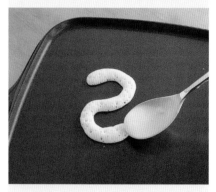

Draw a mirror image of the desired initial (a spoon, squeeze bottle or turkey baster works well).

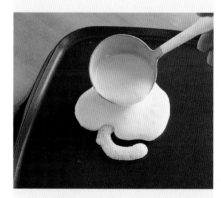

Completely cover the initial with more batter.

Ta-da! Once flipped, everyone knows whose pancake is whose.

Piña Colada Pancakes with Tropical Fruit Topping

These tropical-tasting pancakes are filled with our favourite Caribbean flavours—coconut, banana, pineapple, mango, and even a little rum.

TROPICAL FRUIT TOPPING

Shredded coconut	1/2 cup	125 mL
Cooking oil	1 tbsp.	15 mL
Medium bananas, cut into 1/2 inch (12 mm) slices	2	2
Rum (or 1/4 tsp., 1 mL, rum flavouring), optional	1 tbsp.	15 mL
Can of pineapple chunks, drained	14 oz.	398 mL
Fresh ripe mango, diced	1	1
Golden corn syrup	1 cup	250 mL

PIÑA COLADA PANCAKES

All-purpose flour	2 cups	500 mL
Brown sugar, packed	1/2 cup	125 mL
Baking soda	2 tsp.	10 mL
Salt	1/2 tsp.	2 mL
Egg yolks (large)	3	3
Pineapple juice	1 1/2 cups	375 mL
Cooking oil	2 tbsp.	30 mL
Coconut flavouring	1/4 tsp.	1 mL
Egg whites (large)	3	3

Tropical Fruit Topping: Toast coconut in large ungreased frying pan on medium until lightly browned. Transfer to small serving dish. Set aside.

Heat cooking oil in same frying pan on medium. Add banana. Sauté for 1 minute.

Add next 4 ingredients. Bring to a gentle boil on medium. Reduce heat to low. Simmer, uncovered, for about 10 minutes, stirring occasionally, until fruit is hot and sauce is slightly reduced. Transfer to separate serving dish. Cover to keep warm. Makes 3 cups (750 mL) topping.

Piña Colada Pancakes: Sift first 4 ingredients together into large bowl. Make a well in centre.

Beat egg yolks in separate large bowl until light and fluffy. Add next 3 ingredients. Stir. Pour into well. Mix until just moistened.

Beat egg whites in medium bowl until stiff but not dry. Fold into batter. Heat greased frying pan or electric griddle on medium-high until drops of water dance around on surface. For each 4 inch (10 cm) pancake, spoon 1/4 cup (60 mL) batter into frying pan. Cook until bubbles appear on surface and edges are lightly browned. Flip over. Cook until lightly browned. Serve with warm topping and toasted coconut. Makes about 20 (4 inch, 10 cm) pancakes.

1 pancake with 2 1/2 tbsp. (37 mL) topping: 199 Calories; 4.6 g Total Fat; 222 mg Sodium; 3 g Protein; 39 g Carbohydrate; 1 g Dietary Fibre

Pictured below.

Gingerbread Pancakes with Pear and Maple Pecan Topping

Fans of both gingerbread and pancakes will go for these flapjacks. Topped with a chunky fruit and nut combination, these are a nice change from the usual pancakes.

PEAR AND MAPLE PECAN TOPPING

Butter (or hard margarine)	1/4 cup	60 mL
Can of pear halves, drained and coarsely chopped	28 oz.	796 mL
Pecans, toasted and coarsely chopped◆	1 cup	250 mL
Maple syrup	1 1/2 cups	375 mL
Ground cinnamon	1/2 tsp.	2 mL
Ground nutmeg, just a pinch		

GINGERBREAD PANCAKES

All-purpose flour	2 cups	500 mL
Brown sugar, packed	1/4 cup	60 mL
Baking soda	2 tsp.	10 mL
Salt	1/2 tsp.	2 mL
Ground ginger	1/2 tsp.	2 mL
Ground cinnamon	1/4 tsp.	1 mL
Ground cloves	1/8 tsp.	0.5 mL
Large eggs	3	3
Fancy (mild) molasses	3 tbsp.	50 mL
Buttermilk	1 3/4 cups	425 mL

Pear and Maple Pecan Topping: Melt butter in large saucepan on medium-high. Add pear and pecans. Sauté for 1 minute until coated.

Add next 3 ingredients. Bring to a gentle boil. Reduce heat to low. Simmer, uncovered, for 5 minutes, stirring occasionally, to blend flavours. Cover to keep warm. Makes 3 cups (750 mL) topping.

Gingerbread Pancakes: Sift first 7 ingredients together into large bowl. Make a well in centre.

Beat eggs until light and fluffy. Add molasses and buttermilk. Stir. Pour into well. Mix until just moistened. Heat greased frying pan or electric griddle on medium-high until drops of water dance around on surface. For each 4 inch (10 cm) pancake, spoon 1/4 cup (60 mL) batter into frying pan. Cook until bubbles appear on surface and edges are lightly browned. Flip over. Cook until lightly browned. Serve with warm topping. Makes about 20 (4 inch, 10 cm) pancakes.

1 pancake with 2 1/2 tbsp. (37 mL) topping: 241 Calories; 8.2 g Total Fat; 265 mg Sodium; 4 g Protein; 39 g Carbohydrate; 2 g Dietary Fibre

◆To toast pecans, place in single layer in ungreased shallow pan. Bake in 350°F (175°C) oven for 5 to 10 minutes, stirring or shaking often, until desired doneness.

Over-the-Top Ideas

When you want to break with the butter-and-maple-syrup tradition, give one of these toppings a try.

Peaches and Cream: Canned sliced peaches with whipped cream

Black Forest: Bing cherries, whipped cream and chocolate shavings or chocolate sauce

Warm Berry Compote: Frozen mixed berries simmered to a thick sauce (with a little liqueur, if you like)

Bella Italia: Ricotta cheese mixed with orange zest and vanilla sugar, and topped with broiled grapefruit segments

Also good on waffles, French toast, or any plain cake.

The Heat is On

The griddle is at the right cooking temperature when water dances on the surface.

Flip your pancake when bubbles cover the surface of the uncooked side and the edge is lightly browned.

Jason's Breakfast Burritos

"My husband, Jason, and I used to drive truck as a team. Each week we travelled to the U.S. West Coast, gaining a real appreciation for Mexican food. Our favourite warehouse to load produce for home was in Yuma, Arizona, where a little catering booth served lots of Mexican dishes, including bacon and egg burritos, our favourite! Jason created this recipe, and these burritos taste every bit as good as the ones in Yuma. We make it two or three times per week, and overnight guests always request it." Serve with salsa and additional sour cream, taco sauce and diced tomatoes.

— Robyn Larabee, Lucknow, Ontario

Large eggs	8	8
Sour cream	1/4 cup	60 mL
Grated Cheddar cheese	1/2 cup	125 mL
Taco sauce	2 tbsp.	30 mL
Hot pepper sauce	1 tsp.	5 mL
Bacon slices, chopped	7	7
Frozen hash brown potatoes	1 cup	250 mL
Chopped onion	2 tbsp.	30 mL
Flour tortillas (10 inch, 25 cm, size)	4	4
Grated Cheddar cheese	1/2 cup	125 mL

Combine first 5 ingredients in medium bowl. Mix well. Set aside.

Cook bacon in frying pan on medium-high for 6 minutes until almost crisp. Remove bacon to paper towel to drain. Drain all but 1 tbsp. (15 mL) drippings from pan.

Sauté hash browns and onion in reserved drippings for about 8 minutes until hash browns are crisp and browned. Add egg mixture and bacon. Heat and stir on low for 5 minutes until eggs are just set. Remove from heat.

Divide and spread egg filling down centre of each tortilla. Roll up to enclose filling. Place tortillas, seam side down, in lightly greased baking dish.

Sprinkle with second amount of cheese. Bake in 350°F (175°C) oven for about 5 minutes until cheese is melted. Serves 4.

1 serving: 572 Calories; 34.1 g Total Fat; 729 mg Sodium; 29 g Protein; 36 g Carbohydrate; 3 g Dietary Fibre

Do-Ahead Breakfast Bake, below

Do-Ahead Breakfast Bake

Whip this up the night before and bake it for about an hour the next morning as you squeeze some oranges for juice and make the coffee. Makes a hungry throng very happy.

Loaf of Texas toast, crusts removed and cut into 1 inch (2.5 cm) cubes	1/2	1/2
Bacon slices, cooked crisp and crumbled	6	6
Grated Cheddar cheese	1/2 cup	125 mL
Green onions, chopped	4	4
Small red peppers, chopped	2	2
Large eggs	8	8
Milk	2 cups	500 mL
Mayonnaise	2 tbsp.	30 mL
Dry mustard	1 tsp.	5 mL
Chopped fresh sweet basil	1/4 cup	60 mL
Salt, to taste		
Pepper, to taste		

Arrange bread in bottom of greased deep 3 quart (3 L) baking dish. Sprinkle with next 4 ingredients.

Stir remaining 7 ingredients together in medium bowl. Pour evenly over bread. Cover. Chill overnight. Bake, uncovered, in 350°F (175°C) oven for 50 to 60 minutes until set and golden. Serve warm. Serves 6 to 8.

1 serving: 376 Calories; 19.6 g Total Fat; 546 mg Sodium; 20 g Protein; 30 g Carbohydrate; 2 g Dietary Fibre

Pictured above.

Poached Salmon with Herbed Mayonnaise

Salmon fillets infused with the delicate flavours of citrus and wine are a perfect complement to the fresh, herbed mayonnaise. A light and elegant make-ahead dish for spring.

Medium lemons, quartered	2	2
Medium onions, sliced	2	2
White (or alcohol-free) wine	1 cup	250 mL
Whole black peppercorns	12	12
Bay leaves	4	4
Water	2 cups	500 mL
Salmon fillets, trimmed, skin removed, cut into 12 equal pieces◆	3 1/2 lbs.	1.6 kg

HERBED MAYONNAISE

Large eggs	3	3
Dijon mustard	1 tbsp.	15 mL
Salt	1/4 tsp.	1 mL
Freshly ground pepper, just a pinch		
Olive (or cooking) oil	1 cup	250 mL
White wine vinegar	2 tbsp.	30 mL
Cooking oil	1/2 cup	125 mL
Finely chopped fresh chives	2 tbsp.	30 mL
Finely chopped fresh dill	1 tbsp.	15 mL
Finely grated lemon zest	1 tsp.	5 mL
Freshly squeezed lemon juice	1 tbsp.	15 mL

Combine first 6 ingredients in large saucepan. Bring to a boil on medium-high. Reduce heat to medium-low. Cover. Simmer for 20 minutes, stirring occasionally. Strain into large frying pan. Discard solids.

Bring wine mixture to a simmer on medium-low. Add half of salmon. Cover. Poach for 15 minutes until fish flakes easily when tested with fork. Carefully remove to parchment-lined baking sheet with sides. Repeat with remaining salmon. Discard poaching liquid. Chill salmon for 2 hours or overnight. Remove any gelatin or fat before serving.

Herbed Mayonnaise: Combine first 4 ingredients in food processor or blender.

With motor running, slowly add next 3 ingredients, in order given, in steady stream through feed chute. Process until mixture has the consistency of thin mayonnaise.

Tomato Tart, below

Add remaining 4 ingredients. Process for minute until well combined. Chill for at least hour to blend flavours. (Mayonnaise can be refrigerated for up to 4 days.) Makes 2 1/3 cups 575 mL). Serve with salmon. Serves 12.

piece salmon with 2 tbsp. (30 mL) Herbed Mayonnaise: 07 Calories; 31.2 g Total Fat; 122 mg Sodium; 25 g Protein; g Carbohydrate; trace Dietary Fibre

ictured below.

For even cooking, choose salmon from the hicker centre of the fillet, rather than from he thinner tail end.

Smoked Salmon and Brie Frittatas

wonderful brunch table addition, these muffin-shaped frittatas also work well as a light lunch. Just pair them with baby potatoes and teamed asparagus tossed in lemon juice and oasted almond slices.

arge eggs, fork-beaten	6	6
moked salmon, coarsely chopped	6 oz.	170 g
Brie cheese, chopped	3 1/2 oz.	100 g
Chopped fresh dill	1 1/2 tbsp.	25 mL
Capers, finely chopped	1 1/2 tbsp.	25 mL
reshly ground pepper	1/2 tsp.	2 mL

Combine all 6 ingredients in large bowl. Fill greased muffin cups with 1/3 cup (75 mL) almon mixture. Cover with foil. Bake in 375°F 190°C) oven for 10 minutes. Remove foil. ake for further 10 minutes until set. Let stand n pan for 2 minutes before turning out onto erving plates. Makes 8 frittatas.

frittata: 124 Calories; 8.2 g Total Fat; 319 mg Sodium; 1 g Protein; 1 g Carbohydrate; trace Dietary Fibre

Poached Salmon with
Herbed Mayonnaise, above

Tomato Tart

There's a lovely hint of Mediterranean flavour in this pretty, quiche-like tart. Don't be afraid of the anchovies—chop them up finely and nobody will guess the source of the salty tang.
— Jo-Anne Penston, Winnipeg, Manitoba

SHORTCRUST PASTRY

All-purpose flour	1 cup	250 mL
Finely grated Parmesan cheese	1 tbsp.	15 mL
Salt	1/8 tsp.	0.5 mL
Cold butter (or hard margarine)	3 tbsp.	50 mL
Lard (or shortening)	2 tbsp.	30 mL
Cold water	3 tbsp.	50 mL

FILLING

Olive (or cooking) oil	2 tbsp.	30 mL
Medium onion, chopped	1	1
Garlic clove, crushed	1	1
Dried whole oregano	1 tbsp.	15 mL
Anchovy fillets, rinsed and chopped (optional)	6	6
Large tomatoes, peeled, seeded and chopped	2	2
Sharp Cheddar cheese, grated	1/4 cup	60 mL
Large eggs	2	2
Salt	1/8 tsp.	0.5 mL
Freshly ground pepper	1/8 tsp.	0.5 mL
Whipping cream	1/2 cup	125 mL
Chopped pitted kalamata olives	1/4 cup	60 mL

Shortcrust Pastry: Combine first 3 ingredients in medium bowl. Cut in butter and lard until mixture is crumbly.

Add cold water. Mix until soft dough forms, adding more cold water, if necessary, 1/2 tsp. (2 mL) at a time. Shape into flattened ball. Cover with plastic wrap. Chill for 15 minutes. Roll out dough on lightly floured surface to fit 8 inch (20 cm) tart pan with removable bottom. Line tart pan with pastry. Cover with plastic wrap. Chill for 30 minutes. Remove plastic wrap. Place tart pan on baking sheet with sides. Lay 16 inch (40 cm) circle of parchment paper on top of pastry shell. Gently press down. Fill with dried beans, rice or pastry weights. Tuck edge of paper under tart pan. Bake in 400°F (205°C) oven for 15 minutes. Carefully lift and remove parchment paper and dried beans.

Filling: Heat olive oil in medium frying pan on medium. Add onion. Sauté for about 5 minutes until onion is softened.

Add garlic and oregano. Heat and stir for 1 minute until fragrant. Spoon into pastry crust.

Sprinkle next 3 ingredients over onion mixture.

Whisk next 3 ingredients together in small bowl. Add whipping cream. Whisk until well combined. Pour over tomato mixture. Sprinkle olives over top. Bake in 400°F (205°C) oven for about 35 minutes until filling is set and golden brown. (Once baked, the tart can be cooled, covered and refrigerated for up to 2 days. To reheat, cover with aluminum foil and bake in 350°F (175°C) oven for about 25 minutes until warm.) Cuts into 12 wedges.

1 wedge: 174 Calories; 12.9 g Total Fat; 139 mg Sodium; 4 g Protein; 11 g Carbohydrate; 1 g Dietary Fibre

Pictured above.

Eggs Florentine on
Cream Puff Pastry, below

Eggs Florentine on Cream Puff Pastry

Rich-tasting Cheese Sauce, fresh spinach and
Cream Puff Pastry offer a simple yet elegant
variation on traditional Eggs Benedict.

CREAM PUFF PASTRY

Water	1 cup	250 mL
Hard margarine (or butter), cut up	1/4 cup	60 mL
Granulated sugar	1 tsp.	5 mL
Salt	1/4 tsp.	1 mL
All-purpose flour, sifted	1 cup	250 mL
Large eggs	4	4

CHEESE SAUCE

Hard margarine (or butter)	2 tbsp.	30 mL
All-purpose flour	2 tbsp.	30 mL
Salt	1/4 tsp.	1 mL
Paprika	1/8 tsp.	0.5 mL
Pepper, sprinkle		
Milk	1 cup	250 mL
White (or alcohol-free) wine	1/4 cup	60 mL
Lemon juice	1/2 tsp.	2 mL
Grated sharp Cheddar cheese	1/2 cup	125 mL
Water	6 cups	1.5 L
White vinegar	3 tbsp.	50 mL
Large eggs	8	8

Fresh baby spinach leaves	2 cups	500 mL
Black Forest ham, thinly sliced	1 lb.	454 g
Paprika, sprinkle		

Cream Puff Pastry: Combine first 4 ingredients
in medium saucepan. Bring to a boil. Remove
from heat.

Immediately add flour all at once, stirring
vigorously. Return to heat. Heat and stir for
about 30 seconds until mixture pulls away
from sides of pan and forms a ball. Remove
from heat. Cool for 5 minutes.

Add eggs, 1 at a time, beating thoroughly after
each addition. Dough should look smooth
and shiny, but still hold its shape. Pipe or spoon
8 circles, 3 1/2 inch (9 cm) in diameter and
3/4 inch (2 cm) thick, onto greased baking
sheet. Bake in 425°F (220°C) oven for
15 minutes. Reduce heat to 400°F (205°C).
Bake for 15 minutes until browned. Remove
to wire racks to cool.

Cheese Sauce: Melt margarine in small
saucepan on medium. Stir in next 4 ingredients
until smooth. Heat and stir for 1 to 2 minutes
until bubbling. Gradually whisk in milk. Heat
and stir until boiling and thickened.

Add next 3 ingredients. Heat and stir until cheese
is melted. Makes 1 1/2 cups (375 mL) sauce.

Bring water and vinegar to a simmer in large
frying pan. Break egg into small bowl. Gently
slide into simmering water. Repeat with
remaining eggs. Poach for 3 to 5 minutes until
just set. Remove with slotted spoon.

Cut tops off cream puffs. Reserve tops. Layer
1/4 cup (60 mL) spinach, 2 oz. (57 g) ham,
1 poached egg and about 2 tbsp. (30 mL)
sauce on each cream puff. Sprinkle with
paprika. Replace top of cream puff or place
on the side. Serves 8.

1 serving: 426 Calories; 24.3 g Total Fat; 1952 mg Sodium;
31 g Protein; 19 g Carbohydrate; 1 g Dietary Fibre

Pictured above.

Make-Ahead Eggs Benedict

If a one-dish main course is more your style,
this classic brunch dish from the Company's
Coming recipe collection offers great
convenience and taste.

English muffins, split	4	4
Bacon slices	16	16
Water	6 cups	1.5 L
White vinegar	3 tbsp.	50 mL
Large eggs	8	8
SAUCE		
Hard margarine (or butter)	1/4 cup	60 mL
All-purpose flour	1/4 cup	60 mL
Paprika	1 tsp.	5 mL
Pepper	1/4 tsp.	1 mL
Ground nutmeg	1/8 tsp.	0.5 mL
Milk	2 cups	500 mL
Grated Swiss cheese	2 cups	500 mL

Asparagus with Lemon
Herb Dressing, page 180

White (or alcohol-free) wine	1/2 cup	125 mL

TOPPING

Hard margarine (or butter)	1 tbsp.	15 mL
Coarsely crushed corn flakes cereal	1/2 cup	125 mL

Arrange muffin halves, cut side up, in greased 9 x 13 inch (22 x 33 cm) pan.

Cook bacon in frying pan until crisp. Remove to paper towel to drain. Place 2 slices on each muffin half.

Bring water and vinegar to a simmer in large frying pan. Break egg into small bowl. Gently slide into simmering water. Repeat with remaining eggs. Poach 3 to 5 minutes until just set. Remove with slotted spoon. Place eggs on bacon.

Sauce: Melt margarine in large saucepan. Stir in first 4 ingredients. Heat and stir for 1 to 2 minutes until bubbling. Gradually whisk in milk. Heat and stir until boiling and thickened.

Add cheese and wine. Heat and stir until cheese melts. Spoon sauce over eggs.

Topping: Melt margarine in small saucepan. Stir in cereal. Sprinkle over sauce. Cover. Chill overnight. Remove cover. Bake in 375°F (190°C) oven for 20 to 25 minutes until heated through. Serves 8.

1 serving: 463 Calories; 27.9 g Total Fat; 708 mg Sodium; 24 g Protein; 26 g Carbohydrate; trace Dietary Fibre

Potato Cakes

If you like hashbrowns or fried potatoes, serve Eggs Florentine, page 54, on top of these seasoned patties instead of on Cream Puff Pastry.

Large baking potatoes, peeled and shredded	3	3
Finely chopped onion (about 1 small)	1/2 cup	125 mL
Seasoned salt	1 tsp.	5 mL
Freshly ground pepper	1/2 tsp.	2 mL
Large egg	1	1
Fine dry bread crumbs	1/4 cup	60 mL
Green onions, chopped	2	2
Cooking oil	2 tbsp.	30 mL

Combine first 7 ingredients in large bowl.

Shape 1/4 cup (60 mL) mixture into 1/2 inch (12 mm) thick cake. Repeat with remaining mixture. Heat cooking oil in frying pan on medium. Add cakes. Cook for 12 minutes. Turn over. Cook for 5 minutes. Remove to paper towel to drain. Makes 8 cakes.

1 cake: 103 Calories; 4.4 g Total Fat; 191 mg Sodium; 3 g Protein; 14 g Carbohydrate; 1 g Dietary Fibre

Sweet Potato, Spinach and Bacon Frittata

Italy's famous flat omelette is substantial enough for supper—just add a mixed green salad and crusty bread.

Medium leek (white and tender parts only), thinly sliced	1	1
Garlic cloves, crushed	2	2
Bacon slices, diced	6	6
Olive oil	1 tbsp.	15 mL
Bag of spinach (or 2 bundles, trimmed)	10 oz.	285 g
Can of sweet potatoes, drained	19 oz.	540 mL
Large eggs	6	6
Milk	1/3 cup	75 mL
Freshly grated Parmesan cheese	1/4 cup	60 mL
Freshly grated Parmesan cheese	1/4 cup	60 mL

Sauté first 3 ingredients in large non-stick frying pan on medium-high for about 7 minutes until leek is soft.

Add spinach and sweet potatoes. Heat, stirring occasionally, for about 2 minutes until spinach is wilted.

Whisk next 3 ingredients together in medium bowl. Add to spinach mixture. Stir gently to combine. Cook on medium for about 7 minutes until egg is almost set.

Sprinkle with remaining Parmesan cheese. Broil 3 inches (7.5 cm) from heat for about 5 minutes until cheese is melted and golden. Cuts into 6 wedges.

1 wedge: 357 Calories; 23.2 g Total Fat; 490 mg Sodium; 17 g Protein; 21 g Carbohydrate; 3 g Dietary Fibre

Pictured below.

Sweet Potato, Spinach
and Bacon Frittata, above

Fresh Veggie Rice Wraps

Delicate, light-tasting and very pretty, these colourful wraps use rehydrated rice paper rounds to form the wrap for a vegetarian filling. Create more filling versions with the addition of cooked shrimp, chicken, pork or fish.

Warm water		
Rice paper rounds (9 inch, 22 cm, size)	12	12
Medium carrots, cut julienne◆	2	2
Pea sprouts	1 1/4 cups	300 mL
Baby spinach leaves	1 1/4 cups	300 mL
Grated fresh beets◆◆	1/2 cup	125 mL
Coarsely chopped fresh mint leaves	1/4 cup	60 mL
Coarsely chopped fresh cilantro	1/4 cup	60 mL
Thinly sliced yellow pepper	1 1/3 cups	325 mL

PEANUT SAUCE

Crunchy peanut butter	1/2 cup	125 mL
Chili sauce	2 tbsp.	30 mL
Lime juice	2 tbsp.	30 mL
Hot water	6 tbsp.	100 mL
Soy sauce	1 tbsp.	15 mL
Sesame oil	1 tsp.	5 mL
Chili paste	1 tsp.	5 mL

Fill large pie plate 1/2 full with warm water. Soak rice paper rounds, a few at a time, for 2 to 3 minutes until soft. Remove to tea towel to drain, being careful not to rip rounds when removing from water (see photo 1). Line up rounds on working surface.

Divide and layer next 7 ingredients down centre top half of each round (see photo 2). Carefully fold bottom edges over vegetables. Fold one side over filling (see photo 3). Roll up each round to enclose filling, leaving tops open.

Peanut Sauce: Whisk all 7 ingredients together in small bowl until smooth. Makes 1 cup (250 mL) sauce. Serve with wraps. Makes 12 wraps.

1 wrap with 1 1/2 tbsp. (25 mL) sauce: 136 Calories; 6.3 g Total Fat; 162 mg Sodium; 5 g Protein; 18 g Carbohydrate; 1 g Dietary Fibre

Pictured above.

◆To julienne, cut into thin slices, then cut each slice into thin strips.

◆◆To prevent hands from staining, wear rubber gloves while handling beets.

The Wrap Report

Rice paper rounds are transparent wraps made from compressed rice flour. Packages of small and large sizes can be found in the Asian section of your grocery store. When rehydrated, they're terrific wrapped around vegetables and more—like sliced cooked shrimp or leftover chicken.

1

2

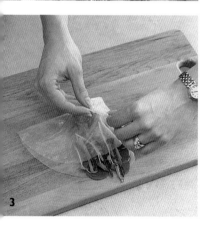

3

Peached Pork Lettuce Wraps

Pork is a very fruit-friendly meat and the pairing of it here in the form of pork tenderloin with peach is inspired. Fast, easy and a sure-fire winner.

Rice vermicelli	3 oz.	85 g
Hot water, to cover		
Sesame oil	1 tbsp.	15 mL
Garlic clove, minced	1	1
Pork tenderloin, cut julienne♦	3/4 lb.	340 g
Ground ginger	1/2 tsp.	2 mL
Hoisin sauce	1 tbsp.	15 mL
Salt	1/2 tsp.	2 mL
Freshly ground pepper, sprinkle		
Can of sliced peaches, drained and juice reserved	14 oz.	398 mL
Salad dressing (or mayonnaise)	2 tbsp.	30 mL
SAUCE		
Reserved peach juice	2/3 cup	150 mL
Soy sauce	2 tbsp.	30 mL
Rice vinegar	3 tbsp.	50 mL
Dried crushed chilies	1/4 tsp.	1 mL
Iceberg lettuce leaves	8	8
Chopped cashews	1/3 cup	75 mL

Cover rice vermicelli with hot water in small bowl. Let stand for 5 minutes. Drain. Rinse with cold water. Drain well. Set aside.

Heat sesame oil in wok or frying pan. Add garlic and pork strips. Stir-fry for 1 minute.

Add next 4 ingredients. Stir to combine.

Add peaches and salad dressing. Stir-fry until hot and well-coated.

Sauce: Combine first 4 ingredients in small bowl. Let stand for 10 minutes to allow flavours to blend. Makes about 1 cup (250 mL) sauce.

Divide vermicelli among lettuce leaves. Divide and spoon pork mixture onto vermicelli. Sprinkle cashews over top. Drizzle with about 1 tbsp. (15 mL) sauce. Wrap lettuce around filling. Makes 8 wraps.

1 wrap: 201 Calories; 8.4 g Total Fat; 542 mg Sodium; 11 g Protein; 22 g Carbohydrate; 1 g Dietary Fibre

♦To julienne, cut into thin slices, then cut each slice into thin strips.

A Bunch of Lunch Ideas

Looking for new ways to make everyone want to grab their lunch bags on the way out the door? Try these suggestions to perk up mid-day meals.

Cheese, Carrot and Ham Wraps: Combine grated cheese, grated carrot, chopped celery and mayonnaise and spread over tortilla. Lay slices of ham on top. Roll up to enclose filling. Cut into thick slices.

Almost Caesar: Combine shredded romaine lettuce, chopped ham, chopped boiled egg and Caesar dressing. Spoon mixture onto split focaccia bread. Top with other half of bread and cut into wedges. For a change, toast the focaccia bread.

Double Decker: Spread one slice of white bread with process cheese spread, top with ham, a slice of whole wheat bread, then potato salad and another slice of white bread. Cut into three fingers.

Chicken Salad: Combine finely chopped cooked chicken, red pepper, green onion and celery with a little mayonnaise and sour cream. Make two vertical cuts in a bread roll, cutting almost all the way through. Fill each cut with chicken salad.

Chicken and Cranberry Onion Roll: Spread a soft, split onion roll with cream cheese on one side and cranberry sauce on the other. Add shredded cooked chicken and shredded romaine lettuce, then put it all together.

Chicken and Bacon Bagel: Combine chopped cooked chicken, chopped crispy bacon, sliced green onion, sour cream and honey mustard. Spread on bagel half, then add butter lettuce leaves and a slice of cheese. Top with other half of bagel.

Tuna and Egg Combo: Combine mashed hard-boiled eggs, flaked tuna, mayonnaise, mild curry powder and chopped red onion. Spread on a thick slice of French loaf and add baby spinach leaves. Top with another slice of French bread.

Tuna Pita Pockets: Combine flaked tuna and tabbouleh. Split pita and spread pocket with cream cheese. Fill with tuna mixture.

Tuna, Raisin, Celery and Walnut Wrap: Combine honey mustard and sour cream. Add flaked tuna, golden raisins, finely chopped celery and chopped walnuts. Place in tortilla wrap and roll up.

Nori Cones

These attractive cones make a lovely first course or appetizer.

Short grain white rice	2/3 cup	150 mL
Water	1 1/3 cups	325 mL
Rice (or white) vinegar	1 tbsp.	15 mL
Granulated sugar	2 tsp.	10 mL
Salt	1/2 tsp.	2 mL
Rice wine (sake), or dry (or alcohol-free) sherry	1 tbsp.	15 mL
Nori (roasted seaweed) sheets	4	4
SAUCE		
Wasabi paste	1 1/2 tsp.	7 mL
Mayonnaise (not salad dressing)	1/4 cup	60 mL
Chopped fresh dill	1 tbsp.	15 mL
FILLING		
Small red onion, thinly sliced	1/2	1/2
Smoked salmon, sliced into long strips	3 oz.	85 g
Medium English cucumber, sliced into thin strips	1/4	1/4
Medium yellow pepper, cut julienne♦	1/2	1/2

Combine first 5 ingredients in medium saucepan. Cover. Simmer for 25 to 30 minutes until rice is tender and most of liquid is absorbed.

Stir in rice wine. Cool.

Cut nori sheets in half widthwise with kitchen scissors. Lay on cloth napkins. Using wet fork, spread 1/4 cup (60 mL) rice over 2/3 of each sheet, leaving 1/3 inch (1 cm) edge plain (see photo 1).

Sauce: Combine all 3 ingredients in small bowl. Spread 1 to 1 1/2 tsp. (5 to 7 mL) over rice on each sheet.

Filling: Divide and layer all 4 ingredients diagonally across rice on each sheet (see photo 2). Dampen plain edge of nori with water. Roll up diagonally, starting with a rice corner and ending with the plain edge to form a cone (see photo 3). Serve immediately. Makes 8 cones.

1 cone: 145 Calories; 6.5 g Total Fat; 276 mg Sodium; 4 g Protein; 17 g Carbohydrate; trace Dietary Fibre

Pictured below.

♦To julienne, cut into thin slices, then cut each slice into thin strips.

1

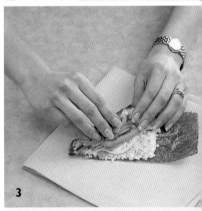

2

3

Nori Know-How

Nori is the dark green roasted seaweed sheet commonly used in Japanese sushi. Look for packages of nori in the Asian section of your grocery store. When you open the package, you'll find a stack of thin, shiny, brittle sheets. As nori absorbs moisture from the rice, it becomes soft and pliable, wrapping easily around the filling. Once you get the hang of this, you'll want to wrap nori around all kinds of flavourful fillings.

Salami Pineapple Wraps, below

Salami Pineapple Wraps

This is a lunch that can be made by many hands. Set out the fillings, and let everyone roll up their own easy and delicious wraps.

Mayonnaise	1/2 cup	125 mL
Chopped fresh mint leaves	3 tbsp.	50 mL
Prepared grainy mustard	2 tbsp.	30 mL
Flour tortillas (10 inch, 25 cm, size)	8	8
Thin slices of salami	24	24
Avocados, peeled, pitted and thinly sliced	2	2
Can of pineapple slices, drained and halved	14 oz.	398 mL
Mixed baby lettuce leaves	2 cups	500 mL

Combine first 3 ingredients in small bowl. Divide and spread on tortillas.

Layer remaining 4 ingredients, in order given, down centre of each tortilla, leaving 2 inch (5 cm) edge at bottom. Fold bottom edge over filling. Roll up sides to enclose filling, leaving top open. Makes 8 wraps.

1 wrap: 514 Calories; 35.7 g Total Fat; 1205 mg Sodium; 14 g Protein; 36 g Carbohydrate; 4 g Dietary Fibre

Pictured above.

Chicken Crunch Pitas

Definitely not your average chicken salad filling. This version packs lots of nutrition and crunch, thanks to fresh bean sprouts, grated carrot, a bit of green onion and nutty sesame seeds. Terrific picnic fare.

Chopped cooked chicken	1/2 cup	125 mL
Chopped fresh bean sprouts	1/2 cup	125 mL
Grated carrot	2 tbsp.	30 mL
Finely sliced green onion	2 tbsp.	30 mL
Sesame seeds, toasted◆	1 tsp.	5 mL
Light mayonnaise (not salad dressing)	1 1/2 tbsp.	25 mL
Soy sauce	2 tsp.	10 mL
Lemon juice	1 tsp.	5 mL

Ground ginger, sprinkle
Garlic powder, sprinkle

Spinach leaves	4 - 6	4 - 6
Pita (6 inch, 15 cm, size)	2	2

Combine first 5 ingredients in medium bowl.

Combine next 3 ingredients in small bowl. Drizzle over chicken mixture.

Sprinkle with ginger and garlic powders. Toss. Makes 1 1/3 cups (325 mL) filling.

Divide and lay spinach leaves down centre of pita. Spoon filling onto spinach. Roll up sides to enclose filling. Makes 2 pitas.

1 pita: 292 Calories; 7.6 g Total Fat; 791 mg Sodium; 17 g Protein; 39 g Carbohydrate; 2 g Dietary Fibre

◆To toast the sesame seeds, place them in an ungreased frying pan. Heat on medium, stirring often, until golden.

Taco Potato Wedges with
Guacamole, page 178

Mini-Cheeseburgers, below

Mini-Cheeseburgers

These pint-sized burgers appeal to kid-sized appetites. Perfect for lunches or even after-school snacks. Mini-burgers—maxi-taste!

Lean ground beef	1/2 lb.	225 g
Small onion, finely diced	1	1
Barbecue sauce	2 tbsp.	30 mL
Large egg, fork-beaten	1	1
Dry bread crumbs	1/4 cup	60 mL
Seasoned salt	1/2 tsp.	2 mL
Cooking oil	1 tsp.	5 mL
Small round dinner rolls, split	6	6
Cheese slices, cut into quarters	3	3

Combine first 6 ingredients in large bowl. Mix well. Form into 6 patties, about 2 inches (5 cm) in diameter.

Heat cooking oil in large non-stick frying pan on medium. Cook patties for about 3 minutes. Turn patties over. Cook for another 3 to 4 minutes until browned and no longer pink inside.

Place patties on bottom half of rolls. Top each with 2 pieces of cheese. Cover with top half of rolls. Makes 6 snack-size burgers.

1 burger: 271 Calories; 14.6 g Total Fat; 590 mg Sodium; 15 g Protein; 20 g Carbohydrate; 2 g Dietary Fibre

Pictured above.

Mm-Mm-Meatballs

It's hard to find anything more kid-friendly than good old meatballs, and this easy recipe is no exception. Pack the meatballs with a barbecue dipping sauce—if frozen, let the meatballs thaw right in the lunch box where they'll keep things cool, or slice and layer them with cheese for a great sandwich.

Ground beef	1 lb.	454 g
Package of sausage meat	13 oz.	375 g
Small onion, finely chopped	1	1
Small carrot, grated	1	1
Celery rib, finely chopped	1	1
Chopped fresh parsley	2 tbsp.	30 mL
Ketchup	2 tbsp.	30 mL
Worcestershire sauce	1 tbsp.	15 mL
Fine dry bread crumbs	1/2 cup	125 mL
Large egg, fork-beaten	1	1

Combine all 10 ingredients in large bowl. Shape into 24 balls. Arrange in single layer on lightly greased baking sheets. Bake in 350°F (175°C) oven for 15 to 20 minutes until browned and no longer pink inside. Remove to paper towels to drain. Cool completely before storing. Makes 24 meatballs.

1 meatball: 79 Calories; 5.2 g Total Fat; 114 mg Sodium; 5 g Protein; 3 g Carbohydrate; trace Dietary Fibre

Tourtières

French Canada's tribute to the savoury meat pie, tourtière is one of the best choices for outdoor eating—it's just as delicious served cold as hot. Pack along some pickled beets or onions, or a piquant chutney to serve alongside. Store in the refrigerator in a large shallow container and remember to remove from the cooler about 15 minutes before serving.

Small onion, finely chopped	1	1
Garlic cloves, crushed	2	2
Cooking oil	1 tbsp.	15 mL
Ground pork	3/4 lb.	340 g
Ground beef	3/4 lb.	340 g
Ground allspice	1/2 tsp.	2 mL
Ground cloves	1/4 tsp.	1 mL
Salt	1/2 tsp.	2 mL
Freshly ground pepper	1/2 tsp.	2 mL
Water	3/4 cup	175 mL
Dry bread crumbs	3/4 cup	175 mL
Pastry for 4 pie crusts, your own or a mix	1 1/2 lbs.	680 g
Egg yolk (large), fork-beaten	1	1
Water	1 tbsp.	15 mL

Sauté onion and garlic in cooking oil in large saucepan on medium for about 5 minutes until soft.

Add next 7 ingredients. Bring to a boil on high. Reduce heat to medium. Simmer, uncovered, for about 20 minutes, stirring occasionally, breaking up larger pieces of meat, until mixture is reduced by half.

Add bread crumbs. Mix well. Cool.

Roll out pastry to 1/8 inch (3 mm) thickness. Cut into sixteen 4 inch (10 cm) and sixteen 3 inch (7.5 cm) circles. Line ungreased muffin pans with the 4 inch (10 cm) circles, bringing pastry slightly up over edge. Divide filling among pastry-lined muffin cups. Top with 3 inch (7.5 cm) pastry circles. Press and crimp edges together to seal. Trim overhang. Cut slits in pastry tops.

Combine egg yolk and second amount of water in small cup. Brush tops with egg yolk mixture. Bake in 375°F (190°C) oven for 40 minutes until golden. Cool in pan on wire rack for 15 minutes. Remove from pan to wire rack to cool completely. Store in airtight container. Makes 16 tourtières.

1 tourtière: 319 Calories; 22 g Total Fat; 352 mg Sodium; 9 g Protein; 20 g Carbohydrate; trace Dietary Fibre

Pictured below.

Shishkabobs with
Peanut Sauce, below

Shishkabobs with Peanut Sauce

"I have two very fussy eaters to cook for, but a main course with peanut butter goes over huge at my house. My two daughters ask for this meal often—my 16-year-old, Charlotte, has been asking me to make it so that she can invite her friend over to try it. So maybe this recipe will become someone else's favourite! Goes well with rice."

— Laurel Loewen, Calgary, Alberta

Italian salad dressing	1/2 cup	125 mL
Soy sauce	2 tbsp.	30 mL
Brown sugar, packed	1 tbsp.	15 mL
Boneless sirloin steak, thinly sliced	1 1/2 lbs.	680 g
8 inch (20 cm) bamboo skewers, soaked in water for 10 minutes	14	14

PEANUT SAUCE

Peanut butter	1/2 cup	125 mL
Barbecue sauce	1/4 cup	60 mL
Water	2/3 cup	150 mL
Soy sauce	1 tbsp.	15 mL
Lemon juice	1 tbsp.	15 mL
Hot pepper sauce	1/2 tsp.	2 mL

Combine first 3 ingredients in resealable plastic bag. Add beef. Turn to coat. Marinate in refrigerator for 4 hours.

Preheat grill to high. Thread 3 to 4 slices of beef, accordion-style, onto each skewer. Cook kabobs for about 3 minutes on each side until desired doneness. Makes 14 kabobs.

Peanut Sauce: Combine all 6 ingredients in small saucepan. Heat on low for 5 minutes, stirring occasionally, until smooth and warm. Do not overheat. Makes 1 1/4 cups (300 mL) sauce. Serve with kabobs.

1 kabob with 1 tbsp. (15 mL) sauce: 172 Calories; 12.9 g Total Fat; 468 mg Sodium; 11 g Protein; 4 g Carbohydrate; 1 g Dietary Fibre

Pictured above.

Pineapple Pepper Burgers

The sweet tastes of red pepper and honeyed pineapple set this burger apart—in looks and taste-appeal.

Lean ground beef	1 1/2 lbs.	680 g
Fresh bread crumbs	3/4 cup	175 mL
Large egg	1	1
Ketchup	1/3 cup	75 mL
Sweet chili sauce	2 tbsp.	30 mL
Very finely chopped onion	1/4 cup	60 mL
Very finely chopped red pepper	3/4 cup	175 mL
Chopped fresh cilantro	2 tbsp.	30 mL
Salt	1 1/2 tsp.	7 mL
Pepper	1/4 tsp.	1 mL
Pineapple rings	6	6
Soy sauce	2 tbsp.	30 mL
Liquid honey	1 tbsp.	15 mL
Kaiser buns, split	6	6
Red leaf lettuce leaves	6	6

Preheat grill to medium-low. Combine first
10 ingredients in large bowl. Mix well. Divide
and shape into 6 patties, about 4 inches
(10 cm) across. Poke hole through centre of
each patty with finger. Grill for 5 to 6 minutes
per side until no longer pink inside.

Blot pineapple rings dry on paper towel.
Combine soy sauce and honey in small bowl.
Brush over pineapple. Grill for 2 to 3 minutes
per side.

Place buns, cut sides down, on grill. Toast until
lightly browned.

Place 1 lettuce leaf on bottom half of each
bun. Layer each with burger, pineapple slice
and top half of bun. Makes 6 burgers.

burger: 500 Calories; 14.3 g Total Fat; 1690 mg Sodium;
30 g Protein; 63 g Carbohydrate; 3 g Dietary Fibre

Beef Stew with Caramelized Root Vegetables

"Browning the beef and root vegetables adds a
layer of flavour to this classic stew. Partnered with
biscuits, it's supper in a hurry. Served with garlic
mashed potatoes and a hearty red wine, it's a
casual but classy dinner."
— Cinda Chavich, author of *125 Best Pressure*
Cooker Recipes (Robert Rose Inc., 2004)

Thick slices of double-smoked (or European) bacon (about 3 oz., 85 g), chopped	3	3
Butter	2 tbsp.	30 mL
Lean beef stew meat (or braising steak, cut into 2 inch, 5 cm, cubes)	3 lbs.	1.4 kg
Baby carrots	2 cups	500 mL
Parsnips, cut into large chunks	1 cup	250 mL
Tiny white pearl onions, parboiled and peeled◆	3 cups	750 mL
Salt	1 tsp.	5 mL
Freshly ground pepper	1/2 tsp.	2 mL
Dried sweet basil	2 tsp.	10 mL
Dried thyme	2 tsp.	10 mL
Garlic cloves, minced	4	4
Dry red wine	1 cup	250 mL
Brown sugar, packed	1/4 cup	60 mL
Brandy	1/4 cup	60 mL
Tomato paste	2 tbsp.	30 mL
Butter	2 tbsp.	30 mL
All-purpose flour	3 tbsp.	50 mL

Sauté bacon in first amount of butter in
pressure cooker on medium-high for 3 to
5 minutes until bacon begins to brown.
Cook beef, in batches, on medium-high until
browned. Remove bacon and beef to large
bowl. Set aside.

Combine next 3 ingredients in pressure
cooker. Heat and stir on medium-high for
5 minutes until vegetables are lightly browned.

Add next 5 ingredients. Cook for 2 minutes
until fragrant.

Add next 4 ingredients. Add beef and bacon
mixture. Mix well. Lock lid in place. Bring up
to pressure on medium-high. Reduce heat to
medium-low just to maintain even pressure.
Cook for 25 minutes. Remove from heat.
Release pressure. Remove lid.

Stir second amount of butter into flour in
small bowl until smooth. Gradually stir into
beef mixture. Heat and stir on high for about
3 minutes until boiling and thickened. Cook,
uncovered, a few minutes longer if necessary
to thicken. Serves 6 to 8.

1 serving: 519 Calories; 19.8 g Total Fat; 666 mg Sodium;
40 g Protein; 32 g Carbohydrate; 3 g Dietary Fibre

Pictured below.

◆*To parboil pearl onions, place in rapidly boiling*
water. Boil for 4 minutes. Drain. Rinse under cold
running water until cool.

Beef Stew with
Caramelized Root
Vegetables, above

Stir-Fried Beef with Assorted Peppers

"A very tender cut, such as beef tenderloin or sirloin, is the best choice for this dish. It's important not to overcook the meat. For a slightly different taste, I sometimes substitute green onions for the shallots. The combination of sugar and salt is very common in Chinese dishes as a flavour enhancer. Wonderful served over rice."
— Peter Cheung, Edmonton, Alberta

Light soy sauce	1/2 tbsp.	7 mL
Dark soy sauce	1 tsp.	5 mL
Granulated sugar	1/2 tsp.	2 mL
Sesame oil, dash		
Pepper, dash		
Cornstarch	2 tsp.	10 mL
Sirloin steak, sliced into 1/8 inch (3 mm) thin strips	3/4 lb.	340 g
Cooking oil	1 tsp.	5 mL
Chinese cooking wine♦	2 tbsp.	30 mL
Cooking oil	1 tsp.	5 mL
Small green pepper, thinly sliced	1	1
Small red pepper, thinly sliced	1	1
Small yellow pepper, thinly sliced	1	1
Cooking oil	1 tbsp.	15 mL
Whole shallots, sliced	2 - 3	2 - 3
Chinese cooking wine♦	1 tsp.	5 mL

SEASONING SAUCE

Water	2 tbsp.	30 mL
Light soy sauce	2 1/2 tsp.	12 mL
Granulated sugar	3/4 tsp.	4 mL
Salt, sprinkle		
Pepper, sprinkle		
Green onions, diagonally sliced	3	3

Combine first 5 ingredients in medium bowl. Stir in cornstarch until smooth. Add beef. Cover. Chill for 30 minutes.

Add first amount of cooking oil to hot wok or frying pan. Stir-fry beef mixture on high for 3 to 4 minutes until almost cooked. Sprinkle with first amount of cooking wine. Remove to bowl. Set aside.

Add second amount of cooking oil to hot wok. Add all 3 peppers. Stir-fry for 3 to 4 minutes until tender-crisp. Remove to bowl. Set aside.

Add third amount of cooking oil to hot wok. Sauté shallots until soft. Add beef mixture. Sprinkle with second amount of cooking wine.

Seasoning Sauce: Combine first 5 ingredients in small cup. Add to wok. Add peppers. Stir-fry for about 2 minutes until beef is no longer pink.

Garnish with green onion. Serves 4.

1 serving: 231 Calories; 10.4 g Total Fat; 708 mg Sodium; 21 g Protein; 12 g Carbohydrate; 1 g Dietary Fibre

♦*Dry (or alcohol-free) sherry can be substituted for Chinese cooking wine.*

Pictured below.

Spaghetti with Bolognese Sauce

Everyone enjoys the classic flavour of this traditional Italian pasta dish. Serve with warm garlic and cheese bread and a fresh green salad.

Spaghetti pasta	12 oz.	340 g
Boiling water	12 cups	3 L
Salt	2 tsp.	10 mL
Lean ground beef	1 lb.	454 g
Cooking oil	1 1/2 tsp.	7 mL
Chopped onion (about 1 medium)	1 cup	250 mL
Chopped green pepper (about 1 small)	1 cup	250 mL
Chopped celery	1 cup	250 mL
Cooking oil	1 1/2 tsp.	7 mL
Envelopes of spaghetti sauce mix (1 1/2 oz., 43 g, each)	4	4
Water	6 cups	1.5 L
Can of tomato paste	5 1/2 oz.	156 mL
Can of stewed tomatoes	14 oz.	398 mL
Salt	2 tsp.	10 mL
Pepper	1 tsp.	5 mL
Chopped fresh oregano	2 tbsp.	30 mL
Chopped fresh sweet basil	1/4 cup	60 mL

Cook spaghetti in boiling water and salt in large uncovered pot or Dutch oven for 8 to 10 minutes, stirring occasionally, until tender but firm. Drain well. Turn into large bowl.

Scramble-fry ground beef in first amount of cooking oil in frying pan until no pink remains in beef. Drain. Transfer to large pot or Dutch oven.

Sauté next 3 ingredients in second amount of cooking oil in frying pan until soft. Add to beef.

Stir in remaining 8 ingredients. Bring to a boil. Reduce heat. Simmer, uncovered, for 30 minutes, stirring occasionally, until thickened. Makes 8 cups (2 L) sauce. Serve over pasta. Serves 8.

1 serving: 369 Calories; 7.8 g Total Fat; 2613 mg Sodium; 19 g Protein; 57 g Carbohydrate; 4 g Dietary Fibre

Eggplant with Tomato and Mushrooms, page 181

Stir-Fried Beef with Assorted Peppers, above

Spiced Burgers with Mint Yogurt Sauce

These burgers are filled with exotic Middle Eastern flavours, which means ground lamb works very well as a substitute for beef. The Mint Yogurt Sauce provides the perfect accent.

Medium onions, halved and thinly sliced	3	3
Hard margarine (or butter)	2 tbsp.	30 mL
Salt	1/4 tsp.	1 mL
Ground cinnamon, sprinkle		
Paprika, sprinkle		
Cayenne pepper, light sprinkle		
Lean ground beef	1 1/2 lbs.	680 g
Garlic cloves, minced	2	2
Seasoned salt	1 tsp.	5 mL
Ground cinnamon	1 tsp.	5 mL
Paprika	1 tsp.	5 mL
Cayenne pepper	1/4 tsp.	1 mL
Freshly ground pepper, heavy sprinkle		
Water	2 tbsp.	30 mL
Whole wheat hamburger buns, split	6	6

MINT YOGURT SAUCE

Plain yogurt	1 cup	250 mL
Small garlic clove, minced	1	1
Finely chopped fresh mint leaves	2 tbsp.	30 mL
Thin slices English cucumber	18	18
Fresh mint leaves, for garnish	6	6

Sauté onion in margarine in large frying pan on medium-low for about 15 minutes until soft. Sprinkle with next 4 ingredients. Cook for 15 to 20 minutes until golden brown. Keep warm.

Preheat grill to medium. Combine next 8 ingredients in large bowl. Divide and shape into 6 patties, about 4 inches (10 cm) across. Poke hole in centre of each patty with finger. Grill for about 6 minutes per side until no longer pink inside.

Place buns, cut sides down, on grill. Toast until lightly browned.

Chicken and Avocado Burgers, page 127

Spiced Burgers with Mint Yogurt Sauce, left

Veggie Burgers with Chili Cream Sauce, page 120

Mint Yogurt Sauce: Combine first 3 ingredients in small bowl. Let stand for 10 minutes to allow flavours to blend. Makes 1 cup (250 mL) sauce.

Place patties on bottom half of buns. Layer each with onion mixture, yogurt sauce and 3 cucumber slices. Garnish with mint leaves. Top with other half of buns. Makes 6 burgers.

1 burger: 316 Calories; 19.9 g Total Fat; 427 mg Sodium; 24 g Protein; 9 g Carbohydrate; 1 g Dietary Fibre

Pictured above.

Spicy Cheeseburgers

Taco seasoning and a hint of lime give these burgers a Tex-Mex zing. The cheesy surprise inside will have everyone asking for seconds.

Lean ground beef	1 lb.	454 g
Fresh bread crumbs	1/4 cup	60 mL
Large egg, fork-beaten	1	1
Very finely chopped red onion	1/4 cup	60 mL
Taco seasoning mix (stir before measuring)	3 tbsp.	50 mL
Chopped fresh oregano	1 tbsp.	15 mL
Lime juice	2 tbsp.	30 mL
Freshly ground pepper, to taste		
Cheddar cheese slices	4	4
Hamburger buns, split	4	4
Sour cream	1/4 cup	75 mL
Tomato, thinly sliced	1	1
Salsa	1/4 cup	75 mL

Preheat grill to medium-high. Combine first 8 ingredients in medium bowl. Mix well. Divide and shape into 8 thin patties, about 5 inches (12.5 cm) across.

Place 1 cheese slice on each of 4 patties. Top with remaining patties. Pinch edges to seal. Grill for 6 to 8 minutes per side until no longer pink inside.

Place buns, cut sides down, on grill. Toast until lightly browned.

Place patties on bottom half of buns. Dollop with sour cream. Layer each with tomato, salsa and top half of bun. Makes 4 burgers.

1 burger: 523 Calories 26.1 g Total Fat; 1868 mg Sodium; 35 g Protein; 37 g Carbohydrate; 2 g Dietary Fibre

Ali Beef Curry, below

Teriyaki Ribs

When rib-lovers crave meaty, sticky ribs, these are the kind they're thinking about—slow-cooked beef ribs smothered in teriyaki sauce with mustard, honey and a little hot sauce. You can add a chopped fresh chili pepper or two if you're a heat-lover.

Beef back rib racks (about 5 1/2 lbs., 2.7 kg)	2	2
Teriyaki sauce	1/2 cup	125 mL
Prepared grainy mustard	1/3 cup	75 mL
Liquid honey	1/2 cup	125 mL
Worcestershire sauce	1/4 cup	60 mL
Hot pepper sauce	1 tbsp.	15 mL
Garlic cloves, crushed	4	4

Place ribs in long shallow dish.

Combine remaining 6 ingredients in small bowl. Pour over ribs. Turn to coat. Cover. Chill for 6 hours or overnight, turning several times. Drain, reserving marinade in small saucepan. Bring marinade to a boil. Boil for 5 minutes.

Preheat grill to medium-low. Place ribs on grill over drip pan. Close lid. Cook, using indirect cooking method (see Indirectly Speaking, page 67), for about 1 1/2 hours, turning occasionally, basting with reserved marinade, until tender and glazed. Serves 6 to 8.

1 serving: 454 Calories; 18.3 g Total Fat; 1484 mg Sodium; 37 g Protein; 35 g Carbohydrate; trace Dietary Fibre

Pictured below.

Ali Beef Curry

"My mum serves this with rice, naan or pita bread and a favourite chutney. Use a good-quality curry powder for best results. In our house, of course, we use Homemade Magic Curry Powder (available in Edmonton and Calgary), which is based on our family recipe."

— Naazima Ali, Edmonton, Alberta

Chopped onion	1/4 cup	60 mL
Cooking oil	2 - 3 tbsp.	30 - 50 mL
Crushed garlic (2 - 3 cloves)	1 tbsp.	15 mL
Curry powder♦	1 1/2 tbsp.	25 mL
Paprika	2 tsp.	10 mL
Chili powder	2 - 3 tsp.	10 - 15 mL
Boneless stewing beef, cut into 3/4 inch (2 cm) cubes	1 lb.	454 g
Salt	1/4 tsp.	1 mL
Water, to cover		
Chopped fresh cilantro	1 - 2 tbsp.	15 - 30 mL

Sauté onion in cooking oil in large saucepan on medium-high for about 2 minutes until soft.

Add next 4 ingredients. Cook on medium for 2 to 3 minutes, stirring constantly, until fragrant.

Add beef and salt. Stir. Cover. Cook on medium-low for about 5 minutes, stirring occasionally. Add enough water to just cover beef. Cover. Cook, adding more water as needed, until beef is tender and water is absorbed to desired thickness of sauce. (This may take 1 to 1 1/4 hours depending on the quality of beef used.)

Sprinkle with cilantro. Makes 2 cups (500 mL). Serves 3.

1 serving: 348 Calories; 20.9 g Total Fat; 233 mg Sodium; 35 g Protein; 5 g Carbohydrate; 1 g Dietary Fibre

Pictured above.

♦*The original recipe gave a range of 1 1/2 to 2 1/2 tbsp. (25 to 37 mL) of curry powder in total.*

Teriyaki Ribs, above

Vegetable Skewers with Pesto Dressing, page 182

ndirectly Speaking

There are different ways to do indirect cooking. Unless noted otherwise, we tested our recipes on a gas barbecue using the following method. Start by lighting the barbecue, then preheat with the lid closed.

For a two or three-burner gas barbecue:
Turn off one burner after preheating (on three-burner barbecues, it should be the centre one). Place a drip pan on the rocks above the burner that's been turned off. Replace the grill and place the food on the grill above the drip pan. Close the lid and cook as directed in the recipe.

For a charcoal barbecue:
Move the hot coals to the outer edges of the barbecue in two equal piles. Option 1: Place a drip pan in the cleared centre area of the barbecue. Replace the grill and place the food on the grill over the drip pan. Option 2: Remove the grill, set a foil or metal pan directly in the cleared centre area with the hot coals around it and place the food in the pan.

Close the lid and cook as directed in the recipe, adding more charcoal or briquets as needed.

Keep a lid on it:
Every time you lift the lid, heat escapes and cooking time is increased, so resist the temptation to keep checking ... and checking ... and checking ... on how things are going.

Sesame Pepper-Crusted Beef Roast

Garlic, sesame seeds, pepper and curry powder lend their exotic flavours to beef in this impressive entree. If your roast has a little excess fat, trim a piece and use it to grease down the grill. Looks nice served with grilled red onion wedges.

Rib-eye roast	3 lbs.	1.4 kg
Garlic cloves, halved	3	3
Olive (or cooking) oil	1 tbsp.	15 mL
Sesame seeds	1/4 cup	60 mL
Coarsely crushed peppercorns	2 tbsp.	30 mL
Curry powder	2 tsp.	10 mL

Trim excess fat from roast. Cut 6 shallow slits in roast at random. Poke garlic into each slit. Rub olive oil over roast.

Combine remaining 3 ingredients in small bowl. Spread in ungreased baking sheet. Roll roast in mixture to coat well. Preheat grill to medium-high. Place roast on greased grill over drip pan. Close lid. Cook, using indirect cooking method (see Indirectly Speaking, at left), for 30 minutes. Reduce heat to medium. Cook for 30 minutes until meat thermometer inserted in centre reads 135°F (57°C) for rare to 165°F (72°C) for well-done. Let roast stand, covered, for 10 minutes before carving. Carve into 1/2 inch (12 mm) slices to serve. Serves 10.

1 serving: 206 Calories; 10.6 g Total Fat; 69 mg Sodium; 20 g Protein; 2 g Carbohydrate; 1 g Dietary Fibre

Pictured above.

Is It Done Yet?

Differences in barbecues, outside temperatures and even wind can affect cooking time. With large pieces of meat, the only sure-fire way to know when they're done is to check the internal temperature with a meat thermometer.

Super Oz Burgers, below

Dijon Bacon Burgers

Go beyond the traditional . . . and try this terrific horseradish cheese sauce on lamb burgers, chicken burgers or salmon burgers.

Lean ground beef	1 lb.	454 g
Dijon mustard	3 tbsp.	50 mL
Crumbled cooked bacon	1/4 cup	60 mL
Onion salt	1 tsp.	5 mL
Freshly ground pepper, sprinkle		
Hamburger buns, split	4	4
HORSERADISH CHEESE SAUCE		
Process cheese spread	1/3 cup	75 mL
Prepared horseradish	1 tsp.	5 mL
Chopped green onion	2 tbsp.	30 mL
Grated sharp Cheddar cheese	1/3 cup	75 mL

Preheat grill to medium. Combine first 5 ingredients in medium bowl. Divide and shape into 4 patties, about 4 inches (10 cm) across. Poke hole through centre of each patty with finger. Grill for about 6 minutes per side until no longer pink inside.

Place buns, cut sides down, on grill. Toast until lightly browned.

Horseradish Cheese Sauce: Combine all 4 ingredients in small bowl. Makes 1/2 cup (125 mL) sauce. Place dollop of sauce on each patty. Grill for 1 minute until sauce is melted. Place patties on bottom half of buns. Top with other half of buns. Makes 4 burgers.

1 burger: 399 Calories; 29 g Total Fat; 1053 mg Sodium; 30 g Protein; 3 g Carbohydrate; trace Dietary Fibre

Super Oz Burgers

If you have travelled "Down Under" to Australia, you may have already experienced these hamburgers-with-the-works. Stacked high with sliced beets, bacon, egg, cheese, fried onions and more, this meal-in-a-bun is a must-try!

Medium onions, thinly sliced	3	3
Cooking oil	1 tbsp.	15 mL
Lean ground beef	1 lb.	454 g
Finely chopped onion (about 1 medium)	3/4 cup	175 mL
Fresh bread crumbs	1/3 cup	75 mL
Large egg, fork-beaten	1	1
Barbecue sauce	2 tbsp.	30 mL
Salt	1/4 tsp.	1 mL
Pepper	1/4 tsp.	1 mL
Hamburger buns, split	6	6
Barbecue sauce	1/3 cup	75 mL
Canned beet slices	12 - 18	12 - 18
Cheese slices (if small, use 12 slices)	6	6
Fried eggs	6	6
Medium tomatoes, sliced	2	2
Bacon slices, cooked (not crisp)	6	6
Lettuce leaves	6	6

Sauté onion in cooking oil on barbecue hot plate (or in frying pan) over medium heat for 15 minutes until soft and browned.

Preheat grill to medium-high. Combine next 7 ingredients in large bowl. Mix well. Divide and shape into 6 patties, about 5 inches (12.5 cm) across. Poke hole through centre of each patty with finger. Grill for about 6 minutes per side until no longer pink inside.

Place buns, cut sides down, on grill. Toast until lightly browned.

Spread bottom half of buns with barbecue sauce. Layer each with patty, onion and remaining 7 ingredients in order given. Top with other half of buns. Makes 6 burgers.

1 burger: 626 Calories; 32.3 g Total Fat; 1364 mg Sodium; 35 g Protein; 43 g Carbohydrate; 4 g Dietary Fibre

Pictured above.

Under-the-Grill Drip Pans

Disposable aluminum pans work well and can be re-used.

Or designate an old, rectangular baking pan solely for use in the barbecue. It'll get pretty dark and abused-looking, but will do a good job of catching drips and holding liquids for several seasons.

In a pinch, use several layers of heavy-duty foil with edges folded up to create a makeshift pan.

Minted Beef with Almond Couscous

Middle Eastern flavours in the middle of the week! Liven up dinner with this multi-flavoured dish that will fill your house with exotic aromas as it cooks.

Cooking oil	1 tbsp.	15 mL
Small onion, sliced	1	1
Garlic cloves, crushed	2	2
Ground cumin	2 tsp.	10 mL
Ground coriander	2 tsp.	10 mL
Ground ginger	2 tsp.	10 mL
Chili powder (optional)	1 tsp.	5 mL
Can of diced tomatoes, with juice	14 oz.	398 mL
Chopped dates	1/2 cup	125 mL
Cooking oil	1 tbsp.	15 mL
Sirloin steak, sliced into 1/8 inch (3 mm) thin strips	1 3/4 lbs.	790 g
Chopped fresh mint leaves	1/3 cup	75 mL
Salt	1/2 tsp.	2 mL
Can of condensed chicken broth	10 oz.	284 mL
Water	2 tbsp.	30 mL
Hard margarine (or butter)	1 tbsp.	15 mL
Couscous	1 1/2 cups	375 mL
Slivered almonds, toasted◆	1/3 cup	75 mL

Heat first amount of cooking oil in large saucepan on medium. Add next 6 ingredients. Sauté for 5 minutes until onion is soft.

Add tomatoes and dates. Simmer, uncovered, for 5 minutes, stirring occasionally, until thickened.

Heat 1/2 of second amount of cooking oil in frying pan on medium-high. Stir-fry 1/2 of beef strips for 2 to 3 minutes until browned. Add to tomato mixture. Stir. Repeat with remaining cooking oil and beef strips.

Add mint and salt to beef mixture. Stir. Makes 5 cups (1.25 L) minted beef.

Bring next 3 ingredients to a boil in small saucepan. Add couscous. Remove from heat. Cover. Let stand for 5 minutes.

Add almonds. Fluff with fork. Makes 4 cups (1 L) couscous. Serve beef over couscous. Serves 6.

serving: 598 Calories; 21 g Total Fat; 737 mg Sodium; 41 g Protein; 62 g Carbohydrate; 6 g Dietary Fibre

◆To toast the almonds, place them in an ungreased frying pan. Heat on medium, stirring often, until golden.

Tortilla Wraps

The kids can help you make these savoury Tex-Mex-style wraps that feature ground beef, beans, Cheddar cheese and the wonderful flavour of fresh cilantro. Serve with your favourite salsa and a little sour cream.

Finely chopped onion	1 1/4 cups	300 mL
Garlic cloves, crushed	2	2
Cooking oil	1 tsp.	5 mL
Lean ground beef	1 1/2 lbs.	680 g
Can of red kidney beans, drained, rinsed and chopped	14 oz.	398 mL
Envelope of taco seasoning mix	1 1/4 oz.	35 g
Water	1/2 cup	125 mL
Condensed beef bouillon	2/3 cup	150 mL
Tomato paste	1/4 cup	60 mL
Chopped fresh oregano	1 tbsp.	15 mL
Flavoured tortillas, your choice (10 inch, 25 cm, size)	6	6
Chopped fresh cilantro	1/3 cup	75 mL
Grated medium Cheddar cheese	1 cup	250 mL
Cilantro sprigs, for garnish		

Sauté onion and garlic in cooking oil in frying pan on medium-high until onion is soft.

Add ground beef. Scramble-fry until no pink remains in beef. Drain.

Add beans to beef mixture. Stir.

Stir in next 5 ingredients. Simmer, uncovered, for 10 minutes until boiling and thickened.

Spoon 2/3 cup (150 mL) beef mixture down center of 1 tortilla. Sprinkle on 2 1/2 tsp. (12 mL) cilantro. Roll up tightly. Repeat with remaining beef mixture, cilantro and tortillas. Place on greased baking sheet. Sprinkle with cheese. Bake in 350°F (175°C) oven for 15 minutes until cheese is melted and tortillas are golden.

Garnish with cilantro sprigs. Makes 6 wraps.

1 wrap: 460 Calories; 17.9 g Total Fat; 1249 mg Sodium; 30 g Protein; 45 g Carbohydrate; 3 g Dietary Fibre

Pictured below.

Tortilla Wraps, above

Tuscan Beef and Bean Stew

"Like many other cuisines, this Italian region also has a stew, Spezzatino di Manzo. *It's a simple dish, but very Tuscan. The bite-sized cubes of meat become very tender and absorb the seasonings as they slowly simmer in red wine and beef broth. Basil adds a real taste of the Mediterranean."*

— Kathy Kerr and Richard Turner
  Edmonton, Alberta

Beef stew meat (chuck), cubed	2 1/4 lbs.	1 kg
Cooking oil	2 tbsp.	30 mL
Medium onion, chopped	1	1
Garlic cloves, crushed	4	4
Olive oil	1 tbsp.	15 mL
All-purpose flour	2 tbsp.	30 mL
Red (or alcohol-free) wine	1 cup	250 mL
Prepared beef broth	1 cup	250 mL
Can of diced tomatoes, with juice	14 oz.	398 g
Salt	1/2 tsp.	2 mL
Freshly ground pepper	1/2 tsp.	2 mL
Cans of cannellini (or white kidney) beans (19 oz., 540 mL, each)	2	2
Chopped fresh sweet basil	2 tbsp.	30 mL

Sauté beef, in 2 batches, in cooking oil in large pot or Dutch oven on medium-high for about 5 minutes until browned. Remove from pan.

Sauté onion and garlic in olive oil in same pan on medium for about 5 minutes until soft.

Add flour. Heat and stir for about 1 minute until grainy.

Add beef and next 5 ingredients. Bring to a boil. Reduce heat to low. Cover. Cook for 1 3/4 hours until beef is very tender.

Add beans. Cook, uncovered, for 15 minutes until thickened.

Add basil. Stir. Serves 6.

1 serving: 656 Calories; 22.4 g Total Fat; 608 mg Sodium; 53 g Protein; 54 g Carbohydrate; trace Dietary Fibre

Pictured below.

Tuscan Beef and Bean Stew, above

Beef and Eggplant Stew with Couscous

Eggplant, olives, red pepper and, of course, couscous, lend their exotic influences to humble stewing beef to make this great, one-pot dish. This recipe also works well with a boneless lamb shoulder.

Olive (or cooking) oil	1 1/2 tsp.	7 mL
Beef stew meat	1 lb.	454 g
Olive (or cooking) oil	1 1/2 tsp.	7 mL
Medium onion, sliced	1	1
Garlic cloves, crushed	4	4
Medium red pepper, chopped	1	1
Can of diced tomatoes	28 oz.	796 mL
Tomato paste	3 tbsp.	50 mL
Red (or alcohol-free) wine	1/2 cup	125 mL
Can of condensed beef broth	10 oz.	284 mL
Salt	1 tsp.	5 mL
Freshly ground pepper	1 tsp.	5 mL
Medium eggplant, chopped	1	1
Pitted green olives, halved lengthwise	1/2 cup	125 mL
Couscous	1 1/4 cups	300 mL
Balsamic (or red wine) vinegar	3 tbsp.	50 mL
Chopped fresh parsley	1/3 cup	75 mL

Heat first amount of olive oil in large pot or Dutch oven until hot. Add beef. Cook on medium-high for about 8 minutes, stirring occasionally, until browned. Remove from pot.

Heat second amount of olive oil in same pot until hot. Add next 3 ingredients. Cook on medium for about 5 minutes, stirring occasionally, until onion and red pepper are softened.

Add beef and next 6 ingredients. Cover. Simmer on low for 1 hour, stirring occasionally.

Add eggplant. Simmer, uncovered, for 20 minutes, stirring occasionally, until eggplant is tender. Remove from heat.

Add remaining 4 ingredients. Mix well. Cover. Let stand for 5 minutes until couscous is tender. Serve immediately. Serves 6.

1 serving: 412 Calories; 11.6 g Total Fat; 1300 mg Sodium; 26 g Protein; 49 g Carbohydrate; 4 g Dietary Fibre

Sweet-and-Sour Meatballs

"This is an old childhood favourite of mine that my mother used to make. I usually serve it with steaming hot rice and green peas. It is also a dish that often comes to mind as a 'second meat' when serving guests. I'm sure there are hundreds of versions of this meal, but I've made this one my own by adding pineapple to the sauce. I really have a sweet tooth, and this recipe provides lots of sauce to smother the rice with and satisfy my craving. This is a meal I will make on the weekend, sometimes doubling the recipe so we have leftovers for quick meals during the week."

— Shauna Robertson, Unity, Saskatchewan

MEATBALLS

Lean ground beef	2 lbs.	900 g
Large eggs	2	2
Fine dry bread crumbs	1/2 cup	125 mL
Seasoned salt	1 tsp.	5 mL
Pepper	1/4 tsp.	1 mL
Worcestershire sauce	1/2 tbsp.	7 mL
Garlic powder	1/4 tsp.	1 mL

SAUCE

Brown sugar, packed	1 cup	250 mL
Cornstarch	3 tbsp.	50 mL
Reserved pineapple juice, plus water to equal	1 3/4 cups	425 mL
White vinegar	1/4 cup	60 mL
Soy sauce	1 1/2 tbsp.	25 mL
Worcestershire sauce	1/2 tbsp.	7 mL
Can of pineapple tidbits, drained and juice reserved	14 oz.	398 mL

Meatballs: Combine first 7 ingredients in medium bowl. Mix well. Shape into 1 inch (2.5 cm) balls. Cook meatballs, in 3 batches, in non-stick frying pan on medium for about 10 minutes until browned all over. Drain on paper towel. Set aside.

Sauce: Combine brown sugar and cornstarch in large saucepan. Whisk in pineapple juice mixture until smooth. Add next 3 ingredients. Stir. Simmer, uncovered, on medium-low for 3 minutes until thickened.

Add meatballs and pineapple. Stir gently until meatballs are well coated. Simmer, uncovered, on low for 20 minutes until no pink remains in meatballs. Serves 6.

1 serving: 497 Calories; 15.1 g Total Fat; 714 mg Sodium; 31 g Protein; 59 g Carbohydrate; 1 g Dietary Fibre

Pictured on this page.

Sweet and Sour Meatballs, left

Taco Pizza, below

Variation: Instead of simmering the meatballs and sauce for 20 minutes in saucepan, place meatballs and sauce in ungreased 2 quart (2 L) casserole. Bake in 350°F (175°C) oven for 30 minutes.

Taco Pizza

"This pizza recipe is inspired by specialty pizza take-out restaurants in Unity. We sampled their menus, then I set out to create similar recipes of my very own. I use the pizza dough recipe supplied with my breadmaker and set the timer so that the dough is ready when I get home from work. I roll the dough onto my 16-inch pizza stone and leave it to rise while I prepare the rest of the ingredients. A pre-packaged seasoning mix works fine, but I usually use my own less-spicy seasoning blend. Taco condiments such as shredded lettuce, diced tomatoes, green onions, taco sauce and sour cream go on the table and everyone can dress up their own slices to taste."

— Shauna Robertson, Unity, Saskatchewan

Lean ground beef	1 1/2 lbs.	680 g
All-purpose flour	2 tsp.	10 mL
Salt	1 tsp.	5 mL
Paprika	1 tsp.	5 mL
Onion flakes	1 tsp.	5 mL
Garlic powder	1/2 tsp.	2 mL
Chili powder	1/2 tsp.	2 mL
Granulated sugar	1 tsp.	5 mL
Water	1/2 cup	125 mL
Partially baked commercial pizza crust (12 inch, 30 cm)♦	1	1
Salsa	2/3 cup	150 mL
Grated Cheddar cheese	2 cups	500 mL

Scramble-fry ground beef on medium for 8 minutes until no longer pink. Drain.

Combine next 7 ingredients in small cup. Add to beef. Stir in water. Simmer, uncovered, on low until thickened. Remove from heat.

Place pizza crust on ungreased baking sheet. Spread salsa evenly over crust. Top with beef mixture. Sprinkle with cheese. Bake in 450°F (230°C) oven for about 20 minutes until crust is golden. Cool on wire rack for 5 minutes before slicing. Cuts into 8 wedges.

1 wedge: 437 Calories; 21.6 g Total Fat; 936 mg Sodium; 27 g Protein; 33 g Carbohydrate; 2 g Dietary Fibre

Pictured above.

♦We tested this recipe with a partially baked commercial pizza crust, but you can use your own pizza dough as Shauna did. Baking time will be the same.

Connie's Mexican Meatloaf, below

Connie's Mexican Meatloaf

Connie's recipe won first prize in our Mighty Marvellous Meatloaf Contest. One taste, and your family will vote for more.
— Connie Johnson, Edmonton, Alberta

Lean ground beef	2 lbs.	900 g
Medium onion, very finely chopped	1	1
Garlic cloves, crushed	4	4
Fine dry bread crumbs	1 cup	250 mL
Finely ground nacho chips	1/2 cup	125 mL
Chili powder	1 tbsp.	15 mL
Jalapeño peppers, seeds and ribs removed, finely chopped◆	2	2
Large eggs, fork-beaten	2	2
Mild chunky salsa	1/2 cup	125 mL
Medium Cheddar cheese, cut into 1/4 inch (6 mm) cubes	8 oz.	225 g
Brown sugar, packed	1/4 cup	60 mL
Chili sauce	1/4 cup	60 mL
Prepared mustard	1 tbsp.	15 mL

Combine first 7 ingredients in large bowl. Mix well.

Add eggs and salsa. Stir. Add cheese. Mix well. Press evenly into ungreased 9 x 5 x 3 inch (22 x 12.5 x 7.5 cm) loaf pan.

Combine remaining 3 ingredients in small bowl. Mix well. Spread over beef mixture. Bake, uncovered, in 350°F (175°C) oven for 80 to 90 minutes until firm and meat thermometer inserted in centre registers 170°F (77°C). Carefully drain any excess drippings from pan. Let stand for 10 minutes. Cuts into eighteen 1/2 inch (12 mm) slices.

1 slice: 226 Calories; 13.2 g Total Fat; 276 mg Sodium; 15 g Protein; 12 g Carbohydrate; 1 g Dietary Fibre

Pictured above.

◆Wear rubber gloves when chopping jalapeño peppers, and avoid touching your eyes.

Apricot Meatloaf

"My family loves this meatloaf, so I make it quite often."
— Gwen Pecaric, Burnaby, British Columbia

GLAZE		
Apricot jam	1/2 cup	125 mL
Ketchup	2 tbsp.	30 mL
MEATLOAF		
Lean ground beef	1 lb.	454 g
Ground pork	1/2 lb.	225 g
Medium onion, finely chopped	1	1
Fine dry bread crumbs	2 tbsp.	30 mL
Large egg, fork-beaten	1	1
Salt	1/4 tsp.	1 mL
Freshly ground pepper, just a pinch		
Chopped fresh parsley	1/4 cup	60 mL
Fine dry bread crumbs	6 tbsp.	100 mL
Finely chopped dried apricots	1 1/4 cups	300 mL
Finely chopped green onion	1/2 cup	125 mL
Finely chopped almonds, toasted◆	1/2 cup	125 mL

Glaze: Combine jam and ketchup in small bowl. Set aside.

Meatloaf: Combine first 7 ingredients in large bowl. Mix well. Turn out onto sheet of ungreased foil. Shape into rectangle, 9 x 15 inches (22 x 38 cm) and 1/2 inch (12 mm) thick.

Sprinkle with parsley and second amount of bread crumbs.

Combine remaining 3 ingredients in separate small bowl. Spread over meatloaf to within 2 inches (5 cm) of edge. Starting from short end, roll up tightly, jelly roll-style, pulling foil back as you roll. Discard foil. Place meatloaf, seam-side down, on greased baking sheet with sides. Bake, uncovered, in 350°F (175°C) oven for 30 minutes. Spread 1/2 of glaze over meatloaf. Bake, uncovered, for 15 minutes further. Spread remaining glaze over meatloaf. Bake, uncovered, for 20 to 25 minutes further until meatloaf is firm and meat thermometer inserted in centre registers 170°F (77°C). Let stand for 10 minutes before cutting. Cuts into eighteen 1/2 inch (12 mm) slices.

1 slice: 177 Calories; 9.0 g Total Fat; 113 mg Sodium; 9 g Protein; 16 g Carbohydrate; 1 g Dietary Fibre

Pictured below.

◆To toast the almonds, place them in an ungreased frying pan. Heat on medium, stirring often, until golden.

Apricot Meatloaf, left

Stuffed Roast Beef with Red Wine Sauce

Never underestimate the appeal of perfectly roasted beef for a celebration. It has everything it takes to please a crowd and make the cook a hero. In this presentation, horseradish and bacon pair beautifully with an au jus-like red wine sauce.

HORSERADISH STUFFING

Cooking oil	2 tsp.	10 mL
Small onion, finely chopped	1	1
Bacon slices, finely chopped	3	3
Coarse dry bread crumbs	2 cups	500 mL
Chopped fresh parsley	3 tbsp.	50 mL
Creamed horseradish	2 tbsp.	30 mL
Freshly ground pepper	1 tsp.	5 mL
Top sirloin roast, trimmed of fat	4 1/2 lbs.	2 kg
Water	1/2 cup	125 mL

RED WINE SAUCE

All-purpose flour	1/4 cup	60 mL
Prepared beef broth	2 cups	500 mL
Red (or alcohol-free) wine	1 cup	250 mL
Creamed horseradish	2 tbsp.	30 mL
Salt, sprinkle		
Freshly ground pepper, sprinkle		

Horseradish Stuffing: Heat cooking oil in medium frying pan on medium-high. Add onion. Sauté for about 5 minutes until softened.

Add bacon. Fry for about 5 minutes until bacon is crisp.

Combine next 4 ingredients in medium bowl. Add bacon mixture. Mix well.

Cut a long deep pocket in one long side of roast almost through to other side. Spoon stuffing into pocket. Tie with butcher's string at 1 1/4 inch (3 cm) intervals. Place on greased wire rack in roasting pan. Pour water in bottom of pan. Roast, uncovered, in 350°F (175°C) oven about 1 3/4 hours (for medium doneness) until tender, or until internal temperature reaches 155°F (68°C). Remove from oven. Cover with foil. Let stand for 10 minutes before carving into 1/2 inch (12 mm) slices.

Red Wine Sauce: Drain all but 2 tbsp. (30 mL) pan drippings from roasting pan. Stir in flour. Heat and stir on medium for 1 minute until grainy.

Add remaining 5 ingredients. Stir. Bring to a boil. Boil, uncovered, for 10 to 12 minutes, stirring occasionally, until sauce is thickened. Strain. Makes about 1 1/4 cups (300 mL) sauce. Serve drizzled over beef slices. Serves 10.

1 serving: 455 Calories; 16 g Total Fat; 547 mg Sodium; 50 g Protein; 20 g Carbohydrate; 1 g Dietary Fibre

Liver with Bacon and Onions

There's a very good reason why this traditional combination is enjoying renewed popularity: it's nourishing, fast and easy to put together, inexpensive and satisfying. Team it with your best mashed potatoes and your favourite winter vegetable.

Bacon slices, chopped	6	6
Sliced onion	1 cup	250 mL
All-purpose flour	1/4 cup	60 mL
Salt, just a pinch		
Freshly ground pepper, just a pinch		
Baby beef (or calf) liver, trimmed and sliced	10 oz.	285 g

Fry bacon in large cast iron or heavy frying pan on medium for about 5 minutes until crisp. Drain and discard all but 2 tbsp. (30 mL) drippings. Set reserved drippings aside. Leave bacon in frying pan.

Add onion to bacon. Sauté for about 5 minutes until onion is softened. Remove from pan. Keep warm.

Mix next 3 ingredients in shallow dish or on waxed paper. Dredge liver in flour mixture. Shake gently to remove excess. Heat reserved drippings in same pan on medium-low. Add liver. Cook for 3 to 4 minutes per side for medium or 5 to 6 minutes per side for well done. Serve topped with bacon mixture. Serves 2.

1 serving: 509 Calories; 28.8 g Total Fat; 394 mg Sodium; 34 g Protein; 27 g Carbohydrate; 2 g Dietary Fibre

Pictured above.

Liver with Bacon and Onions, below

Beef Stroganoff

"This low-fat version of an old comfort-food favourite doesn't sacrifice taste. It's perfect served over yolk-free egg noodles or mashed potatoes."
— Kit Price, Edmonton, Alberta

Inside round steak, cut into 1/4 inch (6 mm) thick strips	1 1/2 lbs.	680 g
Prepared beef broth	2 1/2 cups	625 mL
Dry white (or alcohol-free) wine (optional)	1/2 cup	125 mL
Tomato paste	1 tbsp.	15 mL
Dried tarragon leaves	2 tsp.	10 mL
Medium onion, diced	1	1
Sliced fresh mushrooms	2 cups	500 mL
Light sour cream	1/3 cup	75 mL
All-purpose flour	3 tbsp.	50 mL

Lightly spray large non-stick frying pan with cooking spray. Heat on medium-high. Add beef. Cook, stirring occasionally, for about 5 minutes until browned.

Add next 4 ingredients. Bring to a boil. Reduce heat to low. Cover. Simmer for about 2 hours until beef is tender.

Lightly spray medium non-stick frying pan with cooking spray. Heat on medium-high. Add onion. Sauté for 3 minutes. Add mushrooms. Sauté for 5 minutes until onion and mushrooms are softened. Remove from frying pan. Set aside.

Combine sour cream and flour in small bowl. Stir 1/3 cup (75 mL) pan juices from beef mixture into sour cream mixture until smooth. Stir into beef mixture. Add onion mixture. Heat and stir on medium for about 10 minutes until sauce is boiling gently and thickened. Serves 4.

1 serving: 304 Calories; 9.3 g Total Fat; 623 mg Sodium; 43 g Protein; 11 g Carbohydrate; 1 g Dietary Fibre

Steak and Kidney Pie

A taste of tradition with simmered beef, kidney and onions in a rich sauce beneath a golden pastry crust—reserve this hearty, comforting English specialty for the coldest day of the year. Great with a pint of dark ale.

FILLING

All-purpose flour	1/4 cup	60 mL
Salt	1/2 tsp.	2 mL
Pepper	1/2 tsp.	2 mL
Round steak, cut into 1 inch (2.5 cm) cubes	2 lbs.	900 g
Cooking oil	1 tbsp.	15 mL
Cooking oil	1 tbsp.	15 mL
Medium onions, cut into 1 inch (2.5 cm) pieces	3	3
Prepared beef broth	2 cups	500 mL
Bay leaves	2	2
Fresh beef kidney♦	1 lb.	454 g
Cooking oil	2 tbsp.	30 mL

PASTRY

All-purpose flour	1 1/2 cups	375 mL
Salt	1/2 tsp.	2 mL
Lard (or shortening), cut up	3/4 cup	175 mL
Egg yolks (large)	2	2
White vinegar	1/2 tsp.	2 mL
Cold water, approximately	2 tbsp.	30 mL
Large egg	1	1
Milk	1 tbsp.	15 mL

Filling: Combine first 3 ingredients in shallow bowl or on waxed paper. Dredge beef in flour mixture. Shake gently to remove excess. Reserve remaining flour mixture.

Heat first amount of cooking oil in large, deep, frying pan or Dutch oven on medium-high. Add 1/2 of beef. Sauté for about 5 minutes until browned. Remove from pan.

Repeat with remaining beef and second amount of cooking oil. Remove from pan.

Add onion to same pan. Sauté on medium-high for about 5 minutes until softened. Add reserved flour mixture. Heat and stir for 1 minute until onion is well coated.

Gradually stir broth into onion mixture until smooth. Add beef and bay leaves. Bring to

a boil. Reduce heat to medium-low. Cover. Simmer for 1 hour, stirring occasionally, until beef is fork-tender. Remove and discard bay leaves. Remove beef and onion with slotted spoon to large bowl. Strain liquid into 2 cup (500 mL) liquid measure. If more than 1 cup (250 mL) liquid, boil in same frying pan until reduced to 1 cup (250 mL). Add to beef mixture.

Trim kidney of fat and veins. Cut into 3/4 inch (2 cm) cubes. Heat third amount of cooking oil in large frying pan on medium. Add kidney. Sauté for about 3 minutes, until lightly browned. Add to beef mixture. Stir. Set filling aside.

Pastry: Combine flour and salt in medium bowl. Cut in lard until mixture is crumbly.

Whisk egg yolks, vinegar and 2 tbsp. (30 mL) water together in small bowl. Add to flour mixture. Mix until soft dough forms. If dough is too dry, add more cold water, 1 tbsp. (15 mL) at a time. Shape into flattened ball. Cover with plastic wrap. Chill for 15 minutes. Roll out pastry on lightly floured surface to 1/8 inch (3 mm) thickness. Cut out 10 inch (25 cm) circle. Set aside. Roll out pastry trimmings to 1/8 inch (3 mm) thickness. Cut into 1 inch (2.5 cm) wide strips. Dampen and press ends of strips together to make 1 strip long enough to circle the rim of 9 inch (22 cm) pie plate. Fold and press strip over rim of pie plate. Roll out remaining pastry trimmings to 1/8 inch (3 mm) thickness. Cut into leaves or shapes to decorate pie top. Set aside. Pour filling into pie plate.

Whisk egg and milk together in small cup until combined. Brush over top of pastry strip. Place pastry circle on top. Press down gently all around edge. Crimp edge. To allow steam to escape and reduce likelihood of gravy splashing onto pastry top, make a "chimney." Cut a 6 x 12 inch (15 x 30 cm) piece of foil. Fold into 2 x 12 inch (5 x 30 cm) strip. Roll foil strip around 3/4 inch (2 cm) diameter wooden spoon handle or dowel to make 2 inch (5 cm) high cylinder. Make 3/4 inch (2 cm) hole in centre of pie. Insert chimney, leaving about 1/2 inch (12 mm) protruding. Decorate top with pastry cut-outs. Brush with egg mixture. Bake in 375°F (190°C) oven for 30 to 35 minutes until filling is bubbly and pastry is flaky and deep golden. Let stand for 10 minutes. Remove chimney. Serves 8.

1 serving: 607 Calories; 36.2 g Total Fat; 678 mg Sodium; 41 g Protein; 27 g Carbohydrate; 2 g Dietary Fibre

♦For a less pronounced kidney taste, soak whole kidneys overnight, in refrigerator, in lightly salted water or milk.

Beef Wellington

Variety meats are part of some favourite and classic dishes, such as this one. Liver paté is a fundamental component of this time-honoured recipe. Don't let the length of the recipe put you off—it's not hard to make. And what an impressive and elegant main dish for a special dinner party.

Cooking oil	1 tbsp.	15 mL
Beef tenderloin, trimmed of silver skin and fat♦	3 lbs.	1.4 kg
Butter (or hard margarine)	1 tbsp.	15 mL
Finely chopped fresh mushrooms	1 1/2 cups	375 mL
Finely chopped shallots	3/4 cup	175 mL
Liver paté (cognac or country-style)	1/2 cup	125 mL
Salt	1/8 tsp.	0.5 mL
Pepper	1/8 tsp.	0.5 mL
Package of frozen puff pastry, thawed according to package directions	14 oz.	397 g
Large egg	1	1
Milk	1 tbsp.	15 mL
RED WINE SAUCE		
Thinly sliced onion	2 cups	500 mL
Butter (not margarine)	1 tbsp.	15 mL
Salt, just a pinch		
Red (or alcohol-free) wine	1 cup	250 mL
Fresh thyme sprigs	3	3
Bay leaves	3	3
Whole black (or white) peppercorns	8	8
Cans of condensed beef broth (10 oz., 284 mL, each)	2	2
Cornstarch	2 tbsp.	30 mL
Cold water	3 tbsp.	50 mL
Cold butter (not margarine), optional, cut into 1/2 inch (12 mm) cubes♦♦	1/4 cup	60 mL

Heat cooking oil in large frying pan on medium-high. Add tenderloin. Sear on all sides until browned. Remove to wire rack set on baking sheet with sides.

Melt butter in same frying pan on medium. Add mushrooms and shallots. Sauté for 10 to 15 minutes until liquid from mushrooms has evaporated. Remove from heat.

Remove and discard any gelatin from paté. Add paté to mushroom mixture. Add salt and pepper. Stir until well combined. Set aside.

Roll out puff pastry on lightly floured surface to about 11 x 15 inch (28 x 38 cm) rectangle. Cut 2 x 2 x 3 inch (5 x 5 x 7.5 cm) triangle from each corner of pastry. Set aside for decoration. Spread mushroom mixture on pastry, leaving about 2 inch (5 cm) edge on all sides. Place tenderloin in centre of mushroom mixture. Bring long sides of pastry up over beef to overlap. Bring up each end of pastry. Press to seal. Place, seam-side down, on lightly greased baking sheet. Cut reserved pastry triangles into decorative shapes. Place on top.

Whisk egg and milk together in small bowl until combined. Brush on pastry. Bake, uncovered, in 375°F (190°C) oven for 45 to 60 minutes until meat thermometer inserted in centre of meat registers 135°F (57°C) for medium doneness. Remove from oven. Let stand for 15 to 20 minutes before serving.

Red Wine Sauce: Combine first 3 ingredients in large saucepan. Cover. Cook on medium for about 5 minutes, stirring occasionally, until onion is softened. Remove cover. Cook for about 10 minutes, stirring frequently, until onion is rich brown colour.

Add next 4 ingredients. Bring to a boil on medium-high. Boil for 5 to 10 minutes, stirring occasionally, until liquid is reduced by half.

Add broth. Bring to a boil. Reduce heat to medium.

Combine cornstarch and cold water in small bowl until smooth paste forms. Add to wine mixture. Stir until boiling and thickened. Boil for 1 minute.

Strain wine mixture into medium saucepan. Discard solids. Bring to a gentle boil on medium. Add butter, 1 cube at a time, while swirling saucepan. When nearly melted, add next cube. Makes 2 2/3 cups (650 mL) sauce. (Sauce can be prepared and chilled a few hours in advance, but add butter just before serving.) Cut Beef Wellington into 8 slices, being sure to cut end pieces slightly larger so they contain filling, not just pastry. Serve sauce on the side. Serves 8.

1 serving: 662 Calories; 38.2 g Total Fat; 803 mg Sodium; 40 g Protein; 33 g Carbohydrate; 1 g Dietary Fibre

Pictured above.

♦*Silver skin is the thin, light-coloured membrane that covers part of the tenderloin. Trim using a thin, sharp knife, removing as little of the meat as possible.*

♦♦*Swirling in cold butter to finish a sauce is a common technique in classic French cuisine. The butter adds a little extra body to the sauce, gives it a nice shine and rounds out the taste. Butter also prevents the sauce from forming a skin as it cools.*

Beef with Red Wine and Rosemary Sauce

If there's such a thing as an elegant pot roast, this is it. The cross-rib is often overlooked for the pricier roasts but, pound for pound, you won't find more flavour than in this user-friendly cut.

Boneless cross-rib roast	2 3/4 lbs.	1.25 kg
Garlic cloves, quartered	2	2
Cooking oil	1 tbsp.	15 mL
Cooking oil	1 tbsp.	15 mL
Medium onions, sliced	2	2
Garlic cloves, crushed	2	2
Red (or alcohol-free) wine	3/4 cup	175 mL
Prepared beef broth	1 cup	250 mL
Dried rosemary	1 1/2 tsp.	7 mL
Freshly ground pepper	1/2 tsp.	2 mL
Blueberry (or blackberry) jam	3 tbsp.	50 mL

Make 8 small slits at regular intervals in roast using sharp knife. Insert garlic quarters into slits.

Heat first amount of cooking oil in large pot or Dutch oven on medium-high. Sear roast for about 10 minutes until browned on all sides. Remove roast from pot.

Heat second amount of cooking oil in same pot on medium-high. Add onion and crushed garlic. Sauté for about 5 minutes until onion is softened.

Add next 4 ingredients. Stir. Add roast. Bring to a boil. Reduce heat to low. Cover. Simmer for 1 1/2 to 1 3/4 hours until roast is tender. Remove roast to serving plate. Cover with foil. Let stand for 10 to 15 minutes before carving.

Strain drippings into medium frying pan. Discard solids. Add jam. Heat and stir on medium-high until jam is dissolved. Bring to a boil. Boil, uncovered, for about 10 minutes, stirring occasionally, until sauce is reduced to about 3/4 cup (175 mL). Serve with roast. Serves 4.

1 serving: 871 Calories; 57.5 g Total Fat; 386 mg Sodium; 61 g Protein; 17 g Carbohydrate; 1 g Dietary Fibre

Groundnut Stew

"We were first served this delicious stew while visiting family in Chicago and it's now a favourite recipe in our household. This is such a simple dish to prepare and yet really tastes like something special."

— Deborha Kerr, Fort St. John, British Columbia

Cooking oil	1 1/2 tbsp.	25 mL
Beef stew meat, trimmed of fat and cut into 1 1/2 inch (3.8 cm) pieces	2 lbs.	900 g
Can of Roma (plum) tomatoes, with liquid	14 oz.	398 mL
Water	1 cup	250 mL
Dried crushed chilies	1 tbsp.	15 mL
Beef bouillon powder	1 tsp.	5 mL
Salt	1 tsp.	5 mL
Smooth peanut butter	2/3 cup	150 mL
Sweet potatoes (or yams), about 2 medium, cut into 1 inch (2.5 cm) pieces	2 lbs.	900 g
Large onion, cut into 1 inch (2.5 cm) pieces	1	1
Medium green peppers, cut into 1 inch (2.5 cm) pieces	2	2

Heat cooking oil in large heavy pot or Dutch oven on medium-high. Sear beef, in 2 batches, until browned on all sides.

Add next 5 ingredients. Stir. Bring to a boil. Reduce heat to medium-low. Cover. Simmer for 1 1/2 hours, stirring occasionally.

Add peanut butter. Stir. Add remaining 3 ingredients. Stir. Cover. Bring to a boil. Reduce heat. Simmer for about 1 hour, stirring occasionally, until vegetables are tender. Makes 11 1/2 cups (2.9 L).

1 cup (250 mL): 271 Calories; 12.7 g Total Fat; 429 mg Sodium; 18 g Protein; 23 g Carbohydrate; 4 g Dietary Fibre

Pictured below.

Creamy Veal Stew

"This is a stew I like putting together on a weekend afternoon. It goes into the oven, my husband and I take a long walk through the woods, and we come home to the wonderful smell of supper cooking. We enjoy this slightly spicy stew with mashed potatoes, hot biscuits and red wine."

— Kirstin Piché, Ottawa, Ontario

All-purpose flour	1/4 cup	60 mL
Salt	1 tsp.	5 mL
Freshly ground pepper	1/4 tsp.	1 mL
Boneless veal shoulder, trimmed of fat and cut into 1 1/2 inch (3.8 cm) pieces	2 lbs.	900 g

Groundnut Stew, above

Creamy Veal Stew, above

Cooking oil	2 tbsp.	30 mL
Dry white (or alcohol-free) wine	1 cup	250 mL
Cooking oil	2 tsp.	10 mL
Medium onions, chopped	2	2
Medium carrots, chopped	3	3
Chopped fresh mushrooms	1/2 cup	125 mL
Prepared chicken broth	1 cup	250 mL
Bay leaf	1	1
Dried thyme	1/4 tsp.	1 mL
Cayenne pepper	1/4 tsp.	1 mL
Whipping cream	1/4 cup	60 mL

Combine first 3 ingredients in shallow bowl or on waxed paper. Pat veal dry with paper towels. Dredge in flour mixture. Shake gently to remove excess. Discard any remaining flour mixture.

Heat first amount of cooking oil in large non-stick frying pan on medium-high. Sear veal, in 2 batches, until browned on all sides. Remove to plate.

Add wine to same frying pan. Bring to a boil, scraping up any browned bits from bottom of frying pan. Remove from heat.

Heat second amount of cooking oil in large heavy pot or Dutch oven on medium. Add next 3 ingredients. Sauté for about 5 minutes until onion is softened.

Add veal, wine mixture and next 4 ingredients. Stir. Bring to a boil. Cover. Bake in 350°F (175°C) oven for about 1 1/4 hours, stirring occasionally, until veal is tender.◆

Add cream. Stir until well combined. Makes 7 cups (1.75 L).

1 cup (250 mL): 294 Calories; 12.4 g Total Fat; 594 mg Sodium; 28 g Protein; 11 g Carbohydrate; 2 g Dietary Fibre

Pictured on page 76.

◆For a thicker sauce, remove the lid and bake the stew for a further 15 minutes until the sauce is the desired consistency.

Creamy Veal with Apples and Rosemary, below

Creamy Veal with Apples and Rosemary

These tender veal chops are a fabulous special occasion dish, served with delightful apple sauce enriched with cream. Garnish with fresh rosemary sprigs.

Cooking oil	1 tbsp.	15 mL
Veal rib (or loin) chops, 3/4 inch (2 cm) thick (about 1 lb., 454 g)	4	4
Cooking oil	1 tbsp.	15 mL
Garlic cloves, crushed	4	4
Red (or alcohol-free) wine	1/4 cup	60 mL
Medium Granny Smith apples, peeled, cored and cut into 8 wedges	2	2
Chopped fresh rosemary	2 tsp.	10 mL
Freshly squeezed orange juice	1/4 cup	60 mL
Strip of orange peel (3 inch, 7.5 cm, length)	1	1
Whipping cream	1 cup	250 mL
Salt	1/2 tsp.	2 mL
Freshly ground pepper	1/2 tsp.	2 mL

Heat first amount of cooking oil in large frying pan. Cook chops on medium-high for 3 to 5 minutes on each side until lightly browned. Remove from pan.

Heat second amount of cooking oil in same pan. Add garlic. Heat and stir on medium for 30 seconds.

Add remaining 8 ingredients. Mix well. Add chops to pan. Simmer, uncovered, for 20 to 25 minutes, turning chops over once and stirring mixture several times, until chops are tender and sauce is thickened. Serves 4.

1 serving: 519 Calories; 38.9 g Total Fat; 427 mg Sodium; 25 g Protein; 15 g Carbohydrate; 1 g Dietary Fibre

Pictured above.

Veal in Creamy Caper Mustard Sauce

This simple yet impressive entree requires little effort, but delivers great taste. Serve with a lively green salad and pasta tossed with butter and chopped fresh herbs.

All-purpose flour	1/4 cup	60 mL
Veal inside round fillets, about 1/4 inch (6 mm) thick◆	1 lb.	454 g
Cooking oil	1 tbsp.	15 mL
Cooking oil	2 tsp.	10 mL
Garlic cloves, crushed	4	4
Dry white (or alcohol-free) wine	1/4 cup	60 mL
Whipping cream	1 cup	250 mL
Dijon mustard	2 tsp.	10 mL
Capers, coarsely chopped	2 tsp.	10 mL
Salt	1/4 tsp.	1 mL
Freshly ground pepper	1/4 tsp.	1 mL

Put flour into resealable plastic bag. Add veal. Seal. Shake to coat.

Heat first amount of cooking oil in large frying pan on medium-high. Sear veal, in 2 batches, for about 2 minutes per side until lightly browned. Remove from frying pan. Keep warm.

Heat second amount of cooking oil in same frying pan on medium. Add garlic. Sauté for about 1 minute until fragrant.

Add remaining 6 ingredients. Stir. Bring to a boil on medium-high. Boil for about 5 minutes until sauce is thickened. Add veal. Turn to coat. Serves 4.

1 serving: 498 Calories; 37.9 g Total Fat; 397 mg Sodium; 27 g Protein; 10 g Carbohydrate; trace Dietary Fibre

Pictured below.

◆*Veal inside round fillets are also called scaloppine steaks.*

Veal in Creamy Caper Mustard Sauce, above

Veal Chops with Orange and Peppercorns

The naturally mild flavour of veal chops gets a lift with this combination of sweet orange flavours and piquant green peppercorns. Serve with a brilliant green vegetable like broccoli or spinach, and your very best creamy mashed potatoes. Great for a cold winter evening.

All-purpose flour	2 tbsp.	30 mL
Paprika	2 tsp.	10 mL
Chopped fresh sage (or 3/4 tsp., 4 mL, ground)	1 tbsp.	15 mL
Freshly ground pepper	1 tsp.	5 mL
Veal chops	4	4
Cooking oil	1 tbsp.	15 mL
Cooking oil	1/2 tbsp.	7 mL
Medium onion, thinly sliced	1	1
Garlic cloves, crushed	4	4
Slices of prosciutto, chopped into 1 inch (2.5 cm) pieces◆	4	4
Dry vermouth◆◆	1/2 cup	125 mL
Freshly grated orange zest	2 tsp.	10 mL
Freshly squeezed orange juice	1/2 cup	125 mL
Green peppercorns in brine, drained, slightly crushed	1 tbsp.	15 mL

Combine first 4 ingredients in shallow dish. Dredge veal chops in flour mixture.

Heat first amount of cooking oil on medium in large frying pan. Cook chops for about 5 minutes per side until browned. Remove from pan.

Heat second amount of cooking oil in same frying pan on medium. Add onion and garlic. Sauté for 5 minutes until onion is softened.

Add prosciutto. Sauté for 5 minutes until prosciutto is crisp.

Add chops and remaining 4 ingredients. Stir. Bring to a boil. Reduce heat to medium-low. Cover. Simmer for 10 minutes. Remove cover. Simmer for about 5 minutes further until sauce is thickened and chops are tender. Serves 4.

1 serving: 384 Calories; 14.3 g Total Fat; 873 mg Sodium; 45 g Protein; 13 g Carbohydrate; 1 g Dietary Fibre

◆*Prosciutto is a salt-cured, unsmoked, air-dried ham sold in very thin slices in the deli section of your grocery store.*

◆◆*You can substitute dry white wine, dry sherry, or an alcohol-free variety of either.*

Kate's Roast Potatoes, page 192

Pepper and Mushroom Salad with Basil Honey Dressing, page 159

Baked Salmon Spanakopita, below

Baked Salmon Spanakopita

Here's a Canadian update of the classic Greek spanakopita. Chef Al Barriault, formerly of Billy's Seafood Company, liked to wrap fresh spinach-filled salmon in phyllo for a great Maritime variation.

— Billy's Seafood Company, Old City Market, Saint John, New Brunswick

Spinach leaves, trimmed	8 oz.	225 g
Feta cheese, crumbled	4 oz.	113 g
Salmon fillet, cut into 6 pieces	1 1/2 lbs.	680 g
Salt	1/2 tsp.	2 mL
Pepper	1/2 tsp.	2 mL
Hard margarine (or butter), melted	6 tbsp.	100 mL
Phyllo pastry sheets	6	6

Cook spinach in large saucepan on low until just wilted. Drain. Cool. Squeeze excess liquid from spinach. Chop finely. Combine spinach and feta cheese in medium bowl.

Cut lengthwise pocket down 1 side of each salmon piece almost, but not quite, cutting through. Pack 1/3 cup (75 mL) spinach mixture into each pocket. Sprinkle with salt and pepper.

Brush margarine on 1 side of each pastry sheet. Fold each sheet to width of fillets. Place fillets on top. Wrap up to form parcels. Brush tops with margarine. Bake in 400°F (205°C) oven for 12 to 15 minutes until pastry is browned. Serves 6.

1 serving: 546 Calories; 24.6 g Total Fat; 1315 mg Sodium; 52 g Protein; 42 g Carbohydrate; 23 g Dietary Fibre

Pictured above.

Maple Salmon

"This is a must at a fly-in fishing camp. At home, we serve it with a Parmesan cheese and asparagus risotto."

— Scott Middleton, Pigeon Lake, Alberta

Soy sauce	1/2 cup	125 mL
Olive oil	3/4 cup	175 mL
Maple syrup	1 cup	250 mL
Rye whisky	3/4 cup	175 mL
Chopped fresh parsley	1 cup	250 mL
Garlic cloves, crushed	4	4
Freshly ground pepper	1 tsp.	5 mL
Whole salmon fillet	2 1/2 lbs.	1.1 kg

Combine first 7 ingredients in medium saucepan. Heat and stir on medium for 3 to 5 minutes until hot. Cool. Makes about 3 1/3 cups (825 mL) marinade. Reserve 1/2 of marinade.

Place remaining marinade in long shallow dish. Add salmon. Cover. Chill for 12 to 24 hours, turning several times. Remove salmon, discarding marinade. Preheat grill to medium-high. Place salmon in lightly greased disposable foil baking pan or on several layers of greased foil. Cook, using indirect cooking method (see Indirectly Speaking, page 67), omitting drip pan, for 10 minutes per side, basting with reserved marinade several times during cooking. Cook until salmon flakes easily when tested with a fork. Do not overcook. Discard any leftover marinade. Serves 8.

1 serving: 343 Calories; 20 g Total Fat; 347 mg Sodium; 29 g Protein; 8 g Carbohydrate; trace Dietary Fibre

Sole with Lemon
Dill Sauce, below

Mussels with White Wine and Basil Sauce

This creamy, fragrant wine sauce goes perfectly with the texture of sweet mussel meat, freshly cooked pasta and a bright garden salad. You could vary this recipe by using freshly chopped coriander in place of the basil.

Ingredient	Imperial	Metric
Fresh (blue) mussels (about 3 1/2 dozen), scrubbed clean◆	3 1/4 lbs.	1.5 kg
Butter (not margarine)	3 tbsp.	50 mL
Medium onion, finely chopped	1	1
Garlic cloves, crushed	2	2
All-purpose flour	2 tbsp.	30 mL
Dry white (or alcohol-free) wine	1/4 cup	60 mL
Half-and-half cream	1 cup	250 mL
Salt	1/4 tsp.	1 mL
Fresh sweet basil leaves, cut chiffonade◆◆	1/4 cup	60 mL
Fresh sweet basil leaves, for garnish		

Place mussels in large pot or Dutch oven 1/3 full of boiling water. Reduce heat to low. Cover. Simmer for about 3 to 5 minutes until shells are open and mussels are tender. Drain, reserving 1/2 cup (125 mL) liquid. Set mussels aside, discarding any that are unopened.

Melt butter in same pot. Sauté onion and garlic for about 5 minutes until onion is soft.

Stir in flour. Cook for 2 minutes until flour is grainy.

Stir in next 3 ingredients and reserved mussel liquid. Cook on medium for 5 to 8 minutes, stirring occasionally, until mixture is thickened.

Add mussels and basil. Stir until mussels are well coated.

Garnish with basil leaves. Serves 6.

1 serving: 224 Calories; 12.7 g Total Fat; 498 mg Sodium; 15 g Protein; 10 g Carbohydrate; trace Dietary Fibre

◆Mussels occasionally have a "beard" (black stringy filament) when purchased. Clip it off with scissors or a paring knife. If you choose to pull the beard off, make sure to pull towards the hinge.

◆◆To cut chiffonade, stack a few basil leaves at a time and roll up tightly. Slice crosswise into very thin strips.

Sole with Lemon Dill Sauce

As classic as the combination of sole and lemon is, you'll want to try this aromatic sauce with halibut, haddock, red snapper, sea bass and especially salmon. It's also great with shrimp and scallops.

Ingredient	Imperial	Metric
Garlic clove, crushed	1	1
Hard margarine (or butter)	1 tbsp.	15 mL
LEMON DILL SAUCE		
Finely grated lemon zest	1 tbsp.	15 mL
Whipping cream	1 cup	250 mL
Chopped fresh dill	1 tbsp.	15 mL
Salt	1/4 tsp.	1 mL
Pepper, sprinkle		
Sole fillets	1 1/2 lbs.	680 g

Sauté garlic in margarine in medium saucepan on medium-low for 1 minute.

Lemon Dill Sauce: Add next 5 ingredients. Stir. Simmer, uncovered, for about 12 minutes until slightly thickened. Makes 1 cup (250 mL) sauce.

Roll up sole, starting from small end. Bring 1 inch (2.5 cm) water to a boil in non-stick frying pan on medium low. Add sole. Cover. Poach for 6 to 8 minutes, turning over once, until sole flakes easily when tested with a fork. Serve sauce over sole. Serves 4.

1 serving: 420 Calories; 30.4 g Total Fat; 369 mg Sodium; 33 g Protein; 2 g Carbohydrate; trace Dietary Fibre

Pictured above.

Honey Mustard Scallop Kabobs

Pretty, elegant and so easy to prepare, this recipe is a wonderful blend of textures—the crunch of snow peas, the softness of scallops and the warmed juices of the tomatoes. Serve with steamed rice.

Ingredient	Imperial	Metric
Snow peas	10 oz.	285 g
Large fresh (or frozen, thawed) sea scallops	36	36
Grape tomatoes	36	36
Liquid honey	3 tbsp.	50 mL
Prepared grainy mustard	2 tbsp.	30 mL
Balsamic vinegar	2 tsp.	10 mL
Garlic clove, crushed	1	1
Ground cumin	1 tsp.	5 mL

Alternate first 3 ingredients on 12 skewers.

Preheat grill to medium-high. Combine remaining 5 ingredients in small bowl. Place skewers on greased grill. Grill for 5 minutes, turning several times. Baste with honey mixture. Grill for 2 minutes, basting constantly, until scallops are just cooked. Makes 12 kabobs.

1 kabob: 79 Calories; 0.8 g Total Fat; 113 mg Sodium; 9 g Protein; 10 g Carbohydrate; 1 g Dietary Fibre

Risotto with Shrimp and Peas

"The creamy risotto that comes out of this pressure cooker in seven minutes is a real revelation. You won't believe that it works as perfectly as it does. If you can, spring for the saffron; it gives the dish a great earthy flavour and bright golden hue. Try substituting some crab and rings of baby squid for half of the shrimp, or using lightly steamed asparagus instead of peas. Garnish with shaved Parmesan cheese."

— Cinda Chavich, author of *125 Best Pressure Cooker Recipes* (Robert Rose Inc., 2004)

Crushed saffron threads (optional)	1/4 tsp.	1 mL
Chicken (or vegetable) broth	2 cups	500 mL
Small onion, chopped	1	1
Butter	1 tbsp.	15 mL
Olive oil	1 tbsp.	15 mL
Arborio rice	1 cup	250 mL
Dry white (or alcohol-free) wine	1/4 cup	60 mL
Large shrimp, peeled, deveined and halved lengthwise	3/4 lb.	340 g
Frozen peas, thawed (or chopped asparagus, lightly steamed)	1 cup	250 mL
Finely grated Parmesan cheese	1/2 cup	125 mL
Freshly ground pepper, to taste		

Combine saffron and chicken broth in medium bowl. Let stand for 2 minutes. Set aside.

Sauté onion in butter and olive oil in pressure cooker on medium-high for about 3 to 5 minutes until softened. Add rice. Stir until well-coated. Add wine. Mix well.

Add broth mixture. Lock lid in place. Bring pressure cooker up to pressure on high heat. Reduce heat to medium-low just to maintain even pressure. Cook for 7 minutes. Release pressure. Remove from heat. Remove lid.

Add shrimp and peas. Stir. Cover, but do not secure lid. Let stand for 10 minutes until shrimp are pink and curled.

Add Parmesan cheese and pepper. Serve immediately. Serves 4 as a first course or side dish, 2 as a main dish.

1 main dish serving: 924 Calories; 26 g Total Fat; 1712 mg Sodium; 62 g Protein; 100 g Carbohydrate; 4 g Dietary Fibre

Pictured below.

Photo by: Ian Grant

Paella, below

Paella

Spain's national dish, paella (pi-AY-yuh), combines assorted seafood with spicy sausage, chicken, sweet red peppers, tomatoes and rice. It's conveniently cooked in one large pan and is well worth the extra bit of preparation time required.

Fresh clams	1 lb.	454 g
Salt	2 tsp.	10 mL
Cold water, to cover		
Saffron threads◆	1/2 tsp.	2 mL
Dry white (or alcohol-free) wine	1 1/2 cups	375 mL
Olive (or cooking) oil	1 tbsp.	15 mL
Chicken drumettes	10	10
Chorizo sausages, sliced	4	4
Chopped red onion	1 1/3 cups	325 mL
Garlic cloves, crushed	4	4
Long grain white rice	3 cups	750 mL
Diced red pepper	1 1/4 cups	300 mL
Cans of condensed chicken broth (10 oz., 284 mL, each)	2	2
Water	2 1/2 cups	625 mL
Medium tomatoes, diced	4	4
Fresh (or frozen, thawed) medium shrimp, peeled and deveined	1 lb.	454 g
Sliced green beans	1 1/2 cups	375 mL
Frozen peas	1 cup	250 mL
Fresh (or frozen, thawed) scallops	14 oz.	395 g

Place clams and salt in large bowl. Cover with water. Let stand for 30 minutes. Drain.

Combine saffron and wine in small bowl. Let stand for 20 minutes.

Heat olive oil in large pot or Dutch oven. Cook chicken on medium-high for 8 to 10 minutes until browned and no pink remains. Remove chicken. Set aside. Drain all but 2 tsp. (10 mL) oil.

Add next 3 ingredients to pot. Sauté on medium for about 5 minutes, stirring occasionally, until onion is soft.

Mussels with Fresh Tomato and Chili Peppers

This spiced tomato sauce is wonderful with mussels. Serve with hot pasta and some good, crusty bread to mop up every last bit!

Medium onion, finely chopped	1	1
Garlic cloves, crushed	3	3
Small red chili peppers, finely chopped♦	2	2
Olive (or cooking) oil	1 tbsp.	15 mL
Medium tomatoes, coarsely chopped	8	8
Dry white (or alcohol-free) wine	1/3 cup	75 mL
Tomato paste	3 tbsp.	50 mL
Chopped fresh whole oregano leaves	1 tbsp.	15 mL
Chopped fresh thyme leaves	1 tsp.	5 mL
Salt	1 tsp.	5 mL
Frozen New Zealand green (green-lipped) mussels, thawed and scrubbed clean♦♦	3 1/4 lbs.	1.5 kg

Sauté first 3 ingredients in olive oil in large pot or Dutch oven on medium for about 5 minutes until onion is soft.

Process tomatoes in food processor until smooth. Add to onion mixture.

Add next 5 ingredients to tomato mixture. Stir. Bring to a boil. Reduce heat to medium-low. Simmer, uncovered, for 20 to 25 minutes, stirring occasionally, until sauce is thickened. Makes 6 cups (1.5 L) sauce.

Place mussels in large pot or Dutch oven 1/3 full of boiling water. Reduce heat to low. Cover. Simmer for about 5 minutes until shells are open and mussels are tender. Drain. Discard any unopened mussels. Add remaining mussels to sauce. Stir until mussels are well coated. Serves 6.

1 serving: 183 Calories; 5.5 g Total Fat; 739 mg Sodium; 16 g Protein; 17 g Carbohydrate; 3 g Dietary Fibre

♦*Wear gloves when chopping chili peppers, and avoid touching your eyes.*

♦♦*Mussels occasionally have a "beard" (black stringy filament) when purchased. Clip it off with scissors or a paring knife. If you choose to pull the beard off, make sure to pull towards the hinge.*

Spaghetti with Clam Sauce

This is the easiest clam sauce you'll ever make. The wonderful blend of clams, garlic, cheese and onions is great with spaghetti or linguine.

Spaghetti	1 lb.	454 g
Boiling water	12 cups	3 L
Salt	2 tsp.	10 mL
Medium onion, finely chopped	1	1
Garlic cloves, crushed	2	2
Hard margarine (or butter)	1 tbsp.	15 mL
Can of condensed New England clam chowder	10 oz.	284 mL
Milk	1/4 cup	60 mL
Can of clams, with liquid	10 oz.	284 mL
Cream cheese, cut up	1/3 cup	75 mL
Freshly grated lemon zest	1/2 tsp.	2 mL
Freshly grated Parmesan cheese	1/4 cup	60 mL
Chopped fresh parsley, for garnish	2 tbsp.	30 mL
Freshly ground pepper, for garnish		
Finely shaved fresh Parmesan cheese, for garnish		

Cook spaghetti in boiling water and salt in large uncovered pot or Dutch oven for 8 to 10 minutes, stirring occasionally, until tender but firm. Drain well. Keep warm.

Sauté onion and garlic in margarine in medium saucepan for 5 minutes until onion is soft.

Add next 5 ingredients. Stir until sauce is hot and cream cheese is melted. Makes 2 3/4 cups (675 mL) sauce.

Combine spaghetti, sauce and grated Parmesan cheese in large bowl.

Garnish with remaining 3 ingredients. Serves 6.

1 serving: 435 Calories; 10.6 g Total Fat; 600 mg Sodium; 19 g Protein; 65 g Carbohydrate; 2 g Dietary Fibre

Add rice and red pepper. Stir. Add saffron mixture. Heat and stir on medium until liquid is absorbed.

Add next 3 ingredients. Bring to a boil. Reduce heat to very low. Cover. Cook for 15 minutes.

Add clams and next 3 ingredients. Cook for to 10 minutes.

Add chicken and scallops. Cover. Cook for minutes until scallops are tender. Makes 0 cups (5 L). Serves 6 to 8.

serving: 1097 Calories; 36.7 g Total Fat; 1927 mg Sodium; 6 g Protein; 100 g Carbohydrate; 4 g Dietary Fibre

Pictured above.

Saffron threads can be substituted with 1/2 tsp. 2 mL) turmeric. If using turmeric, eliminate the oaking step.

Butterflied Salmon with Wild Rice and Seafood Stuffing

Whole stuffed salmon makes an impressive main course dish, especially when every tasty morsel can be enjoyed without having to pick out a single bone.

Small leek (white and tender parts only), chopped	1	1
Cooking oil	1 tbsp.	15 mL
Small red pepper, finely chopped	1	1
Celery rib, finely chopped	1	1
Brown sugar, packed	2 tsp.	10 mL
Raw medium shrimp, peeled and deveined, chopped	12 1/4 oz.	350 g
Raw medium scallops, halved	6 oz.	175 g
Cooked white and wild rice blend	1 1/2 cups	375 mL
Feta cheese, crumbled	1/3 cup	75 mL
Freshly ground pepper	1 tsp.	5 mL
Whole salmon, clean gutted and scaled	6 lbs.	2.7 kg
Cooking oil	1 tbsp.	15 mL
Salt	1 tsp.	5 mL
Freshly ground pepper	1 tsp.	5 mL

Sauté leek in cooking oil in large frying pan on medium-low for about 10 minutes until very soft.

Add red pepper and celery. Cook for 10 minutes, stirring occasionally, until soft.

Add brown sugar. Stir until dissolved.

Add shrimp and scallops. Cook on high for about 3 minutes until just cooked. Transfer to large bowl.

Add next 3 ingredients. Mix well. Cool. Makes 3 1/2 cups (875 mL).

Preheat grill to medium-high. Butterfly salmon (see Butterflying Salmon, page 85). Lay, skin side down, on cutting board. Place stuffing down centre of salmon. Fold over to enclose filling. Tie with butcher's string in 5 or 6 places at equal intervals to secure. Rub both sides of salmon with cooking oil. Sprinkle with salt and second amount of pepper. Place on 10 x 24 inch (25 x 60 cm) piece of greased foil. Cook salmon with lid closed for about 30 minutes until fish flakes easily when tested with a fork. Serves 8.

1 serving: 803 Calories; 43 g Total Fat; 682 mg Sodium; 82 g Protein; 16 g Carbohydrate; 1 g Dietary Fibre

Pictured at left.

Butterflying Salmon

You'll need a filleting or medium flexible knife and small needle-nose pliers (or tweezers for smaller fish). You may find it easier on some repeat steps to turn the fish 180°. Start with cleaned and scaled fish, gills removed.

Photos by: Bluefish Studios

1. Release the backbone. Cut through the rib bones to a depth of about 1 inch (2.5 cm) on one side of the backbone, from head to tail. Angle the blade against the backbone to cleanly cut away the most flesh and ride along the backbone to guide the knife. Repeat on the other side of the backbone.

**2. Trim the flesh away from both sides of the exposed backbone.

3. Remove the backbone. Starting at the head end, cut underneath the backbone, lifting it up and out of the way as you cut. Snap the backbone off at the tail.

4. Remove the rib bones. Starting at the head end, cut the rib bones away from the flesh, making sure to angle the knife to ride along the underside of the bones.

5. Lift the rib bones out of the way as you trim. Repeat on the other side.

6. Pull out the pin bones. Starting again at the head end and going down each side of the fish, feel for the small individual pin bones with your fingertips. Use the pliers to remove them, pulling in the direction they grow.

Trout with Horseradish Cream Sauce

When the fishermen—or women!—in your family bring home their catch, this is the recipe to remember. Easy to prepare, quick to cook and very tasty, trout and horseradish have a natural affinity.

Whole rainbow trout (about 14 oz., 395 g, each), clean gutted and scaled	8	8
Salt	2 tsp.	10 mL
Freshly ground pepper	2 tsp.	10 mL

HORSERADISH CREAM SAUCE

Small onion, finely chopped	1	1
Cooking oil	2 tsp.	10 mL
Creamed horseradish	1 1/2 tbsp.	25 mL
Whipping cream	1 1/4 cups	300 mL
Chopped fresh dill	2 tbsp.	30 mL

Preheat grill to medium. Pat trout dry. Cut 3 slashes into flesh at an angle on each side. Sprinkle both sides with salt and pepper. Cook trout on well-greased grill for 5 to 7 minutes per side until fish flakes easily when tested with fork. Cover to keep warm.

Horseradish Cream Sauce: Sauté onion in cooking oil in frying pan on medium for about 5 minutes until soft. Add horseradish and whipping cream. Bring to a simmer. Heat and stir for about 2 minutes until thickened. Remove from heat. Add dill. Stir. Makes 1 2/3 cups (400 mL) sauce. Drizzle over trout. Serves 8.

1 serving: 680 Calories; 35.2 g Total Fat; 749 mg Sodium; 83 g Protein; 3 g Carbohydrate; trace Dietary Fibre

Creamy Seafood Pizza

We've combined shrimp, scallops, mussels and a creamy tomato sauce for a fresh take on seafood pizza. Asiago cheese and a hint of lemon add a lively nip of flavour to every bite.

Thick-Crust Dough (see Roasted Pepper, Sausage and Pesto Pizza, page 112)		
Chopped fresh thyme	1 tbsp.	15 mL
TOPPING		
Pizza sauce	2/3 cup	150 mL
Whipping cream	1/3 cup	75 mL
Butter (or hard margarine)	1 tbsp.	15 mL
Olive (or cooking) oil	1 tbsp.	15 mL
Garlic cloves, crushed	3	3
Fresh (or frozen, thawed) medium shrimp, peeled and deveined	12 oz.	340 g
Fresh (or frozen, thawed) scallops, halved if large	8 1/2 oz.	250 g
Finely grated lemon zest	1/2 tsp.	2 mL
Salt	1/4 tsp.	1 mL
Freshly ground pepper	1/2 tsp.	2 mL
Grated Asiago cheese	3/4 cup	175 mL

Prepare pizza dough according to directions, adding thyme after olive oil.

Topping: Combine pizza sauce and whipping cream in medium saucepan. Boil gently on medium-low for about 10 minutes, stirring occasionally, until reduced to 1/2 cup (125 mL). Set aside.

Heat butter and olive oil in large frying pan on medium. Add garlic. Heat and stir for 1 minute. Add shrimp and scallops. Heat and stir for 3 to 5 minutes until shrimp is just beginning to turn pink. Remove from heat. Drain and discard any juices from frying pan.

Add next 3 ingredients to seafood mixture. Mix well. Set aside.

Turn out dough onto lightly floured surface. Shape into a ball. Roll out or press in lightly greased 12 inch (30 cm) pizza pan. Spread pizza sauce mixture evenly over crust to within 1/2 inch (12 mm) of edge. Top with seafood mixture. Sprinkle cheese over top. Bake in 500°F (260°C) oven for 15 to 18 minutes until crust is golden and crispy. Cuts into 8 wedges.

1 wedge: 365 Calories; 15.2 g Total Fat; 512 mg Sodium; 21 g Protein; 35 g Carbohydrate; 2 g Dietary Fibre

Fish Cakes with Sun-Dried Tomatoes and Couscous

We think this recipe is the best thing to happen to fish cakes in a long time. These patties are moist, colourful and full of flavour. Lovely as an appetizer or light lunch too.

Chicken broth (or water)	1 cup	250 mL
Couscous	1 cup	250 mL
Olive (or cooking) oil	1 tbsp.	15 mL
Halibut fillets, cut up	1 lb.	454 g
Large egg	1	1
Crunchy peanut butter	3 tbsp.	50 mL
Chili paste	1 tsp.	5 mL
Garlic cloves	2	2
Chopped fresh sweet basil	3 tbsp.	50 mL
Sun-dried tomatoes, in oil, drained and chopped	1/4 cup	60 mL
Green onions, finely sliced	6	6
Crumbled feta cheese	2/3 cup	150 mL
Freshly grated Parmesan cheese	1/4 cup	60 mL
Olive (or cooking) oil	2 tbsp.	30 mL
TOMATO AND LEMON SALSA		
Roma (plum) tomatoes, seeded and finely chopped	6	6
Finely chopped red onion	1/4 cup	60 mL
Freshly squeezed lemon juice	1 tbsp.	15 mL
Olive (or cooking) oil	1 tbsp.	15 mL
Chopped fresh sweet basil	1 tbsp.	15 mL
Salt, to taste		
Pepper, to taste		

Bring broth to a boil in medium saucepan. Remove from heat. Add couscous and olive oil. Stir. Cover. Let stand for 5 minutes. Fluff with fork.

Put next 6 ingredients in food processor. Process until almost smooth. Turn into large bowl. Add couscous mixture. Stir.

Add next 4 ingredients. Mix well. Shape into 8 patties, using 1/2 cup (125 mL) mixture for each.

Heat second amount of olive oil in large frying pan. Cook patties, in 2 batches, on medium for 3 to 4 minutes per side until lightly browned. Makes 8 patties.

Tomato and Lemon Salsa: Combine all 7 ingredients in small bowl. Makes 2 cups (500 mL) salsa. Serve with Fish Cakes.

1 fish cake with 1/4 cup (60 mL) salsa: 355 Calories; 17.1 g Total Fat; 410 mg Sodium; 24 g Protein; 27 g Carbohydrate; 3 g Dietary Fibre

Seafood Stew

"This hearty stew lends itself well to interpretation, so feel free to use any seafood you like—cod, snapper, lobster, shrimp . . . All you need is a napkin, a spoon and some crusty bread, and you're ready to dig in."

— **Kit Price, Edmonton, Alberta**

Cooking oil	2 tsp.	10 mL
Medium onion, chopped	1	1
Garlic clove, crushed	1	1
Medium green pepper, chopped	1	1
Can of diced tomatoes	28 oz.	796 mL
Can of tomato sauce	14 oz.	398 mL
Prepared chicken broth	1 cup	250 mL
Dry white (or alcohol-free) wine	1 cup	250 mL
Dried sweet basil	1 tbsp.	15 mL
Halibut fillets, cut into 1 inch (2.5 cm) pieces	12 oz.	340 g
Medium shrimp, peeled and deveined, leaving tails intact	12 oz.	340 g
Scallops	4 oz.	113 g
Imitation lobster	4 oz.	113 g
Mussels, scrubbed clean♦	1 lb.	454 g

Heat cooking oil in large pot or Dutch oven on medium-high. Add next 3 ingredients. Sauté for about 5 minutes until onion is softened.

Add next 5 ingredients. Mix well. Bring to a boil. Reduce heat to medium. Simmer, uncovered, for 30 minutes, stirring occasionally, until thickened.

Add next 4 ingredients. Layer mussels over top. Cover. Simmer for about 5 minutes until mussels have opened and seafood is just cooked. Discard any unopened mussels. Stir. Serves 4.

1 serving: 458 Calories; 8.7 g Total Fat; 1721 mg Sodium; 57 g Protein; 28 g Carbohydrate; 4 g Dietary Fibre

Pictured below.

♦Mussels occasionally have a "beard" (black stringy filament) when purchased. Clip it off with scissors or a paring knife. If you choose to pull the beard off, make sure to pull towards the hinge.

Seafood Stew, above

Mustard-and-Dill-Crumbed Halibut

Firm, mild halibut gets a zing of flavour from grainy mustard and lemon zest in this super-easy fish dish. Garnish with more fresh dill and wedges of lemon.

Grainy mustard	1/3 cup	75 mL
Halibut fillets, skin removed, cut into 4 equal pieces	1 1/2 lbs.	680 g
Fresh bread crumbs	2 cups	500 mL
Chopped fresh dill	3 tbsp.	50 mL
Finely grated lemon zest	2 tsp.	10 mL
Freshly ground pepper	1 tsp.	5 mL
Salt	1/2 tsp.	2 mL
Cooking oil	1/3 cup	75 mL

Liberally spread mustard on both sides of fish.

Combine next 5 ingredients in shallow dish. Coat fish in bread crumb mixture.

Heat cooking oil in large frying pan on medium. Cook fish, in 2 batches, for 3 to 4 minutes per side (depending on thickness of fish) until lightly browned and fish flakes easily when tested with fork. Serves 4.

1 serving: 609 Calories; 27.6 g Total Fat; 1166 mg Sodium; 45 g Protein; 43 g Carbohydrate; 3 g Dietary Fibre

Cornmeal-Crusted Fish with Jalapeño Mayonnaise

Easily made in half an hour, this seafood dish partners well with potato wedges and a salad.

Large egg	1	1
Halibut (or haddock) fillets, cut into 12 equal pieces	1 1/3 lbs.	600 g
Yellow cornmeal	1/4 cup	60 mL
Fine dry bread crumbs	1/4 cup	60 mL
Ground cumin	1 tsp.	5 mL
Ground coriander	1 tsp.	5 mL
Salt	1/2 tsp.	2 mL
Freshly ground pepper	1/2 tsp.	2 mL

JALAPEÑO MAYONNAISE

Mayonnaise (not salad dressing)	1/4 cup	60 mL
Sour cream	2 tbsp.	30 mL
Chopped pickled jalapeño peppers	2 1/2 tbsp.	37 mL
Chopped fresh chives	2 tbsp.	30 mL
Finely grated lemon zest	1/2 tsp.	2 mL

Lightly beat egg in medium bowl. Add fish. Gently stir to coat.

Combine next 6 ingredients in shallow dish or on waxed paper. Press fish into cornmeal mixture to coat completely. Arrange in single layer on greased baking sheet with sides. Lightly spray fish with cooking spray. Bake in 425°F (220°C) oven for about 10 minutes, turning once, until golden and fish flakes easily when tested with fork.

Jalapeño Mayonnaise: While fish is baking, combine all 5 ingredients in small bowl. Makes 1/2 cup (125 mL) mayonnaise. Serve with fish. Serves 4.

1 serving: 370 Calories; 18.3 g Total Fat; 598 mg Sodium; 35 g Protein; 14 g Carbohydrate; 1 g Dietary Fibre

Baked Cod Parcels with Asian Cucumber Salad

"Inside these parchment parcels you'll find moist, flaky cod fragrant with Asian spices. A lime and ginger-spiced cucumber salad provides a fresh and crunchy contrast."
— **Kit Price, Edmonton, Alberta**

Soy sauce	3 tbsp.	50 mL
Finely grated gingerroot	2 tsp.	10 mL
Garlic cloves, crushed	2	2
Liquid honey	2 tbsp.	30 mL
Cod fillets, cut into 4 equal pieces	1 1/2 lbs.	680 g

ASIAN CUCUMBER SALAD

Medium English cucumber (about 15 oz., 425 g)	1	1
Small red pepper, finely chopped	1	1
Small red onion, thinly sliced	1	1
Soy sauce	3 tbsp.	50 mL
Lime juice	3 tbsp.	50 mL
Chopped fresh cilantro	3 tbsp.	50 mL
Cooking oil	2 tbsp.	30 mL
Sweet chili sauce	1 tbsp.	15 mL
Finely grated gingerroot	2 tsp.	10 mL
Fish sauce	2 tsp.	10 mL

Combine first 4 ingredients in small bowl.

Place 1 piece of cod, lengthwise, in centre of 10 inch (25 cm) piece of parchment paper. Drizzle 1/4 of soy sauce mixture over cod. Bring long sides of parchment paper together. Fold parchment paper over 2 to 3 times to form seam. Fold short ends over seam to form parcel. Place, seam-side down, on lightly greased baking sheet with sides. Repeat with remaining cod pieces and soy sauce mixture. Bake in 400°F (205°C) oven for 12 to 15 minutes until cod flakes easily when tested with fork.

Asian Cucumber Salad: Cut cucumber in half lengthwise. Scoop out and discard seeds. Cut diagonally into 1/4 inch (6 mm) thick slices. Transfer to large bowl.

Add red pepper and onion. Stir.

Combine remaining 7 ingredients in jar with tight-fitting lid. Shake well. Makes 2/3 cup (150 mL) dressing. Drizzle over cucumber mixture. Toss. Makes 4 cups (1 L) salad. Serve with cod. Serves 4.

1 cod parcel and 1 cup (250 mL) salad: 294 Calories; 8.4 g Total Fat; 1896 mg Sodium; 35 g Protein; 21 g Carbohydrate; 2 g Dietary Fibre

Lamb with Wine Sauce and Soft Polenta

Naturally tender lamb pairs beautifully with creamy smooth polenta in this impressive, yet simple to prepare, entree.

POLENTA

Cans of condensed chicken broth (10 oz., 284 mL, each)	2	2
Water	3 1/2 cups	875 mL
Cornmeal	1 1/2 cups	375 mL
Freshly grated Parmesan cheese	1/3 cup	75 mL
Sour cream	2 tbsp.	30 mL
Salt	1/4 tsp.	1 mL
Pepper, to taste		
Rack of lamb (8 ribs), trimmed of fat and blotted dry	1 lb.	454 g
Cooking oil	2 tsp.	10 mL
WINE SAUCE		
Red (or alcohol-free) wine	1/2 cup	125 mL
Condensed beef broth	1/2 cup	125 mL
Cranberry jelly	2 tbsp.	30 mL
Salt	1/4 tsp.	1 mL
Whole black peppercorns, cracked	1/4 tsp.	1 mL
Cornstarch	1 tsp.	5 mL
Water	1 tbsp.	15 mL

Polenta: Bring chicken broth and water to a boil in large saucepan on high. Reduce heat to medium-low. Stir in cornmeal. Heat and stir for 15 minutes until thickened and mixture leaves sides of pan.

Add next 4 ingredients Stir. Keep warm. Makes 4 cups (1 L) polenta.

Separate rack of lamb into chops by slicing between rib bones.

Heat cooking oil in large frying pan on medium. Add lamb. Cook, uncovered, for 3 minutes on each side until desired tenderness. Remove from pan. Keep warm.

Wine Sauce: Add first 5 ingredients to same frying pan. Simmer, uncovered, for about 5 minutes.

Stir cornstarch into water in small bowl until smooth. Add to wine mixture. Heat and stir until boiling and thickened. Makes 1/2 cup (125 mL) sauce. To serve, drizzle sauce over lamb and polenta. Serves 4.

1 serving: 442 Calories; 13 g Total Fat; 1551 mg Sodium; 25 g Protein; 49 g Carbohydrate; 3 g Dietary Fibre

Pictured above.

Lamb Shanks in Tomato Wine Sauce

Slow cooking is the secret to this wonderfully tender lamb dish. Sambal oelek, a multi-purpose condiment popular in Indonesia, Malaysia and Southern India, is a blend of chilies, brown sugar and salt. It helps to make this dish what it is—splendid!

Cooking oil	1 tbsp.	15 mL
Lamb shanks, trimmed of fat	6	6
Cooking oil	1 tbsp.	15 mL
Medium onions, thinly sliced	2	2
Garlic cloves, crushed	4	4
Sambal oelek	1/2 tsp.	2 mL
Red (or alcohol-free) wine	1 cup	250 mL
Can of diced tomatoes	28 oz.	796 mL
Tomato paste	1/4 cup	60 mL
Chicken broth	1/2 cup	125 mL
Fresh rosemary sprigs	3	3

Heat first amount of cooking oil in large saucepan. Add lamb. Cook on medium-high, turning occasionally, for about 8 minutes until browned. Remove from saucepan.

Heat second amount of cooking oil in same saucepan. Add next 3 ingredients. Sauté on medium for about 5 minutes until onion is soft.

Return lamb to saucepan. Add remaining 5 ingredients. Bring to a boil. Reduce heat to low. Cover. Cook for 1 1/2 hours. Remove lid. Simmer, uncovered, for 30 minutes until sauce is thickened and lamb is falling off bones. Serves 4.

1 serving: 556 Calories; 33.1 g Total Fat; 524 mg Sodium; 36 g Protein; 19 g Carbohydrate; 3 g Dietary Fibre

Pictured on this page.

Fruited Lamb Curry

The combination is a little out of the ordinary, but the flavour is spectacular. This is one curry that wins raves from everyone.

Boneless lamb shoulder, trimmed of fat and cut into 1 1/2 inch (3.8 cm) cubes	2 lbs.	900 g
Cooking oil	1 tbsp.	15 mL
Seasoned salt	1 tsp.	5 mL
Freshly ground pepper, sprinkle		

Lamb Shanks in Tomato Wine Sauce, left

Coarsely chopped onion	1 1/2 cups	375 mL
Garlic cloves, crushed	2	2
Curry paste	2 tsp.	10 mL
Ground coriander	1/4 tsp.	1 mL
Ground ginger	1/4 tsp.	1 mL
Can of coconut milk Reserved pineapple juice	14 oz.	398 mL
Can of pineapple tidbits, drained and juice reserved	14 oz.	398 mL
Firm bananas, cut into 1/2 inch (12 mm) thick slices	2	2
Water	2 tbsp.	30 mL
Lemon juice	1 tbsp.	15 mL
Cornstarch	1 tbsp.	15 mL
Slivered almonds, toasted (optional)♦	1/4 cup	60 mL

Sear lamb, in batches, in cooking oil in large frying pan on medium-high until browned.

Sprinkle with seasoned salt and pepper. Remove to paper towel to drain.

Add next 5 ingredients to same frying pan. Sauté until onion is soft.

Stir in coconut milk and reserved pineapple juice. Add lamb. Cover. Simmer for 1 to 1 1/2 hours until lamb is tender.

Stir in pineapple and banana.

Stir water and lemon juice into cornstarch in small bowl until smooth. Stir into curry mixture. Heat, uncovered, for about 5 minutes, stirring occasionally, until boiling and slightly thickened.

Sprinkle with almonds just before serving. Makes 6 1/2 cups (1.6 L).

1 cup (250 mL): 418 Calories; 22.9 g Total Fat; 288 mg Sodium; 30 g Protein; 25 g Carbohydrate; 2 g Dietary Fibre

♦To toast the almonds, place them in an ungreased frying pan. Heat on medium, stirring often, until golden.

Lamb Chops with Minted Applesauce

Liven up the flavour of prepared applesauce with chopped fresh mint, the traditional accompaniment to succulent lamb.

MINTED APPLESAUCE

Can of sweetened applesauce	14 oz.	398 mL
Chopped fresh mint leaves	2 tbsp.	30 mL
Brown sugar, packed	1 tbsp.	15 mL
Lemon juice	2 tsp.	10 mL
Garlic clove, cut in half	1	1
Lamb chops (about 1 inch, 2.5 cm, thick), trimmed of fat	4	4
Ground thyme	1/8 tsp.	0.5 mL
Freshly ground pepper, sprinkle		
Salt	1/4 tsp.	1 mL

Minted Applesauce: Combine first 4 ingredients in small bowl. Let stand for 10 minutes to allow flavours to blend. Makes 1 3/4 cups (425 mL) applesauce.

Rub garlic over both sides of chops. Sprinkle with thyme and pepper. Place on broiler pan. Broil 5 to 6 inches (12.5 to 15 cm) from heat for 4 to 5 minutes until browned. Turn over. Broil for 5 minutes.

Sprinkle with salt. Spoon 1 tsp. (5 mL) applesauce onto each chop. Broil for 1 to 2 minutes until desired doneness. Serve with remaining applesauce. Serves 2.

1 serving: 318 Calories; 9.1 g Total Fat; 381 mg Sodium; 28 g Protein; 31 g Carbohydrate; 3 g Dietary Fibre

Rack of Lamb with Kiwi Relish

This marinated rack of lamb with tangy fruit and mint relish is simple to prepare and elegant to serve. A lovely combination of classic flavours with a modern twist.

Garlic clove, minced	1	1
Finely grated lemon zest	1/2 tsp.	2 mL
Crushed dried rosemary	1/4 tsp.	1 mL
Freshly ground pepper, sprinkle		
Lemon juice	1 tsp.	5 mL
Olive oil	2 tsp.	10 mL
Rack of lamb, trimmed of fat	1 1/4 lbs.	560 g
KIWI RELISH		
Medium kiwi fruit, peeled and coarsely chopped	2	2
Chopped fresh mint leaves	1 tbsp.	15 mL
Finely sliced green onion	1 tbsp.	15 mL
Granulated sugar	1 tsp.	5 mL
Lime juice	1 tbsp.	15 mL
Salt, sprinkle		

Combine first 4 ingredients in small dish until paste-like consistency. Stir in lemon juice and olive oil.

Rub garlic mixture on all sides of lamb. Place in resealable plastic bag. Chill for several hours or overnight. Place lamb, meaty side down, on wire rack in shallow baking dish. Bake in 475°F (240°C) oven for 12 to 15 minutes. Reduce heat to 400°F (205°C). Turn lamb over. Bake for 20 to 30 minutes until desired doneness.

Kiwi Relish: Combine all 6 ingredients in small bowl. Let stand at room temperature for about 30 minutes to allow flavours to blend. Makes 2/3 cup (150 mL) relish. Serve with lamb. Serves 2.

1 serving: 330 Calories; 18 g Total Fat; 84 mg Sodium; 27 g Protein; 19 g Carbohydrate; 3 g Dietary Fibre

Pineapple Lamb Kabobs with Spiced Yogurt

Lamb is a great choice for indoor or outdoor grilling. Serve this colourful Mediterranean-style kabob with extra flavourful spiced yogurt.

Lamb tenderloin (or medallions), cut into 1 inch (2.5 cm) cubes	1 1/2 lbs.	680 g
Balsamic vinegar	1/4 cup	60 mL
Garlic cloves, crushed	2	2
Olive oil	2 tbsp.	30 mL
Whole black peppercorns, cracked	2 tsp.	10 mL
Cubed fresh pineapple (about 1 medium)	2 cups	500 mL
Cubed red pepper (about 2 large)	2 cups	500 mL
SPICED YOGURT		
Plain yogurt	1 cup	250 mL
Finely chopped English cucumber	1/4 cup	60 mL
Chopped fresh cilantro	1/4 cup	60 mL
Finely chopped red onion (about 1 small)	1/2 cup	125 mL
Ground cumin	1 tsp.	5 mL

Toss first 5 ingredients together in medium bowl to coat.

Alternate lamb, pineapple and red pepper on 12 skewers. Grill or broil for about 10 minutes, turning occasionally, until lamb reaches desired doneness.

Spiced Yogurt: Combine all 5 ingredients in small bowl. Mix well. Makes 2 1/2 cups (625 mL) spiced yogurt. Serve with kabobs. Serves 4.

1 serving: 411 Calories; 17.5 g Total Fat; 165 mg Sodium; 40 g Protein; 24 g Carbohydrate; 3 g Dietary Fibre

Pictured below.

Choose a Lamb Cut

Choose a Method

Roast, pot roast, casserole or stew:
- shanks
- shoulder
- whole leg

Grill, broil or pan-fry:
- loin chops
- shoulder blade chops
- rib chops
- round leg steak
- medallions
- fillets

Roast:
- whole rack

Cooked to Perfection

Lamb is most flavourful when it is still slightly pink, but doneness is a personal preference. Since lamb tends to dry and become tough, most cuts should be cooked at moderate temperatures and not overcooked.

Lovely with Lamb

rosemary	mint	parsley
curry powder	marjoram	thyme
coriander	caraway	paprika
cinnamon	cloves	garlic
basil	lemon	red wine

Pineapple Lamb Kabobs with Spiced Yogurt, above

Roast Lamb with Baby Vegetables

Instead of the usual roast beef on Sunday night, treat your family to roast lamb. Mini-vegetables and mint jelly-flavoured gravy make this a truly special feast.

Leg of lamb, trimmed of fat	4 1/2 lbs.	2 kg
Garlic cloves, cut into 4 slices	2	2
Fresh rosemary sprigs	8	8
Cooking oil	1 tbsp.	15 mL
Salt	1/2 tsp.	2 mL
Unpeeled baby potatoes	2 lbs.	900 g
Baby carrots	3 cups	750 mL
Small sweet potato, (or yam) cut into pieces, same size as potatoes	1	1
Cooking oil	1 tbsp.	15 mL
Salt	1/2 tsp.	2 mL

GRAVY		
All-purpose flour	2 tbsp.	30 mL
Condensed chicken broth	2 cups	500 mL
Mint jelly	1/4 cup	60 mL

Place lamb on rack in shallow baking dish. Make 8 shallow incisions, about 1/2 inch (12 mm) deep, all over lamb. Press garlic and rosemary into incisions. Rub first amount of cooking oil and salt all over lamb. Bake in 350°F (175°C) oven for 1 1/4 hours.

Combine next 5 ingredients in large bowl. Arrange in single layer on baking sheet. Add to oven. Bake with lamb for 45 to 60 minutes until vegetables are tender-crisp and lamb reaches desired doneness. Remove lamb from oven, reserving pan drippings. Cover. Let stand for 10 minutes before carving into thin slices.

Gravy: Measure 1 tbsp. (15 mL) reserved drippings into small saucepan. Bring to a boil on medium. Stir in flour. Heat and stir for 1 minute until bubbling.

Add broth and jelly. Heat and stir until well combined. Simmer, uncovered, for about 5 minutes until gravy is boiling and thickened. Strain. Serve with lamb and vegetables. Serves 6.

1 serving: 933 Calories; 49.2 g Total Fat; 887 mg Sodium; 73 g Protein; 46 g Carbohydrate; 4 g Dietary Fibre

Pictured above.

Get the Most from your Roast

When roasting, place lamb on a rack in a shallow roasting dish so any fat drains away.

Always cover and allow roast lamb to "stand," or rest, for about 10 minutes, so you don't lose flavourful meat juices when you start carving.

Lamb Stew with Winter Vegetables

We always think of leg of lamb or meaty little chops as the perfect dinner, but flavourful lamb shoulder makes one of the most economical and delicious of suppers. Slow-cooked to perfection with classic winter vegetables, this is a splendid dish to enjoy after a day outdoors.

All-purpose flour	1/4 cup	60 mL
Salt	1/2 tsp.	2 mL
Freshly ground pepper	1/2 tsp.	2 mL
Boneless lamb shoulder, trimmed of fat and cut into 1 1/2 inch (3.8 cm) cubes	1 1/2 lbs.	680 g
Cooking oil	1 tbsp.	15 mL
Cooking oil	1 tbsp.	15 mL
Large onions, cut into 1 inch (2.5 cm) pieces	2	2
Prepared beef broth	4 cups	1 L
Small yellow turnip, cut into 1 inch (2.5 cm) pieces	1	1
Large parsnips, cut into 1 inch (2.5 cm) pieces	2	2
Large carrots, cut into 1 inch (2.5 cm) pieces	2	2
Large potato, cut into 1 inch (2.5 cm) pieces	1	1
Dried whole oregano	1/2 tsp.	2 mL
Dried rosemary	1/2 tsp.	2 mL
Frozen peas	1 cup	250 mL

Combine first 3 ingredients in shallow bowl. Dredge lamb in flour mixture. Shake gently to remove excess. Reserve remaining flour mixture.

Heat first amount of cooking oil in large heavy-bottomed pot or Dutch oven on medium-high. Sear lamb, in 2 batches, for about 5 minutes, until browned on all sides. Remove lamb from pot.

Heat second amount of cooking oil in same pot on medium-high. Add onion. Sauté for about 5 minutes, until softened. Add reserved flour mixture. Heat and stir for 1 minute until onion is well coated.

Add broth. Heat and stir for 2 to 3 minutes until flour is incorporated. Add lamb and next 6 ingredients. Bring to a boil on medium-high. Reduce heat to medium-low. Cover. Simmer for about 1 1/2 hours, stirring occasionally, until lamb is tender.

Add peas. Stir. Heat through. Serves 4.

1 serving: 687 Calories; 26.2 g Total Fat; 1848 mg Sodium; 46 g Protein; 66 g Carbohydrate; 8 g Dietary Fibre

Pictured below.

Lamb Stew with Winter Vegetables, above, with Easy Dumplings, page 182

Ham and Pea Risotto, page 95

Ham and Pea Risotto

Adding the liquid slowly is the key to a successful creamy risotto. Serve larger portions as a main course dish or smaller portions as an accompaniment. Garnish with Parmesan cheese, oregano leaves and freshly ground pepper.

Cans of condensed chicken broth (10 oz., 284 mL, each)	2	2
Water	2 cups	500 mL
Medium onion, finely chopped	1	1
Garlic cloves, crushed	2	2
Finely chopped ham	1 cup	250 mL
Butter (or hard margarine)	1 tbsp.	15 mL
Olive (or cooking) oil	1 tbsp.	15 mL
Arborio rice	2 cups	500 mL
Dry white (or alcohol-free) wine	1/2 cup	125 mL
Frozen peas, thawed	1 cup	250 mL
Grated fresh Parmesan cheese	1/2 cup	125 mL
Chopped fresh parsley	2 tbsp.	30 mL
Chopped fresh oregano leaves	1 tbsp.	15 mL
Salt	1/4 tsp.	1 mL
Freshly ground pepper	1/2 tsp.	2 mL

Combine broth and water in medium saucepan (see photo 1). Cover. Bring to a boil. Reduce heat to very low. Keep covered until needed.

Sauté next 3 ingredients in butter and olive oil in large pot or Dutch oven on medium for about 5 minutes until onion is soft. Add rice. Stir until coated (see photo 2).

Add wine. Cook on medium-low, stirring constantly, until wine is absorbed (see photo 3). Add 1 cup (250 mL) hot broth mixture, stirring constantly, until broth is absorbed. Repeat with remaining broth mixture, 1 cup (250 mL) at a time, until broth is absorbed and rice is tender (see photo 4). Entire process will take about 30 minutes.

Add remaining 6 ingredients. Stir well (see photo 5). Remove from heat. Makes about 6 1/2 cups (1.6 L).

1 1/2 cups (375 mL): 617 Calories; 14.5 g Total Fat; 1676 mg Sodium; 27 g Protein; 87 g Carbohydrate; 2 g Dietary Fibre

Pictured on page 94.

Pork Loin with Orange and Sage

After tasting this dish you'll think pork and fresh sage were made for each other. The combination, along with the fresh-tasting hints of orange and piquant mustard, makes for unbeatable flavour!

Hard margarine (or butter), softened	3 tbsp.	50 mL
Dijon mustard	2 tbsp.	30 mL
Finely grated orange zest	2 tsp.	10 mL
Boneless pork loin roast	4 1/2 lbs.	2 kg
Bacon slices	6	6
Fresh sage leaves, firmly packed	1/3 cup	75 mL
Cooking oil	2 tsp.	10 mL
Salt	1 tsp.	5 mL

Combine first 3 ingredients in small bowl.

Cut strings from pork. Lay pork, fat side down, on cutting board. Spread with mustard mixture.

Layer bacon slices and sage leaves over mustard mixture. Roll up pork firmly to enclose filling. Secure with butcher's string. Drizzle with cooking oil. Sprinkle with salt.

Preheat grill to medium-high. Place roast on greased grill over drip pan. Close lid. Cook, using indirect cooking method (see Indirectly Speaking, page 67), for 30 minutes. Turn roast. Reduce heat to medium. Close lid. Cook for 1 hour until meat thermometer inserted in centre reads 160°F (70°C) for medium to 170°F (75°C) for well-done. Let roast stand, covered, for 10 minutes before carving. Carve into 1/2 inch (12 mm) slices. Serves 12 to 14.

1 serving: 307 Calories; 18.2 g Total Fat; 366 mg Sodium; 33 g Protein; trace Carbohydrate; trace Dietary Fibre

Egg and Spinach Pasta with Pancetta

"In Italy, this dish is called Paglia e Fieno, *which translates literally to 'straw and hay'. It refers to the colours of the yellow egg and green spinach noodles used in this dish. Other ingredients and creaminess of the dish can vary quite a bit. The combination of bacon and pancetta (Italian bacon that's salt-cured but not smoked) gives a distinctive taste to our recipe. The dash of celery salt isn't very Italian, but we like it."*

— Kathy Murrie and Bill Sass, Edmonton, Alberta

Pancetta, chopped	6 oz.	170 g
Bacon (not hickory or maple), chopped	4 oz.	113 g
Medium onion, chopped	1	1
Garlic cloves, crushed	4	4
Small carrot, chopped	1	1
Medium celery rib, chopped	1	1
Olive oil	2 tbsp.	30 mL
Fresh white mushrooms, sliced♦	9 oz.	250 g
Can of diced tomatoes, with juice	14 oz.	398 g
Can of crushed tomatoes	14 oz.	398 g
Dry white (or alcohol-free) wine	3/4 cup	175 mL
Celery salt	1 1/2 tsp.	7 mL
Fettuccine	1/2 lb.	225 g
Spinach fettuccine	1/2 lb.	225 g
Boiling water	16 cups	4 L
Salt	1 tsp.	5 mL
Frozen peas	1/2 cup	125 mL
Chopped fresh Italian (flat leaf) parsley	1/4 cup	60 mL
Shaved fresh Parmesan cheese	1/3 cup	75 mL

Cook pancetta and bacon in large pot or Dutch oven on medium for about 5 minutes until browned. Remove to paper towel to drain. Drain drippings from pot.

Sauté next 4 ingredients in olive oil in same pot on medium for about 5 minutes until onion is soft.

Add mushrooms. Stir. Cook for 3 to 5 minutes until soft.

Add next 4 ingredients. Bring to a boil. Reduce heat to medium-low. Cook, uncovered, for about 15 minutes, stirring occasionally, until slightly thickened.

Cook both pastas in boiling water and salt in separate large pot or Dutch oven for about 12 minutes, stirring occasionally, until just tender. Drain well. Return pasta to same pot.

Add peas and bacon mixture to tomato mixture. Stir until heated through. Add to pasta. Mix well.

Garnish with parsley and Parmesan cheese. Serves 6.

1 serving: 511 Calories; 14.2 g Total Fat; 927 mg Sodium; 20 g Protein; 72 g Carbohydrate; 6 g Dietary Fibre

Pictured below.

♦*Try using a combination of white and brown mushrooms. Or, if available, substitute dried Italian porcini mushrooms. Cover dried mushrooms with boiling water. Soak for 15 minutes. Drain. Chop. Add to onion mixture.*

Glazed Garlic and
Soy Ribs, below

Glazed Garlic and Soy Ribs

These appetizing ribs get their shiny glaze
from honey and their wonderful stickiness
from hoisin sauce. Fans of classic Chinese-style
ribs will love them. Garnish with pieces of
diagonally sliced green onion.

Garlic cloves, crushed	4	4
Finely grated gingerroot	2 tsp.	10 mL
Soy sauce	1/2 cup	125 mL
Hoisin sauce	1/4 cup	60 mL
Liquid honey	2 tbsp.	30 mL
Sesame oil	2 tsp.	10 mL
Sweet-and-sour-cut pork ribs, trimmed of fat, cut into bite-size pieces	3 1/2 lbs.	1.6 kg

Combine first 6 ingredients in large bowl.

Add ribs. Mix well to coat. Cover. Marinate
in refrigerator for 6 hours or overnight. Drain
ribs, reserving marinade in small saucepan.
Bring marinade to a boil. Boil for 5 minutes.
Place ribs in lightly greased shallow roasting
pan. Cover with foil. Bake in 350°F (175°C)
oven for about 1 hour until very tender. Brush
marinade over ribs. Bake, uncovered, for 20 to
25 minutes, stirring twice, until ribs are dark
and sticky. Serves 4.

1 serving: 582 Calories; 27.3 g Total Fat; 1508 mg Sodium;
60 g Protein; 22 g Carbohydrate; trace Dietary Fibre

Pictured above.

Lime Pork Chops with Chili Cilantro Butter

Mild-tasting pork is perfect with the jazzy,
contemporary taste of the accompanying
chili and herb butter. When grilling the red
pepper for the Chili Cilantro Butter, grill extra
red peppers, red onion wedges and some long,
thick zucchini slices to serve with the pork
chops. Add quick-to-make buttered couscous
and your guests won't know how easy it was
to plan this meal.

CHILI CILANTRO BUTTER

Small red pepper, quartered and seeded	1	1
Butter (not margarine), softened	1/2 cup	125 mL
Small red chili peppers, finely chopped◆	2	2
Chopped fresh cilantro	1/3 cup	75 mL
Salt	1/4 tsp.	1 mL
Garlic cloves, crushed	3	3
Finely grated lime zest	2 tsp.	10 mL
Freshly squeezed lime juice	3 tbsp.	50 mL
Brown sugar, packed	2 tsp.	10 mL
Freshly ground pepper	1 1/2 tsp.	7 mL
Peanut (or cooking) oil	1 tbsp.	15 mL
Boneless pork loin chops (1 inch, 2.5 cm, thick)	6	6

Chili Cilantro Butter: Preheat grill to
medium-high. Grill red pepper, skin side down,
for 8 to 10 minutes until skin is blistered and
blackened. Place in bowl. Cover with plastic
wrap. Let stand for 10 minutes until cool
enough to handle. Remove and discard skin.
Finely chop pepper.

Combine next 4 ingredients in small bowl.
Add red pepper. Mix well. Makes 3/4 cup
(175 mL) butter. Spread butter mixture into
6 inch (15 cm) circle on waxed paper. Chill
for 30 minutes until hard. Cut into 6 wedges.

Combine next 6 ingredients in large bowl or
resealable plastic bag. Add pork. Turn to coat.
Cover or seal. Marinate in refrigerator for
30 minutes. Preheat grill to medium-high. Cook
chops on lightly greased grill for 6 to 8 minutes
per side until chops are just tender. Do not
overcook. To serve, place chops on individual
serving plates. Top with wedge of Chili Cilantro
Butter. Serves 6.

1 serving: 343 Calories; 25 g Total Fat; 311 mg Sodium;
24 g Protein; 6 g Carbohydrate; 1 g Dietary Fibre

◆Wear gloves when chopping chili peppers and
avoid touching your eyes.

Crown Roast Pork with Cranberry Orange Gravy

A truly royal presentation, this is one pork roast you'll never tire of serving and enjoying. Traditional gravy is wonderfully enhanced with the addition of orange juice and tangy cranberry jelly.

Pork loin rib half, crown roast (10 - 12 ribs)	7 lbs.	3.2 kg
Cooking oil	1 tbsp.	15 mL
Salt	1/2 tsp.	2 mL

BACON AND APPLE STUFFING

Small onion, finely chopped	1	1
Cooking oil	2 tsp.	10 mL
Bacon slices, chopped	4	4
Medium cooking apples (such as McIntosh), peeled and grated	2	2
Coarse dry bread crumbs	2 cups	500 mL
Large egg, fork-beaten	1	1
Finely grated orange zest	2 tsp.	10 mL
Chopped fresh parsley	1/4 cup	60 mL

CRANBERRY ORANGE GRAVY

All-purpose flour	1/4 cup	60 mL
Freshly squeezed orange juice	1 1/2 cups	375 mL
Chicken broth	1 1/2 cups	375 mL
Cranberry jelly	1/2 cup	125 mL
Fresh (or frozen, thawed) cranberries	1/3 cup	75 mL

Place pork in roasting pan on wire rack with bones pointing up. Rub cooking oil over pork. Sprinkle with salt. Fill cavity with large ball of foil. Cover bone tips with small pieces of foil. Bake, uncovered, in 325°F (160°C) oven for 1 hour.

Bacon and Apple Stuffing: Sauté onion in cooking oil on medium for about 5 minutes until soft.

Add bacon. Cook for about 5 minutes until crisp.

Combine next 5 ingredients in medium bowl. Add onion and bacon mixture. Mix well. Set aside until ready to use. Makes 4 cups (1 L) stuffing. Remove pork from oven. Carefully remove foil from cavity. Spoon stuffing into cavity. Press down lightly. Bake for 1 1/4 to 1 1/2 hours until meat thermometer inserted in thickest part of meat reads 160°F (70°C). Remove from oven. Cover with foil. Let stand for 15 minutes before carving. Remove foil from bones before serving.

Cranberry Orange Gravy: Drain all but 1 tbsp. (15 mL) drippings from roasting pan. Stir in flour. Heat and stir on medium for 1 minute until grainy.

Add orange juice and broth. Bring to a boil on high, stirring constantly. Add jelly. Stir until jelly is dissolved. Boil, uncovered, for 10 to 12 minutes, stirring occasionally, until gravy is thickened. Strain, discarding solids. Add cranberries. Simmer 5 minutes until cranberries "pop." Makes 3 1/2 cups (875 mL) gravy. Serve pork with stuffing and gravy. Serves 8.

1 serving: 821 Calories; 40.9 g Total Fat; 876 mg Sodium; 62 g Protein; 49 g Carbohydrate; 2 g Dietary Fibre

Pictured at right.

Done Just Right

The days of cooking pork until it was really, really well done are long gone. According to the Canadian Pork Council, pork is at its tender and juicy best when cooked to an internal temperature of 160°F (70°C), with just a hint of pink in the centre. Thanks to years of continual improvements in both feeding practices and monitoring procedures, Canadian pork is safe, wholesome and nutritious.

Spiced Grilled Pork Pitas

The Mediterranean flavour of this build-your-own dish will have you thinking of Greek island vacations.

Ground cumin	2 tsp.	10 mL
Ground coriander	1 tsp.	5 mL
Chili powder	1 tsp.	5 mL
Freshly ground pepper	1/2 tsp.	2 mL
Garlic cloves, crushed	4	4
Liquid honey	2 tbsp.	30 mL
Olive (or cooking) oil	3 tbsp.	50 mL
Lemon juice	3 tbsp.	50 mL
Chopped fresh oregano leaves	3 tbsp.	50 mL
Boneless pork loin roast, cut into 1/4 inch (6 mm) thick strips	1 2/3 lbs.	760 g
8 inch (20 cm) bamboo skewers, soaked in water for 10 minutes	12	12
Plain yogurt	1 cup	250 mL
Chopped fresh mint leaves	1/3 cup	75 mL
Finely chopped English cucumber	1/2 cup	125 mL
Pita breads (6 inch, 15 cm, size), halved	6	6
Medium tomatoes, halved and thinly sliced	2	2
Small red onion, halved and thinly sliced	1	1

Combine first 9 ingredients in large bowl. Add pork. Mix well. Cover. Marinate in refrigerator for 3 hours. Drain, discarding marinade.

Preheat grill to medium. Thread pork, accordion-style, onto skewers. Grill for about 10 minutes, turning occasionally, until just tender.

Combine yogurt, mint and cucumber in small bowl. Makes 1 1/2 cups (375 mL).

To serve, spread yogurt mixture in pita halves. Remove pork from skewers. Stuff pita halves with tomato, onion and pork. Serves 6.

1 serving: 492 Calories; 18.5 g Total Fat; 400 mg Sodium; 33 g Protein; 48 g Carbohydrate; 2 g Dietary Fibre

Pictured below.

Pork Tenderloin with Port and Pears

If you've ever had fresh pears marinated in port for dessert, you'll understand the inspiration for this dish. Delish.

Cooking oil	2 tbsp.	30 mL
Pork tenderloins (2 1/4 lbs., 1 kg)	2	2
All-purpose flour	1/4 cup	60 mL
Port	1 cup	250 mL
Apple juice	1 cup	250 mL
Plum jam	2 tbsp.	30 mL
Chopped fresh thyme leaves	2 tsp.	10 mL
Salt	1/2 tsp.	2 mL
Freshly ground pepper	1 tsp.	5 mL
Unripened pears, peeled and quartered	4	4

Heat cooking oil in large pot or Dutch oven. Add pork. Cook on medium-high for 5 to 7 minutes, turning occasionally, until browned. Remove from pan.

Add flour to same pan. Heat and stir on medium for about 1 minute until grainy.

Add next 6 ingredients. Heat and stir until well combined.

Add pear and pork to pan. Cook, uncovered, for 15 to 20 minutes, turning pork occasionally, until pork is tender. Remove pork from pan. Cover. Set aside. Cook pears a further 10 minutes until tender and sauce is thickened. Cut pork into 1 inch (2.5 cm) thick slices. Serve with pears and sauce. Serves 6.

1 serving: 198 Calories; 5.3 g Total Fat; 205 mg Sodium; 2 g Protein; 32 g Carbohydrate; 4 g Dietary Fibre

Spiced Grilled Pork Pitas, above

Spicy Tofu and Pork

This mildly spicy dish is very similar to one served in Chinese restaurants. The flavours are wonderful together, and the dish offers a good and nutritious way to stretch a pound of ground pork. Garnish with wedges of lime.

Package of extra-firm tofu	14 oz.	350 g
Chicken broth	1/4 cup	60 mL
Soy sauce	2 tbsp.	30 mL
Fish sauce	1 tbsp.	15 mL
Freshly squeezed lime juice	1 tbsp.	15 mL
Granulated sugar	1 tsp.	5 mL
Cornstarch	2 tsp.	10 mL
Peanut (or cooking) oil	1 tbsp.	15 mL
Ground pork	1/2 lb.	225 g
Peanut (or cooking) oil	2 tsp.	10 mL
Garlic cloves, crushed	4	4
Small red chili peppers, finely chopped◆	2	2
Finely grated gingerroot	1 tsp.	5 mL
Green onions, cut into 1 inch (2.5 cm) pieces	8	8
Coarsely chopped peanuts	1/3 cup	75 mL
Coarsely chopped fresh cilantro	1/4 cup	60 mL

Cut tofu into 3/4 inch (2 cm) cubes. Place on paper towel to drain.

Combine next 6 ingredients in small bowl.

Heat first amount of peanut oil in wok or large frying pan. Add ground pork. Scramble-fry on high for about 5 minutes until browned. Transfer pork to second small bowl.

Heat second amount of peanut oil in same wok. Add next 3 ingredients. Stir-fry for 1 minute until fragrant.

Add green onion, pork, tofu and broth mixture. Stir-fry on high for about 3 minutes until hot. Remove from heat.

Stir in peanuts and cilantro. Makes 3 1/2 cups (875 mL). Serves 4.

1 serving: 436 Calories; 31.9 g Total Fat; 886 mg Sodium; 29 g Protein; 13 g Carbohydrate; 3 g Dietary Fibre

Pictured above.

◆Wear gloves when chopping chili peppers, and avoid touching your eyes.

Baked Pork Chops with Apple Rings

Tangy apples and moist, tender pork chops are such a good combination.

— Wayne Shearer, Edmonton, Alberta

Cooking oil	2 tbsp.	30 mL
Pork chops, trimmed of fat	8	8
Ground sage	1/2 tsp.	2 mL
Salt	1/2 tsp.	2 mL
Medium Granny Smith apples, peeled, cored and cut into rings	4	4
Brown sugar, packed	1/4 cup	60 mL
Cooking oil	1 tbsp.	15 mL
All-purpose flour	2 tbsp.	30 mL
Hot water	1 cup	250 mL
Apple cider vinegar	1 tbsp.	15 mL
Raisins	1/2 cup	125 mL

Heat cooking oil in large frying pan. Cook chops, in 2 batches, for 3 to 5 minutes on each side until browned. Sprinkle with sage and salt. Remove chops to ungreased 9 x 13 inch (22 x 33 cm) baking dish.

Place apple rings over chops. Sprinkle with brown sugar.

Heat second amount of cooking oil in same frying pan. Sprinkle with flour. Heat and stir for 1 minute until grainy. Gradually stir in water and vinegar. Cook on medium-high for about 5 minutes, stirring occasionally, until smooth and thickened.

Stir in raisins. Pour over chops. Bake, uncovered, in 350°F (175°C) oven for about 1 hour until tender. Serves 8.

1 serving: 277 Calories; 10.4 g Total Fat; 46 mg Sodium; 21 g Protein; 26 g Carbohydrate; 2 g Dietary Fibre

Pictured above.

Pork Chops with Curried Apple Cream Sauce

Seared and baked pork chops are moist and tender in this quick-fix main dish that's finished with a creamy apple and sweet onion sauce. The hint of ginger and curry makes this a great dish for entertaining.

All-purpose flour	2 tbsp.	30 mL
Curry powder	1 tbsp.	15 mL
Salt	1/2 tsp.	2 mL
Pork chops (about 1 2/3 lbs., 750 g)	4	4
Cooking oil	1 tbsp.	15 mL
Cooking oil	1 tsp.	5 mL
Large sweet onion (such as Vidalia or Walla Walla), chopped	1	1
Large cooking apple (such as McIntosh), chopped	1	1
Large tart cooking apple (such as Granny Smith), chopped	1	1
Granulated sugar	1 tsp.	5 mL
Water	1 cup	250 mL
Whipping cream	1 cup	250 mL
Finely grated gingerroot	2 tsp.	10 mL

Combine first 3 ingredients in shallow bowl. Dredge chops in flour mixture. Shake gently to remove excess. Reserve remaining flour mixture.

Heat first amount of cooking oil in large frying pan on medium-high. Sear chops for about 3 minutes per side until lightly browned. Remove to greased baking sheet with sides. Bake in 350°F (175°C) oven for about 15 minutes until tender.

Heat second amount of cooking oil in same frying pan on medium-high. Add onion. Sauté for about 3 minutes until onion is softened. Add both apples. Sauté for about 5 minutes until apple is softened. Add sugar and reserved flour mixture. Heat and stir for 1 minute until onion and apple are well coated.

Add water. Stir. Reduce heat to medium-low. Simmer, uncovered, for about 5 minutes until thickened. Stir in cream and ginger. Bring to a boil on medium. Serve over pork chops. Serves 4.

1 serving: 543 Calories; 39.7 g Total Fat; 389 mg Sodium; 25 g Protein; 23 g Carbohydrate; 3 g Dietary Fibre

Greek Ribs

"This is one of my most requested entrees. Due to the price of good-quality back ribs, we save this for special celebrations like a birthday, a great report card or a hat trick."

— Linda Rudachyk, Weyburn, Saskatchewan

Pork baby back ribs (about 8 racks)	8 lbs.	3.6 kg
Butter (not margarine), melted	1/2 cup	125 mL
Lemon juice	3 tbsp.	50 mL
Greek seasoning	2 tbsp.	30 mL
Seasoned salt	1 tbsp.	15 mL
Italian seasoning	1 tbsp.	15 mL
Salt	3/4 tsp.	4 mL
Freshly ground pepper	1/2 tsp.	2 mL

Place ribs, meaty side up, on 3 lightly greased baking sheets with sides.

Combine butter and lemon juice in 1 cup (250 mL) liquid measure. Brush 1/2 onto ribs.

Combine remaining 5 ingredients in small bowl. Sprinkle 1/2 over ribs. Turn ribs over. Brush remaining butter mixture onto ribs. Sprinkle remaining spice mixture on top. Cover. Chill for 1 hour. Bake, uncovered, in 375°F (190°C) oven for 45 minutes, turning once, until tender. Serves 16.

1 serving: 457 Calories; 39.4 g Total Fat; 577 mg Sodium; 23 g Protein; 1 g Carbohydrate; trace Dietary Fibre

Pictured on page 27.

Braised Pork Loin with Cream Gravy

"The pressure cooker is perfect for cooking large cuts of meat to tender perfection. For a lighter, but equally flavourful gravy, simply purée the braising vegetables and eliminate the sour cream. The sliced pork is delicious over wide egg noodles or mashed potatoes. Garnish with fresh thyme."

— Cinda Chavich, author of *125 Best Pressure Cooker Recipes* (Robert Rose Inc., 2004)

All-purpose flour	1/4 cup	60 mL
Salt	1/2 tsp.	2 mL
Freshly ground pepper	1/2 tsp.	2 mL
Paprika	1 tsp.	5 mL
Boneless pork loin (or butt) roast, trimmed of fat, rolled and tied	2 1/4 lbs.	1 kg
Olive oil	2 tbsp.	30 mL
Thick slices of double-smoked (or European) bacon (about 2 oz., 57 g), chopped	2	2
Celery ribs, finely chopped	2	2
Medium carrot, finely chopped	1	1
Small onion, finely chopped	1	1
Garlic cloves, minced	2	2
Tomato paste	2 tbsp.	30 mL
Chicken (or beef) broth	1 cup	250 mL
Dry white (or alcohol-free) wine	1/2 cup	125 mL
Dried thyme	1 tsp.	5 mL
Paprika	1 tsp.	5 mL
Sour cream (optional)	1/4 cup	60 mL
Salt, to taste		
Freshly ground pepper, to taste		

Combine first 4 ingredients in shallow bowl. Roll roast in flour mixture to coat completely. If desired, reserve any remaining flour mixture to thicken gravy later.

Heat olive oil in pressure cooker on medium-high. Brown roast well all over. Remove roast to large plate. Set aside.

Add bacon to pressure cooker. Cook for 5 minutes until just cooked.

Add next 4 ingredients. Sauté for 5 minutes until vegetables are tender.

Add next 5 ingredients. Stir. Return roast to cooker. Lock lid in place. Bring up to pressure on high heat. Reduce heat to medium-low just to maintain pressure. Cook for 40 minutes. Release pressure. Remove lid. Remove roast. Cover with foil to keep warm. Put vegetables and bacon mixture with juices in blender or food processor. Process until smooth. Return to pressure cooker. Heat and stir on medium until hot.

For a richer gravy, combine sour cream and reserved flour mixture in small bowl. Whisk into vegetable mixture. Simmer, uncovered, until thickened. Season with salt and pepper. Stir. Makes about 1 1/2 cups (375 mL) gravy. Slice roast. Serve with gravy. Serves 6.

1 serving: 388 Calories; 19 g Total Fat; 505 mg Sodium; 38 g Protein; 12 g Carbohydrate; 1 g Dietary Fibre

Pictured below.

Braised Pork Loin with Cream Gravy, above

Photo by Ian Grant

Stuffed Rolled Ribs

Like most Oktoberfest food, this hearty dish of back ribs rolled around a bread stuffing isn't for the calorie-conscious, warns Mark Bingeman, general manager of Bingemans Inc., which operates three Oktoberfest *Festhallen*. *"When properly cooked, the meat just falls off the bone,"* he says. *"Some people spice it up with apples or sweet peppers."*

— Mark Bingeman, Bingemans Inc., Kitchener, Ontario

STUFFING

Loaf of white bread, cubed (about 9 cups, 2.25 L)	1	1
Large onion, chopped	1	1
Celery ribs, chopped	4	4
Medium red peppers, chopped	2	2
Salt	1 tbsp.	15 mL
Pepper	1 tsp.	5 mL
Garlic cloves, crushed	2	2
Parsley flakes	1/2 cup	125 mL
Chicken broth	1 cup	250 mL
Pork back ribs, whole slab (5 1/4 lbs., 2.4 kg), cut into 2 equal portions	4	4
Seasoned salt	2 tbsp.	30 mL
Gravy browning powder	2 tbsp.	30 mL

Stuffing: Combine first 9 ingredients in large bowl. Mix well.

Place ribs, meaty side down, on work surface. Spoon 1 1/4 cups (300 mL) stuffing onto each rib portion. Roll up tightly. Tie butcher's string around each portion to enclose stuffing. Lay ribs in greased 9 x 13 inch (22 x 33 cm) dish.

Combine seasoned salt and gravy browning powder in small bowl. Sprinkle over ribs. Bake, uncovered, in 350°F (175°C) oven for 1 1/2 to 1 3/4 hours until very tender. Serve whole or cut each portion between rib bones. Serves 8.

1 serving: 675 Calories; 46 g Total Fat; 2383 mg Sodium; 35 g Protein; 28 g Carbohydrate; 2 g Dietary Fibre

Pictued below.

Transylvania Pork Schnitzel

During Octoberfest, the Transylvania Club goes through at least 1,200 schnitzel a day. Their secret is the mixture of day-old bread crumbs purchased at local bakeries, from croissants to rye bread. Chicken breasts or veal chops can be substituted for the pork.

— Transylvania Club, Kitchener, Ontario

Boneless pork loin chops (about 1 3/4 lbs., 790 g), trimmed of fat	6	6
Salt, sprinkle		
Pepper, sprinkle		
All-purpose flour	1/3 cup	75 mL
Garlic powder	1/4 tsp.	1 mL
Paprika	1/4 tsp.	1 mL
Onion powder	1/4 tsp.	1 mL
Large eggs, fork-beaten	3	3
Fine dry bread crumbs	1 1/2 cups	375 mL
Cooking oil	6 tbsp.	100 mL
Fresh dill sprig, for garnish		
Capers, for garnish		
Lemon wedge, for garnish		

Pound chops with mallet or rolling pin to 1/4 inch (6 mm) thickness. Sprinkle with salt and pepper.

Combine next 4 ingredients in small cup.

Place flour mixture, egg and bread crumbs in separate bowls. Dredge chops in flour. Dip into egg. Coat with bread crumbs.

Heat 1 tbsp. (15 mL) of cooking oil per chop in large frying pan on medium-high. Cook chops for 4 minutes per side until browned. Repeat with remaining cooking oil and chops.

Garnish with remaining 3 ingredients. Serves 6.

1 serving: 475 Calories; 23.9 g Total Fat; 337 mg Sodium; 36 g Protein; 27 g Carbohydrate; 1 g Dietary Fibre

Pictured on page 105.

Coleslaw, page 167

Stuffed Rolled Ribs, above

Clockwise from left: Transylvania Pork Schnitzel, page 104; Cabbage Rolls, below; German Potato Salad, page 166

Cabbage Rolls

These plump, delicious rolls are a big seller at the Concordia Club, founded in 1873 when Kitchener was still called Berlin. Instead of softening leaves by boiling, club members freeze whole, trimmed cabbages which, when defrosted, yield limp leaves that are easier or rolling.

– Concordia Club, Kitchener, Ontario

Small head of cabbage	1	1
Ground beef	1/2 lb.	225 g
Ground pork	1/2 lb.	225 g
Cooked long grain white rice	1 cup	250 mL
Large egg	1	1
Envelope of dry onion soup mix	1.4 oz.	38 g
Salt, sprinkle		
Pepper, sprinkle		

Large onion, chopped	1	1
Chopped celery	1/2 cup	125 mL
Hard margarine (or butter)	2 tbsp.	30 mL
Can of condensed tomato soup	10 oz.	284 mL
Water (1/2 of soup can)	5 oz.	142 mL
Freshly squeezed lemon juice (about 1 medium lemon)	1/4 cup	60 mL
Granulated sugar	1 tsp.	5 mL
Parsley flakes	1 tsp.	5 mL

Remove and discard core from cabbage. Place cabbage in resealable freezer bag. Freeze overnight or for up to 2 days. Thaw. Separate into leaves. You will need 10 leaves.

Combine next 7 ingredients in large bowl. Place 1/3 cup (75 mL) pork mixture in centre of each cabbage leaf. Fold sides of leaf towards middle. Roll up to enclose filling. Place in greased 11 x 17 inch (28 x 43 cm) baking dish.◆

Sauté onion and celery in margarine in large frying pan on medium-high for about 5 minutes until softened.

Add remaining 5 ingredients. Stir. Pour over cabbage rolls. Cover. Bake in 325°F (160°C) oven for 1 1/2 hours until cabbage leaves are tender and filling is firm. Makes 10 cabbage rolls.

1 cabbage roll: 250 Calories; 14.6 g Total Fat; 634 mg Sodium; 11 g Protein; 20 g Carbohydrate; 3 g Dietary Fibre

Pictured above.

◆*To ensure even cooking, place cabbage rolls with larger, tougher leaves around outside of baking dish.*

Red-Currant-and-Mustard-Glazed Ham, below

Red-Currant-and-Mustard-Glazed Ham

A glaze of red currant jelly gives a hefty ham an elegant profile. Serve warm or cold. Cut leftover ham into two or three large pieces for quicker cooling before refrigerating or freezing.

GLAZE

Red currant jelly	1/2 cup	125 mL
Dry mustard	1 tbsp.	15 mL
Apple cider vinegar	1/4 cup	60 mL
Cooked leg of ham, rind removed	9 lbs.	4 kg
Whole cloves, approximately	3 tbsp.	50 mL

Glaze: Combine all 3 ingredients in small saucepan. Heat and stir on medium for about 5 minutes until jelly is dissolved. Set aside.

Make shallow cuts in ham, in one direction diagonally across fat at 3/4 inch (2 cm) intervals. Make shallow cuts diagonally in opposite direction, forming diamonds. Push 1 clove into centre of each diamond. Place ham on wire rack in roasting pan. Roast ham in 325°F (160°C) oven for 1 hour. Brush ham with glaze. Roast for 30 to 45 minutes further, brushing with glaze several times, until internal temperature reaches 140°F (60°C) and ham is glazed and golden brown. Serves 14 to 16.

1 **serving:** 678 Calories; 45 g Total Fat; 194 mg Sodium; 57 g Protein; 8 g Carbohydrate; trace Dietary Fibre

Pictured above.

Chili, Pork and Pear Stir-Fry

"Pears and pork make tasty partners in this light stir-fry with a hot pepper zing and a hint of exotic Chinese five-spice."
— **Kit Price, Edmonton, Alberta**

Cooking oil	1 tsp.	5 mL
Pork tenderloin, thinly sliced	1 lb.	454 g
Prepared chicken broth (or water)	2 tbsp.	30 mL
Garlic cloves, crushed	2	2
Fresh small red chilies, finely chopped◆	2	2
Chinese five-spice powder	1/8 tsp.	0.5 mL
Hoisin sauce	2 tbsp.	30 mL
Chinese cooking wine (or dry sherry)	2 tbsp.	30 mL
Soy sauce	1 tbsp.	15 mL
Cornstarch	1 tbsp.	15 mL
Can of pear halves in juice, drained and sliced	14 oz.	398 mL
Green onions, cut into 1 inch (2.5 cm) pieces	8	8
Sugar snap peas (about 8 oz., 225 g)	2 cups	500 mL
Toasted sesame seeds (optional)◆◆	2 tsp.	10 mL

Heat cooking oil in large non-stick wok or deep frying pan on medium-high. Stir-fry pork in 2 batches for about 2 minutes until browned. Remove from wok.

Heat broth in same wok. Add next 3 ingredient Stir-fry for about 1 minute until fragrant.

Combine next 4 ingredients in small bowl. Ad to chili mixture.

Add pork and next 3 ingredients. Stir-fry for about 3 minutes until peas are tender-crisp and mixture is hot.

Sprinkle sesame seeds over top. Serves 4.

1 **serving:** 283 Calories; 6.5 g Total Fat; 552 mg Sodium; 30 g Protein; 25 g Carbohydrate; 4 g Dietary Fibre

◆*Wear gloves when chopping chili peppers, and avoid touching your eyes.*

◆◆*To toast the sesame seeds, place them in an ungreased frying pan. Heat on medium, stirring often, until golden.*

Stuffed Pork Loin Roast

Here's where versatile pork loin really comes into its own. The popular roast lends itself to any number of great stuffing combinations. This one, featuring bright green spinach and pieces of tangy dried apricot, tastes as wonderful as it looks.

– **Marilyn Gillespie, Renfrew, Ontario**

SPINACH APRICOT STUFFING

Bag of fresh spinach leaves, stems removed	10 oz.	300 g
Dried apricots	10	10
Cubed white bread (about 8 slices)	4 cups	1 L
Finely chopped onion	1 cup	250 mL
Butter (or hard margarine), melted	1/2 cup	125 mL
Dry mustard	1 tsp.	5 mL
Dried savory	1/2 tsp.	2 mL
Salt	1/4 tsp.	1 mL
Pepper	1/2 tsp.	2 mL

Boneless pork loin roast	4 1/2 lbs.	2 kg
Maple syrup	2 tbsp.	30 mL
Salt	1 tsp.	5 mL
Pepper	1 tsp.	5 mL
Garlic powder	1 tsp.	5 mL

APPLESAUCE

Medium cooking apples (such as McIntosh), peeled, cored and sliced	4	4
Water	1/4 cup	60 mL

Spinach Apricot Stuffing: Steam spinach in medium saucepan over small amount of boiling water until just wilted. Cool slightly. Squeeze dry. Halve apricots horizontally; soak in warm water 5 to 10 minutes until softened. Drain. Set spinach and apricots aside.

Combine next 7 ingredients in large bowl.

Cut pork loin in half lengthwise through centre to form 2 long pieces. Lay 1 piece of pork loin, cut-side up, on work surface. Spoon 1/2 of bread mixture over pork. Layer spinach over bread mixture. Layer apricots over spinach. Top with remaining bread mixture. Place remaining pork loin half on top. Tie with butcher's string at 1 1/4 inch (3 cm) intervals. Place on greased wire rack in roasting pan.

Drizzle with maple syrup. Sprinkle with next 3 ingredients. Roast, uncovered, in 325°F (160°C) oven for about 2 hours until tender and internal temperature of pork loin reaches 160°F (75°C). Remove from oven. Cover with foil. Let stand for 10 minutes before carving into 1/2 inch (12 mm) slices.

Applesauce: Combine apples and water in medium saucepan. Cook, covered, on medium-low for about 15 minutes until apples are softened. Mash with fork. Makes 2 cups (500 mL) applesauce. Serve with pork. Serves 10.

1 serving: 576 Calories; 26.5 g Total Fat; 564 mg Sodium; 43 g Protein; 42 g Carbohydrate; 5 g Dietary Fibre

Pictured below.

Clockwise, from top: Spinach and Orange Salad, page 170; Coq au Vin, page 126; Shortcut Pork Cassoulet, below; Roasted Vegetables with Aioli, page 176; Buttered Herb Noodles, page 182

Shortcut Pork Cassoulet

Preparation of traditional French cassoulet, a dish of slow-baked beans and assorted meats, begins three days in advance. Happily, this more contemporary version takes a fraction of the usual time but provides all the appeal and great taste of the original version. If you have a large cast iron Dutch oven, use it for this recipe, as you can take it straight from the oven to the buffet table for serving. The cassoulet can be made up to the point where the breadcrumbs are added, and chilled for up to one day. To finish the dish, cover and heat in 350°F (175°C) oven for 30 to 40 minutes, stirring twice, then continue with the recipe.

Dried Great Northern (or dried navy) beans	2 cups	500 mL
Boiling water, to cover		
Water, to cover		
Lean pork sausages	1 3/4 lbs.	790 g
Olive (or cooking) oil	1 tbsp.	15 mL
Pork shoulder picnic roast, cut into 1 inch (2.5 cm) cubes	3 lbs.	1.4 kg
Olive (or cooking) oil	1 tbsp.	15 mL
Medium onions, sliced	2	2
Garlic cloves, crushed	4	4
Thick slices of smoked bacon, chopped	4	4
Prepared chicken broth	2 cups	500 mL
Red (or alcohol-free) wine	3/4 cup	175 mL
Can of tomato paste	5 1/2 oz.	156 mL
Chopped fresh thyme leaves	1 1/2 tbsp.	25 mL
Salt	2 tsp.	10 mL
Freshly ground pepper	1/2 tsp.	2 mL
Fine dry bread crumbs	3/4 cup	175 mL

Place beans in large heatproof bowl. Add boiling water. Let stand for 2 hours until doubled in size. Drain.

Place beans in large saucepan. Add enough water to cover beans by 2 inches (5 cm). Bring to a boil. Reduce heat to low. Simmer, partially covered, for about 1 hour until tender but firm. Drain. Set aside.

Cook sausages in large frying pan on medium for about 15 minutes, turning several times, until cooked. Remove from frying pan. Cut into 2-inch pieces. Set aside. Drain any fat from frying pan.

Heat first amount of olive oil in same frying pan on medium-high. Cook pork, in 2 batches until browned. Remove from frying pan. Set aside.

Heat second amount of olive oil in same frying pan on medium-high. Add onion and garlic. Sauté for about 5 minutes until onion is softened.

Add bacon. Fry for about 10 minutes until bacon is crisp.

Combine beans, sausage, pork and onion mixture in large roasting pan or Dutch oven. Add next 6 ingredients. Cover. Cook in 350°F (175°C) oven for about 1 1/2 hours until pork is tender.

Sprinkle with bread crumbs. Cook, uncovered for 20 minutes until top is crunchy. Broil 6 inches from heat for about 5 minutes until golden. Serves 8 to 12.

1 serving: 828 Calories; 44 g Total Fat; 1675 mg Sodium; 45 g Protein; 60 g Carbohydrate; 8 g Dietary Fibre

Pictured above.

Gourmet Pizza

This delicate pizza is based on phyllo pastry, which gives it a light-as-air quality. Also really nice cut into small squares and served as an appetizer.

— Trudi MacMillan, Dartmouth, Nova Scotia

Sun-dried tomatoes	10	10
Water, to cover		
Frozen phyllo pastry sheets, thawed according to package directions	12	12
Butter (or hard margarine), melted	1/2 cup	125 mL
Garlic cloves, thinly sliced	3	3
Sliced portobello mushrooms	1 cup	250 mL
Calabrese (or Genoa) salami slices, halved	8 - 10	8 - 10
Finely grated Parmesan cheese	1 cup	250 mL
Grated Asiago cheese	1 cup	250 mL

Combine sun-dried tomatoes and water in small saucepan. Bring to a boil on medium-high. Boil for 7 to 10 minutes until sun-dried tomatoes are softened. Drain. Cut in half lengthwise. Set aside.

Lay one pastry sheet on ungreased 10 x 15 inch (25 x 38 cm) baking sheet with sides. (Cover remaining pastry sheets with slightly damp tea towel.) Press pastry to fit in and up sides of baking sheet. Working quickly, brush pastry sheet with butter. Lay second pastry sheet on top, also pressing to fit in and up sides. Brush with butter. Repeat with remaining pastry sheets and butter.

Scatter garlic, mushrooms and sun-dried tomato over pastry. Arrange salami over top. Sprinkle with both cheeses. Bake in 375°F (190°C) oven for about 15 minutes until pastry is golden and crispy. Pizza will puff up during baking but will deflate once removed from oven. Cuts into 8 pieces.

1 piece: 365 Calories; 25.9 g Total Fat; 847 mg Sodium; 14 g Protein; 19 g Carbohydrate; trace Dietary Fibre

Pictured below.

Quick and Easy Ham Loaf

"This is a good alternative to your regular meatloaf. I found that when I made this, I had requests to make it again."

— Pat McNeice, Edmonton, Alberta

GLAZE

Brown sugar, packed	1 cup	250 mL
White vinegar	1 tbsp.	15 mL
Dry mustard	1 tsp.	5 mL
Ground cloves, just a pinch		

MEATLOAF

Cooked ham, ground or processed in food processor	1 1/2 lbs.	680 g
Lean ground beef	1/2 lb.	225 g
Ground pork	1/2 lb.	225 g
Large eggs, fork-beaten	2	2
Milk	1 cup	250 mL
Crisp rice cereal	1/2 cup	125 mL
Worcestershire sauce	2 tsp.	10 mL
Dry mustard	1 tsp.	5 mL

Glaze: Combine all 4 ingredients in small bowl. Set aside.

Meatloaf: Combine all 8 ingredients in large bowl. Mix well. Press evenly into ungreased 9 x 5 x 3 inch (22 x 12.5 x 7.5 cm) loaf pan. Bake, uncovered, in 350°F (175°C) oven for 45 minutes. Spread glaze over meatloaf. Bake, uncovered, for 45 minutes further, basting occasionally with drippings, until meatloaf pulls away from sides of pan and meat thermometer inserted in centre registers 170°F (77°C). Carefully drain any excess drippings from pan. Let stand for 10 minutes. Cuts into eighteen 1/2 inch (12 mm) slices.

1 slice: 208 Calories; 8.9 g Total Fat; 74 mg Sodium; 17 g Protein; 14 g Carbohydrate; trace Dietary Fibre

Pictured above.

Quick and Easy Ham Loaf, left

Gourmet Pizza, above

Satay Pork and Peanut Noodles

"Satay, a popular marinated and skewered meat dish, is usually served with high-fat peanut sauce. Here, light peanut butter is used for a lower-fat, but still tasty, dish."

— Kit Price, Edmonton, Alberta

Lime juice	2 tbsp.	30 mL
Soy sauce	1 tbsp.	15 mL
Garlic clove, crushed	1	1
Minced gingerroot	1 tsp.	5 mL
Ground coriander	1/2 tsp.	2 mL
Ground cumin	1/2 tsp.	2 mL
Pork tenderloin, cut into 3/4 inch (2 cm) cubes	1 1/2 lbs.	680 g
Package dried rice noodles (1 lb., 454 g, size)	1/2	1/2
Boiling water, to cover		
Bamboo skewers, 8 inch (20 cm) length, soaked in water for 10 minutes	12	12

PEANUT SAUCE

Light coconut milk	1/4 cup	60 mL
Unsweetened pineapple juice	1/3 cup	75 mL
Water	1/2 cup	125 mL
Light crunchy peanut butter	2 tbsp.	30 mL
Brown sugar, packed	2 tbsp.	30 mL
Tamari sauce (or low-sodium soy sauce)	2 tbsp.	30 mL
Fish sauce	1 tbsp.	15 mL
Minced gingerroot	2 tsp.	10 mL
Garlic clove, crushed	1	1
Ground coriander	1 tsp.	5 mL
Ground cumin	1 tsp.	5 mL
Dried crushed chilies	1/2 tsp.	2 mL
Coconut flavouring	1/4 tsp.	1 mL
Carrots, sliced diagonally	2	2
Snow peas, trimmed (about 9 oz., 255 g)	2 cups	500 mL
Fresh cilantro, chopped	2 tbsp.	30 mL

Combine first 6 ingredients in small bowl. Place pork in shallow dish or resealable freezer bag. Pour lime juice mixture over pork. Stir or turn to coat. Cover or seal. Marinate in refrigerator for 2 hours or overnight, turning several times. Remove meat. Discard marinade.

Place rice noodles in large bowl. Cover with boiling water. Let stand for 20 minutes until softened. Drain.

Thread 3 or 4 pork cubes onto each skewer. Broil 6 inches (15 cm) from heat for 5 to 8 minutes per side, turning once, until tender.

Peanut Sauce: Combine first 13 ingredients in medium saucepan. Heat and stir on medium-low for about 5 minutes until heated through and well combined. Set aside. Makes 1 cup (250 mL) sauce.

Heat lightly greased wok or large non-stick frying pan. Add carrot. Stir-fry on high for about 5 minutes until tender-crisp. Add snow peas and cilantro. Add noodles and 1/2 of peanut sauce. Stir-fry until hot and snow peas are tender-crisp. Makes 6 cups (1.5 L) noodle mixture. Arrange noodle mixture in large shallow serving bowl or on platter. Top with pork skewers. Drizzle with remaining peanut sauce. Serves 6.

1 serving: 419 Calories; 9.5 g Total Fat; 730 mg Sodium; 31 g Protein; 52 g Carbohydrate; 2 g Dietary Fibre

Pictured below.

Sausage Ragout

A nice change from serving sausages solo, this preparation is easy enough for every day, yet certainly special enough for company. Choose mild or hot Italian sausages to suit your taste for heat. Or if your butcher makes a specialty in-house sausage—maybe lamb with garlic, or pork or beef with red wine, cheese and other herbs—give it a try in this recipe.

Olive (or cooking) oil	2 tsp.	10 mL
Italian sausages, uncooked, (about 1 1/3 lbs., 600 g)	8	8
Large onion, sliced	1	1
Garlic cloves, crushed	4	4
Green pepper, cut into 1 inch (2.5 cm) pieces	1	1
Can of diced tomatoes	28 oz.	796 mL
Tomato paste	1/4 cup	60 mL
Prepared beef broth	1 cup	250 mL
Granulated sugar	1 tsp.	5 mL
Hot pepper sauce (optional)	1 tsp.	5 mL
Dried sweet basil	1 tsp.	5 mL
Salt	1/4 tsp.	1 mL
Freshly ground pepper	1/2 tsp.	2 mL

Heat olive oil in large, deep frying pan on medium. Add sausages. Cook for about 15 minutes, turning occasionally, until browned. Remove sausages from frying pan. Cut diagonally into 1/2 inch (12 mm) slices.

Drain all but 1 tbsp. (15 mL) drippings from frying pan. Heat on medium-high. Add next 3 ingredients Sauté for about 5 minutes until onion is softened.

Add sausage and remaining 8 ingredients to onion mixture. Stir. Bring to a boil on medium-high. Reduce heat to medium. Gently boil, uncovered, for about 30 minutes, stirring occasionally, until sauce is thickened. Serves 4.

1 serving: 634 Calories; 50.2 g Total Fat; 1795 mg Sodium; 26 g Protein; 21 g Carbohydrate; 4 g Dietary Fibre

Pictured at right.

Sausage Ragout, left, with
Soft Polenta, page 188

Grilled Pork Chops with Lentils and Spinach

Add some strips of red pepper to the grill and a dollop of yogurt and mango chutney to the pork chops for a fast, flavourful meal.

Plain yogurt	1/3 cup	75 mL
Finely chopped fresh mint	1 tbsp.	15 mL
Finely grated orange zest	1 tsp.	5 mL
Garlic cloves, crushed	2	2
Salt	1/2 tsp.	2 mL
Freshly ground pepper	1/2 tsp.	2 mL
Bone-in pork chops (about 1 3/4 lbs., 790 g)	4	4

LENTILS AND SPINACH

Cooking oil	1 tbsp.	15 mL
Medium onions, sliced	2	2
Brown sugar, packed	2 tsp.	10 mL
Can of brown lentils, drained and rinsed	19 oz.	540 mL
Fresh spinach leaves, packed	2 cups	500 mL
Plain yogurt	1/3 cup	75 mL
Salt	1/2 tsp.	2 mL
Freshly ground pepper	1/2 tsp.	2 mL

Combine first 6 ingredients in medium bowl. Add pork chops. Mix well to coat. Cook pork chops on greased grill over medium-high for 5 to 6 minutes per side until tender.

Lentils and Spinach: While pork chops are grilling, heat cooking oil in large frying pan on medium. Add onion. Sauté for about 10 minutes, stirring occasionally, until lightly browned.

Add brown sugar. Stir for 1 to 2 minutes until dissolved.

Add remaining 5 ingredients. Heat and stir for 3 to 5 minutes until spinach is just wilted and mixture is hot. Makes 2 2/3 cups (650 mL). Serve lentils and spinach with pork chops. Serves 4.

1 serving: 474 Calories; 23.2 g Total Fat; 907 mg Sodium; 40 g Protein; 27 g Carbohydrate; 5 g Dietary Fibre

Roasted Pepper, Sausage and Pesto Pizza

Sweet red peppers, spicy chorizo sausage, tangy feta cheese and fragrant pesto combine their intense flavours in this cosmopolitan pizza.

THICK-CRUST DOUGH

Active dry yeast (or 1/4 oz., 8 g, envelope)	2 1/4 tsp.	11 mL
Granulated sugar	1/2 tsp.	2 mL
Warm water	1 1/4 cups	300 mL
All-purpose flour, approximately	2 1/4 cups	550 mL
Salt	1/2 tsp.	2 mL
Olive (or cooking) oil	2 tbsp.	30 mL

TOPPING

Large red pepper	1	1
Chorizo (or hot Italian) sausages (about 7 oz., 200 g), casings removed, chopped	2	2
Medium onions, thinly sliced	2	2
Granulated sugar	1 tbsp.	15 mL
Basil pesto (prepared or your own)	1/3 cup	75 mL
Feta cheese, crumbled	1/3 cup	75 mL
Finely grated Parmesan cheese	1/3 cup	75 mL

Thick-Crust Dough: Combine first 3 ingredients in small bowl. Cover. Let stand in warm place for 10 minutes. Stir to dissolve yeast.

Combine flour and salt in large bowl. Stir in yeast mixture and olive oil. Mix, adding more flour as needed, until dough just comes together. Turn out onto lightly floured surface. Knead for about 5 minutes, adding little or no extra flour, until smooth and elastic. Place dough in large greased bowl, turning once to grease top. Cover with greased waxed paper and tea towel. Let stand in warm place for about 1 hour until doubled in bulk.

Topping: Place red pepper on ungreased baking sheet. Bake in 400°F (205°C) oven for about 25 minutes, turning once, until skin is blistered and slightly blackened. Put into small bowl. Cover tightly. Let stand for 10 minutes until cool enough to handle. Remove and discard skin and seeds. Cut into 1/3 inch (8 mm) thick strips. Set aside.

Heat medium frying pan on medium-high. Add sausage. Fry for about 5 minutes, stirring occasionally, until lightly browned. Remove to paper towel to drain. Discard all but 1 tbsp. (15 mL) drippings from frying pan.

Sauté onion in same frying pan on medium for 15 minutes, stirring occasionally, until very soft and lightly browned. Add sugar. Stir for 1 minute until sugar is dissolved. Remove from heat. Set aside.

Turn out dough onto lightly floured surface. Shape into a ball. Roll out or press in lightly greased 12 inch (30 cm) pizza pan or 10 x 15 inch (25 x 38 cm) baking sheet with sides. Spread pesto evenly over crust to within 1/2 inch (12 mm) of edge. Top with red pepper, sausage and onion. Sprinkle both cheeses over top. Bake in 500°F (260°C) oven for 15 to 18 minutes until crust is golden and crispy. Cuts into 8 wedges or pieces.

1 wedge or piece: 386 Calories; 20.8 g Total Fat; 617 mg Sodium; 14 g Protein; 35 g Carbohydrate; 2 g Dietary Fibre

Pictured below.

Roasted Pepper, Sausage and Pesto Pizza, above

Tomato, Basil and Garlic Thin-Crust Pizza, page 122

Main Courses: *Meatless*

Gnocchi with Spinach and
Sun-Dried Tomatoes, below

Gnocchi with Spinach and Sun-Dried Tomatoes

One of the quickest meals to prepare—just five minutes! This recipe goes to show why it's a good idea to keep a couple of bags of potato gnocchi in your freezer.

Medium red onion, sliced	1	1
Garlic cloves, crushed	2	2
Olive oil	1 tbsp.	15 mL
Whipping cream	2/3 cup	150 mL
Cans of diced tomatoes, (14 oz., 398 mL, each), with juice	2	2
Sun-dried tomatoes in oil, drained and chopped	3/4 cup	175 mL
Kalamata olives	1/3 cup	75 mL
Potato gnocchi pasta	1 1/2 lbs.	680 g
Boiling water	8 cups	2 L
Salt	1/4 tsp.	1 mL
Bag of spinach (or 2 bundles, trimmed)	10 oz.	285 g
Chopped pistachio nuts	1/2 cup	125 mL

Sauté onion and garlic in olive oil in large frying pan on medium-high for about 3 minutes until onion is soft.

Add whipping cream and tomatoes with juice. Bring to a boil. Reduce heat to medium. Simmer, uncovered, for about 5 minutes until sauce is reduced and thickened.

Add sun-dried tomatoes and olives. Simmer, uncovered, for 2 minutes until heated through.

Cook gnocchi in boiling water and salt in large uncovered pot or Dutch oven for about 5 minutes until gnocchi floats to surface. Remove with slotted spoon to tomato mixture.

Gently stir in spinach and pistachios. Heat and stir for about 3 minutes until spinach is wilted. Makes 8 cups (2 L).

1 cup (250 mL): 281 Calories; 18.2 g Total Fat; 557 mg Sodium; 6 g Protein; 28 g Carbohydrate; 5 g Dietary Fibre

Pictured above.

Pasta Primavera

Bright, colourful and ideal for a light spring meal. Pasta Primavera is a terrific way to enjoy an assortment of vegetables in one easy dish. To save time, prepare all the vegetables the day before and refrigerate until needed.

Spinach fettuccine pasta	12 oz.	340 g
Boiling water	12 cups	3 L
Salt	2 tsp.	10 mL
Chopped onion (about 1 medium)	1 cup	250 mL
Sliced carrot	1/2 cup	125 mL
Garlic cloves, minced	2	2
Olive oil	1 tbsp.	15 mL
Sliced small fresh mushrooms	2/3 cup	150 mL
Slivered red pepper	2/3 cup	150 mL
Slivered yellow pepper	1/2 cup	125 mL
Chopped broccoli	1 cup	250 mL
Can of skim evaporated milk	13 1/2 oz.	385 mL
White (or alcohol-free) wine	1/2 cup	125 mL
Cornstarch	4 tsp.	20 mL
Grated light Parmesan cheese	1/3 cup	75 mL
Chopped fresh parsley	1/4 cup	60 mL
Chopped fresh sweet basil	1 tbsp.	15 mL
Freshly ground pepper	1/4 tsp.	1 mL

Cook pasta in boiling water and salt in large uncovered pot or Dutch oven for 8 to 10 minutes, stirring occasionally, until tender but firm. Drain well. Turn into large bowl.

Sauté next 3 ingredients in olive oil in large frying pan on medium for 2 minutes.

Stir in next 4 ingredients. Cover. Cook for about 2 minutes, stirring once.

Combine next 3 ingredients in small dish until smooth. Add to vegetables.

Add remaining 4 ingredients. Stir. Cover. Heat for 2 minutes until bubbling and thickened. Serve over pasta. Serves 6.

1 serving: 359 Calories; 4.4 g Total Fat; 207 mg Sodium; 17 g Protein; 60 g Carbohydrate; 3 g Dietary Fibre

Bean Dish

When you're invited to an impromptu backyard barbecue and have no time and no clue as to what to bring along, make this easy, great-tasting baked bean dish. Let it cook away in the oven while you get ready.

Can of beans in tomato sauce	14 oz.	398 mL
Can of chick peas (garbanzo beans), drained	19 oz.	540 mL
Can of kidney beans, drained	14 oz.	398 mL
Chopped onion	1 1/2 cups	375 mL
Cooking oil	2 tsp.	10 mL
All-purpose flour	2 tbsp.	30 mL
Can of tomato sauce	7 1/2 oz.	213 mL
Ketchup	1/2 cup	125 mL
Brown sugar, packed	1/4 cup	60 mL
White vinegar	2 tbsp.	30 mL
Hot pepper sauce	1/2 - 3/4 tsp.	2 - 4 mL

Combine first 3 ingredients in ungreased 2 quart (2 L) casserole.

Sauté onion in cooking oil in medium frying pan until soft.

Mix in flour. Add tomato sauce. Heat and stir until boiling and thickened. Add remaining 4 ingredients. Stir. Add to beans. Stir gently. Bake, uncovered, in 350°F (175°C) oven for about 45 minutes. Serves 8.

1 serving: 218 Calories; 2.5 g Total Fat; 734 mg Sodium; 9 g Protein; 44 g Carbohydrate; 9 g Dietary Fibre

Roasted Red Pepper Pasta, below

Roasted Red Pepper Pasta

A flavourful sauce packed with plump sweet peppers and fresh herbs. The whole wheat pasta not only adds a nutty flavour, but important nutrients, too.

Whole wheat penne pasta, (about 9 oz., 350 g)	3 cups	750 mL
Boiling water	9 cups	2.25 L
Salt	2 tsp.	10 mL
Cans of red peppers (14 oz., 398 mL, each), drained	2	2
Chopped fresh sweet basil	2/3 cup	150 mL
Garlic cloves, crushed	2	2
Green onions, thinly sliced	6	6
Hard margarine (or butter)	1 tsp.	5 mL
Can of skim evaporated milk	13 1/2 oz.	385 mL
All-purpose flour	1 1/2 tbsp.	25 mL
Chopped fresh oregano	2 tbsp.	30 mL
Chopped fresh marjoram	2 tsp.	10 mL
Chopped fresh thyme	2 tsp.	10 mL
Salt	1 tsp.	5 mL
Freshly ground pepper	1/2 tsp.	2 mL
White (or alcohol-free) wine	1/4 cup	60 mL

Cook pasta in boiling water and first amount of salt in large uncovered pot or Dutch oven for 7 to 9 minutes, stirring occasionally, until tender but firm. Drain well. Turn into large bowl.

Place peppers on ungreased baking sheet. Broil 3 inches from heat for 15 minutes, turning several times, until browned. Remove from oven. Reserve any juice.

Combine peppers, reserved juice and basil in blender. Process until very finely chopped.

Sauté garlic and green onion in margarine in frying pan until green onion is soft.

Whisk evaporated milk into flour in small cup until smooth. Add next 5 ingredients. Stir. Add to garlic mixture. Add pepper mixture. Heat and stir until boiling and thickened.

Stir in wine. Makes 2 2/3 cups (650 mL) sauce. Serve over pasta. Serves 8.

1 serving: 233 Calories; 1.5 g Total Fat; 1173 mg Sodium; 10 g Protein; 43 g Carbohydrate; 2 g Dietary Fibre

Pictured above.

Four-Cheese Fettuccine

A little garlic makes all the difference in this sumptuous pasta and cheese dish. Serve with a bright green salad and crusty bread.

Fresh fettuccine pasta	12 oz.	340 g
Boiling water	12 cups	3 L
Salt	2 tsp.	10 mL
Garlic clove, minced	1	1
Hard margarine (or butter), melted	1 tbsp.	15 mL
All-purpose flour	1 tbsp.	15 mL
Milk	2/3 cup	150 mL
Dry (or alcohol-free) sherry	2 tbsp.	30 mL
Grated Edam cheese	1/4 cup	60 mL
Grated German butter cheese	1/4 cup	60 mL
Grated Gruyère cheese	1/4 cup	60 mL
Grated Parmesan cheese	1/4 cup	60 mL
Salt, sprinkle		
Pepper, light sprinkle		

Cook pasta in boiling water and salt in large uncovered pot or Dutch oven for about 5 minutes, stirring occasionally, until tender but firm. Drain well. Turn into large bowl.

Sauté garlic in margarine in medium saucepan on low for 1 minute. Stir in flour. Gradually whisk in milk and sherry. Heat and stir about 5 minutes until smooth and thickened.

Stir in remaining 6 ingredients until cheese is melted. Makes 2 1/4 cups (550 mL) sauce. Serve over pasta. Serves 9.

1 serving: 220 Calories; 6.2 g Total Fat; 152 mg Sodium; 10 g Protein; 30 g Carbohydrate; 1 g Dietary Fibre

Pineapple Beans

The humble baked bean is elevated to regal status with the addition of crushed pineapple. For extra pineapple pizzazz, grill slices of the tropical fruit and serve as a garnish. Vegetarians can sustitue 2 tsp (10 mL) cooking oil for the bacon. No draining will be required.

Bacon slices, chopped	6	6
Chopped onion	1 1/2 cups	325 mL
Cans of baked beans in tomato sauce (14 oz., 398 mL, each)	2	2
Chili sauce	2 tbsp.	30 mL
Fancy (mild) molasses	1 tbsp.	15 mL
Prepared mustard	1 tsp.	5 mL
Can of crushed pineapple, drained	14 oz.	398 mL
Salt	1/4 tsp.	1 mL
Freshly ground pepper	1/8 tsp.	0.5 mL
Freshly ground pepper, sprinkle		

Sauté bacon and onion in large saucepan until bacon is crisp and onion is soft. Drain, discarding fat.

Add next 7 ingredients. Bring to a boil. Cover. Simmer for at least 30 minutes.

Sprinkle with pepper. Serves 8.

1 serving: 163 Calories; 3 g Total Fat; 644 mg Sodium; 7 g Protein; 31 g Carbohydrate; 9 g Dietary Fibre

Pictured below.

Note: This may be cooked on the stove and kept warm on the grill, or cook it directly on the barbecue.

Homecoming Beans

A version of this oh-so-easy and popular dish has been served to many a large gathering. The original recipe served 50, but we've altered it to serve six. Top with grated Cheddar cheese during the last half-hour of cooking as a crowning touch.

Cans of beans in tomato sauce (14 oz., 398 mL, each)	2	2
Onion flakes	2 tsp.	10 mL
Brown sugar, packed	2 tbsp.	30 mL
Ketchup	1/2 cup	125 mL
Worcestershire sauce	3/4 tsp.	4 mL

Combine all 5 ingredients in ungreased 1 quart (1 L) casserole. Bake, uncovered, in 350°F (175°C) oven for about 1 hour until bubbling and darkening around sides, stirring halfway through cooking time. Serves 6.

1 serving: 174 Calories; 0.7 g Total Fat; 826 mg Sodium; 7 g Protein; 40 g Carbohydrate; 11 g Dietary Fibre

Pineapple Beans, above

Olive, Feta and Chili Pasta

If you enjoy the flavours found in a classic Greek salad, you'll love this satisfying pasta dish. Add more fresh chilies to suit your own personal heat level!

Rotini (spiral) pasta, about 1 lb. (454 g)	6 cups	1.5 L
Boiling water	12 cups	3 L
Salt	2 tsp.	10 mL
Medium red onion, sliced	1	1
Garlic cloves, crushed	2	2
Small red chili peppers, finely chopped♦	2	2
Olive oil	1 tbsp.	15 mL
Cherry (or grape) tomatoes (about 1 1/2 lbs., 680 g)	4 cups	1 L
Kalamata olives, stones in	1/2 cup	125 mL
Chopped fresh sweet basil	1/2 cup	125 mL
Crumbled Feta cheese	2 cups	500 mL
Pine nuts, toasted♦♦	1/3 cup	75 mL

Cook pasta in boiling water and salt in large uncovered pot or Dutch oven for 10 to 12 minutes, stirring occasionally, until tender but firm. Drain well. Turn into large bowl.

Sauté next 3 ingredients in olive oil in large frying pan on medium for 1 minute. Add tomatoes. Heat, stirring occasionally, for 4 minutes until tomatoes are just starting to soften.

Stir in remaining 4 ingredients. Add to pasta. Toss to coat. Serves 10.

1 serving: 273 Calories; 9.2 g Total Fat; 269 mg Sodium; 11 g Protein; 38 g Carbohydrate; 3 g Dietary Fibre

Pictured at left.

♦Wear gloves when chopping chili peppers, and avoid touching your eyes.

♦♦To toast the pine nuts, place them in an ungreased frying pan. Heat on medium, stirring often, until golden.

Broccoli-Stuffed Pasta Shells, below

Layered Butternut Squash and Mushroom Pie

This savoury main course is as satisfying as any pasta dish that contains meat. Don't be put off by the length of this recipe; it's easy to put together the layers once the fillings are prepared.

Spinach lasagna noodles	9	9
Boiling water	16 cups	4 L
Salt	4 tsp.	20 mL
SAUCE		
Butternut squash, peeled, seeded and cut into 1/2 inch (12 mm) cubes (about 6 cups, 1.5 L)	3 lbs.	1.4 kg
Boiling water	1 cup	250 mL
Salt	1 tsp.	5 mL
Finely chopped onion	1/2 cup	125 mL
Garlic cloves, crushed	2	2
Hard margarine (or butter)	2 tbsp.	30 mL
Coarsely chopped brown mushrooms	2 cups	500 mL
Sherry (or alcohol-free sherry)	2 tbsp.	30 mL
Milk	4 cups	1 L
All-purpose flour	1/4 cup	60 mL
Dried whole oregano	1/4 tsp.	1 mL
Dried thyme	1/4 tsp.	1 mL
Salt	1 tsp.	5 mL
Freshly ground pepper	1/4 tsp.	1 mL
Crumbled feta cheese	1 cup	250 mL
Freshly ground pepper, to taste		

Cook noodles in boiling water and salt in large uncovered pot or Dutch oven for about 12 minutes until tender but firm. Drain. Rinse with cold water. Drain well. Set aside.

Sauce: Cook squash in boiling water and salt in large saucepan on medium for about 9 minutes until tender. Drain well. Set aside.

Sauté onion and garlic in margarine in large frying pan for 5 minutes until softened. Add mushrooms. Cook on high, stirring occasionally, until liquid has evaporated.

Stir in sherry. Reduce heat to medium. Gradually whisk milk into flour in medium bowl until smooth. Stir into mushroom mixture. Cook for about 10 minutes, stirring occasionally, until boiling and thickened.

Broccoli-Stuffed Pasta Shells

"This recipe is brand new—I've only made it twice. It's really tasty." This filling and satisfying dish needs only a side salad and supper is ready.
— Pat McNeice, Edmonton, Alberta

Jumbo shell pasta (4 oz., 113 g)	20	20
Boiling water	12 cups	3 L
Salt	1 tsp.	5 mL
Ricotta cheese	1 cup	250 mL
Large egg, fork-beaten	1	1
Chopped cooked broccoli	2 cups	500 mL
Grated Monterey Jack cheese	1 cup	250 mL
Chopped onion	1/4 cup	60 mL
Hard margarine (or butter)	1 tbsp.	15 mL
Can of crushed tomatoes	28 oz.	796 mL
Envelope of ranch dressing mix	1 oz.	28 g
Grated Parmesan cheese	1/4 cup	60 mL

Cook pasta in boiling water and salt in large uncovered pot or Dutch oven for 8 to 10 minutes, stirring occasionally, until tender but firm. Drain. Rinse under cold water. Drain well.

Combine ricotta and egg in large bowl. Add broccoli and Monterey Jack cheese. Mix well. Fill each pasta shell with 2 tbsp. (30 mL) broccoli mixture. Set aside.

Sauté onion in margarine in frying pan on medium for about 5 minutes until soft. Remove from heat. Add tomatoes and ranch dressing mix. Mix well. Pour 1/3 of tomato mixture into lightly greased 9 x 13 inch (22 x 33 cm) pan. Spread over bottom. Arrange pasta shells over tomato mixture. Spoon remaining tomato mixture over pasta shells.

Sprinkle with Parmesan cheese. Cover. Bake in 350°F (175°C) oven for 10 minutes. Remove cover. Bake for 25 to 30 minutes until lightly browned and bubbly. Serves 4.

1 serving: 478 Calories; 24.8 g Total Fat; 1234 mg Sodium; 27 g Protein; 39 g Carbohydrate; 4 g Dietary Fibre

Pictured above.

Gently stir in all but 1 cup (250 mL) squash. Add next 4 ingredients. Stir. Makes 5 1/2 cups (1.4 L) sauce.

Grease 10 inch (25 cm) springform pan and layer as follows:

1. 1 cup (250 mL) sauce
2. 3 noodles, cut to fit in a single layer
3. 1 1/2 cups (375 mL) sauce
4. 1/3 cup (75 mL) feta cheese
5. 3 noodles, cut to fit in a single layer
6. 1 1/2 cups (375 mL) sauce
7. 1/3 cup (75 mL) feta cheese
8. 3 noodles, cut to fit in a single layer
9. 1 1/2 cups (375 mL) sauce
10. 1 cup (250 mL) reserved squash
11. 1/3 cup (75 mL) feta cheese

Sprinkle with pepper. Cover with greased foil. Bake in 350°F (175°C) oven for 30 minutes. Remove foil. Bake, uncovered, for about 20 minutes further until heated through. Broil on centre rack for 10 minutes to brown cheese, if desired. Let stand for 10 minutes before cutting. Remove side of pan. Cut into 8 or 10 wedges. Serves 8 to 10.

1 serving: 295 Calories; 9.2 g Total Fat; 638 mg Sodium; 12 g Protein; 42 g Carbohydrate; 4 g Dietary Fibre

Vegetable Shepherd's Pie

"Shepherd's pie is traditionally made with ground lamb. This version is chock full of tomatoes, mushrooms, lentils and so many vegetables you won't think a single thing is missing from this delicious dish."

— Kit Price, Edmonton, Alberta

Large red potatoes, quartered (about 2 3/4 lbs., 1.25 kg)	4	4
Water, to cover		
Salt	1 tsp.	5 mL
Light sour cream	1/3 cup	75 mL
Cooking oil	2 tsp.	10 mL
Medium onion, diced	1	1
Garlic clove, crushed	1	1
Medium carrots, sliced	2	2
Sliced fresh mushrooms	1 cup	250 mL
Medium zucchini, diced	1	1
Can of diced tomatoes, drained	28 oz.	796 mL
Vegetable bouillon cube (1/5 oz., 6 g)	1	1
Can of lentils, rinsed and drained	19 oz.	540 mL
Dried sweet basil	1 tsp.	5 mL
Dried whole oregano	1 tsp.	5 mL
Salt	1/4 tsp.	1 mL
Freshly ground pepper	1/2 tsp.	2 mL
Finely grated Parmesan cheese	3 tbsp.	50 mL

Place first 3 ingredients in large saucepan. Bring to a boil. Cook on medium-high for about 25 minutes until potatoes are tender. Drain well. Mash until no lumps remain.

Add sour cream. Stir until smooth. Cover. Set aside.

Heat cooking oil in large pot or Dutch oven on medium-high. Add next 3 ingredients. Sauté for 5 minutes. Add mushrooms and zucchini. Sauté for 5 minutes until carrot is tender-crisp.

Add next 5 ingredients. Stir. Reduce heat to low. Simmer, uncovered, for about 20 minutes until slightly reduced.

Add salt and pepper. Spoon into lightly greased 3 quart (3 L) ovenproof casserole dish. Spread potatoes over top. Sprinkle with Parmesan cheese. Bake in 350°F (175°C) oven for 35 minutes. Broil 5 inches (12.5 cm) from heat until golden. Serves 8.

1 serving: 173 Calories; 3.2 g Total Fat; 561 mg Sodium; 8 g Protein; 31 g Carbohydrate; 5 g Dietary Fibre

Chili with Vegetables and Mixed Beans

"Beans are one of the whole foods that truly shine in the pressure cooker. Most dry beans can be cooked in 10 minutes or less, and you can substitute any varieties that you have on hand. The green onions and dill add colour and fresh flavour to this vegetarian chili, which is also low in fat. Chop the veggies while the beans cook and your chili will be done in a flash."

— Cinda Chavich, author of *125 Best Pressure Cooker Recipes* (Robert Rose Inc., 2004)

Dried mixed beans (such as red, black, pinto or white kidney beans)	1 1/2 cups	375 mL
Water	5 cups	1.25 L
Small zucchini (about 1 lb., 454 g), cut into 1/2 inch (12 mm) cubes	2	2
Large onion, chopped	1	1
Garlic cloves, minced	4	4
Large red pepper, chopped	1	1
Large yellow pepper, chopped	1	1
Jalapeño pepper, chopped♦	1	1
Olive oil	1/4 cup	60 mL
Can of tomatoes, with juice, puréed	28 oz.	796 mL
Water	1/4 cup	60 mL
Chili powder	2 tbsp.	30 mL
Ground cumin	1 tbsp.	15 mL
Dried sweet basil	1 tbsp.	15 mL
Dried whole oregano	1 tbsp.	15 mL
Fennel seed	2 tsp.	10 mL
Dijon mustard	2 tbsp.	30 mL
Liquid honey	1 tbsp.	15 mL
Chopped fresh dill (or 1 tsp., 5 mL, dried)	1 tbsp.	15 mL
Green onions, chopped	2	2
Salt, to taste		
Freshly ground pepper, to taste		

Place beans in pressure cooker. Cover with water. Lock lid in place. Bring up to pressure on high heat. Cook for 8 minutes. Remove from heat. Allow pressure to drop naturally for 10 minutes. Release steam. Drain. Set beans aside. Clean pressure cooker.

Sauté next 6 ingredients in olive oil in pressure cooker on medium-high for 5 minutes.

Add next 7 ingredients and cooked beans. Lock lid in place. Bring up to pressure on high heat. Reduce heat to medium-just to maintain even pressure. Cook for 7 minutes. Remove from heat. Allow pressure to drop naturally. Remove lid. If beans are not cooked, bring up to pressure for 2 to 3 minutes longer.

Just before serving, add remaining 6 ingredients. Stir. Serves 6 to 8.

1 serving: 365 Calories; 12 g Total Fat; 526 mg Sodium; 16 g Protein; 54 g Carbohydrate; 8 g Dietary Fibre

♦*Wear rubber gloves when chopping jalapeño peppers, and avoid touching your eyes.*

Baked Beans

Jewett family members are free to use as much maple syrup as they want during the year. *"They know where to find the keys to the shed,"* says Howard Jewett. The pale gold, almost spicy syrup produced from their maple trees sweetens these slow-cooked beans. Omit the bacon to make vegetarians happy.

— Anne Jewett-Pagé, Knowlton, Quebec

Dried navy beans (about 2 1/3 cups, 575 mL)	1 lb.	454 g
Water, to cover		
Water	5 cups	1.25 L
Cooking oil	1 tbsp.	15 mL
Bacon slices, chopped	4	4
Chopped onion	1 cup	250 mL
Fancy (mild) molasses	1/2 cup	125 mL
Maple syrup	1/2 cup	125 mL
Dry mustard	1 tsp.	5 mL
Ketchup	1/2 cup	125 mL
Salt	1 tsp.	5 mL
Freshly ground pepper	1/4 tsp.	1 mL

Soak beans in water in large bowl overnight. Drain. Put into large pot or Dutch oven.

Add water and cooking oil. Bring to a boil on high. Cover. Boil hard for 2 minutes. Remove from heat. Let stand, covered, for 1 hour.

Add bacon and onion. Bring to a boil on medium-high, stirring occasionally. Reduce heat to medium-low. Cover. Simmer for about 40 minutes, stirring occasionally, until beans are just softened. Transfer to lightly greased 3 quart (3 L) casserole dish.

Combine remaining 6 ingredients in medium bowl. Add to bean mixture. Stir. Cover. Bake in 300°F (150°C) oven for 4 to 4 1/2 hours, adding more water as needed to keep beans covered in liquid, until beans are dark brown and soft. Makes 6 cups (1.5 L).

1/2 cup (125 mL): 263 Calories; 5.2 g Total Fat; 382 mg Sodium; 10 g Protein; 46 g Carbohydrate; 7 g Dietary Fibre

Pictured below.

Veggie Burgers with Chili Cream Sauce

If you think veggie burgers lack zip, try these patties. They're big on colour and flavour. The spicy sauce is a snap to make and gives them even more appeal.

Can of chick peas (garbanzo beans)	19 oz.	540 mL
Fresh bread crumbs	2/3 cup	150 mL
Chopped fresh parsley	1/4 cup	60 mL
Lemon juice	2 tbsp.	30 mL
Mild curry powder	1 tbsp.	15 mL
Large egg	1	1
Hamburger buns, split	4	4
Sweet chili sauce	1/4 cup	60 mL
Light sour cream	1/4 cup	60 mL
Shredded spinach leaves, lightly packed	2 cups	500 mL
Large red onion, thinly sliced	1	1
Jar of roasted red peppers, drained and sliced	12 oz.	340 mL

Preheat grill to medium-high. Combine first 6 ingredients in blender or food processor. Process until almost smooth. Divide and shape into 4 patties, about 4 inches (10 cm) across. Grill for 3 to 4 minutes per side until browned

Place buns, cut sides down, on grill. Toast until lightly browned.

Combine chili sauce and sour cream in small bowl. Spread on bottom half of buns.

Layer with patties and remaining 3 ingredients in order given. Top with other half of buns. Makes 4 burgers.

1 burger: 438 Calories; 7.7 g Total Fat; 971 mg Sodium; 17 g Protein; 77 g Carbohydrate; 3 g Dietary Fibre

Pictured on page 65.

Couscous and Roasted Vegetables with Yogurt, page 121

Baked Beans, above

Photo by: Ian Grant

Couscous and Roasted Vegetables with Yogurt

Vibrant colour, great texture and big flavour make this dish impressive enough to serve on its own as a hearty meatless main course or as the perfect accompaniment to chicken, lamb or pork. Look for dark orange yams or sweet potatoes to contrast with the purple of the beets.

Medium carrots, peeled and quartered	4	4
Medium red onion, cut into 8 wedges	1	1
Yam (or sweet potato), peeled and cut into 1 inch (2.5 cm) pieces (about 3 cups, 750 mL)	1 1/2 lbs.	680 g
Olive (or cooking) oil	2 tbsp.	30 mL
Ground cumin	2 tsp.	10 mL
Garlic cloves, bruised◆	4	4
Salt	1 tsp.	5 mL
Freshly ground pepper	1 tsp.	5 mL
Large beets, scrubbed clean and trimmed◆◆	3	3
Chicken broth	1 1/2 cups	375 mL
Couscous	1 1/2 cups	375 mL
Olive (or cooking) oil	2 tbsp.	30 mL
Lemon juice	2 tbsp.	30 mL
Brown sugar, packed	2 tsp.	10 mL
Salt	1/2 tsp.	2 mL
Freshly ground pepper	1/2 tsp.	2 mL
Can of chickpeas (garbanzo beans), drained and rinsed	19 oz.	540 mL
Plain yogurt	1 cup	250 mL
Chopped fresh cilantro	1/4 cup	60 mL

Combine first 8 ingredients in large bowl. Arrange mixture in single layer on lightly greased baking sheet with sides. Wrap beets in foil. Bake beets and vegetable mixture in 375°F (190°C) oven for about 1 hour until vegetables are lightly browned and beets are tender. Set aside roasted vegetables. Remove foil and peel beets. Cut each beet into 8 wedges. Set aside in separate bowl.

Bring broth to a boil in large saucepan. Remove from heat. Add couscous and olive oil. Stir. Cover. Let stand for 5 minutes. Fluff with fork.

Add next 5 ingredients. Stir. Combine roasted vegetables and couscous mixture in large serving bowl. Add beets. Do not stir, as beets will colour the mixture.

Combine yogurt and cilantro in small bowl. Drizzle over top. Serves 6 to 8 as a main course or 10 to 12 as an accompaniment.

1 serving (main course): 562 Calories; 12.1 g Total Fat; 994 mg Sodium; 17 g Protein; 98 g Carbohydrate; 11 g Dietary Fibre

Pictured above.

Crea...

Change th...
in the pack...
couscous, a...
and you've ...
some flavou...
started.

Apple Cranberry
apple juice
butter
chopped dried cranberries
chopped walnuts

Pine Nut Orange
orange juice
olive oil
ground cumin
pine nuts
chopped dried apple
orange zest

Balsamic Roasted Pepper
chicken broth
olive oil
chopped roasted peppers
sliced red onions
dash of balsamic vinegar
chopped fresh parsley

Minted Almond
water
butter
toasted sliced almonds
currants rehydrated in orange juice
chopped fresh mint and cilantro

Chili Mushroom
vegetable broth
olive oil
chopped red chili peppers
sautéed sliced mushrooms
chopped fresh tomatoes

◆To bruise garlic, press with flat side of knife blade until flattened slightly. This releases the flavour while leaving the garlic whole.

◆◆To prevent hands from staining, wear rubber gloves while handling beets.

...o, Basil and Garlic ...hin-Crust Pizza

...sting the tomato, onion and garlic intensifies their flavours and makes for a delicious sauce. If you like, garnish the pizza with more fresh basil leaves.

THIN-CRUST DOUGH

Active dry yeast	2 tsp.	10 mL
Granulated sugar	1/4 tsp.	1 mL
Warm water	1/4 cup	60 mL
Large egg	1	1
All-purpose flour	1 cup	250 mL
Salt	1/2 tsp.	2 mL
All-purpose flour, approximately	1/4 cup	60 mL

TOPPING

Large Roma (plum) tomatoes, quartered	2	2
Small onion, cut into 6 wedges	1	1
Garlic cloves, unpeeled	4	4
Salt	1/2 tsp.	2 mL
Freshly ground pepper	1/4 tsp.	1 mL
Granulated sugar	1 tsp.	5 mL
Olive (or cooking) oil	1 tbsp.	15 mL
Balsamic (or red wine) vinegar	2 tsp.	10 mL
Garlic cloves, thinly sliced	2	2
Large Roma (plum) tomatoes, cut into 1/8 inch (3 mm) thick slices	2	2
Fresh sweet basil leaves, torn	1/4 cup	60 mL
Finely grated Parmesan cheese	2/3 cup	150 mL

Thin-Crust Dough: Combine first 3 ingredients in small bowl. Cover. Let stand in warm place for 10 minutes. Stir to dissolve yeast.

Add egg. Whisk to combine.

Combine flour and salt in large bowl. Stir in yeast mixture. Mix until dough just comes together. Turn out onto lightly floured surface. Knead for about 5 minutes, adding second amount of flour, 1 tbsp. (15 mL) at a time, until smooth and elastic. Place dough in large greased bowl, turning once to grease top. Cover with greased waxed paper and tea towel. Let stand in warm place for about 1 hour until doubled in bulk.

Topping: Combine first 7 ingredients in small bowl. Turn out onto baking sheet with sides.

Bake in 350°F (175°C) oven for about 30 minutes, stirring once, until vegetables are softened. Cool slightly. Squeeze flesh from garlic cloves. Discard skins.

Put roasted vegetables into food processor. Add vinegar. Process until smooth. Set aside.

Turn out dough onto lightly floured surface. Shape into a ball. Roll out or press in lightly greased 12 inch (30 cm) pizza pan. Spread tomato mixture evenly over crust to within 1/2 inch (12 mm) of edge. Top with next 3 ingredients. Sprinkle Parmesan cheese over top. Bake in 500°F (260°C) oven for about 15 minutes until crust is golden and crispy. Cuts into 8 wedges.

1 wedge: 211 Calories; 5.6 g Total Fat; 477 mg Sodium; 9 g Protein; 31 g Carbohydrate; 2 g Dietary Fibre

Pictured on page 112.

Mushroom, Spinach and Goat Cheese Pizza

Anyone who thinks they don't like mushrooms or spinach will change their tune after one bite of this pizza.

WHOLE WHEAT CRUST DOUGH

Active dry yeast (or 1/4 oz., 8 g, envelope)	2 1/4 tsp.	11 mL
Granulated sugar	1/2 tsp.	2 mL
Warm water	3/4 cup	175 mL
All-purpose flour, approximately	1 1/4 cups	300 mL
Whole wheat flour	1/2 cup	125 mL
Salt	3/4 tsp.	4 mL
Finely grated Parmesan cheese	1/2 cup	125 mL

TOPPING

Butter (or hard margarine)	1 tbsp.	15 mL
Olive (or cooking) oil	1 tbsp.	15 mL
Sliced brown (cremini) mushrooms (about 12 1/2 oz., 350 g)	5 cups	1.25 L
Balsamic (or red wine) vinegar	1 tbsp.	15 mL
Chopped fresh oregano leaves (or 3/4 tsp., 4 mL, dried)	1 tbsp.	15 mL
Goat cheese, chopped	4 1/2 oz.	125 g
Baby spinach leaves, packed	1 1/2 cups	375 mL
Walnuts, coarsely chopped	1/3 cup	75 mL
Finely grated Parmesan cheese	1/2 cup	125 mL

Whole Wheat Crust Dough: Combine first 3 ingredients in small bowl. Cover. Let stand in warm place for 10 minutes. Stir to dissolve yeast.

Combine next 3 ingredients in large bowl. Stir in yeast mixture and Parmesan cheese. Mix, adding more all-purpose flour as needed, until dough just comes together. Turn out onto lightly floured surface. Knead for about 5 minutes, adding little or no extra flour, until smooth and elastic. Place dough in large greased bowl, turning once to grease top. Cover with greased waxed paper and tea towel. Let stand in warm place for about 1 hour until doubled in bulk.

Topping: Heat butter and olive oil in large frying pan on medium-high. Add mushrooms. Sauté for 5 to 7 minutes, stirring occasionally, until browned and liquid from mushrooms has evaporated. Reduce heat to low.

Add vinegar, oregano and 1/2 of goat cheese. Stir until cheese is melted. Remove from heat.

Turn out dough onto lightly floured surface. Shape into a ball. Roll out or press in lightly greased 12 inch (30 cm) pizza pan. Spread mushroom mixture evenly over crust to within 1/2 inch (12 mm) of edge. Top with spinach and walnuts. Sprinkle Parmesan cheese and remaining goat cheese over top. Bake in 500°F (260°C) oven for 15 to 18 minutes until crust is golden and crispy. Cuts into 8 wedges.

1 wedge: 301 Calories; 15.6 g Total Fat; 576 mg Sodium; 15 g Protein; 27 g Carbohydrate; 3 g Dietary Fibre

Dough Notes

- If a light, crisp and slightly chewy pizza crust is the goal, the dough is the starting point. Use all-purpose or bread flour, which are higher in gluten, for the best results.

- For a tender crust, try to use little or no extra flour during kneading.

- Dough can be made a day ahead, covered and stored in the refrigerator. Let it come to room temperature before shaping and finishing with toppings.

- You can double these dough recipes with no problem.

Tortellini and Vegetables in Creamy Wine Sauce

Make this a meal with a tossed salad and slices of garlic bread.

Package of fresh three-cheese tortellini	12 1/3 oz.	350 g
Boiling water	8 cups	2 L
Salt	2 tsp.	10 mL
Olive (or cooking) oil	1 tbsp.	15 mL
Garlic cloves, crushed	2	2
Medium red peppers, cut into 1/2 inch (12 mm) pieces	2	2
Medium yellow peppers, cut into 1/2 inch (12 mm) pieces	2	2
Medium red onion, cut into 1/2 inch (12 mm) pieces	1	1
Dry white (or alcohol-free) wine	1/2 cup	125 mL
Half-and-half cream	1 cup	250 mL
Finely grated lemon zest	1 tsp.	5 mL
Chopped fresh parsley	1/3 cup	75 mL
Salt	1/2 tsp.	2 mL
Freshly ground pepper	1/2 tsp.	2 mL
Chopped fresh sweet basil	1/4 cup	60 mL
Freshly grated Parmesan cheese	1/3 cup	75 mL

Cook tortellini in boiling water and first amount of salt in large uncovered pot or Dutch oven for 8 to 10 minutes, stirring occasionally, until tender but firm. Drain well. Return to pot.

While tortellini is cooking, heat olive oil in large frying pan or wok on medium-high. Add next 4 ingredients. Sauté for about 5 minutes until onion is softened.

Add next 6 ingredients. Stir. Bring to a boil on medium-high. Boil for about 5 minutes to blend flavours.

Add basil and vegetable mixture to cooked tortellini. Heat and stir for about 3 minutes until tortellini is coated.

Sprinkle Parmesan cheese over individual servings. Makes about 8 cups (2 L).

cup (250 mL): 225 Calories; 11.9 g Total Fat; 366 mg Sodium; 0 g Protein; 18 g Carbohydrate; 1 g Dietary Fibre

Pictured at right.

Penne Fagioli

Pasta with fagioli (fa-ZHOH-lee), or beans, is a traditional Tuscan favourite that's easy to make at home using canned beans and broth. *Buon appetito!*

Butter (or hard margarine)	3 tbsp.	50 mL
Chopped onion	1 cup	250 mL
Garlic cloves, crushed	3	3
Chopped fresh mushrooms	1 1/2 cups	375 mL
Cooked or canned navy beans	1 cup	250 mL
Can of condensed chicken (or vegetable) broth	10 oz.	284 mL
Salt	1/2 tsp.	2 mL
Freshly ground pepper	1 tsp.	5 mL
Whipping cream	1/2 cup	125 mL
Penne pasta	2 1/2 cups	625 mL
Boiling water	12 cups	3 L
Salt	1 tsp.	5 mL
Chopped fresh parsley	1/4 cup	60 mL
Freshly grated Parmesan cheese	3/4 cup	175 mL

Heat butter in large frying pan on medium. Add onion and garlic. Sauté for about 5 minutes until onion is softened.

Add mushrooms. Sauté for 3 to 4 minutes until liquid from mushrooms has evaporated.

Add next 4 ingredients. Bring to a boil on medium-high. Reduce heat to medium-low. Simmer, uncovered, for 10 minutes, stirring occasionally.

Add whipping cream. Simmer, uncovered, for 5 minutes until reduced slightly. Remove from heat.

Cook pasta in boiling water and second amount of salt in large uncovered pot or Dutch oven for 10 to 12 minutes, stirring occasionally, until tender but firm. Drain well. Transfer to serving bowl.

Add bean mixture and parsley to pasta. Toss. Sprinkle with Parmesan cheese. Serves 4.

1 serving: 641 Calories; 27.2 g Total Fat; 1363 mg Sodium; 27 g Protein; 73 g Carbohydrate; 6 g Dietary Fibre

Tortellini and Vegetables in Creamy Wine Sauce, left

Soy-and-Lime-Glazed Turkey

"Choose a turkey based on the number of people you're feeding, but ensure it's small enough that the lid of the barbecue can close when the turkey is sitting on the grill. Oven-roasted turkeys take about 20 minutes per pound, but I find barbecued turkey cooks much faster—I usually figure on 10 to 15 minutes per pound, on high, if it's a hot day with little wind. I use the indirect cooking method that leaves all the burners on, with liquid in the drip pan under the turkey."

— Cliff Higuchi, Edmonton, Alberta

SOY AND LIME GLAZE

Olive oil	1/3 cup	75 mL
Soy sauce	1/3 cup	75 mL
Juice of 2 limes		

Whole turkey, pan ready	10-12 lbs.	5-5.5 kg
Salt	1 tsp.	5 mL
Pepper	1 tsp.	5 mL
Poultry seasoning	1 tsp.	5 mL
Garlic powder	1 tsp.	5 mL

Soy and Lime Glaze: Mix first 3 ingredients in small bowl.

Remove grills from barbecue. Put drip pan (large enough to extend the width and length of turkey) on top of ceramic bricks or lava rocks. Fill pan with water 1 1/2 to 2 inches (3.8 to 5 cm) deep. Replace grills. Preheat grill to high. Sprinkle turkey with remaining 4 ingredients. To keep turkey from sticking to grill, place a small piece of ungreased foil (about 5 inches, 12.5 cm, square) on grill over drip pan. Place turkey on foil square. Close lid and cook, using indirect cooking (see Indirectly Speaking, page 67), for 2 to 2 1/2 hours until thermometer inserted in thigh reads 180°F (82°C). Baste with glaze about 3 times during last hour of cooking. To avoid flare-ups, add water to drip pan as needed. Let turkey stand for 15 minutes before carving. Serves 8 to 10

1 serving: 734 Calories; 38.8 g Total Fat; 1233 mg Sodium; 86 g Protein; 6 g Carbohydrate; 1 g Dietary Fibre

Pictured above.

Variation: Add a smoked flavour to the turkey by using wood chips (cherry or apple wood) in a barbecue smoker box. Soak wood chips first, according to package directions.

Sweet Heat Peanut Chicken

With a little crunch from the peanut butter and some heat from the sweet chili sauce, this dish was made for the barbecue. If your grill is large enough, start cooking the chicken, then add Vegetable Skewers with Pesto Dressing, page 182. If you can only fit one or the other on, cook the chicken first, then cover and keep it warm while grilling the vegetables.

Crunchy peanut butter	1/3 cup	75 mL
Sweet chili sauce	1/4 cup	60 mL
Lime juice	2 tbsp.	30 mL
Garlic cloves, crushed	2	2
Finely grated gingerroot	1 tsp.	5 mL
Water	3 tbsp.	50 mL
Skinless chicken breast halves, bone-in	6	6

Combine first 6 ingredients in large bowl. Makes 1 cup (250 mL) sauce.

Preheat grill to medium. Add chicken to sauce. Mix to coat well. Cook chicken on greased grill for about 20 minutes, turning often, until no longer pink. Serves 6.

1 serving: 260 Calories; 10 g Total Fat; 236 mg Sodium; 35 g Protein; 7 g Carbohydrate; 2 g Dietary Fibre

Pictured at right.

Chicken and Sweet Pepper Ragout

Boneless, skinless chicken thighs are rich and tender in this colourful dish that's perfect to serve, cacciatore-style, over pasta. Make it in the fall when bell peppers are plentiful and inexpensive in the local markets. Or substitute a large jar of sliced roasted peppers—just stir them in after you release the steam."

– Cinda Chavich, author of *125 Best Pressure Cooker Recipes* (Robert Rose Inc., 2004)

Boneless, skinless chicken thighs	3 lbs.	1.4 kg
Butter	1 tbsp.	15 mL
Olive oil	1 tbsp.	15 mL
Garlic cloves, peeled	8	8
Thick slices of double-smoked (or European) bacon (about 4 oz., 113 g), julienned♦	4	4
Brandy (or cognac)	2 tbsp.	30 mL
Dry white wine	1/2 cup	125 mL
Bay leaf	1	1
Italian seasoning	1 tbsp.	15 mL
Medium onions, quartered and sliced	2	2
Medium ripe tomatoes, seeded and chopped (or can of crushed tomatoes, 14 oz., 398 mL, size)	3	3
Medium red pepper, sliced	1	1
Medium green pepper, sliced	1	1
Medium yellow pepper, sliced	1	1
Salt, to taste		
Freshly ground pepper, to taste		
Water	1/4 cup	60 mL
Cornstarch	2 - 3 tbsp.	30 - 50 mL

Cut each chicken thigh into 2 or 3 pieces. Heat butter and olive oil in pressure cooker on medium-high. Cook chicken, in batches, with garlic and bacon until chicken is browned. Remove to large bowl. Set aside. Drain all but 2 tsp. (10 mL) drippings from pressure cooker.

Add brandy. Stir to loosen any browned bits from pressure cooker. Add next 10 ingredients. Add chicken mixture. Stir. Lock lid in place. Bring up to pressure on medium-high. Reduce heat to medium-low, just to maintain even pressure. Cook for 12 minutes. Release pressure. Check to ensure chicken is tender. Remove and discard bay leaf.

Stir water into cornstarch in small bowl until smooth. Gradually stir into chicken mixture. Bring to a boil. Reduce heat to medium. Heat and stir for 1 to 2 minutes until thickened. Serves 4 to 6.

1 serving: 653 Calories; 35 g Total Fat; 674 mg Sodium; 50 g Protein; 26 g Carbohydrate; 4 g Dietary Fibre

♦*To julienne, cut into thin slices, then cut each slice into thin strips.*

Vegetable Skewers with Pesto Dressing, page 182

Sweet Heat Peanut Chicken, this page

Chicken with Sage and Cherries

"When it comes to cherries, fresh may be best, but this recipe can also be made with canned sweet or sour cherries. It's nice to be able to enjoy this dish even when fresh cherries aren't in season."
— Christine Dendy, Kelowna, British Columbia

All-purpose flour	1/2 cup	125 mL
Salt	1/2 tsp.	2 mL
Pepper	1/4 tsp.	1 mL
Boneless, skinless chicken breast halves (about 1 lb., 454 g)	4	4
Hard margarine (or butter)	2 tbsp.	30 mL
Garlic clove, crushed	1	1
Shallots, minced	2	2
Sour cherry juice (or chicken broth)	1/2 cup	125 mL
Sour cherries, pitted and coarsely chopped♦	1/2 cup	125 mL
Brown sugar, packed	1 tsp.	5 mL
Finely chopped fresh sage	1 tbsp.	15 mL

Combine first 3 ingredients in shallow dish. Dredge chicken in flour mixture until well coated.

Melt margarine in non-stick frying pan. Add chicken. Cover. Cook on medium-high for about 6 minutes until browned.

Turn chicken over. Add garlic and shallots. Cover. Cook for 6 minutes until chicken is no longer pink. Remove and keep warm.

Add cherry juice and cherries to same frying pan. Add brown sugar. Add sage. Simmer for 8 minutes until thickened. Spoon over chicken. Serves 4.

1 serving: 289 Calories; 7.9 g Total Fat; 369 mg Sodium; 28 g Protein; 26 g Carbohydrate; 1 g Dietary Fibre

Pictured below.

♦As we weren't able to get fresh cherries for testing, we used the sour cherry version of Christine's recipe. If canned sweet cherries or fresh are used, Christine recommends adding brown sugar and/or lemon juice to taste.

Butterflied Herb Chicken

Butterflying the bird ensures that the meat cooks evenly and quickly. Once you taste how good chicken is prepared in this fashion, you may never barbecue it any other way!

Whole roasting chicken	4 lbs.	1.8 kg
Hard margarine (or butter), softened	2 tbsp.	30 mL
Prepared grainy mustard	1 tbsp.	15 mL
Chopped fresh sweet basil	2 tbsp.	30 mL
Chopped fresh parsley	2 tbsp.	30 mL
Salt	1/2 tsp.	2 mL
Freshly ground pepper	1/2 tsp.	2 mL

Place chicken, breast side down, on cutting board. Using kitchen shears or sharp knife, cut down both sides of backbone to remove. Turn chicken, skin side up. Press chicken out flat.

Combine remaining 6 ingredients in small bowl. Carefully loosen, but do not remove, skin. Stuff margarine mixture between flesh and skin, spreading mixture as evenly as possible. Preheat grill to medium. Place chicken, skin side down, on greased grill over drip pan. Close lid. Cook, using indirect cooking method (see Indirectly Speaking, page 67), for 45 minutes. Turn chicken. Cook for 40 to 45 minutes until meat thermometer inserted in breast reads 180°F (82°C). Cut into serving size pieces. Serves 4 to 6.

1 serving: 483 Calories; 30.3 g Total Fat; 564 mg Sodium; 49 g Protein; 1 g Carbohydrate; trace Dietary Fibre

Coq au Vin

In place of the whole chicken called for in the original French recipe, we're using economical and flavourful chicken thighs. Any good dry red wine delivers great results. This dish tastes even better if made a day ahead of serving. Coq au Vin can be made up to the point where the mushrooms are added, then chilled for up to one day in a sealable container. To finish the dish, place in large pot or Dutch oven. Cover. Heat on low for about 30 minutes, stirring several times during cooking, then continue with the recipe.

All-purpose flour	3 tbsp.	50 mL
Salt	1/2 tsp.	2 mL
Boneless, skinless chicken thighs	16	16
Olive (or cooking) oil	1 tbsp.	15 mL
Olive (or cooking) oil	1 tbsp.	15 mL
Medium onions, thickly sliced	2	2
Garlic cloves, crushed	4	4
Bacon slices, chopped	4	4
Bay leaves	2	2
Chopped fresh thyme leaves (or 3/4 tsp., 4 mL, dried)	1 tbsp.	15 mL
Red (or alcohol-free) wine	1 cup	250 mL
Prepared chicken broth	1 cup	250 mL
Olive (or cooking) oil	1 tbsp.	15 mL
Small mushrooms, halved	9 oz.	255 g

Chicken with Sage and Cherries, above

Combine flour and salt in resealable plastic bag. Add chicken. Toss to coat.

Heat first amount of olive oil in large pot or Dutch oven on medium-high. Cook chicken, in 2 batches, for about 4 minutes per side, until lightly browned. Remove from pot. Set aside.

Heat second amount of olive oil in same pot on medium-high. Add onion and garlic. Sauté for about 5 minutes until onion is softened.

Add bacon. Fry for about 10 minutes until bacon is crisp.

Add chicken. Add next 4 ingredients. Mix well. Reduce heat to low. Cover. Simmer for 1 hour. Remove and discard bay leaves.

Heat last amount of olive oil in large frying pan on medium-high. Add mushrooms. Sauté for 5 to 8 minutes until lightly browned. Add to chicken mixture. Cook, uncovered, on medium for about 15 minutes until sauce is slightly thickened. Serves 8 to 10.

1 serving: 285 Calories; 13.8 g Total Fat; 305 mg Sodium; 27 g Protein; 7 g Carbohydrate; 1 g Dietary Fibre

Pictured on page 108.

Curry Yogurt Chicken with Tomato Salsa

The best thing about curry is layer upon layer of flavour, and this recipe is a perfect example. Easy and delicious.

Mild curry paste (available in Asian section of grocery store)	1/4 cup	60 mL
Plain yogurt	1/2 cup	125 mL
Boneless, skinless chicken breast halves (about 1 lb., 454 g)	4	4

TOMATO SALSA

Finely chopped seeded tomato	2 cups	500 mL
Chopped red onion (about 1 small)	1/2 cup	125 mL
Chopped fresh cilantro	1 tbsp.	15 mL
Lime juice	1/2 tbsp.	7 mL
Olive oil	2 tsp.	10 mL
Garlic clove, crushed	1	1
Salt	1/4 tsp.	1 mL

Preheat grill to medium. Combine curry paste and yogurt in large bowl. Add chicken. Stir to coat chicken. Grill chicken for 4 to 6 minutes per side until tender.

Grilled Spiced Chicken, below.

Tomato Salsa: Combine all 7 ingredients in medium bowl. Makes 3 cups (750 mL) salsa. Serve with chicken. Serves 4.

1 serving: 368 Calories; 13.7 g Total Fat; 261 mg Sodium; 50 g Protein; 10 g Carbohydrate; 2 g Dietary Fibre

Chicken and Avocado Burgers

A wonderful alternative to beef, these full-flavoured chicken burgers provide a fast, easy supper everyone will enjoy.

Boneless, skinless chicken breast halves (about 1 1/2 lbs., 680 g)	6	6
Ciabatta (or hamburger) buns, split	6	6
Sour cream	1/3 cup	75 mL
Prepared grainy mustard	2 tbsp.	30 mL
Gouda cheese slices, cut in half	6	6
Medium tomatoes, sliced	2	2
Medium ripe avocados, peeled, pitted and sliced	2	2

Preheat grill to medium-high. Lightly pound chicken until 1/2 inch (12 mm) thick. Grill for about 7 minutes per side until juices run clear.

Place buns, cut sides down, on grill. Toast until lightly browned.

Combine sour cream and mustard in small bowl. Spread on bottom and top half of buns.

Place chicken on bottom half of buns. Layer with remaining 3 ingredients in order given. Top with other half of buns. Makes 6 burgers.

1 burger: 506 Calories; 23.5 g Total Fat; 424 mg Sodium; 43 g Protein; 31 g Carbohydrate; 2 g Dietary Fibre

Pictured on page 65.

Grilled Spiced Chicken

"Every Caribbean cook boasts the best secret mix of herbs and spices for jerked meats. Jerking is the traditional Caribbean way of preserving meat."
— Jennifer Cockrall-King, Edmonton, Alberta

Garlic cloves	4	4
Green onions, chopped	4	4
Green curry paste	2 tbsp.	30 mL
Fresh thyme leaves	1 tbsp.	15 mL
Ground nutmeg	1/2 tsp.	2 mL
Finely grated lime zest	1 tsp.	5 mL
Cooking oil	1/4 cup	60 mL
Boneless, skinless chicken breast halves (about 1 1/2 lbs., 680 g)	6	6
Freshly squeezed lime juice (about 2 small)	1/4 cup	60 mL

Combine first 7 ingredients in blender or food processor. Process until paste-like consistency.

Rub garlic mixture on all sides of chicken. Place chicken in shallow dish. Cover. Chill for 6 hours or overnight.

Add lime juice. Mix well. Preheat grill to high. Grill chicken for 7 to 8 minutes per side, brushing with any remaining paste, until tender. Serves 6.

1 serving: 268 Calories; 13.9 g Total Fat; 2 mg Sodium; 32 g Protein; 3 g Carbohydrate; trace Dietary Fibre

Pictured above.

Pineapple and Coconut Chicken

Don't shy away from the adventurous blend of flavours in this dish. You won't believe the wonderful taste of lemon grass, pineapple and spicy curry in a creamy coconut milk sauce. A terrific special occasion taste that's great any day.

Cooking oil	1 tbsp.	15 mL
Garlic cloves, crushed	2	2
Freshly grated gingerroot	1 tsp.	5 mL
Red curry paste	2 tbsp.	30 mL
Can of coconut milk	14 oz.	400 mL
Lemon grass stalk (white part only), cut in half crosswise	1	1
Water	1/3 cup	75 mL
Fish sauce	1 tsp.	5 mL
Brown sugar, packed	2 tsp.	10 mL
Freshly squeezed lime juice	2 tsp.	10 mL
Salt	1/2 tsp.	2 mL
Boneless, skinless chicken breast halves (about 6), cut into cubes	1 1/2 lbs.	680 g
Can of pineapple chunks, drained	14 oz.	398 mL
Green onions, cut into 1 inch (2.5 cm) pieces	6	6

Heat cooking oil in large wok or frying pan. Add next 3 ingredients. Cook on high for 1 minute, stirring constantly, until fragrant.

Add next 7 ingredients. Simmer, uncovered, on medium-high for about 10 minutes until thickened. Remove and discard lemon grass.

Add chicken and pineapple. Simmer, uncovered, on medium for 5 to 7 minutes until chicken is no longer pink.

Stir in green onions. Serves 6.

1 serving: 347 Calories; 20.1 g Total Fat; 267 mg Sodium; 33 g Protein; 9 g Carbohydrate; 1 g Dietary Fibre

Pictured below.

More Ways with Coconut Milk

Breakfast bonus:
- In pancakes, crepes, waffles and muffins, on its own or mixed with dairy milk
- In omelets or scrambled eggs

A drizzle here, a drop there:
- As an extra smooth and creamy finish for risotto
- Over steamed vegetables with a squeeze of lime juice

Saucy options:
- In an exotic white sauce or salad dressing
- In place of cream in a mushroom sauce for steaks and chops

Asian addition:
- In stir-fries or satay sauce
- In chili-flavoured marinades

Shake things up:
- In a milkshake or fruit smoothie
- With a favourite liqueur

Pineapple and Coconut Chicken, above, with Thai-Style Coconut Rice, page 183

Phyllo-Wrapped Chicken with Port Wine Sauce

"Chicken breasts stuffed with savoury leek filling are wrapped in layers of phyllo, then baked to crisp perfection. Guests will love this dish, especially with the sauce, never guessing it's easy on the waistline."
— Kit Price, Edmonton, Alberta

Cooking oil	I tsp.	5 mL
Thinly sliced leek (white and tender parts only)	I cup	250 mL
Garlic cloves, crushed	2	2
Finely grated orange zest	I tsp.	5 mL
Freshly ground pepper	1/4 tsp.	I mL
Boneless, skinless chicken breast halves (about I lb., 454 g)	4	4
Frozen phyllo pastry sheets, thawed according to package directions	8	8
PORT WINE SAUCE		
Prepared chicken broth	I tbsp.	15 mL
Finely chopped onion	1/2 cup	125 mL
Port	1/2 cup	125 mL
Prepared chicken broth	1/2 cup	125 mL
Red currant jelly	3 tbsp.	50 mL
Salt, to taste		

Heat cooking oil in medium non-stick frying pan on medium-low. Add leek and garlic. Cook for about 10 minutes, stirring occasionally, until leek is softened.

Add orange zest and pepper. Stir. Makes about 3/4 cup (175 mL) filling.

Cut deep pocket into side of each chicken breast almost through to other side. Fill each pocket with 1/4 of filling. Press to seal openings.

Lay 1 pastry sheet on waxed paper or parchment paper on counter. Cover remaining pastry with slightly damp tea towel. Lightly spray pastry sheet with cooking spray. Working quickly, lay second pastry sheet on top. Spray with cooking spray. Repeat with 2 more pastry sheets and cooking spray. Cut pastry in half crosswise. Place 1 stuffed chicken breast 1 inch (2.5 cm) from short end. Fold in each long side, slightly overlapping chicken. Roll up to enclose chicken. Place, seam-side down, on lightly greased baking sheet with sides. Repeat

Phyllo-Wrapped Chicken with Port Wine Sauce, left

with remaining pastry and chicken. Lightly spray chicken parcels with cooking spray. Bake in 400°F (205°C) oven for about 15 minutes until pastry is browned.

Port Wine Sauce: Heat first amount of broth in medium frying pan on medium. Add onion. Cook for 5 minutes until onion is softened.

Add remaining 4 ingredients. Heat and stir until jelly melts. Bring to a boil on medium-high. Boil, uncovered, for about 10 minutes until thickened. Makes 2/3 cup (150 mL). Serve with chicken parcels. Serves 4.

I serving: 401 Calories; 6.9 g Total Fat; 429 mg Sodium; 31 g Protein; 47 g Carbohydrate; I g Dietary Fibre

Pictured above.

Helen's Chicken Satay Stew with Dried Fruit

This *stew*pendous mix of chicken and dried fruit won first prize in our Simmering Stews Contest. Inspired by her mom's curries, Helen created a wonderfully saucy, sweet-savoury dish.
— Helen Yeung, Edmonton, Alberta

Boneless, skinless chicken thighs, cut into I inch (2.5 cm) pieces	I 1/2 lbs.	680 g
Cooking oil (or butter)	I tbsp.	15 mL
Medium onion, chopped	I	I
Garlic cloves, crushed	2	2
Curry paste	2 tsp.	10 mL
Ground coriander	I tsp.	5 mL
Low-sodium prepared chicken broth	I 1/2 cups	375 mL
Can of light coconut milk	14 oz.	398 mL
Light peanut butter	1/3 cup	75 mL
Dried apricots	1/2 cup	125 mL
Dried currants	1/2 cup	125 mL
Brown sugar, packed	3 tbsp.	50 mL
Fish sauce	2 tbsp.	30 mL
Lime juice	2 tbsp.	30 mL
Salt	I tsp.	5 mL
Water	2 tbsp.	30 mL
Arrowroot (or cornstarch)	I tbsp.	15 mL
Chopped fresh cilantro, for garnish		
Crushed dry-roasted peanuts, for garnish		

Spray large non-stick frying pan with cooking spray. Heat on medium-high. Sear chicken until browned on all sides. Remove from pan.

Heat cooking oil in same frying pan on medium. Add onion. Sauté for about 5 minutes until softened. Add garlic. Sauté for 2 minutes until onion is golden.

Add curry paste and coriander. Cook for 1 minute until fragrant.

Add chicken and next 9 ingredients. Stir. Bring to a boil. Reduce heat to medium-low. Cover. Simmer for about 1 hour, stirring occasionally, until chicken is tender.

Stir water into arrowroot in small bowl until smooth. Add to chicken mixture. Heat and stir until boiling and thickened.

Garnish individual servings with cilantro and peanuts. Makes 4 1/2 cups (1.1 L).

I cup (250 mL): 500 Calories; 25 g Total Fat; 1246 mg Sodium; 26 g Protein; 47 g Carbohydrate; 3 g Dietary Fibre

Pictured on page 141.

Deluxe Raspberry Pie with
Butter Pastry, page 254

Potato and Green Bean Salad with
Vinaigrette Dressing, page 161

Leek-and-Ham-Stuffed
Chicken, page 131

Leek-and-Ham-Stuffed Chicken

Now this is a recipe that truly benefits from being made a day in advance of your outing —in fact, we recommend it! When cool, wrap each chicken bundle in foil or arrange on a serving platter and cover tightly.

Leek (white and tender parts only), thinly sliced	1	1
Garlic cloves, crushed	4	4
Cooking oil	1 tbsp.	15 mL
Deli ham, finely chopped (about 3/4 cup, 175 mL)	4 1/2 oz.	128 g
Grated fresh Parmesan cheese	1/3 cup	75 mL
Marinated artichokes, drained and chopped	1/3 cup	75 mL
Salt	1/2 tsp.	2 mL
Large boneless, skinless chicken breast halves (1 1/2 lbs., 680 g)	6	6
All-purpose flour	1/2 cup	125 mL
Seasoned salt	1 tsp.	5 mL
Dry bread crumbs	1 cup	250 mL
Large eggs, fork-beaten	2	2
Cooking oil	1/4 cup	60 mL

Sauté leek and garlic in first amount of cooking oil in large frying pan for 5 minutes until leek is soft.

Add ham. Cook for 2 minutes. Combine leek mixture and next 3 ingredients in medium bowl. Makes 1 1/2 cups (375 mL) stuffing.

Cut deep pocket in side of each chicken breast almost through to other side. Fill each pocket with 1/4 cup (60 mL) stuffing. Secure openings with wooden picks.

Combine flour and seasoned salt in shallow bowl. Place bread crumbs in separate shallow bowl. Dredge chicken in flour mixture. Dip in egg. Coat in bread crumbs. Heat second amount of cooking oil in large frying pan. Cook chicken on medium for 8 minutes per side until golden and tender. Cool. Cover. Chill for about 3 hours until cold. Remove wooden picks. Cut cold chicken into 1 inch (2.5 cm) slices. Serves 6 to 8.

1 serving: 487 Calories; 21.2 g Total Fat; 1001 mg Sodium; 44 g Protein; 28 g Carbohydrate; 2 g Dietary Fibre

Pictured on page 130.

Grilled Satay Chicken Burgers

Flavours from the Thai pantry make these large, stylish chicken patties really tasty. Adding a little Asian or Thai chili sauce to the ingredient mix gives an extra-spicy kick.

Medium carrots	2	2
English cucumber, halved crosswise	1	1
Ground chicken	2 1/2 lbs.	1.1 kg
Dry bread crumbs	1 1/2 cups	375 mL
Chopped fresh cilantro	1/3 cup	75 mL
Satay (or peanut) sauce	2/3 cup	150 mL
Kaiser rolls, split	8	8
Plain yogurt	1 cup	250 mL
Satay (or peanut) sauce	1/3 cup	75 mL

Peel carrots and cucumbers into long thin strips with vegetable peeler. Set aside.

Preheat grill to high. Combine next 3 ingredients in large bowl. Add first amount of satay sauce. Mix well. Shape into 8 patties. Cook on greased grill for 4 to 5 minutes per side until browned and no longer pink inside.

Grill rolls, cut side down, for about 2 minutes until lightly toasted.

Combine yogurt and second amount of satay sauce. Makes 1 1/3 cups (325 mL) sauce. Spread both halves of each roll with sauce. Place patty, carrot and cucumber on bottom roll. Cover with top half of roll. Makes 8 burgers.

1 burger: 653 Calories; 29.1 g Total Fat; 1152 mg Sodium; 39 g Protein; 58 g Carbohydrate; 2 g Dietary Fibre

Pictured below.

Grilled Satay Chicken Burgers, above

Photo by: Bluefish Studios

Crazy Cousin Susan's Caribbean Chicken

"This is the easiest thing in the world to make. Serve chicken with jasmine or coconut rice."
Try this recipe served over our Thai-Style Coconut Rice, page 183.
— KJ MacAlister, Edmonton, Alberta

Tikka masala curry paste♦	2 tbsp.	30 mL
Medium onion, chopped	1	1
Medium green peppers, chopped	2	2
Cans of stewed tomatoes (14 oz., 398 mL, each), with juice, chopped	2	2
Small ripe pineapple, peeled, cored and chopped (about 4 cups, 1 L)	1	1
Boneless, skinless chicken breast halves (about 1 lb., 454 g), chopped	4	4
Salt	1/4 tsp.	1 mL
Pepper, sprinkle		
Medium firm bananas	2	2

Combine first 6 ingredients in large pot or Dutch oven. Bring to a boil. Reduce heat to medium-low. Simmer, uncovered, for about 40 minutes until sauce is thickened.

Add salt and pepper.

Before serving, cut bananas in half lengthwise. Cut each half crosswise into 8 pieces. Add to chicken mixture. Stir. Serves 4 to 6.

1 serving: 368 Calories; 5 g Total Fat; 699 mg Sodium; 30 g Protein; 57 g Carbohydrate; 7 g Dietary Fibre

Pictured below.

♦Substitute with curry paste of your choice.

Crazy Cousin Susan's Caribbean Chicken, above

Roast Turkey with Pear and Walnut Stuffing

Fresh pears provide an unmistakable moistness to this stuffing that also features crunchy, chopped walnuts and fragrant thyme. Take the time to carefully toast the nuts beforehand, as this step adds to the overall flavour and texture of the stuffing. Wonderful with the cranberry-apple gravy.

CRANBERRY BASTE

Cranberry sauce	1/3 cup	75 mL
Apple juice	1/4 cup	60 mL
Butter (or hard margarine), melted	3 tbsp.	50 mL

PEAR AND WALNUT STUFFING

Loaf of unsliced white bread, crust removed	1	1
Medium onion, finely chopped	1	1
Cooking oil	2 tsp.	10 mL
Bacon slices, finely chopped	4	4
Firm pears, peeled and grated	2	2
Raisins, chopped	2/3 cup	150 mL
Walnut halves, toasted and chopped♦	2/3 cup	150 mL
Chopped fresh thyme leaves	2 tbsp.	30 mL
Cranberry sauce	2 tbsp.	30 mL
Salt	1/2 tsp.	2 mL
Freshly ground pepper	1/2 tsp.	2 mL
Whole turkey, pan ready	12 lbs.	5.4 kg
Water	1 cup	250 mL

CRANBERRY GRAVY

All-purpose flour	1/3 cup	75 mL
Brandy (optional!)	1/3 cup	75 mL
Can of condensed chicken broth♦♦	10 oz.	284 mL
Water	1 cup	250 mL
Apple juice	1 cup	250 mL
Cranberry sauce	2/3 cup	150 mL
Salt	1/2 tsp.	2 mL
Freshly ground pepper	1/2 tsp.	2 mL

Cranberry Baste: Combine all 3 ingredients in small bowl. Cover. Set aside.

Pear and Walnut Stuffing: Tear bread into large pieces. Place in blender or food processor. Process until bread forms coarse crumbs.

Clockwise from top: Marmalade-Glazed Yams, page 180; Roast Turkey with Pear and Walnut Stuffing, page 132; Cranberry Sauce with Apricots and Ginger, page 147; Brussels Sprouts and Green Beans in Almond Citrus Butter, page 179

Sauté onion in cooking oil in frying pan on medium for 5 minutes until soft. Add bacon. Fry for about 10 minutes until bacon is crisp and onion is browned. Transfer to large bowl.

Add bread crumbs and next 7 ingredients. Mix well.

Loosely fill both body and neck cavities of turkey with stuffing. Secure with wooden picks or small skewers. Tie legs together. Fold wings behind. Place turkey on wire rack in roasting pan. Pour water into bottom of roasting pan. Cover turkey loosely with greased foil. Roast in 325°F (160°C) oven for 3 hours. Remove foil. Brush with Cranberry Baste. Roast for a further 45 to 60 minutes, brushing with Cranberry Baste several times, until thermometer inserted into thigh reads 180°F (82°C). Transfer turkey to cutting board or serving platter. Remove stuffing to serving dish. Cover to keep warm. Cover turkey with foil. Let stand for 15 minutes before carving.

Cranberry Gravy: Drain pan juices, reserving 2/3 cup (150 mL). Heat 1/2 of reserved pan juices in same roasting pan. Whisk in flour. Heat and stir on medium for 1 to 2 minutes until boiling. Stir in brandy.

Add remaining pan juices and remaining 6 ingredients. Bring to a boil. Reduce heat to medium. Simmer, uncovered, for 15 to 20 minutes, stirring occasionally, until gravy is thickened. Strain. Makes about 3 cups (750 mL) gravy. Serve with stuffing and turkey. Serves 8 to 10.

1 serving: 1258 Calories; 54.5 g Total Fat; 1189 mg Sodium; 113 g Protein; 70 g Carbohydrate; 4 g Dietary Fibre

Pictured above.

◆ To toast walnuts, place them in an ungreased frying pan. Heat on medium, stirring often, until golden.

◆◆If you prefer, omit the condensed chicken broth and water in the gravy and use 2 cups (500 mL) of your own homemade stock.

Photo by: Ian Grant

Glazed Cornish Hens with Apricot Couscous Stuffing

Who says all stuffings have to start with bread crumbs? Couscous is a wonderful alternative and can be combined with no end of interesting ingredients. Vary the fruit and nut component in this recipe by substituting dates and toasted pine nuts. Serve with a simple side dish such as sautéed bell peppers and mushrooms.

APRICOT COUSCOUS STUFFING

Large onion, halved and sliced	1	1
Garlic cloves, crushed	2	2
Olive (or cooking) oil	1 tbsp.	15 mL
Liquid honey	1 tbsp.	15 mL
Chicken broth	1 cup	250 mL
Couscous	1 cup	250 mL
Hard margarine (or butter)	1 tbsp.	15 mL
Cashews, chopped	1/2 cup	125 mL
Dried apricots, finely chopped	1/2 cup	125 mL
Chopped fresh mint leaves	1/4 cup	60 mL
Salt	1/2 tsp.	2 mL
Freshly ground pepper	1/2 tsp.	2 mL
Finely grated orange zest	1 tsp.	5 mL
Cornish game hens, pan ready	4	4

GLAZE

Freshly squeezed orange juice	1/2 cup	125 mL
Liquid honey	3 tbsp.	50 mL
Chili sauce	2 tbsp.	30 mL

Apricot Couscous Stuffing: Sauté onion and garlic in olive oil in large frying pan on medium for about 20 minutes until onion is browned. Remove from heat. Stir in honey.

Bring broth to a boil in medium saucepan. Remove from heat. Add couscous and margarine. Stir. Cover. Let stand for 5 minutes. Fluff with fork. Transfer couscous mixture to large bowl. Add onion mixture.

Add next 6 ingredients. Mix well. Makes 4 cups (1 L) stuffing.

Loosely fill cavity of hen with stuffing. Secure opening with wooden picks or small metal skewers. Tie legs together. Tuck wings behind. Place on greased wire rack in baking pan. Repeat with remaining hens and stuffing.

Glaze: Combine all 3 ingredients in small bowl. Brush hens with glaze. Bake, uncovered, in 375°F (190°C) oven for about 45 minutes, brushing with glaze several times during cooking, until juices run clear. Serve whole or cut hens in half using knife or kitchen shears. Serves 4.

1 stuffed cornish hen: 1096 Calories; 57.4 g Total Fat; 810 mg Sodium; 63 g Protein; 82 g Carbohydrate; 5 g Dietary Fibre

Pictured above.

Orange Spice Chicken Casserole

When the right fruit is paired with the right meat—as in this wonderful winter warmer—it makes for a very satisfying entree. This casserole's slightly spicy sauce has aroma and flavour appeal.

Ground coriander	2 tsp.	10 mL
Ground cumin	2 tsp.	10 mL
Ground ginger	2 tsp.	10 mL
Chili powder	1 tsp.	5 mL
Freshly ground pepper	1 tsp.	5 mL
Ground cinnamon	1/2 tsp.	2 mL
Salt	1/2 tsp.	2 mL
Freshly squeezed orange juice	1 cup	250 mL
Dry white (or alcohol-free) wine	1/2 cup	125 mL
Liquid honey	1/4 cup	60 mL
Olive (or cooking) oil	2 tbsp.	30 mL
Pitted prunes	1 cup	250 mL
Dried apricots, halved	1 cup	250 mL
Pimiento-stuffed olives	1/2 cup	125 mL
Boneless, skinless chicken thighs, halved	2 1/4 lbs.	1 kg
Medium orange, cut into 1/4 inch (6 mm) slices	1	1

Combine first 11 ingredients in small bowl.

Place next 3 ingredients in 3 quart (3 L) casserole. Arrange chicken over top. Pour orange juice mixture over chicken.

Arrange orange slices over chicken. Cover. Bake in 350°F (175°C) oven for 30 minutes.

Remove cover. Bake for 50 minutes, basting twice, until sauce is slightly thickened and chicken is tender. Serves 8.

1 serving: 372 Calories; 11.3 g Total Fat; 390 mg Sodium; 26 g Protein; 43 g Carbohydrate; 4 g Dietary Fibre

Pictured below

Chicken Enchiladas

"Layers of flavour and lots of textures make this low-fat dish a high-scoring hit. Stay on the mild side, or turn up the heat by adding cayenne or dried pepper flakes to the tomato sauce mix."
— **Kit Price, Edmonton, Alberta**

Can of tomato sauce	24 oz.	680 mL
Tomato paste	2 tbsp.	30 mL
Chili powder	1 tbsp.	15 mL
Ground cumin	1 tsp.	5 mL
Dried whole oregano	1 tsp.	5 mL
Garlic clove, crushed	1	1
FILLING		
Boneless, skinless chicken breast halves, cubed (about 1 lb., 454 g)	4	4
Chili powder	1 tbsp.	15 mL
Medium onion, diced	1	1
Green pepper, diced	1/2	1/2
Medium zucchini, diced	1	1
Sliced fresh mushrooms	2 cups	500 mL
Frozen kernel corn	1/2 cup	125 mL
Can of diced green chilies, drained	4 oz.	113 g

Flour tortillas (10 inch, 25 cm, size)	8	8
Grated light Cheddar cheese	1/2 cup	125 mL
Chopped fresh cilantro (optional)	1/4 cup	60 mL

Combine first 6 ingredients in large saucepan. Bring to boil. Reduce heat to medium-low. Simmer, uncovered, for about 20 minutes, stirring occasionally, until thickened. Remove from heat. Set aside.

Filling: Lightly spray large non-stick frying pan with cooking spray. Heat on medium-high. Add chicken and chili powder. Cook, stirring occasionally, for about 5 minutes until chicken is no longer pink. Remove from frying pan. Set aside.

Add onion to same frying pan. Sauté on medium-high for 5 minutes until softened.

Add next 5 ingredients. Heat and stir for 5 minutes until vegetables are softened. Add chicken. Mix well.

Spread 1/2 cup (125 mL) tomato sauce mixture in bottom of lightly greased 9 x 13 inch (22 x 33 cm) pan. Place about 2/3 cup (150 mL) chicken mixture down centre of each tortilla. Roll up to enclose filling. Arrange in single layer, seam-side down, in pan. Pour remaining tomato sauce mixture over top.

Sprinkle with cheese. Cover with foil. Bake in 350°F (175°C) oven for about 30 minutes until heated through.

To serve, sprinkle with cilantro. Serves 4.

1 serving: 79 Calories; 6.9 g Total Fat; 1956 mg Sodium; 49 g Protein; 79 g Carbohydrate; 9 g Dietary Fibre

Orange Rice Pilaf, page 183

Orange Spice Chicken Casserole, above

Roast Duck with Apple Mustard Baste

The naturally rich quality of duck meat pairs well with the sweet-sharp acidity of apples. Both the baste and a side of Apple Relish, page 153, make this a truly wonderful dish. Garnished with fresh herbs, pearl onions and apple wedges, this is also a feast for the eyes.

Apple juice	3/4 cup	175 mL
Brown sugar, packed	1/4 cup	60 mL
Dijon mustard	1 tbsp.	15 mL
Salt	1 tsp.	5 mL
Freshly ground pepper	1 tsp.	5 mL
Whole duck (about 5 lbs., 2.3 kg)	1	1

Combine first 5 ingredients in medium saucepan. Heat and stir on medium until sugar is dissolved. Bring to a boil. Reduce heat to medium-low. Simmer, uncovered, for 5 to 10 minutes until slightly thickened. Set aside.

Remove and discard neck and giblets from cavity of duck. Rinse duck. Pat dry inside and out with paper towels. Place breast-side up on wire rack in roasting pan. Prick skin all over with metal skewer, being careful not to pierce through to flesh. Roast in 300°F (150°C) oven for 1 hour. Brush with apple juice mixture. Roast a further 2 hours, brushing with apple juice mixture several times, until duck is tender and skin is crisp. Meat thermometer inserted into the breast (or thickest part) should register 180°F (82°C). Cover to keep warm. Let stand for 10 minutes before carving. Serve with Apple Relish. Serves 4.

1 serving without skin: 260 Calories; 10.2 g Total Fat; 710 mg Sodium; 21 g Protein; 21 g Carbohydrate; trace Dietary Fibre

Pictured below.

Apple Relish, page 153

Roast Duck with Apple Mustard Baste, above

Grilled Chicken Dijonnaise

"I made this dish for a dinner party . . . It was a hit. Everyone I serve it to constantly asks me for the recipe, so I thought I would share it. My husband, who isn't a great lover of mustard, loves this dish."
— Sabrina Guard, Aurora, Ontario

Cooking oil	1/4 cup	60 mL
Lemon juice	1/4 cup	60 mL
Salt	1/2 tsp.	2 mL
Freshly ground pepper	1/2 tsp.	2 mL
Boneless, skinless chicken breast halves (about 1 lb., 454 g)	4	4

DIJONNAISE SAUCE

White wine vinegar	3 tbsp.	50 mL
Dry white (or alcohol-free) wine	2 1/2 tbsp.	37 mL
Dried tarragon leaves	1/8 tsp.	0.5 mL
Cold butter (or hard margarine), chopped	1/4 cup	60 mL
Dijon mustard	3 tbsp.	50 mL

Combine first 4 ingredients in medium bowl. Add chicken. Turn to coat. Cover. Marinate in refrigerator for 1 1/2 hours. Remove chicken. Discard any leftover marinade. Grill chicken over medium-high heat for 7 to 8 minutes per side until no longer pink inside.

Dijonnaise Sauce: Combine first 3 ingredients in small saucepan. Bring to a boil on high. Reduce heat to medium-low.

Add butter and mustard. Heat and stir for about 3 minutes until butter is melted. Makes about 1/2 cup (125 mL) sauce. Serve drizzled over chicken. Serves 4.

1 serving: 386 Calories; 29.5 g Total Fat; 579 mg Sodium; 26 g Protein; 3 g Carbohydrate; trace Dietary Fibre

Two-Toned Scalloped Potatoes, page 192, with Crisp Basil Leaves, page 192

Walnut-Crumbed Chicken with Mushroom and Peppercorn Sauce, below

Walnut-Crumbed Chicken with Mushroom and Peppercorn Sauce

Tender chicken breast is coated in a crunchy walnut crust filled with spinach, sweet pimiento and artichoke, and finished with a mélange of mushrooms in a red wine peppercorn sauce. Pair it with market-fresh buttered beans and creamy Two-Toned Scalloped Potatoes, page 192. The chicken can be stuffed and crumbed in advance, then stored in a covered plate in the refrigerator until ready to cook.

SPINACH ARTICHOKE STUFFING

Fresh spinach leaves, stems removed, lightly packed (about 3 1/2 oz., 100 g)	2 cups	500 mL
Boiling water		
Jar of sliced pimientos, drained, finely chopped	2 oz.	57 mL
Garlic cloves, crushed	2	2
Finely chopped canned artichoke hearts	1/2 cup	125 mL
Freshly grated Parmesan cheese	1/3 cup	75 mL
Salt	1/4 tsp.	1 mL
Freshly ground pepper	1/4 tsp.	1 mL
Large boneless, skinless chicken breast halves (1 1/3 lbs., 600 g)	4	4

WALNUT CRUMB COATING

Fresh bread crumbs	1 1/4 cups	300 mL
Walnuts, finely chopped	3/4 cup	175 mL
Finely sliced fresh sweet basil	1/4 cup	60 mL
Freshly grated Parmesan cheese	1/4 cup	60 mL
Large eggs	2	2
All-purpose flour	1/2 cup	125 mL
Seasoned salt	1/2 tsp.	2 mL
Cooking oil	3 tbsp.	50 mL

MUSHROOM AND PEPPERCORN SAUCE

Butter (or hard margarine)	2 tbsp.	30 mL
Garlic cloves, crushed	2	2
Fresh mushrooms, sliced (a mix of oyster, brown, button and enoki)	2 cups	500 mL
Red (or alcohol-free) wine	2/3 cup	150 mL
Prepared chicken broth	1/3 cup	75 mL
Green peppercorns in brine, drained and crushed	1 tbsp.	15 mL
Salt	1/4 tsp.	1 mL
Whipping cream (optional)	1 tbsp.	15 mL

Spinach Artichoke Stuffing: Steam spinach in medium saucepan over small amount of boiling water on high until just wilted. Cool slightly. Squeeze dry. Chop. Place in medium bowl.

Add next 6 ingredients. Mix well.

Cut deep pocket in thick portion of chicken breast, almost through to other side. Fill each pocket with 1/4 cup (60 mL) stuffing. Secure with wooden picks.

Walnut Crumb Coating: Combine first 4 ingredients in shallow dish or on waxed paper.

Whisk eggs in shallow bowl. Combine flour and seasoned salt in shallow dish or on waxed paper. Dredge chicken in flour mixture. Dip in egg. Press chicken in bread crumb mixture to coat completely.

Heat cooking oil in large frying pan on medium. Cook chicken, uncovered for about 10 minutes per side until golden and tender. Remove from frying pan. Keep warm.

Mushroom and Peppercorn Sauce: Melt butter in same large frying pan on medium-high. Add garlic and mushrooms. Cook for 3 minutes, stirring occasionally.

Add remaining 5 ingredients. Bring to a boil. Reduce heat to medium. Simmer, uncovered, for about 5 minutes until thickened. Makes 1 cup (250 mL) sauce. Serves 4.

1 serving: 876 Calories; 42.7 g Total Fat; 1527 mg Sodium; 61 g Protein; 59 g Carbohydrate; 8 g Dietary Fibre

Pictured above.

Thai Chicken Pizza

You can make this pizza in no time using a few convenience products and some leftover cooked chicken.

Prebaked pizza crust (12 inch, 30 cm, size)	1	1

TOPPING

Thai peanut sauce	1/3 cup	75 mL
Chopped cooked chicken	1 1/2 cups	375 mL
Can of pineapple tidbits, drained	8 oz.	227 mL
Thinly sliced red onion	1/2 cup	125 mL
Fresh mint leaves, cut chiffonade◆	2 tbsp.	30 mL
Sweet chili sauce	2 tbsp.	30 mL
Grated smoked mozzarella cheese	2/3 cup	150 mL
Fresh bean sprouts	1/2 cup	125 mL
Fresh cilantro leaves	2 tbsp.	30 mL
Diagonally sliced green onion	2 tbsp.	30 mL

Place pizza crust on 12 inch (30 cm) pizza pan.

Topping: Spread peanut sauce evenly over crust to within 1/2 inch (12 mm) of edge. Top with next 4 ingredients. Drizzle chili sauce over all. Sprinkle cheese over top. Bake in 500°F (260°C) oven for about 12 minutes until crust is crispy.

Scatter sprouts, cilantro and green onion over top. Cuts into 8 wedges.

1 wedge: 214 Calories; 7 g Total Fat; 473 mg Sodium; 16 g Protein; 22 g Carbohydrate; 1 g Dietary Fibre

Pictured on this page.

Thai Chicken Pizza, left

◆*To cut chiffonade, stack a few mint leaves at a time, roll up tightly, then slice crosswise into very thin strips.*

Pizza Possibilities

- Prepare topping ingredients while your pizza dough is rising.

- Explore the possibilities: mix and match toppings and crusts. Just remember—use less topping on thinner crusts.

- When the dough is on the pan, gently poke your fingers over the surface to create dimples for the sauce to pool in.

- Don't overload your pizza. If you have too much topping or topping that's too wet, you can end up with a soggy crust.

Saucy Winter Chicken

More and more home cooks are discovering the wonderful versatility of this inexpensive chicken cut that's packed with flavour. Mushrooms, mustard and lemon lend a robust accent to skinless chicken thighs.

Olive (or cooking) oil	1 tbsp.	15 mL
Skinless chicken thighs, with bone (about 2 1/4 lbs., 1 kg)	8	8
Sliced small mushrooms (about 5 oz., 140 g)	2 cups	500 mL
Olive (or cooking) oil	1 tbsp.	15 mL
Medium onions, chopped	2	2
Garlic cloves, crushed	2	2
Celery rib, chopped	1	1
Paprika	2 tsp.	10 mL
Dijon mustard	3 tbsp.	50 mL
Prepared chicken broth	2 cups	500 mL
Chopped fresh parsley	3 tbsp.	50 mL
Finely grated lemon zest	1 tsp.	5 mL
Sour cream	1/3 cup	75 mL
Salt	1/2 tsp.	2 mL
Freshly ground pepper	1/2 tsp.	2 mL
Water	1 tbsp.	15 mL
Cornstarch	2 tsp.	10 mL

Heat first amount of olive oil in large pot or Dutch oven on medium-high. Sear chicken, in 2 batches, for 5 minutes per side until lightly browned. Remove chicken from pot.

Reduce heat to medium. Add mushrooms to same pot. Sauté for about 5 minutes, stirring occasionally, until lightly browned. Remove mushrooms from pot.

Heat second amount of olive oil in same pot on medium. Add next 4 ingredients. Sauté for about 5 minutes, stirring occasionally, until onion is softened.

Add mustard, broth and chicken. Stir. Reduce heat to medium-low. Simmer, uncovered, stirring occasionally, for about 20 minutes, until chicken is tender.

Add mushrooms and next 5 ingredients. Stir. Increase heat to medium-high.

Stir water into cornstarch in small bowl until smooth. Gradually stir into chicken mixture. Heat and stir for 2 to 3 minutes until sauce is slightly thickened. Serves 4.

1 serving: 329 Calories; 18.3 g Total Fat; 886 mg Sodium; 30 g Protein; 12 g Carbohydrate; 2 g Dietary Fibre

Pictured on page 187.

Mediterranean Chicken and Bean Casserole

Baked slowly in a fragrant tomato broth, this nourishing casserole is ideal for a relaxed dinner with friends. Lemon and parsley add a fresh touch.

Dried navy beans (about 2 1/3 cups, 575 mL)	1 lb.	454 g
Water, to cover		
Olive (or cooking) oil	1 tbsp.	15 mL
Bone-in chicken thighs, skin removed	8	8
Chopped onion	2 cups	500 mL
Chopped fennel bulb (or celery)	1 cup	250 mL
Prepared low-sodium chicken broth	3 cups	750 mL
Can of diced tomatoes, with juice	14 oz.	398 mL
Garlic cloves, crushed	6	6
Bay leaves	2	2
Freshly ground pepper	1 tsp.	5 mL
Medium lemon, ends removed, cut into 8 slices	1	1
Chopped fresh parsley	1/2 cup	125 mL
Salt	1 tsp.	5 mL

Soak beans in water in large bowl overnight. Drain. Put into lightly greased 4 quart (4 L) casserole dish.

Heat olive oil in large frying pan on medium-high. Add chicken. Sear until browned on both sides. Remove from frying pan. Set aside.

Add onion and fennel to same frying pan. Sauté for about 5 minutes until onion is softened.

Add onion mixture and next 5 ingredients to beans. Mix well. Nestle chicken into bean mixture.

Place 1 lemon slice over each chicken thigh. Cover. Bake in 350°F (175°C) oven for 3 1/2 hours until beans are softened.

Remove and discard lemon slices and bay leaves. Remove chicken. Add parsley and salt to beans. Stir. Serve with chicken. Serves 8.

1 serving: 343 Calories; 6.7 g Total Fat; 620 mg Sodium; 28 g Protein; 45 g Carbohydrate; 11 g Dietary Fibre

Pictured on front cover and at right.

Duck with Cranberry and Sage

This is a wonderfully festive main course that's so easy to prepare. Make sure to allow yourself enough time to marinate the duck the night before.

Whole duck, (about 5 lbs., 2.3 kg)	1	1
Whole cranberry sauce	1/2 cup	125 mL
White (or alcohol-free) wine	1/2 cup	125 mL
Chopped fresh sage	3 tbsp.	50 mL
Cranberry juice	1 cup	250 mL
Salt	1/2 tsp.	2 mL
Freshly ground pepper	1/2 tsp.	2 mL

Remove and discard neck and giblets from cavity of duck. Rinse duck. Pat dry inside and out with paper towels. Place duck, breast-side down, on cutting board. Using kitchen shears or sharp knife, cut down both sides of backbone. Remove. Turn duck skin-side up. Press out flat. Cut duck into 2 halves through breastbone. Cut each half into 2 pieces. Place in large shallow dish.

Combine remaining 6 ingredients in small bowl. Pour over duck. Stir or turn to coat. Cover. Marinate in refrigerator for 6 hours or overnight, turning several times. Remove meat, reserving marinade. Place duck skin-side up on wire rack in roasting pan. Prick skin all over with metal skewer, being careful not to pierce through to flesh. Roast in 300°F (150°C) oven for about 2 1/2 hours until duck is tender and skin is crisp. Place marinade in large saucepan. Bring to a boil. Boil for about 20 minutes until thickened. Makes 3/4 cup (175 mL) sauce. Serve with duck. Serves 4.

1 serving without skin: 360 Calories; 13.7 g Total Fat; 390 mg Sodium; 29 g Protein; 25 g Carbohydrate; trace Dietary Fibre

Mediterranean Chicken and Bean Casserole, left

Warm Chicken Salad

"Lemon dressing adds a taste of spring to this grilled chicken and vegetable salad."
— Kit Price, Edmonton, Alberta

Liquid honey	3 tbsp.	50 mL
Ground cumin	2 tsp.	10 mL
Water	2 tsp.	10 mL
Salt	1/2 tsp.	2 mL
Freshly ground pepper	1/4 tsp.	1 mL
Boneless, skinless chicken breast halves (about 4)	1 lb.	454 g
Fresh asparagus, trimmed of tough ends, halved	1 lb.	454 g
Boiling water		
Ice water		
Brown (cremini) mushrooms (about 10 1/2 oz., 300 g), sliced	3 cups	750 mL
Balsamic (or red wine) vinegar	1 tbsp.	15 mL
Can of chickpeas (garbanzo beans), drained and rinsed	19 oz.	540 mL

LEMON DRESSING

Freshly squeezed lemon juice	1/3 cup	75 mL
Chopped fresh oregano leaves	1/4 cup	60 mL
Fresh small red chili, finely chopped♦	1	1
Garlic clove, crushed	1	1
Olive (or cooking) oil	2 tbsp.	30 mL
Liquid honey	2 tbsp.	30 mL
Salt	1/4 tsp.	1 mL

Combine first 5 ingredients in small bowl. Place chicken in shallow dish or resealable plastic bag. Pour honey mixture over chicken. Stir or turn to coat. Cover or seal. Marinate in refrigerator for 3 hours or overnight, turning several times. Remove chicken. Cook on greased grill on medium for about 7 minutes per side until no longer pink inside. Cut chicken across grain into 1/4 inch (6 mm) thick slices. Keep warm.

Blanch asparagus in boiling water in large pot or Dutch oven for 3 minutes. Drain. Put asparagus into large bowl of ice water. Let stand for 5 to 7 minutes until cold. Drain.

Heat large non-stick frying pan on medium-high. Add mushrooms and vinegar. Cook for about 5 minutes until mushrooms are lightly browned and liquid is evaporated. Transfer to large serving bowl.

Add asparagus, chicken and chickpeas. Toss.

Lemon Dressing: Combine all 7 ingredients in jar with tight-fitting lid. Shake well. Makes about 2/3 cup (150 mL). Drizzle dressing over salad. Toss. Makes about 9 cups (2.25 L) salad.

1 cup (250 mL): 187 Calories; 4.9 g Total Fat; 265 mg Sodium; 16 g Protein; 22 g Carbohydrate; 2 g Dietary Fibre

Pictured below.

♦Wear gloves when chopping chili peppers, and avoid touching your eyes.

Anise Chicken

Toss steamed snow peas with toasted sesame seeds and add some jasmine rice to the menu for an Asian-inspired meal.

Cooking oil	1 tbsp.	15 mL
Boneless, skinless chicken thighs (about 1 3/4 lbs., 790 g)	8	8
Garlic cloves, crushed	2	2
Finely grated gingerroot	1 tbsp.	15 mL
Chinese cooking wine (or dry sherry)	1 tbsp.	15 mL
Prepared chicken broth	1/4 cup	60 mL
Liquid honey	1/4 cup	60 mL
Low-sodium soy sauce	3 tbsp.	50 mL
Star anise♦	1	1
Freshly ground pepper	1/2 tsp.	2 mL
Water	1 tbsp.	15 mL
Cornstarch	1 1/2 tsp.	7 mL

Heat cooking oil in wok or large frying pan on medium-high. Cook chicken, in 2 batches, for 3 minutes per side until lightly browned. Remove from wok.

Add garlic and ginger to same wok. Sauté for about 1 minute until fragrant.

Add next 6 ingredients. Bring to a boil on high. Reduce heat to medium-high. Add chicken. Cover. Simmer for 10 to 15 minutes until chicken is no longer pink inside. Remove and discard star anise.

Stir water into cornstarch in small bowl until smooth. Stir into chicken mixture. Heat and stir for 1 to 2 minutes until sauce is boiling and thickened. Serves 4.

1 serving: 377 Calories; 14.2 g Total Fat; 345 mg Sodium; 39 g Protein; 22 g Carbohydrate; trace Dietary Fibre

Pictured on page 141.

♦Star anise is a star-shaped spice with a mild licorice flavour. Look for it in grocery, spice and specialty food stores.

Warm Chicken Salad, above

Helen's Chicken Satay Stew
with Dried Fruit, page 129

Anise Chicken,
page 140

Marinades, Sauces & More

Red Wine, Mustard and Garlic Marinade, below

Teriyaki Marinade, page 143

Spice and Herb Marinade, below

Marinating Time

The food: Soaking time varies based on the food group and type of food (for example, more delicate, white-fleshed trout versus firmer, "meatier" salmon). In the case of meat, cut and size are also significant. Experience is the best teacher.

Your goal: Bear in mind your marinating goal: is it flavouring, tenderizing or both? Poultry, fish and seafood, for example, don't need much tenderizing, so flavour is what you're looking for from the marinades.

A general guideline: Marinating times can and should increase as you go from fish and chicken to veal, pork and lamb to beef and game, which need or can handle the longest soak.

Natural tenderness: Some foods might require as little as 15 minutes to absorb flavour; less tender meats might need to marinate overnight.

The marinade: Different ingredient combinations deliver different results. For example, kiwi fruit's enzyme-rich juice is a quick-acting tenderizer. Soy sauce adds flavour but also takes the place of the more common vinegar or wine as a marinade acid.

Red Wine, Mustard and Garlic Marinade

Red wine and mustard are classic marinade partners, especially when teamed with garlic and pepper as in this recipe. Beef, poultry, veal, lamb and game are excellent candidates for this marinade.

Red (or alcohol-free) wine	1 cup	250 mL
Prepared grainy mustard	2 tbsp.	30 mL
Barbecue sauce	2 tbsp.	30 mL
Worcestershire sauce	1 tbsp.	15 mL
Olive (or cooking) oil	1 tbsp.	15 mL
Garlic cloves, crushed	4	4
Freshly ground pepper	1 tsp.	5 mL

Combine all 7 ingredients in small bowl. Makes 1 1/3 cups (325 mL).

1 recipe: 387 Calories; 16.4 g Total Fat; 876 mg Sodium; 5 g Protein; 17 g Carbohydrate; 2 g Dietary Fibre

Pictured above.

Spice and Herb Marinade

The combination of lively spices is tempered nicely with the addition of chopped fresh herbs. This all-purpose sauce can be used with any meat or fish.

Ground cumin	1 tsp.	5 mL
Ground cinnamon	1/2 tsp.	2 mL
Ground ginger	1/2 tsp.	2 mL
Chili powder	1/4 tsp.	1 mL
Finely grated orange zest	1 tsp.	5 mL
Orange juice	1/2 cup	125 mL
White (or alcohol-free) wine	1/2 cup	125 mL
Chopped fresh cilantro	1/4 cup	60 mL
Chopped fresh mint leaves	1/4 cup	60 mL
Olive (or cooking) oil	2 tbsp.	30 mL
Garlic cloves, crushed	2	2
Liquid honey	2 tbsp.	30 mL

Combine all 12 ingredients in small bowl. Makes 1 1/3 cups (325 mL).

1 recipe: 553 Calories; 28.5 g Total Fat; 32 mg Sodium; 3 g Protein; 57 g Carbohydrate; 2 g Dietary Fibre

Pictured above.

Sweet and Sour Marinade, below

Lemon, Thyme and Chili Marinade

Here is a versatile marinade that you'll want to use with everything from boneless chicken breasts, shrimp and scallops to lamb and pork. Just remember to follow these times for effective marinating: for seafood, up to 20 minutes; for chicken, up to one hour; and for lamb, pork or beef, up to three hours.

Finely grated lemon zest	1 tsp.	5 mL
Freshly squeezed lemon juice (about 1 large)	1/3 cup	75 mL
Olive oil	1/4 cup	60 mL
Chopped fresh thyme	2 tbsp.	30 mL
Prepared grainy mustard	1 tbsp.	15 mL
Small fresh red chili peppers, chopped♦	2	2
Garlic cloves, crushed	2	2
Brown sugar, packed	1 tbsp.	15 mL
Whole black peppercorns, cracked	1 tsp.	5 mL

Combine all 9 ingredients in small bowl. Mix well. Makes 1 cup (250 mL).

2 tbsp. (30 mL): 78 Calories; 7.1 g Total Fat; 27 mg Sodium; trace Protein; 4 g Carbohydrate; trace Dietary Fibre

♦Wear gloves when chopping chili peppers, and avoid touching your eyes.

Teriyaki Marinade

"This very tasty marinade came from my late wife Marilyn's collection of recipes that she accumulated over many years." Partner this with poultry, pork, lamb or fish.

— Wayne Shearer, Edmonton, Alberta

Soy sauce	1/2 cup	125 mL
Cooking oil	2 tbsp.	30 mL
Fancy (mild) molasses	2 tbsp.	30 mL
Dry mustard	2 tsp.	10 mL
Ground ginger	1 tsp.	5 mL
Garlic clove, crushed	1	1
Water	1/4 cup	60 mL

Combine all 7 ingredients in medium bowl. Makes 1 cup (250 mL).

1 recipe: 495 Calories; 29.7 g Total Fat; 8719 mg Sodium; 15 g Protein; 46 g Carbohydrate; 1 g Dietary Fibre

Pictured on page 142.

Sweet-and-Sour Marinade

This particular marinade also lends itself well to serving as a sauce—just double the recipe so you have enough for double-duty. Boiling releases the green pepper flavour as a nice accent to the subtle Asian taste of this sauce. Excellent with fish, poultry or pork.

Brown sugar, packed	1/2 cup	125 mL
Red wine vinegar	1/3 cup	75 mL
Unsweetened pineapple juice	1/3 cup	75 mL
Finely chopped green pepper	1/4 cup	60 mL
Soy sauce	1 tbsp.	15 mL
Garlic clove, minced	1	1
Freshly grated gingerroot	1/2 tsp.	2 mL

Combine all 7 ingredients in medium saucepan. Heat and stir on medium-high until boiling. Makes 1 cup (250 mL).

1 recipe: 526 Calories; 0.2 g Total Fat; 1093 mg Sodium; 2 g Protein; 135 g Carbohydrate; 1 g Dietary Fibre

Pictured above.

Marinating 101

Choose a Container

Material: A shallow ceramic or glass dish works best; a plastic container is also fine, though it may stain. Don't use anything made of metal, as a chemical reaction with the acid in the marinade can discolour the dish and sometimes give the meat or seafood a funny taste. Another option is a heavy-duty resealable plastic freezer bag, which makes clean-up a breeze.

Size: If possible, pick a dish that accommodates a single layer to be well covered in marinade, or one that allows room for the food to be stirred or turned.

Make the Marinade

Use a separate bowl or the marinating container.

Add the Food

Turn the meat several times to coat it thoroughly. Cover or seal the container tightly. Place it in the refrigerator if the food will be soaking for longer than 30 minutes.

Let It Marinate

Turn the items occasionally during the suggested marinating time.

Grill It

Remove the meat or seafood and let the excess liquid drip back into the container. Bear in mind that marinating has tenderized the food, so it may cook in slightly less time than if it hadn't been marinated.

The used marinade should be discarded, or if you want to use it for basting the food during cooking, the Beef Information Centre advises boiling it first for five to 10 minutes. If you don't want to boil and re-use the marinade, make a double batch and use half for marinating and the balance for basting or as a sauce.

Hot and Spicy Rub

For timid tasters, a little can go a long way, but those who enjoy flavourful steaks or burgers will love this spicy combination.

Chili powder	1 tsp.	5 mL
Garlic salt	1 tsp.	5 mL
Paprika	1 tsp.	5 mL
Brown sugar, packed	1 tsp.	5 mL
Freshly ground pepper	1 tsp.	5 mL

Combine all 5 ingredients in small cup. Rub on both sides of steaks. Use as little or as much as desired. Makes about 1 1/2 tbsp. (25 mL).

1 recipe: 36 Calories; 0.8 g Total Fat; 1216 mg Sodium; 1 g Protein; 8 g Carbohydrate; 1 g Dietary Fibre

Pictured below.

Middle Eastern Rub

The heady aromas of this rub whisk you off to old spice markets in hot climates. Delicious on chicken and beef.

Garlic salt	1 tsp.	5 mL
Ground cumin	1 tsp.	5 mL
Ground coriander	1 tsp.	5 mL
Ground ginger	1 tsp.	5 mL
Ground cinnamon	1/2 tsp.	2 mL

Combine all 5 ingredients in small cup. Rub on both sides of steaks. Use as little or as much as desired. Makes 4 1/2 tsp. (22 mL).

1 recipe: 24 Calories; 0.7 g Total Fat; 1193 mg Sodium; 1 g Protein; 5 g Carbohydrate; 1 g Dietary Fibre

Pictured below.

Curry Garlic Rub

Let your seasoned meat absorb the flavour of a rub for several hours in the refrigerator. But if you're in a hurry, apply the rub liberally and start grilling right away.

Curry powder	1 tbsp.	15 mL
Garlic powder	2 tsp.	10 mL
Dried sweet basil	1 tsp.	5 mL

Combine all 3 ingredients in small cup. Rub on both sides of steaks. Use as little or as much as desired. Makes 2 tbsp. (30 mL).

1 recipe: 43 Calories; 1 g Total Fat; 5 mg Sodium; 2 g Protein; 9 g Carbohydrate; 1 g Dietary Fibre

Pictured below.

Parsley Mustard Rub

As with any rub, you can boost the impact of this parsley/mustard combination by cutting small slits in the meat and massaging the spices into the openings.

Parsley flakes, crumbled	2 tbsp.	30 mL
Dry mustard	2 tsp.	10 mL
Lemon pepper	1 tsp.	5 mL
Brown sugar, packed	1 tsp.	5 mL

Combine all 4 ingredients in small cup. Rub on both sides of steaks. Use as little or as much as desired. Makes about 2 1/2 tbsp. (37 mL).

1 recipe: 56 Calories; 2.1 g Total Fat; 14 mg Sodium; 3 g Protein; 8 g Carbohydrate; 1 g Dietary Fibre

Pictured below.

Middle Eastern Rub, above

Curry Garlic Rub, above

Hot and Spicy Rub, above

Parsley Mustard Rub, above

Basic White Sauce

White sauce, also known as béchamel (bay-shah-MEHL), starts with a roux (roo), which is a mixture of fat and flour. Onion can also be a part of this mixture, but is optional. Liquid is gradually added, and the sauce is cooked until thickened. This is the point where people often have problems and end up with a lumpy sauce. Not any more! Follow these easy steps and you'll never again have to strain lumps out of your white sauce!

Hard margarine (or butter)	3 tbsp.	50 mL
Finely chopped onion (about 1 small), optional	1/2 cup	125 mL
All-purpose flour	3 tbsp.	50 mL
Milk♦	2 cups	500 mL
Salt	1/4 tsp.	1 mL
Pepper	1/4 tsp.	1 mL
Ground nutmeg	1/4 tsp.	1 mL

Melt hard margarine in small saucepan on medium heat (see photo 1). Add onion. Sauté for 5 minutes until soft.

Stir in flour until well mixed (see photo 2). Cook and stir for 1 to 2 minutes until bubbling and grainy but not browned.

Gradually whisk in 1/4 cup (60 mL) milk until combined. Whisk in remaining milk, salt and pepper (see photo 3).

Simmer, uncovered, on low for about 10 minutes, stirring occasionally, until sauce is thickened (see photo 4). Stir in nutmeg or other seasonings of your choice (see Saucy Variations, left).

♦For a richer sauce, substitute half-and-half cream for milk.

Saucy Variations

Make the Basic White Sauce, remove the saucepan from the heat, then get fancy! Here are a few ideas:

Add to Basic White Sauce ...

Mornay
3 tbsp. (50 mL) Parmesan cheese
3 tbsp. (50 mL) of Cheddar or Gruyère cheese
1 egg yolk (large)

Goes great with ...
vegetables, fish, seafood, eggs, chicken or pasta

Mustard
2 tbsp. (30 mL) of Dijon mustard

Goes great with ...
vegetables, fish, seafood, chicken or red meat

Herb
2 tbsp. (30 mL) each of chopped fresh parsley and basil

Goes great with ...
vegetables, fish, seafood, eggs, chicken, red meat or pasta

In-a-Jiffy Barbecue Sauce, page 148

Curried Yogurt Basting Sauce, below

Green Peppercorn Sauce, below

Curried Yogurt Basting Sauce

Plan a South Asian-style barbecue and use this basting sauce to add great flavour and a tenderizing quality to meat. We have used a mild curry paste in this recipe but you can use a hotter version if you prefer.

Plain yogurt	1 1/4 cups	300 mL
Mild curry paste	1/4 cup	60 mL
Chopped fresh mint leaves	1/4 cup	60 mL
Chopped fresh cilantro	1/4 cup	60 mL
Mango chutney	2 tbsp.	30 mL

Combine all 5 ingredients in medium bowl. Makes 1 1/2 cups (375 mL).

1 recipe: 463 Calories; 26 g Total Fat; 247 mg Sodium; 20 g Protein; 42 g Carbohydrate; 3 g Dietary Fibre

Pictured above.

Green Peppercorn Sauce

Look no further for the world's greatest steak sauce. It's peppery, yet mild and creamy, and absolutely made for a big, hefty grilled T-bone or porterhouse steak.

Small onion, finely chopped	1	1
Garlic cloves, crushed	2	2
Hard margarine (or butter)	1 tbsp.	15 mL
Brandy	2 tbsp.	30 mL
Can of green peppercorns, in brine, drained	1.06 oz.	30 g
Whipping cream	1 1/2 cups	375 mL
Prepared mustard	1 tsp.	5 mL
Salt	1/4 tsp.	1 mL

Sauté onion and garlic in margarine in large frying pan on medium for about 5 minutes until onion is soft.

Add brandy. Ignite with a match to burn off alcohol.

Add remaining 4 ingredients. Heat and stir on medium for 5 to 7 minutes until thickened. Makes 1 1/2 cups (375 mL).

1 recipe: 1368 Calories; 133.5 g Total Fat; 2136 mg Sodium; 10 g Protein; 24 g Carbohydrate; 2 g Dietary Fibre

Pictured above.

Best Time to Baste

Steaks, chops, fish, chicken pieces: Apply sauce anytime, including as soon as the food is on the grill.

Larger cuts such as roasts: Brush on the sauce toward the end so it doesn't burn during the longer cooking time.

Blueberry Sauce

A fruity change of pace for a serving sauce. Fresh rosemary combined with blueberry will have you wanting to try this on everything from steak to barbecued beef ribs and roasts.

Blueberry jam	1/3 cup	75 mL
Can of condensed chicken broth	10 oz.	284 mL
Chopped fresh rosemary leaves	1 tsp.	5 mL
Salt	1/4 tsp.	1 mL
Freshly ground pepper	1/2 tsp.	2 mL
Water	2 tsp.	10 mL
Cornstarch	2 tsp.	10 mL
Fresh (or frozen) blueberries	1 cup	250 mL

Combine first 5 ingredients in medium saucepan. Cook on medium-high for 10 to 12 minutes until sauce is thickened. Strain. Return strained mixture to same pan.

Stir water into cornstarch in small cup until smooth. Add to jam mixture.

Add blueberries. Heat and stir for about 5 minutes until berries are hot and sauce is thickened. Makes about 1 1/2 cups (375 mL).

1 recipe: 477 Calories; 4.7 g Total Fat; 2528 mg Sodium; 15 g Protein; 101 g Carbohydrate; 7 g Dietary Fibre

Cranberry Sauce with Apricots and Ginger

Of all the condiments you may attempt, nothing is easier to make than cranberry sauce. This one is a cut above the rest thanks to flavour boosts from apricot and gingerroot.

Granulated sugar	1 1/2 cups	375 mL
Freshly squeezed orange juice	3/4 cup	175 mL
Chopped dried apricots	1/2 cup	125 mL
Finely grated gingerroot	1/2 tsp.	2 mL
Salt	1/2 tsp.	2 mL
Fresh or frozen cranberries	4 cups	1 L

Combine first 5 ingredients in large saucepan. Heat and stir on low until sugar is dissolved. Bring to a boil. Simmer, uncovered, on medium-low for 10 minutes.

Add cranberries. Simmer for 15 minutes until sauce is thickened.◆ Makes 3 2/3 cups (900 mL).

2 tbsp. (30 mL): 55 Calories; 0.1 g Total Fat; 39 mg Sodium; trace Protein; 14 g Carbohydrate; 1 g Dietary Fibre

Pictured on page 133.

◆*Sauce will thicken further upon cooling.*

Raspberry Coulis

A coulis (koo-LEE) is a thick sauce made from fruit or vegetables. A sweet fruit coulis such as this raspberry one can enhance the flavours of ice creams, puddings and custards, as well as your favourite cheesecake. Spoon some on a plate and place a delicious dessert in the centre. For an extra-special touch, decorate the plate with Saucy Hearts, page 216.

Frozen raspberries in syrup, thawed	15 oz.	425 g
Water		
Granulated sugar	2 tbsp.	30 mL
Cornstarch	4 tsp.	20 mL

Strain raspberries through sieve. Reserve and measure syrup. Add water to make 1 1/4 cups (300 mL). Pour into saucepan.

Add sugar and cornstarch. Stir. Heat, stirring constantly, until mixture boils and thickens. Cool. Makes 1 1/4 cups (300 mL).

2 tbsp. (30 mL): 55 Calories; 0.1 g Total Fat; 1 mg Sodium; trace Protein; 14 g Carbohydrate; 2 g Dietary Fibre

Pictured below.

Raspberry Coulis, above, with
Saucy Hearts, page 216

Lively Flavoured Butters

Dressed-up butters infuse everyday meals with a whole new taste. Try the Cajun Garlic on your garlic bread, or drop a dollop of the Lemon Mint on a bowl of peas. Even better: make both butters for a good ol' fashioned corn roast!

Cajun Garlic: Add 2 tsp. (10 mL) Cajun seasoning and a crushed garlic clove to 1/2 cup (125 mL) of butter. Pictured below and on page 190.

Lemon Mint: Mix 2 tbsp. (30 mL) of chopped fresh mint, 1 tsp. (5 mL) lemon zest and 1 tsp. (5 mL) freshly ground pepper with 1/2 cup (125 mL) of butter. Pictured below and on page 190.

Cajun Garlic Butter, above

Lemon Mint Butter, above

In-a-Jiffy Barbecue Sauce

Here's what we knew about this recipe when we got it: *"This is an easy, sweet and tangy basting sauce for beef cooked in a slow cooker. My mom always served this with rice. It's also great with chicken."* We think you'll agree that it's also a wonderful basting sauce for grilled steaks.
— Denise Decoux, Edmonton, Alberta

Chopped onion	3/4 cup	175 mL
Ketchup	1 cup	250 mL
Water	1 cup	250 mL
Worcestershire sauce	1 1/2 tsp.	7 mL
Prepared mustard	1 1/2 tsp.	7 mL
Granulated sugar	1/4 cup	60 mL

Combine all 6 ingredients in medium saucepan. Simmer for 10 minutes. Cool. Makes 2 1/2 cups (625 mL).

1 recipe: 531 Calories; 1.7 g Total Fat; 3219 mg Sodium; 7 g Protein; 134 g Carbohydrate; 6 g Dietary Fibre.

Pictured on page 146.

Liquid Gravy Browner

Sometimes homemade gravy is paler than you'd like. A liquid browner enhances the colour without affecting the flavour. Here's an age-old recipe.

Granulated sugar	2 tbsp.	30 mL
Salt, just a pinch		
Water	2 tsp.	10 mL
Water	1 cup	250 mL

Combine sugar and salt in small saucepan. Heat and stir until sugar is melted and very dark brown.

Add first amount of water, stirring constantly. It will spatter.

Gradually stir in second amount of water until all hard sugar syrup is dissolved. Cool. Cover and refrigerate for up to 6 months. Makes 1 cup (250 mL) gravy browner.

Pictured below.

Liquid Gravy Browner, above

Lemon Garlic Butter

Especially good as a dipping sauce for artichokes or lobster, this butter is also delicious drizzled over baked potatoes or steamed vegetables such as asparagus.

Butter (not margarine)	1 cup	250 mL
Garlic cloves, crushed	4	4
Freshly squeezed lemon juice	2 tbsp.	30 mL
Chopped fresh parsley	2 tsp.	10 mL

Heat butter and garlic in small saucepan on medium until butter is melted. Remove from heat. Add lemon juice and parsley. Stir. Serve warm. Makes 1 cup (250 mL).

1 tbsp. (15 mL): 210 Calories; 23.4 g Total Fat; 238 mg Sodium; trace Protein; 1 g Carbohydrate; trace Dietary Fibre

Chive Mayonnaise

Delicious with seafood, particularly salmon, or as a dip for steamed artichokes. This flavourful mayonnaise also livens up a cold chicken or tuna salad, and makes a good sandwich spread.

Mayonnaise (not salad dressing)	1 cup	250 mL
Chopped fresh chives	1 tsp.	5 mL
Freshly squeezed lemon juice	2 tsp.	10 mL
Freshly ground pepper, just a pinch		

Combine all 4 ingredients in small bowl. Stir. Chill for at least 1 hour to blend flavours. Makes 1 cup (250 mL).

1 tbsp. (15 mL): 102 Calories; 11.2 g Total Fat; 72 mg Sodium; trace Protein; trace Carbohydrate; 0 g Dietary Fibre

Get on Board the Gravy Train

- Use the same pan you cooked your poultry in; any baked-on bits will add colour and flavour to the gravy

- Reserve the drippings from the pan for added flavour

- Use the amount of fat recommended so the gravy isn't greasy

- Cook the flour thoroughly in the fat (the mixture is called a "roux") to avoid a raw flour taste and to ensure the gravy thickens properly

- Add liquid slowly and stir constantly to prevent lumps

Poultry Gravy

We tested this with a 3 1/2 lb. (1.6 kg) chicken. The recipe can easily be doubled.

Fat from pan drippings	1/4 cup	60 mL
All-purpose flour	1/4 cup	60 mL
Drippings without fat, plus poultry stock or prepared broth to equal	2 cups	500 mL
Salt, to taste		
Pepper, to taste		

Remove poultry from roasting pan. Cover loosely to keep warm. Pour pan drippings into large liquid measure. Allow fat to rise to surface (see photo 1). Skim off 1/4 cup (60 mL) fat. Add to same roasting pan. Spoon off remaining fat and discard. Reserve any remaining pan drippings.

Place roasting pan on burner on medium. If pan is large, you may need to use two burners. Heat and stir until hot. Add flour. Heat and stir for 1 minute until bubbling (see photo 2).

Gradually stir in broth mixture and reserved pan drippings. Heat and stir on medium for 10 minutes, scraping up any browned bits from bottom of pan, until gravy is boiling and thickened (see photo 3). Add salt and pepper. Stir. Strain gravy, if desired. Makes 2 cups (500 mL).

1/4 cup (60 mL): 87 Calories; 7.2 g Total Fat; 206 mg Sodium; 2 g Protein; 3 g Carbohydrate; trace Dietary Fibre

Pictured on this page.

Tasty Variations to Consider

Rosemary Wine

Substitute ...	For ...	And add ...
1/2 cup (125 mL) white or alcohol-free wine	1/2 cup (125 mL) broth	1 - 2 tbsp. (15 - 30 mL) chopped fresh rosemary

Orange Mustard

Substitute ...	For ...	And add ...
1 cup (250 mL) orange juice	1 cup (250 mL) broth	1 - 2 tbsp. (15 - 30 mL) grainy mustard

Port Wine and Blackberry

Substitute ...	For ...	And add ...
1/2 cup (125 mL) port	1/2 cup (125 mL) broth	2 - 3 tbsp. (30 - 50 mL) blackberry jam

Cooked Tomato Chutney. below

Puri, page 41

Pumpkin Curry, page 178

Cooked Tomato Chutney

"My mum's cooked chutney is delicious made with beefsteak tomatoes fresh from the garden—but is still good with any in-season tomatoes. Serve at room temperature with Pumpkin Curry, page 178, and Puri, page 41. It's also good with other curries." Fenugreek can be found in the spice section of large grocery stores. Fresh curry leaves are available in specialty spice stores.

— Naazima Ali, Edmonton, Alberta

Cooking oil	1 tbsp.	15 mL
Mustard seed	1/4 tsp.	1 mL
Cumin seed	1/2 tsp.	2 mL
Fenugreek	1/4 tsp.	1 mL
Fresh curry leaves	3 - 4	3 - 4
Medium onion, coarsely chopped	1/2	1/2
Finely grated gingerroot	1/2 tsp.	2 mL
Garlic cloves, chopped	2	2
Small red chili peppers, chopped◆	2 - 3	2 - 3
Ripe medium tomatoes, coarsely chopped	4	4
Salt, to taste		

Heat cooking oil in large frying pan on high. Add mustard seed, cumin seed and fenugreek. Cook for about 30 seconds until browned and fragrant. Stir in curry leaves.

Add next 3 ingredients. Cook on medium for 2 to 3 minutes until onion is soft.

Add remaining 3 ingredients. Cook, uncovered, for about 10 minutes, stirring occasionally, until oil starts to come to surface. Makes 2 3/4 cups (675 mL).

1 tbsp. (15 mL): 7 Calories; 0.4 g Total Fat; 1 mg Sodium; trace Protein; 1 g Carbohydrate; trace Dietary Fibre

Pictured above.

◆*Wear gloves when chopping chili peppers, and avoid touching your eyes.*

Cilantro Chutney

"This is my mum's recipe. It's a spicy dish, but you can use fewer chilies and/or remove the ribs and seeds of the chilies before processing to lessen the heat. Fresh tomatoes can be added to this chutney for a nice variation. Add as much tomato as you like to make the consistency you prefer. Serve with beef or vegetable curries or dal."

— Naazima Ali, Edmonton, Alberta

Bunch of fresh cilantro, coarsely chopped (about 2 cups, 500 mL)	1	1
Small garlic clove	1	1
Small red chili peppers	3	3
Freshly squeezed lemon juice	1/4 tsp.	1 mL
Salt, to taste		

Process all 5 ingredients in blender or food processor until very finely chopped. Makes about 1/3 cup (75 mL).

1 tbsp. (15 mL): 22 Calories; 0.4 g Total Fat; 17 mg Sodium; 2 g Protein; 4 g Carbohydrate; trace Dietary Fibre

Rhubarb Pineapple Jam

Pearl Hunter's bakery was long a fixture at the historic Old City Market in St. John. This recipe, from her family's collection, makes good use of spring's first rhubarb.

Fresh (or frozen, thawed and drained) chopped rhubarb	3 cups	750 mL
Can of crushed pineapple, drained	19 oz.	540 mL
Granulated sugar	5 cups	1.25 L
Pouches of liquid pectin (3 oz., 85 mL, each)	2	2

Combine first 3 ingredients in large saucepan. Heat and stir on low until sugar is dissolved. Bring to a boil. Boil, uncovered, for 30 minutes, stirring occasionally and skimming off any foam.

Stir in pectin until mixture reaches a full rolling boil. Boil hard for 1 minute. Remove from heat. Skim off foam. Pour hot jam into hot sterilized half pint jars to within 1/4 inch (6 mm) of top. Place sterilized metal lids on jars and screw metal bands on securely. Process in a boiling water bath for 5 minutes. Makes 7 cups (1.75 L), enough for 7 half pint jars or 3 pints plus 1 half pint jar.

1 tbsp. (15 mL): 80 Calories; 0 g Total Fat; 2 mg Sodium; trace Protein; 21 g Carbohydrate; trace Dietary Fibre.

Gel Test at your Fingertips

To make sure your jams, jellies and marmalades have reached the gelling point, remove them from heat, place a spoonful on a chilled plate and place it in the freezer until the mixture has reached room temperature. Press the length of your finger down the middle of the mixture. If it doesn't run together into the "trench" you've created, the mixture has gelled.

Note: Do not leave your jam or jelly simmering on the stove while you're testing, to ensure it doesn't overcook.

Tomato, Date and Caramelized Onion Jam

We think of this delicious spread as a savoury jam. While it makes a great accompaniment to beef, pork or chicken, it's also wonderful served with a selection of cheeses, paté and bread as an appetizer or light lunch.

Medium onions, thinly sliced	4	4
Cooking oil	1 tbsp.	15 mL
Red wine vinegar	3 tbsp.	50 mL
Brown sugar, packed	1/4 cup	60 mL
Large tomatoes (about 3 lbs., 1.4 kg), peeled and chopped	6	6
Dates, chopped	3 cups	750 mL
Lemon juice	1/2 cup	125 mL
Granulated sugar	4 cups	1 L

Sauté onion in cooking oil in frying pan on low for about 20 minutes until very soft.

Add vinegar and brown sugar. Cook for about 5 minutes, stirring occasionally, until sugar is dissolved. Set aside.

Combine tomatoes and dates in large heavy pot or Dutch oven. Simmer on medium, uncovered, for about 20 minutes, stirring occasionally, until dates are soft and mixture is thickened.

Add lemon juice, sugar and onion mixture. Heat and stir on low until sugar is dissolved. Bring to a boil. Reduce heat to medium. Gently boil, uncovered, for 15 to 20 minutes, stirring occasionally, until jam gels when tested on small cold plate (see Gel Test at your Fingertips, below). Fill hot sterilized half pint jars to within 1/2 inch (12 mm) of top. Place sterilized metal lids on jars and screw metal bands on securely. Process in a boiling water bath for 5 minutes. Makes 8 half pint (1 cup, 250 mL) jars.

2 tbsp. (30 mL): 83 Calories; 0.3 g Total Fat; 2 mg Sodium; trace Protein; 21 g Carbohydrate; 1 g Dietary Fibre

Pictured below.

Tomato, Date and Caramelized Onion Jam, above

Cranberry Chutney, below

Get into Hot Water— You **Can** Do It

Current home-canning research recommends that all high-acid foods be processed in a boiling water bath. Not only does this destroy micro-organisms that enter the jar upon filling, but it also allows air to be vented from the jar to create an airtight vacuum seal. The seal prevents colour and texture changes and keeps micro-organisms from developing.

High-acid foods include all jams, jellies, marmalades, pickles, relishes, salsas, chutney and tomatoes with added acid, as well as all fruits, fruit sauces, fruit syrups, fruit butters and fruit juices.

The bathtub: Any deep pot with a lid, including a stock pot, can be used as a canner, as long as it allows jars, resting on a rack, to be covered with 1 inch (2.5 cm) of water. The traditional enamel canner has the benefit of including a custom-fitted jar rack to prevent the jars from sitting directly on the bottom. You can also use a cake rack or several tied-together screw bands to fit the bottom of your vessel. Sterilize your jar by boiling them rapidly for 15 minutes if your elevation is 1001 to 3000 feet (306 to 915 m) above sea level. (Make adjustment for elevation in your area if necessary.)

Bath time: Once the jars are filled, apply the screw bands just till fingertip tight (to allow air to escape) and place in the canner. Jars should not touch one another. As soon as the water has returned to a rolling boil, begin processing time. Reduce heat to maintain a gentle, steady boil until done.

After the bath: Set the jars upright on a rack, towel or cutting board to cool for 24 hours without being disturbed. At this point, check that all the lids curve downwards, an indication that a good seal has formed. Jars that have not formed a seal may be refrigerated and used immediately.

Cranberry Chutney

This zesty, ruby-red sauce is adapted from a well-loved recipe from Claire's mother-in-law, Margaret. Serve it with everything from the holiday turkey to a simple ham sandwich, or even pork and seafood.

— Claire Doyle, Isle Madame, Nova Scotia

Fresh (or frozen) cranberries	8 cups	2 L
Salt	1 1/2 tsp.	7 mL
Cold water	1 cup	250 mL
All-purpose flour	1/4 cup	60 mL
Dry mustard	1 1/2 tsp.	7 mL
Ground ginger	1/2 tsp.	2 mL
Turmeric	1/4 tsp.	1 mL
Granulated sugar	1 1/2 cups	375 mL
White vinegar	1 1/2 cups	375 mL
Water	1/2 cup	125 mL
Chopped onion	2 cups	500 mL

Combine first 3 ingredients in medium bowl. Cover. Let stand overnight, stirring occasionally.

Combine next 5 ingredients in medium bowl. Add 2 tbsp. (30 mL) of the vinegar and 2 tbsp. (30 mL) of the water. Stir until smooth paste. Set aside.

Combine onion, remaining vinegar and remaining water in large pot or Dutch oven. Add cranberry mixture. Bring to a boil. Reduce heat to medium. Boil gently for 5 minutes. Stir in flour mixture. Boil gently for about 55 minutes, stirring occasionally, until very thick. Fill hot sterilized jars to within 1/2 inch (12 mm) of top. Place sterilized metal lids on jars and screw metal bands on securely. Process in boiling water bath for 5 minutes. Makes 6 half pint (1 cup, 250 mL) jars.

2 tbsp. (30 mL): 38 Calories; 0.1 g Total Fat; 72 mg Sodium; trace Protein; 10 g Carbohydrate; 1 g Dietary Fibre

Pictured above.

Green Tomato and Pear Chutney

When you've had your fill of fried green tomatoes, here's an unusual chutney that will put the rest of your green tomatoes to good use.

Medium firm pears, peeled and chopped	3	3
Medium green tomatoes (about 2 lbs., 900 g), chopped	7	7
Medium onions, chopped	2	2
Golden raisins	1 cup	250 mL
Black mustard seed	1/3 cup	75 mL
Malt vinegar	2 cups	500 mL
Brown sugar, packed	2 cups	500 mL
Salt	2 tsp.	10 mL
Ground cumin	1 tbsp.	15 mL
Ground coriander	1 tbsp.	15 mL
Ground ginger	1 tbsp.	15 mL

Combine all 11 ingredients in a large heavy pot or Dutch oven. Heat and stir on medium for 3 to 5 minutes until sugar is dissolved. Bring to a boil. Reduce heat to medium. Gently boil, uncovered, for about 50 minutes, stirring occasionally, until very thick. Fill hot sterilized half pint jars to within 1/2 inch (12 mm) of top. Place sterilized metal lids on jars and screw metal bands on securely. Process in a boiling water bath for 5 minutes. Makes 6 half pint (1 cup, 250 mL) jars.

2 tbsp. (30 mL): 65 Calories; 0.5 g Total Fat; 102 mg Sodium; 1 g Protein; 16 g Carbohydrate; 1 g Dietary Fibre

Yellow Relish

"This recipe was part of my late wife Marilyn's collection. It was a favourite passed down through the Locke family."
— **Wayne Shearer**, Edmonton, Alberta

Large English cucumbers, unpeeled, chopped	6	6
Coarse (pickling) salt	2 tbsp.	30 mL
Medium green peppers, chopped	3	3
Medium red pepper, chopped	1	1
Medium Granny Smith apples, unpeeled, chopped	3	3
Large head of cauliflower, cut up (about 5 1/2 cups, 1.4 L)	1	1
Medium onions, chopped	4	4
White vinegar	3 cups	750 mL
All-purpose flour	1/2 cup	125 mL
Granulated sugar	5 cups	1.25 L
Ground turmeric	1 tsp.	5 mL
Prepared mustard	1 1/2 tbsp.	25 mL
Mustard seed	1 tsp.	5 mL
Celery seed	1 tsp.	5 mL

Combine cucumber and salt in large bowl. Cover. Chill overnight. Drain. Rinse. Drain well.

Process cucumber mixture and next 5 ingredients in batches in food processor until finely chopped. Place in large heavy 12 quart (12 L) stock pot.♦

Whisk vinegar into flour in large saucepan. Add remaining 5 ingredients. Whisk well. Bring to a boil on high. Reduce heat. Simmer, uncovered, on medium-high for 3 minutes. Add to cucumber mixture. Bring to a boil. Boil gently, uncovered, on medium for 20 to 30 minutes, stirring occasionally, until thickened. Pour into hot sterilized pint jars to within 1/2 inch (12 mm) of top. Place sterilized metal lids on jars and screw metal bands on securely. Process in a boiling water bath for 5 minutes. Makes 9 pint (2 cup, 500 mL) jars.

2 tbsp. (30 mL): 73 Calories; 0.2 g Total Fat; 39 mg Sodium; 1 g Protein; 18 g Carbohydrate; 1 g Dietary Fibre

♦If you don't have a large enough stock pot, a large roaster can be used. Cook on two elements on the stovetop.

Freezer Corn Relish

Enjoy fresh corn at its peak, then put some away for a fresh taste of summer year-round. Here's one of the tried-and-true relish recipes that the Jensen family enjoys.
— **Jensen Family**, Taber, Alberta

Fresh corn kernels (about 5 medium cobs)	3 cups	750 mL
Finely shredded cabbage	2 cups	500 mL
Chopped onion	1 1/2 cups	375 mL
Chopped celery	1 cup	250 mL
Chopped green pepper	1/2 cup	125 mL
Chopped red pepper	1/2 cup	125 mL
White vinegar	2 cups	500 mL
Granulated sugar	1 cup	250 mL
All-purpose flour	4 tsp.	20 mL
Celery seed	2 tsp.	10 mL
Ground turmeric	1/2 tsp.	2 mL

Combine all 11 ingredients in large heavy pot or Dutch oven. Heat and stir on low until sugar is dissolved. Bring to a boil. Simmer, uncovered, on medium for 30 to 40 minutes, stirring occasionally, until thickened. Fill hot, sterilized half pint jars to within 1/2 inch (12 mm) of top. Place sterilized metal lids on jars and screw metal bands on securely. Chill for at least 6 hours or overnight. Store in freezer for up to 12 months. Makes 5 half pint (1 cup, 250 mL) jars.

2 tbsp. (30 mL): 199 Calories; 11 g Total Fat; 354 mg Sodium; 7 g Protein; 21 g Carbohydrate; 3 g Dietary Fibre

Pictured below.

Apple Relish

Wonderfully tasty with poultry. Try this with Roast Duck with Apple Mustard Baste, page 136.
— **Lorraine Marchand**, Regina, Saskatchewan

Thinly sliced apples (such as McIntosh), about 2 medium	1 cup	250 mL
Chopped celery	1/4 cup	60 mL
Chopped red pepper	1/2 cup	125 mL
Chopped green pepper	1/2 cup	125 mL
Chopped onion	1/3 cup	75 mL
Granulated sugar	1/3 cup	75 mL
Water	1/4 cup	60 mL
White vinegar	1/2 cup	125 mL
Dry mustard	1/4 tsp.	1 mL
Turmeric, just a pinch		
Salt	1/4 tsp.	1 mL

Combine all 11 ingredients in large saucepan. Heat and stir on medium for 3 to 5 minutes until sugar is dissolved. Bring to a boil. Reduce heat to medium. Boil gently, uncovered, for 35 to 40 minutes, stirring occasionally, until 1 cup (250 mL). Cool. Cover and chill.

1/4 cup (60 mL) serving: 98 Calories; 0.3 g Total Fat; 156 mg Sodium; 1 g Protein; 25 g Carbohydrate; 1 g Dietary Fibre

Pictured on page 136.

Freezer Corn Relish, above

From left to right: Tomato, Orange and Port Marmalade, below; Spicy Jalapeño Tomato Salsa, page 15; Sweet Tomato Chili Sauce, page 155; Tomato, Zucchini and Red Pepper Relish, page 155; Pineapple and Tomato Jam, below

Tomato, Orange and Port Marmalade

This refreshing citrus marmalade gets a flavour boost from tomatoes and robust port. Great with hearty breakfasts of grilled sausages, smoked fish, scrambled eggs and lots of thick-cut toast.

Medium oranges, cut in half lengthwise	4	4
Medium lemons, cut in half lengthwise	2	2
Water	3 3/4 cups	925 mL
Granulated sugar, approximately	4 cups	1 L
Medium tomatoes (about 2 1/4 lbs., 1 kg), chopped	8	8
Granulated sugar	1 cup	250 mL
Port	1/2 cup	125 mL

Cut orange and lemon halves crosswise into 1/4 inch (6 mm) slices. Reserve seeds. Tie seeds in double layer of cheesecloth to make bag. Place orange and lemon slices, cheesecloth bag and water in large bowl. Cover. Let stand for 8 hours or overnight. Transfer to large heavy pot or Dutch oven. Cover. Simmer for about 1 1/4 hours on medium-low, stirring occasionally, until peel is soft. Cool slightly. Remove and discard cheesecloth bag. Measure orange mixture. Return mixture to same pot.

Allow 1 cup (250 mL) of sugar for each cup of orange mixture. Add measured sugar, tomato and second amount of sugar to orange mixture. Heat and stir on medium for 3 to 5 minutes until sugar is dissolved. Bring to a boil. Reduce heat to medium. Gently boil, uncovered, for about 50 minutes, stirring occasionally, until mixture is reduced by half.

Add port. Mix well. Gently boil, uncovered, on medium for 45 to 50 minutes until marmalade gels when tested on small cold plate (see Gel Test at your Fingertips, page 151). Fill hot sterilized half pint jars to within 1/4 inch (6 mm) of top. Place sterilized metal lids on jars and screw metal bands on securely. Process in a boiling water bath for 5 minutes. Makes about 5 half pint (1 cup, 250 mL) jars.

2 tbsp. (30 mL): 77 Calories; 0.1 g Total Fat; 2 mg Sodium; trace Protein; 20 g Carbohydrate; 1 g Dietary Fibre

Pictured above.

Pineapple and Tomato Jam

The naturally savoury quality of tomato adds a nice balance to the sweetness of fresh pineapple in this gingery jam. Absolutely outstanding with fresh biscuits, French toast, crispy croissants or English muffins.

Medium lemons	2	2
Small oranges	3	3
Chopped fresh pineapple	3 cups	750 mL
Medium tomatoes (about 1 3/4 lbs., 790 g), peeled and chopped	6	6
Finely grated gingerroot	2 1/2 tsp.	12 mL
Ground allspice	1/2 tsp.	2 mL
Granulated sugar	3 2/3 cups	900 mL

Squeeze juice from lemons and oranges to get 1 1/4 cups (300 mL) in total. Reserve seeds. Tie seeds in double layer of cheesecloth to make bag.

Combine juice, cheesecloth bag and next 4 ingredients in large heavy pot or Dutch oven. Bring to a boil. Reduce heat to medium. Cover. Simmer for 20 to 25 minutes until tomatoes are pulpy.

Add sugar. Heat and stir on medium for 3 to 5 minutes until sugar is dissolved. Bring to a boil. Reduce heat to medium. Gently boil, uncovered, for 50 minutes, stirring occasionally, until jam gels when tested on small cold plate (see Gel Test at your Fingertips, page 151). Remove and discard cheesecloth bag. Fill hot sterilized half pint jars to within 1/4 inch (6 mm) of top. Place sterilized metal lids on jars and screw metal bands on securely. Process in a boiling water bath for 5 minutes. Makes 4 half pint (1 cup, 250 mL) jars.

2 tbsp. (30 mL): 105 Calories; 0.2 g Total Fat; 3 mg Sodium; trace Protein; 27 g Carbohydrate; trace Dietary Fibre

Pictured above.

Chow Chow Maritime

This beloved pickle recipe is one of Jean Paré's old family favourites, made by herself and her Prince Edward Island-born mom and grandmother before that. (The original recipe called for a peck, or about eight quarts, of tomatoes.) For gift-giving, pack the Chow Chow in smaller jars.

Medium green tomatoes (about 5 1/3 lbs., 2.5 kg), sliced	18	18
Medium onions, halved lengthwise and sliced	4	4
Coarse (pickling) salt	1/3 cup	75 mL
Granulated sugar	3 1/3 cups	825 mL
Mixed pickling spice, tied in double layer of cheesecloth	4 1/2 tbsp.	67 mL
Turmeric	2 tsp.	10 mL
White vinegar	2 cups	500 mL

Layer first 3 ingredients in large heavy pot or Dutch oven. Cover. Let stand on counter overnight. Drain.

Add remaining 4 ingredients. Heat and stir until sugar is dissolved. Bring to a boil. Reduce heat to medium. Gently boil, uncovered, for 2 hours, stirring occasionally. Fill hot sterilized pint jars to within 1/2 inch (12 mm) of top. Place sterilized metal lids on jars and screw metal bands on securely. Process in a boiling water bath for 5 minutes. Makes 4 pint (2 cup, 500 mL) jars.

2 tbsp. (30 mL): 55 Calories; 0.1 g Total Fat; 290 mg Sodium; 1 g Protein; 14 g Carbohydrate; 1 g Dietary Fibre

Sweet Tomato Chili Sauce

This is a go-with-almost-anything sauce. Great with egg rolls, meatballs and Coconut Shrimp, page 17, it's also a terrific topping for grilled or broiled meats and grilled or steamed fish. A dash or two also adds a spicy zing to stir-fries, dips and wraps.

Medium tomatoes (about 3 lbs., 1.4 kg), chopped	12	12
Salt	2 tsp.	10 mL
Garlic cloves, chopped	8	8
Grated fresh gingerroot	2 tsp.	10 mL
White wine vinegar	1/4 cup	60 mL
Balsamic (or red wine) vinegar	1/4 cup	60 mL
Granulated sugar	2/3 cup	150 mL
Chopped fresh cilantro	1/2 cup	125 mL
Small red chili peppers, chopped♦	4	4

Combine all 9 ingredients in large heavy pot or Dutch oven. Heat and stir on medium for 3 to 5 minutes until sugar is dissolved. Bring to a boil. Reduce heat to medium. Simmer, uncovered, for 35 to 40 minutes, stirring occasionally, until thickened. Cool for 10 minutes. Process mixture in blender or food processor until well combined. Return to same pot. Bring to a boil. Fill hot sterilized half pint jars to within 1/2 inch (12 mm) of top. Place sterilized metal lids on jars and screw metal bands on securely. Process in a boiling water bath for 5 minutes. Makes 3 half pint (1 cup, 250 mL) jars.

2 tbsp. (30 mL): 40 Calories; 0.2 g Total Fat; 197 mg Sodium; 1 g Protein; 10 g Carbohydrate; 1 g Dietary Fibre

Pictured on page 154.

♦Wear gloves when chopping chili peppers, and avoid touching your eyes.

Tomato, Zucchini and Red Pepper Relish

Based on intensely flavoured roasted red peppers, this vibrantly coloured condiment works well with anything grilled, from chicken and pork to hot dogs and sausages. Teaming it with shrimp and freshly cooked pasta is another delicious option.

Medium red peppers, quartered and seeded	3	3
Cooking oil	2 tbsp.	30 mL
Medium onions, sliced	2	2
Garlic cloves, crushed	4	4
Yellow mustard seed	1 tbsp.	15 mL
Ground cumin	1 tbsp.	15 mL
Medium tomatoes (about 1 3/4 lb., 790 g), peeled and chopped	6	6
Medium zucchini, chopped	3	3
White wine vinegar	1 cup	250 mL
Balsamic (or red wine) vinegar	2 tbsp.	30 mL
Brown sugar, packed	1/3 cup	75 mL
Salt	1 1/2 tsp.	7 mL

Broil red peppers, skin side up, for 8 to 10 minutes until skin is blistered and blackened. Place in bowl. Cover with plastic wrap. Let stand for 10 minutes until cool enough to handle. Remove and discard skin. Chop peppers.

Heat cooking oil in large heavy pot or Dutch oven. Add next 4 ingredients. Heat and stir on medium for about 5 minutes until onion is soft.

Add peppers and remaining 6 ingredients to onion mixture. Bring to a boil. Reduce heat to medium. Gently boil, uncovered, for 45 to 50 minutes, stirring occasionally, until mixture is very thick but some liquid is remaining. Fill hot sterilized half pint jars to within 1/2 inch (12 mm) of top. Place sterilized metal lids on jars and screw metal bands on securely. Process in a boiling water bath for 5 minutes. Makes 7 half pint (1 cup, 250 mL) jars.

2 tbsp. (30 mL): 19 Calories; 0.6 g Total Fat; 63 mg Sodium; trace Protein; 3 g Carbohydrate; 1 g Dietary Fibre

Pictured below and on page 154.

Tomato, Zucchini and Red Pepper Relish, above

Honey Beer Mustard

If you've never made your own mustard, you're in for a treat—it's easy and fun and the results are outstanding. This hot mustard recipe produces the perfect beer-lover's mustard, tangy and sweet with a robust flavour. Great with steaks, chicken, pork or shrimp and, of course, smokies.

Liquid honey	1/3 cup	75 mL
Dry mustard	1/4 cup	60 mL
Balsamic (or red wine) vinegar	1 1/2 tbsp.	25 mL
Salt	1 tsp.	5 mL
Brown mustard seeds	1/2 cup	125 mL
Yellow mustard seeds	1/2 cup	125 mL
Beer (or alcohol-free beer)	1 cup	250 mL

Combine first 4 ingredients in small bowl.

Put brown and yellow mustard seeds into blender or coffee grinder. Process until mustard seeds are just crushed. Add to honey mixture. Stir.

Add beer. Mix well. Cover. Chill for at least 24 hours, stirring occasionally, to allow flavours to blend. Makes 1 3/4 cups (425 mL).

1 tbsp. (15 mL): 53 Calories; 2.3 g Total Fat; 82 mg Sodium; 2 g Protein; 6 g Carbohydrate; 1 g Dietary Fibre

Pictured below.

Honey Beer Mustard, above

Orange Mustard Sauce

This warm, creamy sauce is guaranteed to jazz up salmon, pork, chicken or lamb, whether pan-fried or barbecued. It will also impress your guests!

Whipping cream	1 cup	250 mL
Prepared orange juice	1/2 cup	125 mL
Brandy (or 1/2 tsp., 2 mL, brandy flavouring)	1 tbsp.	15 mL
Liquid honey	1 tbsp.	15 mL
Prepared mustard	1 tbsp.	15 mL
Salt	1/4 tsp.	1 mL
Freshly ground pepper	1/2 tsp.	2 mL
Water	2 tbsp.	30 mL
Cornstarch	1 tbsp.	15 mL

Combine first 7 ingredients in medium frying pan. Bring to a boil on medium-high. Reduce heat to medium. Gently boil, uncovered, for 2 to 3 minutes to blend flavours.

Stir water into cornstarch in small cup until smooth. Stir into whipping cream mixture. Heat and stir for 2 to 3 minutes until boiling and thickened. Makes 1 1/2 cups (375 mL).

2 tbsp. (30 mL): 77 Calories; 6.6 g Total Fat; 72 mg Sodium; 1 g Protein; 4 g Carbohydrate; trace Dietary Fibre

Sweet Mustard

"This is a nice sweet mustard that's especially good on ham."
— Kathy Choiniere, Courtenay, British Columbia

Cold water	1/4 cup	60 mL
White vinegar	3 tbsp.	50 mL
Worcestershire sauce	3/4 tsp.	4 mL
Egg yolks (large)	2	2
Granulated sugar	1/3 cup	75 mL
Dry mustard	1/4 cup	60 mL
Salt	1/2 tsp.	2 mL

Whisk first 4 ingredients together in small bowl until well combined.

Combine remaining 3 ingredients in medium saucepan. Add egg yolk mixture. Heat and stir on medium for about 5 minutes until thickened. Chill for at least 24 hours to allow flavours to blend. Makes 2/3 cup (150 mL).

1 tbsp. (15 mL): 55 Calories; 2.1 g Total Fat; 113 mg Sodium; 2 g Protein; 8 g Carbohydrate; trace Dietary Fibre

Cooking with Mustard

- Make an easy sauce by adding grainy mustard and a little cream to pan juices.

- Add Dijon mustard to mayonnaise or yogurt for a zippy dip or sandwich spread.

- Add whole mustard seeds to the water when cooking cabbage or beets.

- Both mustard sprouts and mustard greens, found in supermarkets, make a tasty, slightly sharp addition to salads and sandwiches.

- Dry mustard acts as a meat tenderizer when added to barbecue sauce. It also adds colour and flavour to sauces, salad dressings, baked beans and chowders.

- Mustard helps emulsify mayonnaise and salad dressings by coating the oil and water molecules with a fine film that keeps them suspended together.

- One teaspoon (5 mL) of dry mustard produces about the same flavour hit as 1 tablespoon (15 mL) of prepared Dijon mustard. To replace prepared mustard with dry mustard in a recipe, reconstitute the dry with an equal amount of lukewarm water and let it sit 10 minutes before using.

- Since heating mustard destroys much of its fiery intensity, add mustard late in the cooking process. A little dab will do! Don't let it boil for more than a minute.

Tomato, Tuna and Olive Salad with Croutons, below

Tomato, Tuna and Olive Salad with Croutons

"Our dish is a variation on Panzanella, the Tuscan salad made from day-old bread that is either soaked in water or fried in olive oil. We chose to make homemade croutons instead, which fry up crisp on the outside but softer on the inside than store-bought. Letting the dressed salad sit for a bit made the dressing especially delicious—and the toasted bread absorbed all those rich flavours."

— **Rita and David Penner, Sherwood Park, Alberta**

French baguette, cut into 1/3 inch (1 cm) cubes	3 1/2 cups	875 mL
Olive oil	3 tbsp.	50 mL
Ripe Roma (plum) tomatoes, peeled, seeded and chopped♦	4	4
Medium red onion, halved and thinly sliced	1	1
Black Italian (infornato) olives♦♦	1/2 cup	125 mL
Cans of chunk tuna (6 oz., 170 g, each), drained and flaked	2	2
Bunch of coarsely chopped Italian (flat leaf) parsley	1	1

DRESSING

Garlic cloves, crushed	4	4
Red wine vinegar	3 tbsp.	50 mL
Lemon juice	2 tbsp.	30 mL
Olive oil	3/4 cup	175 mL
Salt	1/2 tsp.	2 mL
Freshly ground pepper	1/2 tsp.	2 mL

Cook bread cubes in olive oil in large frying pan on medium for 5 to 8 minutes, stirring occasionally, until browned. Remove to paper towel to drain.

Combine next 5 ingredients in large serving bowl.

Dressing: Combine all 6 ingredients in jar with tight-fitting lid. Shake well to combine. Makes 1 cup (250 mL) dressing. Drizzle over salad. Toss until well coated. Cover. Chill for 30 minutes. Add bread cubes. Toss. Serves 6.

1 serving: 478 Calories; 39.2 g Total Fat; 622 mg Sodium; 15 g Protein; 18 g Carbohydrate; 2 g Dietary Fibre

Pictured above.

♦For easy peeling, plunge tomatoes into boiling water for a minute or two, then into ice water. The skins should come off easily.

♦♦You can substitute kalamata or ripe olives for infornato olives.

Trayci's Seashell Macaroni Salad

"Listen to the mm-mm's you get for this simple yet ever-so-succulent salad! Hope you enjoy it."

— **Trayci Tiszauer, Minton, Saskatchewan**

Medium shell pasta (about 4 cups, 1 L)	9 oz.	255 g
Boiling water	12 cups	3 L
Large tomato, diced	1	1
English cucumber, with peel, diced	1	1
Green onions, chopped	3	3
Granulated sugar	1/2 cup	125 mL
Cooking oil	1/4 cup	60 mL
Ketchup	1/2 cup	125 mL
White vinegar	1/4 cup	60 mL
Salt	1/2 tsp.	2 mL

Cook pasta in boiling water in large uncovered pot or Dutch oven for about 10 minutes, stirring occasionally, until tender but firm. Drain. Rinse under cold water. Drain well. Cool. Pour into large bowl.

Add next 3 ingredients. Toss well.

Combine remaining 5 ingredients in small bowl. Mix well. Pour over pasta mixture. Toss to coat. Chill for 6 hours or overnight. Makes 8 cups (2 L).

1 cup (250 mL): 247 Calories; 7.9 g Total Fat; 341 mg Sodium; 4 g Protein; 41 g Carbohydrate; 2 g Dietary Fibre

Broccoli Pasta Salad

Whether you serve Olga's pasta salad as a meal or a side dish, you'll love the tasty blend of sweet and savoury flavours.

— Olga Cunningham, Lashburn, Saskatchewan

Conchiglie (small shell) pasta, about 8 oz. (225 g)	2 1/2 cups	625 mL
Boiling water	6 cups	1.5 L
Salt	1 tsp.	5 mL
Olive oil	1 tbsp.	15 mL
Chopped broccoli	4 cups	1 L
Bacon slices, diced and cooked	8	8
Medium red onion, sliced	1	1
Sliced small fresh mushrooms	1 1/2 cups	375 mL
Golden raisins	1 cup	250 mL
Sunflower seeds, toasted◆	2/3 cup	150 mL
DRESSING		
Light mayonnaise (not salad dressing)	1/2 cup	125 mL
Freshly squeezed orange juice (about 1 medium)	1/4 cup	60 mL
Granulated sugar	2 tbsp.	30 mL
White wine vinegar	1 tbsp.	15 mL
Freshly ground pepper	1 tsp.	5 mL

Cook pasta in boiling water and salt in large uncovered pot or Dutch oven for 8 to 10 minutes, stirring occasionally, until tender but firm. Drain. Rinse under cold water. Drain well. Turn into large bowl.

Drizzle olive oil over pasta. Toss to coat.

Add next 6 ingredients. Mix well.

Dressing: Whisk all 5 ingredients in small bowl. Makes about 1 cup (250 mL) dressing. Drizzle over pasta. Toss gently to coat. Makes 12 cups (3 L).

1 cup (250 mL): 254 Calories; 11.4 g Total Fat; 149 mg Sodium; 7 g Protein; 34 g Carbohydrate; 3 g Dietary Fibre

Pictured below.

◆*To toast the sunflower seeds, place them in an ungreased frying pan. Heat on medium, stirring often, until golden.*

Chicken and Avocado Pasta Salad

Tender chicken, crisp vegetables, crunchy almonds and creamy avocado—could a light spring supper get any better?

Bow pasta (about 8 oz., 225 g)	2 1/2 cups	625 mL
Boiling water	8 cups	2 L
Salt	1 tsp.	5 mL
Olive oil	1 tbsp.	15 mL
Chopped cooked chicken	3 cups	750 mL
Diced red pepper (about 2 medium)	2 cups	500 mL
Green onions, sliced	8	8
Sliced celery (about 3 medium ribs)	1 1/3 cups	325 mL
Slivered almonds, toasted◆	1/2 cup	125 mL
DRESSING		
Mayonnaise (not salad dressing)	1/3 cup	75 mL
Lemon juice	2 tbsp.	30 mL
Garlic clove, crushed	1	1
Brown sugar, packed	1 tbsp.	15 mL
Paprika	1 tsp.	5 mL
Ground cumin	1 tsp.	5 mL
Medium ripe avocados, peeled, pitted and diced	2	2

Cook pasta in boiling water and salt in large uncovered pot or Dutch oven for 8 to 10 minutes, stirring occasionally, until tender but firm. Drain. Rinse under cold water. Drain well. Turn into large bowl.

Drizzle olive oil over pasta. Toss to coat.

Add next 5 ingredients. Toss.

Dressing: Whisk first 6 ingredients in small bowl. Add to pasta mixture. Toss to coat. Makes 2/3 cup (150 mL) dressing.

Gently fold in avocado. Makes 12 cups (3 L).

1 cup (250 mL): 196 Calories; 12.7 g Total Fat; 63 mg Sodium; 11 g Protein; 11 g Carbohydrate; 2 g Dietary Fibre

Pictured below.

◆*To toast the almonds, place them in an ungreased frying pan. Heat on medium, stirring often, until golden.*

Broccoli Pasta Salad, above

Chicken and Avocado Pasta Salad, above

Pepper and Mushroom Salad with Basil Honey Dressing

Pair this with Baked Salmon Spanakopita, page 79, and Kate's Roast Potatoes, page 192, for a delightful spring meal.

Mixed baby lettuce leaves	8 cups	2 L
Thinly sliced small fresh mushrooms	1 cup	250 mL
Can of roasted red peppers, drained and sliced	14 oz.	398 mL

BASIL HONEY DRESSING

Olive oil	1/3 cup	75 mL
Balsamic vinegar	2 tbsp.	30 mL
Chopped fresh basil leaves	2 tbsp.	30 mL
Liquid honey	1 tbsp.	15 mL
Garlic clove, crushed	1	1
Salt	1/4 tsp.	1 mL
Whole black peppercorns, cracked	1/4 tsp.	1 mL

Toss first 3 ingredients together in large bowl.

Basil Honey Dressing: Combine all 7 ingredients in sealable jar. Shake well until combined. Makes almost 1/2 cup (125 mL) dressing. Drizzle over salad. Toss gently. Makes 10 cups (2.5 L).

1 cup (250 mL): 87 Calories; 7.8 g Total Fat; 385 mg Sodium; 1 g Protein; 4 g Carbohydrate; 1 g Dietary Fibre

Pictured on page 79.

Honey Lemon Slaw

The sweet, zesty lemon dressing is wonderful with cabbage. *"This is the best coleslaw I have ever made."*

— Casey Vanchie, Port Alberni, British Columbia

Mayonnaise (not salad dressing)	1/2 cup	125 mL
Liquid honey	2 tbsp.	30 mL
Finely grated lemon zest	1/2 tsp.	2 mL
Freshly squeezed lemon juice	2 tbsp.	30 mL
Salt	1/2 tsp.	2 mL
Ground ginger	1/4 tsp.	1 mL
Shredded cabbage	2 cups	500 mL
Shredded red cabbage	2 cups	500 mL

Combine all 8 ingredients in large bowl. Toss to coat well. Cover. Chill for 2 hours before serving. Makes 2 2/3 cups (650 mL).

1/2 cup (125 mL): 200 Calories; 17.7 g Total Fat; 344 mg Sodium; 1 g Protein; 11 g Carbohydrate; 1 g Dietary Fibre

Thai Salad

"This salad is a huge hit with friends. The dressing is hot and very zippy and takes people by surprise."
— Kelly Sorochan, Edmonton, Alberta

Package of vermicelli rice noodles	11 oz.	300 g
Boiling water, to cover		
Pea pods, thinly sliced	1 lb.	454 g
Bean sprouts	1 cup	250 mL
Medium green pepper, sliced	1	1
Medium red pepper, sliced	1	1
Medium orange pepper, sliced	1	1
Medium English cucumber, sliced diagonally	1	1
Green onions, chopped	6	6

SESAME CHILI OIL DRESSING

Soy sauce	1/2 cup	125 mL
Cooking oil	1/4 cup	60 mL
Red wine vinegar	3 tbsp.	50 mL
Sesame oil	2 tbsp.	30 mL
Liquid honey	2 tbsp.	30 mL
Sesame seeds, toasted♦	1/4 cup	60 mL
Chili paste	1 tbsp.	15 mL
Freshly grated gingerroot	1 tsp.	5 mL
Garlic cloves, minced	2	2

Place vermicelli noodles in small bowl. Cover with boiling water. Let stand for 3 minutes. Drain. Turn into salad bowl.

Add next 7 ingredients. Toss.

Sesame Chili Oil Dressing: Combine all 9 ingredients in small bowl until well mixed. Makes 1 1/2 cups (375 mL) dressing. Drizzle over salad. Toss to coat. Serves 6.

1 serving: 442 Calories; 17.8 g Total Fat; 1157 mg Sodium; 7 g Protein; 66 g Carbohydrate; 4 g Dietary Fibre

♦To toast the sesame seeds, place them in an ungreased frying pan. Heat on medium, stirring often, until golden.

Bruce's Own Killer Basil Tomato Salad

"Ideal in the summer when big, scrumptious tomatoes are in season and fresh aromatic basil is waist-high."
— Bruce Daniluck, Edmonton, Alberta

Very ripe large tomatoes, sliced	5	5
Medium red onion, cut in half crosswise, then thinly sliced	1	1

DRESSING

Garlic cloves	4	4
Tomato sauce	1/4 cup	60 mL
Red wine vinegar	1/3 cup	75 mL
Granulated sugar (optional)	1 tbsp.	15 mL
Salt	1/2 tsp.	2 mL
Fresh sweet basil	3 tbsp.	50 mL
Worcestershire sauce	2 tsp.	10 mL
Prepared grainy mustard	1 tsp.	5 mL
Freshly ground pepper	1/2 tsp.	2 mL
Hot pepper sauce	1/2 tsp.	2 mL
Tomato paste	2 tbsp.	30 mL
Olive oil	1 cup	250 mL
Finely chopped parsley, for garnish		
Fresh sweet basil (or parsley) sprigs, for garnish		

Arrange tomato slices, overlapping, on large platter. Scatter onion over top. Cover. Chill.

Dressing: Process garlic cloves in food processor until minced.

Add next 10 ingredients. Process until blended.

With machine running, add olive oil in steady stream through feed chute. Process for 1 minute until smooth. Makes 1 3/4 cups (425 mL) dressing. Drizzle over tomatoes.

Sprinkle with parsley. Garnish with basil. Serves 6.

1 serving: 385 Calories; 38.6 g Total Fat; 323 mg Sodium; 2 g Protein; 11 g Carbohydrate; 2 g Dietary Fibre

Crunchy Cabbage Salad

Chinese cabbage is widely available in supermarkets and fruit and vegetable outlets. Great colour, good crunchy texture and lots of flavour make this salad a festive and tasty choice for any outdoor gathering.

Finely shredded Chinese cabbage	3 cups	750 mL
Finely shredded red cabbage	2 cups	500 mL
Celery ribs, finely sliced	2	2
Green onions, chopped	8	8
Sesame seeds, toasted◆	3 tbsp.	50 mL
Sliced almonds, toasted◆	1/2 cup	125 mL
Steam-fried noodles	2 cups	500 mL
BROWN SUGAR DRESSING		
Cooking oil	1/3 cup	75 mL
White vinegar	1/3 cup	75 mL
Brown sugar, packed	2 tbsp.	30 mL
Soy sauce	2 tsp.	10 mL

Combine first 7 ingredients in large salad bowl.

Brown Sugar Dressing: Combine all 4 ingredients in jar with tight-fitting lid. Shake well. Makes 1 cup (250 mL) dressing. Drizzle over salad. Toss to coat well. Serve immediately. Makes 9 cups (2.25 L). Serves 6.

1 serving: 320 Calories; 25.2 g Total Fat; 213 mg Sodium; 5 g Protein; 22 g Carbohydrate; 4 g Dietary Fibre

Pictured below.

◆Because almonds and sesame seeds toast at different times, they must be toasted separately. To toast, place them in an ungreased frying pan. Heat on medium, stirring often, until golden.

Beef Fajita Salad

This recipe makes four steaks go a long way. If flank steaks are on sale, let them sit in a Mexican-style marinade overnight, then proceed with the recipe.

Taco seasoning mix	2 tbsp.	30 mL
Strip loin steaks (8 oz., 225 g, each)	4	4
Mixed baby lettuce leaves (about 8 oz., 225 g)	12 cups	3 L
Avocados, peeled, pitted and sliced	2	2
Medium red onion, sliced	1	1
Ranch dressing	1 cup	250 mL
Salsa	2/3 cup	150 mL
Sour cream	1/2 cup	125 mL
Canned sliced jalapeño peppers, drained	1/2 cup	125 mL
Corn chips, coarsely crushed	2 cups	500 mL

Preheat grill to medium-high. Rub seasoning mix into both sides of steaks. Cook steaks for 3 to 5 minutes until juices come to surface. Turn steaks over. Cook for 3 to 5 minutes until desired doneness. Let stand for 5 minutes. Cut across the grain into 1/8 inch (3 mm) thick slices.

Combine next 3 ingredients in large bowl. Toss. Divide among individual serving plates. Top with steak. Drizzle with dressing.

Top with salsa and sour cream. Sprinkle with jalapeños and corn chips. Serves 8.

1 serving: 416 Calories; 32.3 g Total Fat; 1033 mg Sodium; 20 g Protein; 14 g Carbohydrate; 3 g Dietary Fibre

Marinated Carrot Salad

"This recipe was given to me by my auntie. If she enjoyed something while she was eating out, she would speak to the chef—and most times she would get the recipe."

— **Jeanne Crocker, Exeter, Ontario**

Grated carrot	4 cups	1 L
Finely chopped onion	1 cup	250 mL
Cooking oil	1/2 cup	125 mL
Dark raisins	1 cup	250 mL
Granulated sugar	1 cup	250 mL
White vinegar	1/2 cup	125 mL
Celery seed	2 tsp.	10 mL

Combine all 7 ingredients in large bowl. Cover. Chill overnight. Makes 5 3/4 cups (1.45 L).

1/2 cup (125 mL): 225 Calories; 10.3 g Total Fat; 17 mg Sodium; 1 g Protein; 35 g Carbohydrate; 2 g Dietary Fibre

Old-Fashioned Creamy Coleslaw

Crunchy coleslaw is a great picnic food and a superb accompaniment to favourite summer fare. Prepare all the ingredients ahead and store in a large airtight container or plastic bowl fitted with a lid. Pack the dressing separately in another sealed container and toss together with salad ingredients up to one hour before serving.

Finely shredded green cabbage	3 1/2 cups	875 mL
Finely shredded red cabbage	3 cups	750 mL
Grated carrot	1 cup	250 mL
Celery rib, finely chopped	1	1
Green onions, chopped	4	4
DRESSING		
Mayonnaise	1/2 cup	125 mL
Apple cider vinegar	1 1/2 tbsp.	25 mL
Granulated sugar	1 1/2 tbsp.	25 mL
Salt	1/4 tsp.	1 mL
Freshly ground pepper	1/4 tsp.	1 mL

Combine first 5 ingredients in large bowl.

Dressing: Combine all 5 ingredients in small bowl. Drizzle over salad. Toss to coat well. Makes 7 1/2 cups (1.9 L).

1/2 cup (125 mL): 77 Calories; 6.4 g Total Fat; 91 mg Sodium; 1 g Protein; 5 g Carbohydrate; 1 g Dietary Fibre

Crunchy Cabbage Salad, above

Potato and Green Bean Salad with Vinaigrette Dressing

What's a picnic without potato salad! This one can be prepared a day ahead. Store the vegetable-herb mix in an airtight container and the dressing in a jar or other container with a secure lid. At serving time, give the vinaigrette a good shake before adding it to the salad.
— Pat Warren, Calgary, Alberta

Unpeeled medium red potatoes	2 lbs.	900 g
Water		
Fresh whole green beans, trimmed	10 1/2 oz.	300 g
Water		
Medium red pepper, thinly sliced	1	1
Chopped fresh sweet basil	3 tbsp.	50 mL

VINAIGRETTE DRESSING

Olive oil	1/3 cup	75 mL
Balsamic (or red wine) vinegar	3 tbsp.	50 mL
Garlic cloves, crushed	3	3
Dijon mustard	2 tsp.	10 mL
Granulated sugar	1/2 tsp.	2 mL
Salt	1/2 tsp.	2 mL
Freshly ground pepper, to taste		

Cook potatoes in water in large saucepan on medium-high for 20 to 25 minutes until tender. Drain. Rinse with cold water. Drain well. Cut each potato into quarters. Set aside.

Blanch beans in boiling water in large saucepan for 3 to 5 minutes until tender-crisp. Drain. Place in bowl of ice water until completely cooled. Drain well.

Combine potatoes, beans, red pepper and basil in large bowl.

Vinaigrette Dressing: Combine all 7 ingredients in jar with tight-fitting lid. Shake well to combine. Makes 1/2 cup (125 mL) dressing. Drizzle over salad just before serving. Toss gently. Makes 9 cups (2.25 L). Serves 6.

1 serving: 272 Calories; 13.1 g Total Fat; 234 mg Sodium; 4 g Protein; 37 g Carbohydrate; 4 g Dietary Fibre

Pictured on page 130.

Apple and Shrimp Salad with Creamy Dill Dressing, below

Apple and Shrimp Salad with Creamy Dill Dressing

This is a delightful salad—fresh and lively in appearance and taste. Great as a lunch or light supper, and a very nice first course before grilled fish, pork tenderloin or chicken. For extra crunch, add some chopped celery or sliced water chestnuts.

Medium cooked prawns, peeled and deveined	1 2/3 lbs.	750 g
Medium Granny Smith apples, unpeeled, quartered and thinly sliced	2	2
Head of romaine lettuce (about 15 cups, 3.74 L), torn bite size	1	1
Walnuts, chopped	1/2 cup	125 mL
Raisins	1/2 cup	125 mL

CREAMY DILL DRESSING

Mayonnaise	1/4 cup	60 mL
Sour cream	1/4 cup	60 mL
Olive (or cooking) oil	3 tbsp.	50 mL
White wine vinegar	2 tbsp.	30 mL
Chopped fresh dill	2 tbsp.	30 mL
Granulated sugar	2 tsp.	10 mL
Salt	3/4 tsp.	4 mL
Freshly ground pepper	1 tsp.	5 mL

Combine first 5 ingredients in large serving bowl.

Creamy Dill Dressing: Process all 8 ingredients in blender until well combined. Makes 3/4 cup (175 mL) dressing. Drizzle over salad. Toss until well coated. Serve immediately. Serves 8.

1 serving: 316 Calories; 18.1 g Total Fat; 479 mg Sodium; 23 g Protein; 17 g Carbohydrate; 2 g Dietary Fibre

Pictured above.

Arugula and Roasted Sweet Potato Salad

If you haven't been introduced to the delights of fresh arugula, this is a great recipe to try. The delicate, slightly bitter, peppery flavour of this green is nicely balanced with the sweet potatoes and the honey dressing. A great summer salad to take to a neighbourhood barbecue.

Cooking oil	1 tbsp.	15 mL
Salt	1/4 tsp.	1 mL
Freshly cracked pepper	1/2 tsp.	2 mL
Cubed sweet potato (or yam)	3 cups	750 mL
Arugula (rocket) leaves, trimmed	1 lb.	454 g
Pine nuts, toasted◆	1/3 cup	75 mL
Bacon slices, cooked crisp and crumbled	6	6
Medium red onion, cut in half and sliced thinly	1	1

HONEY DRESSING

Olive oil	1/3 cup	75 mL
Balsamic vinegar	2 tbsp.	30 mL
Prepared grainy mustard	1 tbsp.	15 mL
Liquid honey	1 tbsp.	15 mL
Garlic clove, crushed	1	1

Combine first 4 ingredients in large bowl. Spread mixture in single layer on ungreased baking sheet. Bake in 375°F (190°C) oven for about 25 minutes until tender and browned. Cool. Turn into large salad bowl.

Add next 4 ingredients.

Honey Dressing: Combine all 5 ingredients in jar with tight-fitting lid. Shake to combine well. Makes 1/2 cup (125 mL) dressing. Drizzle over arugula mixture. Toss gently to coat well. Serves 6 to 8.

1 serving: 332 Calories; 23.7 g Total Fat; 266 mg Sodium; 8 g Protein; 26 g Carbohydrate; 4 g Dietary Fibre

◆To toast the pine nuts, place them in an ungreased frying pan. Heat on medium, stirring often, until golden.

Watercress and Salmon Salad with Creamy Horseradish Dressing

Peppery watercress and a lively dressing go exceptionally well with the natural richness of grilled salmon. Crisp the watercress in the refrigerator ahead of time.

Salmon fillet	13 oz.	370 g
Watercress, trimmed (about 3 bunches)	15 oz.	425 g
Sugar snap peas	2 cups	500 mL
Small red onion, thinly sliced	1	1

CREAMY HORSERADISH DRESSING

Olive oil	1/4 cup	60 mL
White vinegar	1 tbsp.	15 mL
Prepared horseradish	1 tbsp.	15 mL
Garlic clove, crushed	1	1
Chopped fresh chives	3 tbsp.	50 mL
Granulated sugar	1 tsp.	5 mL

A Glossary of Greens

Chicory, chicory chock-full of flavour: *The words "slightly bitter" are most often used in describing the taste of raw chicories—but that doesn't mean they aren't good. Chicories add an edge of interest to any salad (and some cook up nicely as a side vegetable).*

Belgian Endive

Curly Endive

Escarole

Radicchio

Mesclun mates: *So many varieties of baby this and baby that ... a medley of tastes to enjoy on their own or tossed in with more familiar lettuce*

Baby Mustard Greens

Baby Red Oak Leaf

Baby Red Swiss Chard

Mizuna

Preheat grill to medium. Grill salmon for about 4 minutes per side until flakes easily when tested with a fork. Flake into pieces with fork.

Combine salmon and next 3 ingredients in large salad bowl.

Creamy Horseradish Dressing: Combine all 6 ingredients in jar with tight-fitting lid. Shake to combine well. Makes 1/2 cup (125 mL) dressing. Drizzle dressing over watercress mixture. Toss gently to coat well. Serves 6.

1 serving: 237 Calories; 16.6 g Total Fat; 69 mg Sodium; 16 g Protein; 7 g Carbohydrate; 3 g Dietary Fibre

Belgian Endive Salad with Sweet Soy Dressing

Endive is often teamed with milder-tasting salad greens. It's perfect with celery, sunflower seeds, noodles and a sweet Asian-style dressing. Great with grilled shrimp or salmon.

Belgian endive, trimmed (about 6 1/2 cups, 1.6 L)	1 lb.	454 g
Celery ribs, thinly sliced	2	2
Green onions, finely chopped	8	8
Sunflower seeds, toasted◆	1/3 cup	75 mL
Steam-fried noodles◆◆	2 cups	500 mL
SWEET SOY DRESSING		
Olive oil	1/3 cup	75 mL
Lime juice	3 tbsp.	50 mL
Sweet chili sauce	2 tbsp.	30 mL
Soy sauce	1 tsp.	5 mL
Garlic clove, crushed	1	1
Finely grated gingerroot	1/2 tsp.	2 mL

Combine first 5 ingredients in large salad bowl.

Sweet Soy Dressing: Combine all 6 ingredients in jar with tight-fitting lid. Shake to combine well. Makes 2/3 cup (150 mL) dressing. Drizzle dressing over endive mixture. Toss gently to coat well. Serves 6.

1 serving: 262 Calories; 21.6 g Total Fat; 212 mg Sodium; 4 g Protein; 16 g Carbohydrate; 1 g Dietary Fibre

◆To toast the sunflower seeds, place them in an ungreased frying pan. Heat on medium, stirring often, until golden.

◆◆Add noodles just before serving so they stay crunchy.

Mix 'n' match greens: *Leafy vegetables such as these add colour, flavour and texture to a bowl of greens.*

Arugula

Baby Frisée

Spinach

Watercress

Chicories

Belgian Endive (EN-dyv): Slight, distinctive sharpness. Slice into salads, bake whole, sauté for side dishes or use the leaves to hold appetizer fillings.

Curly Endive: Strong, peppery. Usually eaten raw, often in combination with milder lettuces. This one is often called chicory, courtesy of the Americans, and frisée, courtesy of the French.

Escarole (EHS-kuh-rohl): Slightly bitter. Young leaves are tender enough for salads, but otherwise it's best cooked as a side dish or in soups.

Radicchio (rah-DEE-kee-oh): Most distinctly bitter. It's especially good in salads that include fruit or nuts. As a side vegetable, tame the taste by grilling or braising.

Mesclun Mates

Baby Mustard Greens: Pungent, peppery. Mature leaves are better when cooked.

Baby Red Oak Leaf: Mild, sweet. These tender soft leaves have a distinctive shape and make a pretty salad addition.

Baby Red Swiss Chard: Mild, earthy. The red stems and bright green leaves are tasty and attractive.

Mizuna (mih-ZOO-nuh): Pleasant, peppery. This Japanese mustard is much milder than other mustard leaf varieties.

Mix 'n' Match Greens

Arugula (ah-ROO-guh-lah) or **Rocket:** Distinct, spicy, peppery. This member of the cabbage family is rarely served on its own, but it adds real zip to any bowl of greens.

Baby Frisée (free-ZAY): Mildly bitter. Its taste and delicate, slender, feathery leaves are a nice contrast in mixes.

Spinach: Mild. The tender texture of the flat leaf variety is especially suitable for salads.

Watercress: Strong, peppery. It's great for spicing up a salad or sandwich, and for use as a garnish.

Mixed Baby Salad with
Roasted Peppers, below

Mixed Baby Salad with Roasted Peppers

Vibrant colour and a variety of shapes make
for an eye-appealing salad that doesn't
disappoint in taste. Be sure to toss well just
before serving so the ingredients don't get lost
beneath the greens.

CROUTONS

Slices of white bread, crusts removed	4	4
Hard margarine (or butter)	2 tbsp.	30 mL
Red pepper	1	1
Yellow pepper	1	1
Bags of mesclun blend (baby salad greens), 4.5 oz., 128 g, each	2	2
Can of romano beans, drained and rinsed	19 oz.	540 mL
Whole kalamata olives	1/2 cup	125 mL
Medium red onion, halved and thinly sliced	1	1

BASIL DRESSING

Olive oil	1/3 cup	75 mL
Red wine vinegar	2 tbsp.	30 mL
Chopped fresh sweet basil	3 tbsp.	50 mL
Garlic clove	1	1
Granulated sugar	1 tsp.	5 mL
Salt	1/4 tsp.	1 mL
Freshly ground pepper	1/4 tsp.	1 mL

Croutons: Cut bread slices into 1/2 inch
(12 mm) cubes. Sauté in margarine in frying
pan for 4 to 5 minutes until crunchy and
browned. Remove to paper towel to drain.

Preheat grill to high. Cut both peppers into
quarters. Remove seeds and membranes. Place
peppers, skin side down, on grill. Grill until skins
are blackened and blistered, or broil, skin side
up, 6 inches (15 cm) from heat, for 15 minutes.
Place peppers in plastic bag or covered bowl
for 10 minutes. Peel off and discard skins. Cut
into 1/3 inch (1 cm) thick slices.

Combine next 4 ingredients in medium bowl.
Add peppers and croutons.

Basil Dressing: Process all 7 ingredients in
blender until smooth. Makes 1/2 cup (125 mL)
dressing. Drizzle over lettuce mixture. Toss
gently to coat well. Serves 10 to 12.

1 serving: 165 Calories; 10.9 g Total Fat; 259 mg Sodium;
4 g Protein; 15 g Carbohydrate; 2 g Dietary Fibre

Pictured above.

Ladies' Luncheon Salad

*"This is such a nice thing to have on one of those
really hot days when you don't want to heat up the
kitchen."* As a variation, try substituting steak
for the chicken.

— Linda Craig, Edmonton, Alberta

Boneless, skinless chicken breast halves (about 1 lb., 454 g)	4	4
Head of romaine lettuce, torn bite size (about 12 cups, 3 L)	1	1
Sliced fresh strawberries	1 cup	250 mL
Can of mandarin orange segments, drained	10 oz.	284 mL
Medium kiwifruit, peeled and sliced	3	3

RASPBERRY BASIL DRESSING

Raspberry vinegar	6 tbsp.	100 mL
Olive oil	3 tbsp.	50 mL
Dried sweet basil	1 tsp.	5 mL
Salt, sprinkle		
Pepper, sprinkle		

Preheat grill to medium. Grill chicken for
6 to 7 minutes per side until juices run clear.
Chill. Slice thinly across grain.

Combine next 4 ingredients in large salad bowl.

Raspberry Basil Dressing: Combine first 3 ingredients in jar with tight-fitting lid. Add salt and pepper to taste. Shake to combine well. Makes 2/3 cup (150 mL) dressing. Add chicken to lettuce mixture. Drizzle dressing over all. Toss gently to coat well. Serves 8 to 10.

1 serving: 158 Calories; 6.5 g Total Fat; 9 mg Sodium; 15 g Protein; 11 g Carbohydrate; 3 g Dietary Fibre

Pictured on this page.

Radicchio and Pear Salad with Apple Cider Dressing

The slightly bitter taste of radicchio is perfect partnered with sweet, ripe pear and Parmesan cheese.

TOFFEE PECANS

Granulated sugar	1/2 cup	125 mL
Water	3 tbsp.	50 mL
Pecan halves	2/3 cup	150 mL
Heads of radicchio lettuce, trimmed and torn bite size (about 8 cups, 2 L)	2	2
Medium pears, cored and thinly sliced	2	2
Grated fresh Parmesan cheese	1/2 cup	125 mL

APPLE CIDER DRESSING

Olive oil	1/3 cup	75 mL
Apple cider vinegar	3 tbsp.	50 mL
Prepared grainy mustard	1 tbsp.	15 mL
Brown sugar, packed	2 tsp.	10 mL
Garlic clove, crushed	1	1
Salt	1/4 tsp.	1 mL
Freshly ground pepper	1/2 tsp.	2 mL

Toffee Pecans: Combine granulated sugar and water in medium saucepan. Heat and stir on low until sugar is dissolved. Cook, uncovered, on high for 5 minutes, without stirring, until mixture is lightly browned.

Lightly grease baking sheet with cooking spray. Arrange pecans in single layer on sheet. Drizzle with sugar mixture. Cool. Coarsely chop. Makes 1 cup (250 mL).

Combine next 3 ingredients in large salad bowl. Add Toffee Pecans.

Apple Cider Dressing: Combine all 7 ingredients in jar with tight-fitting lid. Shake to combine well. Makes 2/3 cup (150 mL) dressing. Drizzle dressing over lettuce mixture. Toss gently to coat well. Serves 8 to 10.

1 serving: 256 Calories; 18.2 g Total Fat; 233 mg Sodium; 4 g Protein; 21 g Carbohydrate; 1 g Dietary Fibre

Pictured below.

Spinach, Raspberry and Almond Salad

Flavoured with a hint of garlic and orange, this dressing is delicious on dark green spinach with snow-white feta and fresh raspberries.

Baby spinach leaves (about 10 cups, 2.5 L)	10 oz.	300 g
Fresh raspberries	1 1/4 cups	300 mL
Slivered almonds, toasted◆	1/2 cup	125 mL
Feta cheese, crumbled	3 oz.	85 g

RASPBERRY DRESSING

Olive oil	1/3 cup	75 mL
Raspberry vinegar	3 tbsp.	50 mL
Finely grated orange zest	1/2 tsp.	2 mL
Garlic clove	1	1
Salt	1/4 tsp.	1 mL
Freshly ground pepper	1/2 tsp.	2 mL
Granulated sugar	1/2 tsp.	2 mL

Combine first 4 ingredients in large salad bowl.

Raspberry Dressing: Process all 7 ingredients in blender until well combined. Makes 1/2 cup (125 mL) dressing. Drizzle dressing over spinach mixture. Toss gently to coat well. Serves 8 to 10.

1 serving: 175 Calories; 15.7 g Total Fat; 227 mg Sodium; 4 g Protein; 6 g Carbohydrate; 3 g Dietary Fibre

◆*To toast the almonds, place them in an ungreased frying pan. Heat on medium, stirring often, until golden.*

Ladies Luncheon Salad, page 164

Radicchio and Pear Salad with Apple Cider Dressing, left

Warm Spinach and Mushroom
Salad, below

German Potato Salad

Unlike its North American cousins, this perennial German favourite from the Concordia Club contains no eggs or mayonnaise. During Oktoberfest, it's served with schnitzel and a roll. The dressing is poured right over the warm potatoes so they soak up all the flavours. If making the salad in advance, store it in the refrigerator but take the chill off by bringing to room temperature before serving.

— **Concordia Club, Kitchener, Ontario**

Medium onion, diced	1	1
Medium dill pickles, chopped	3 - 4	3 - 4
Red wine vinegar	1/4 cup	60 mL
Large unpeeled Yukon Gold potatoes	7	7
Water		
Vegetable (or chicken) bouillon cubes (1/5 oz., 6 g, each)	3	3
Hot water	1/2 cup	125 mL
Salt	1/4 tsp.	1 mL
Pepper	1/8 tsp.	0.5 mL
Cooking oil	1 tbsp.	15 mL

Combine first 3 ingredients in small bowl. Set aside.

Cook potatoes in water in large saucepan for about 1 hour until tender. Drain well. Cool enough to handle. Peel. Mash very coarsely with fork. Transfer to large bowl.

Combine bouillon cubes and hot water in small bowl. Stir until bouillon cubes are dissolved. Pour over hot potatoes.

Add onion mixture and remaining 3 ingredients. Mix well. Makes 8 cups (2 L).

1 cup (250 mL): 136 Calories; 2.2 g Total Fat; 810 mg Sodium; 3 g Protein; 27 g Carbohydrate; 2 g Dietary Fibre

Pictured on page 105.

Variation: Add 1 tbsp. (15 mL) prepared mustard, 2 tbsp. (30 mL) chopped cooked bacon and 1 tbsp. (15 mL) chopped fresh parsley.

Warm Spinach and Mushroom Salad

Lots of interesting textures and flavours elevate the humble spinach salad to new heights!

Package of firm tofu	14 oz.	350 g
Olive oil	1/2 cup	125 mL
Balsamic (or red wine) vinegar	5 tbsp.	75 mL
Grainy mustard	2 tbsp.	30 mL
Liquid honey	2 tbsp.	30 mL
Garlic cloves, crushed	2	2
Salt	1/2 tsp.	2 mL
Freshly ground pepper	1 tsp.	5 mL
Olive oil	1 tbsp.	15 mL
Brown (crimini) mushrooms, sliced♦	3 1/2 cups	875 mL
Garlic cloves, crushed	2	2
Balsamic (or red wine) vinegar	1 tbsp.	15 mL
Salt, to taste		
Freshly ground pepper, to taste		
Bag of baby spinach leaves	6 oz.	170 g
Pine nuts, toasted♦♦	1/3 cup	75 mL

Cut tofu into 3/4 inch (2 cm) cubes. Place on paper towel to drain.

Combine next 7 ingredients in jar with tight-fitting lid. Shake well. Combine tofu and 1/2 of olive oil mixture in medium bowl. Cover. Marinate in refrigerator for at least 1 hour.

Heat second amount of olive oil in large frying pan. Add mushrooms. Cook on medium-high for 5 to 6 minutes, stirring occasionally, until mushrooms are golden.

Add next 4 ingredients. Cook for 2 to 3 minutes until no liquid remains.

Drain tofu, discarding marinade. Combine spinach leaves, mushroom mixture and tofu in large bowl. Toss. Divide among 4 shallow salad bowls. Sprinkle with pine nuts. Drizzle with remaining olive oil mixture. Serves 4.

1 serving: 482 Calories; 40.4 g Total Fat; 351 mg Sodium; 20 g Protein; 19 g Carbohydrate; 5 g Dietary Fibre

Pictured above and on back cover.

♦Brown (crimini) mushrooms add a nice flavour. White mushrooms may be substituted.

♦♦To toast the pine nuts, place them in an ungreased frying pan. Heat on medium, stirring often, until golden.

Creamy Baby Potato Salad

You can never have too many potato salad recipes and this one is great, whether served warm or cold. Make the dressing up to a couple of days ahead and add the cooked potatoes at the last minute.

Unpeeled baby red potatoes, halved	1 lb.	454 g
Unpeeled baby white potatoes, halved	1 lb.	454 g
Boiling water		
Salt	1/2 tsp.	2 mL
Bacon slices, cooked crisp and crumbled	4	4
Light sour cream	1/4 cup	60 mL
Light mayonnaise (not salad dressing)	1/4 cup	60 mL
Prepared grainy mustard	2 tbsp.	30 mL
Chopped fresh chives	3 tbsp.	50 mL
Freshly ground pepper	1/2 tsp.	2 mL
Fresh chives, cut into 1 inch (2.5 cm) pieces	2 tbsp.	30 mL

Cook potatoes in boiling salted water for 12 to 15 minutes until just tender. Drain well.

Combine next 6 ingredients in large bowl. Makes 1 cup (250 mL) dressing. Add potatoes. Mix to coat well. Spoon into large serving bowl.

Sprinkle with second amount of chives. Makes 6 cups (1.5 L). Serves 6.

1 serving: 183 Calories; 6.5 g Total Fat; 222 mg Sodium; 5 g Protein; 27 g Carbohydrate; 2 g Dietary Fibre

Coleslaw

This classic coleslaw is made year-round by members of the small German-Canadian Hunting & Fishing Club, which opens on weekends during Oktoberfest. The club is also proud of its *Rollbraten am Speiss*, a tantalizing pork loin seasoned with secret spices and roasted on a spit, and its pasta-like *spätzle*. *"Our ladies make everything fresh,"* says the club's Oktoberfest director, Janet Kunsch, who provided the following recipe. *"You can make this salad the night before and it keeps four to five days in the fridge."*

— **German-Canadian Hunting & Fishing Club, Mannheim, Ontario**

Medium head of cabbage, grated (about 12 cups, 3 L)	1	1
Medium yellow (or red) pepper, diced	1	1
Green onions, chopped	3	3
Granulated sugar	2/3 cup	150 mL
White vinegar	1 cup	250 mL
Cooking oil	2/3 cup	150 mL
Salt	1/2 tsp.	2 mL

Layer first 3 ingredients in large bowl.

Combine remaining 4 ingredients in medium saucepan. Heat and stir on medium until sugar is dissolved. Bring to a boil. Pour over cabbage mixture. Do not mix. Cover. Cool. Chill overnight. Toss until well combined. Makes about 12 cups (3 L).

1 cup (250 mL): 184 Calories; 13.1 g Total Fat; 113 mg Sodium; 1 g Protein; 18 g Carbohydrate; 2 g Dietary Fibre

Pictured on page 104.

Mexican Picnic Salad

"We barbecue chicken and pork in the summer, then slice it really thin to wrap in tortillas. In keeping with the Mexican theme, we serve this salad on the side." Adjust the amount of hot sauce to your liking.

— **Jayne Schafer, Cochrane, Alberta**

Medium shell pasta, cooked and drained	1 lb.	454 g
Sliced celery	3/4 cup	175 mL
Chopped red pepper	3/4 cup	175 mL
Green onions, chopped	8	8
Jars of pimientos (2 oz., 57 mL, each), drained and chopped	2	2
Can of diced green chilies	4 oz.	114 mL
Can of kidney beans, drained and rinsed	19 oz.	540 mL
Can of sliced ripe olives	4 1/2 oz.	125 mL
Italian salad dressing	3/4 cup	175 mL
Dashes hot pepper sauce	4	4
Salt	1 tsp.	5 mL
Pepper	1 1/2 tsp.	7 mL
Seasoned salt	1/2 tsp.	2 mL
Salsa	3 tbsp.	50 mL
Mayonnaise (not salad dressing)	1 1/2 cups	375 mL

Combine first 8 ingredients in large salad bowl.

Mix remaining 7 ingredients together in small bowl until combined. Drizzle over pasta mixture. Toss to coat well. Cover. Chill overnight. Makes 12 cups (3 L). Serves 12.

1 serving: 491 Calories; 35.6 g Total Fat; 813 mg Sodium; 7 g Protein; 37 g Carbohydrate; 3 g Dietary Fibre

Pictured below.

Mexican Picnic Salad, above

Sharon's Warm Yam Salad, below

Spinach Salad

"A few summers ago an aunt of mine made this incredibly 'different' spinach salad. As soon as I tasted it, I knew I had to have the recipe. Now it is one of my favourites. I am passing on this delectable salad so your readers can get as much enjoyment out of it as I do."
— Lynne Schurek, Hinton, Alberta

DRESSING

Soy sauce	1/4 cup	60 mL
Cooking oil	1/2 cup	125 mL
Garlic cloves, crushed	3	3
Celery salt	1/8 tsp.	0.5 mL
Cooked rice	2 cups	500 mL
Fresh spinach leaves (1/2 of 10 oz., 285 g, bag)	7 cups	1.75 L
Dark raisins	1/3 cup	75 mL
Cashews	1 cup	250 mL
Chopped celery	1 cup	250 mL
Chopped fresh mushrooms	1/2 cup	125 mL
Chopped green onion	1/2 cup	125 mL
Chopped red pepper	1/2 cup	125 mL

Dressing: Combine first 4 ingredients in jar with tight-fitting lid. Shake to combine well. Chill for 24 hours.

Combine remaining 8 ingredients in large bowl. Shake dressing. Drizzle over salad. Toss until well coated. Let stand for 1 hour before serving. Toss. Makes 12 cups (3 L).

1 cup (250 mL): 227 Calories; 15.4 g Total Fat; 400 mg Sodium; 4 g Protein; 20 g Carbohydrate; 1 g Dietary Fibre

Pictured below.

Sharon's Warm Yam Salad

With this fabulous combination of sweet vegetable, salty cheese and tart balsamic vinegar, it's no wonder that Sharon won first prize in our Starters Contest. *"This Warm Yam Salad is so out of the ordinary and so good. I felt this recipe just had to be shared."* Make sure you look for the dark orange vegetable, known by many as a sweet potato.
— Sharon R. Crowley, Port McNicoll, Ontario

Yam (or sweet potato), cut into 3/4 inch (2 cm) cubes (about 3 cups, 750 mL)	1 1/2 lbs.	680 g
Olive oil	3 tbsp.	50 mL
Brown sugar, packed	1/4 cup	60 mL
Sliced fresh mushrooms	1 cup	250 mL
Bag of spinach, torn bite size	10 oz.	285 g
Garlic cloves, minced	1 - 2	1 - 2
Olive oil	3 tbsp.	50 mL
Crumbled feta cheese (about 4 1/2 oz., 130 g)	1 cup	250 mL
Pine nuts	1/4 cup	60 mL
Balsamic vinegar	2 tbsp.	30 mL

Combine first 3 ingredients in medium bowl. Transfer to ungreased baking sheet. Bake in 350°F (175°C) oven for 45 minutes, stirring occasionally, until tender and golden. Transfer to large bowl. Set aside.

Sauté next 3 ingredients in second amount of olive oil in large frying pan on medium-high for 3 to 5 minutes until mushrooms are soft. Add to yam mixture.

Sprinkle feta cheese and pine nuts over top. Drizzle with vinegar. Toss until well coated. Serve warm. Makes 5 cups (1.25 L).

1 cup (250 mL): 438 Calories; 28.1 g Total Fat; 423 mg Sodium; 10 g Protein; 41 g Carbohydrate; 6 g Dietary Fibre

Pictured above.

Egyptian Lentil Soup, page 199

Spinach Salad, above

Feta Cheese Salad with Balsamic Vinaigrette, below

Broccoli Salad, below

Broccoli Salad

"I make this salad whenever we have a potluck luncheon at work. Everyone asks me for the recipe after lunch is finished!"

— Lynda Dale, Calgary, Alberta

Large head of broccoli (about 9 oz., 255 g), chopped	1	1
Green onions, chopped	2	2
Chopped celery	1 cup	250 mL
Dark seedless raisins	1 cup	250 mL
Shelled sunflower seeds	1 cup	250 mL
Mayonnaise	1 cup	250 mL
Granulated sugar	1/4 cup	60 mL
Freshly squeezed lemon juice	1 tbsp.	15 mL
White vinegar	2 tsp.	10 mL
Bacon slices, cooked crisp and crumbled	2	2

Combine first 5 ingredients in large bowl.

Combine next 4 ingredients in small bowl. Mix well. Pour over broccoli mixture. Toss until well coated. (At this point, salad can be covered and refrigerated for up to 2 days.)

Sprinkle bacon over top. Makes about 8 cups (2 L).

1 cup (250 mL): 555 Calories; 43.6 g Total Fat; 274 mg Sodium; 9 g Protein; 38 g Carbohydrate; 6 g Dietary Fibre

Pictured above.

Feta Cheese Salad with Balsamic Vinaigrette

"When I serve this salad to my three older brothers—two have worked as cooks in the past and one is still a cook—there is never any left. They all comment on how much they love it. (To impress them with a recipe is a triumph!) I don't know how many people I have given this recipe to, but every time I serve it, I'm always asked to share." The salad and vinaigrette can be made ahead and refrigerated in separate airtight containers for up to four hours.

— Rayna Benke, Calgary, Alberta

Head of butter lettuce, cut or torn into bite-size pieces	1	1
English cucumber, with peel, diced	1	1
Large tomatoes, diced	2	2
Diced red onion	3/4 cup	175 mL
Sliced fresh mushrooms	1 cup	250 mL
BALSAMIC VINAIGRETTE		
Balsamic (or red wine) vinegar	1/3 cup	75 mL
Extra-virgin olive (or cooking) oil	2 tbsp.	30 mL
Garlic clove, crushed	1	1
Worcestershire sauce	1 tsp.	5 mL
Dijon mustard	1/2 tsp.	2 mL
Dried sweet basil	1/4 tsp.	1 mL
Dried whole oregano	1/4 tsp.	1 mL
Salt	1/4 tsp.	1 mL
Freshly ground pepper	1/4 tsp.	1 mL
Crumbled feta cheese (about 7 oz., 200 g)	1 1/2 cups	375 mL

Combine first 5 ingredients in large bowl.

Balsamic Vinaigrette: Combine all 9 ingredients in jar with tight-fitting lid. Shake well. Chill until ready to serve. Makes 1/2 cup (125 mL) vinaigrette.

Just before serving, shake vinaigrette. Drizzle over salad. Add half of feta cheese. Toss. Sprinkle remaining feta cheese over top. Serve immediately. Makes about 10 cups (2.5 L).

1 cup (250 mL): 98 Calories; 7.4 g Total Fat; 305 mg Sodium; 4 g Protein; 5 g Carbohydrate; 1 g Dietary Fibre

Pictured above.

Warm Chicken and
Peach Salad, right

Warm Chicken and Peach Salad

This warm salad cooks in minutes and tastes as good as it looks. Serve it with warm crusty bread for a lovely lunch or a light evening meal.

Boneless, skinless chicken breast halves (about 4)	1 lb.	454 g
Grainy mustard	2 tbsp.	30 mL
Liquid honey	2 tbsp.	30 mL
Can of sliced peaches, drained, juice and 1 peach slice reserved	14 oz.	398 mL
Bag of baby spinach leaves	10 oz.	285 g
Medium red onion, halved and sliced	1	1
Unsalted cashews, toasted◆	1/2 cup	125 mL
PEACH DRESSING		
Reserved peach juice	1/4 cup	60 mL
Reserved peach slice	1	1
Olive (or cooking) oil	1/4 cup	60 mL
White wine vinegar	2 tbsp.	30 mL
Grainy mustard	1 tbsp.	15 mL
Granulated sugar	1 tsp.	5 mL
Dry mustard	1/4 tsp.	1 mL
Salt	1/8 tsp.	0.5 mL

Combine first 3 ingredients in large bowl. Stir to coat. Cover. Chill for 1 hour or overnight. Preheat barbecue or electric grill to medium. Cook chicken on greased grill for 7 minutes per side until no longer pink inside. Cut across the grain into 1/4 inch (6 mm) slices.

Combine next 4 ingredients in large bowl. Add chicken.

Peach Dressing: Process all 8 ingredients in blender until smooth. Makes 2/3 cup (150 mL) dressing. Drizzle over salad. Toss gently to coat. Serves 4 to 6.

1 serving: 479 Calories; 25.8 g Total Fat; 299 mg Sodium; 32 g Protein; 34 g Carbohydrate; 4 g Dietary Fibre

Pictured at left.

◆To toast the cashews, place them in an ungreased frying pan. Heat on medium, stirring often, until golden.

Spinach and Orange Salad

We think it's the contrast of flavours, colours and textures that makes this delightful salad such a winner. Add some toasted walnuts or pecans for extra appeal and crunch. To make ahead, wash and chop your salad ingredients and make your vinaigrette several hours before serving. Refrigerate until ready to serve. Then give the dressing a shake and finish off the recipe.

— Susan Taylor, Clarksburg, Ontario

Package of spinach leaves, torn	10 oz.	285 g
Medium oranges, peeled and sectioned	3	3
Medium red onion, thinly sliced	1/2	1/2

VINAIGRETTE		
Raspberry vinegar	1/3 cup	75 mL
Cooking oil	1/4 cup	60 mL
Granulated sugar	1 tbsp.	15 mL
Poppy seeds	1 tsp.	5 mL
Salt	1/4 tsp.	1 mL
Freshly ground pepper, sprinkle		

Combine first 3 ingredients in large serving bowl.

Vinaigrette: Combine all 6 ingredients in jar with tight-fitting lid. Shake well until combined. Makes 2/3 cup (150 mL) dressing. Drizzle over salad. Let stand 5 minutes. Toss gently. Serves 8 to 10.

1 serving: 109 Calories; 7.6 g Total Fat; 105 mg Sodium; 2 g Protein; 10 g Carbohydrate; 1 g Dietary Fibre

Pictured on page 108.

White Bean Salad

Roasted peppers, feta, cumin and pine nuts bring exciting Mediterranean flavours to this colourful salad. Serve as an appetizer or side dish.

Dried navy beans	1 cup	250 mL
Water, to cover		
Water	2 1/2 cups	625 mL
Medium red peppers, quartered	2	2
Baby spinach leaves (about 3 oz., 85 g)	2 1/2 cups	625 mL
Crumbled feta cheese (about 5 oz., 140 g)	1 cup	250 mL
Pine nuts, toasted◆	1/3 cup	75 mL
Olive (or cooking) oil	1/2 cup	125 mL
Lemon juice	3 tbsp.	50 mL
Liquid honey	2 tbsp.	30 mL
Ground cumin	1 tsp.	5 mL
Garlic clove, crushed	1	1
Salt	1/2 tsp.	2 mL
Freshly ground pepper	1/2 tsp.	2 mL

Soak beans in water in large bowl overnight. Drain.

Put beans and second amount of water into large pot or Dutch oven. Bring to a boil on medium. Reduce heat to medium-low. Cover. Simmer, without stirring, for about 50 minutes until tender. Drain. Set aside.

Grill red peppers, skin-side down, over medium-high heat for about 10 minutes until skin is blistered and blackened. Or, broil red peppers, skin-side up, on baking sheet with sides, 5 inches (12.5 cm) from heat until skin is blistered and blackened. Put into small bowl. Cover. Let sweat for 10 minutes until cool enough to handle. Remove and discard skin from peppers. Cut into 1/8 inch (3 mm) pieces. Transfer to large bowl.

Add beans and next 3 ingredients. Toss.

Combine remaining 7 ingredients in small jar with tight-fitting lid. Shake well to combine. Drizzle over salad. Toss to coat. Makes 7 cups (1.75 L).

1 cup (250 mL): 383 Calories; 25.4 g Total Fat; 416 mg Sodium; 13 g Protein; 30 g Carbohydrate; 7 g Dietary Fibre

Pictured below.

◆To toast the pine nuts, place them in an ungreased frying pan. Heat on medium, stirring often, until golden.

Bean Counting

1 cup (250 mL) **dried navy beans** equals about 3 cups (750 mL) cooked beans

2 cups (500 mL) **cooked beans** equals one 19 oz. (540 mL) can navy beans

Walnut Cranberry Salad with
Sweet Mustard Dressing, below

Walnut Cranberry Salad with Sweet Mustard Dressing

This is a great salad for a potluck supper, especially as an accompaniment to lean cuts of meat like chicken breasts or pork tenderloin. Baby spinach leaves are also good with this dressing, which is best made a little ahead of time so the flavours can develop.

Bags of baby greens (4 1/2 oz., 125 g, each), about 8 cups (2 L)	2	2
Walnuts, coarsely chopped	1/2 cup	125 mL
Dried cranberries	1/2 cup	125 mL
Goat cheese, crumbled (about 3/4 cup, 175 mL)	4 1/2 oz.	125 g
Bacon slices, cooked crisp and crumbled	6	6

SWEET MUSTARD DRESSING

Olive (or cooking) oil	1/3 cup	75 mL
White wine vinegar	3 tbsp.	50 mL
Brown sugar, packed	1 tbsp.	15 mL
Chopped fresh oregano leaves	1 tbsp.	15 mL
Prepared mustard	2 tsp.	10 mL
Garlic clove, crushed	1	1
Salt	1/4 tsp.	1 mL
Freshly ground pepper	1/4 tsp.	1 mL

Combine first 3 ingredients in large bowl. Sprinkle cheese and bacon over top.

Sweet Mustard Dressing: Combine all 8 ingredients in small jar with tight-fitting lid. Shake well to combine. Makes about 1/2 cup (125 mL) dressing. Drizzle over salad. Toss. Makes 10 cups (2.5 L).

1 cup (250 mL): 190 Calories; 15.8 g Total Fat; 189 mg Sodium; 6 g Protein; 9 g Carbohydrate; 2 g Dietary Fibre

Pictured above.

Sun-Dried Tomato Dressing

Fresh oregano and a bit of brown sugar add complexity to this dressing. *"This is a favourite of mine."*
— **Nola Ingham, Vancouver, British Columbia**

Olive oil	1/3 cup	75 mL
Red wine vinegar	2 tbsp.	30 mL
Chopped sun-dried tomatoes in oil, drained	2 tbsp.	30 mL
Chopped fresh oregano leaves	2 tsp.	10 mL
Brown sugar, packed	1 tsp.	5 mL
Garlic clove, crushed	1	1
Salt	1/4 tsp.	1 mL
Freshly ground pepper	1/4 tsp.	1 mL

Blend or process all 8 ingredients until smooth. Makes about 2/3 cup (150 mL).

2 tbsp. (30 mL): 131 Calories; 14 g Total Fat; 114 mg Sodium; trace Protein; 2 g Carbohydrate; trace Dietary Fibre

Spinach Orange Salad with Creamy Dressing

Not only is this fresh, light salad pretty to look at and delicious to eat, but your whole kitchen smells wonderful while you're preparing it.

— Patricia Gibb, St. Albert, Alberta

Bags of large spinach leaves (10 oz., 285 g, each) or 4 bundles, trimmed	2	2
Medium grapefruit, peeled and cut bite size	1	1
Medium oranges, peeled and cut bite size	2	2
Small red onion, sliced into rings	1	1

CREAMY DRESSING

Mayonnaise (or salad dressing)	1/2 cup	125 mL
Lemon juice	1 1/2 tsp.	7 mL
Water	1 1/2 tsp.	7 mL
Chopped fresh oregano leaves	1 tsp.	5 mL
Red wine vinegar	1 1/2 tsp.	7 mL
Cooking oil	1 1/2 tsp.	7 mL
Worcestershire sauce	3/4 tsp.	4 mL
Brown sugar, packed	1 1/2 tsp.	7 mL
Garlic clove, minced	1	1

Combine first 4 ingredients in large bowl. Toss.

Creamy Dressing: Combine all 9 ingredients in small bowl. Chill. Makes 3/4 cup (175 mL) dressing. Drizzle over salad. Toss to coat well. Serves 8 to 10.

1 serving: 162 Calories; 12.9 g Total Fat; 138 mg Sodium; 3 g Protein; 11 g Carbohydrate; 3 g Dietary Fibre

Basic Vinaigrette

No matter what kind of salad you make, the dressing is what everyone notices. One of the simplest and most adaptable salad dressings is a basic vinaigrette.

Red wine (or your favourite) vinegar	1/4 cup	60 mL
Olive oil	3/4 cup	175 mL
Salt	1/2 tsp.	2 mL
Freshly ground black pepper	1/2 tsp.	2 mL

Combine all 4 ingredients in jar with tight-fitting lid. Shake well to combine. Makes 1 cup (250 mL).

2 tbsp. (30 mL): 184 Calories; 20.6 g Total Fat; 143 mg Sodium; trace Protein; 1 g Carbohydrate; trace Dietary Fibre

Red Raspberry Vinaigrette

"Serve over a mix of tender greens. Don't worry about what to do with the rest of your jar of grainy Dijon. It's a great complement to other foods, like roast beef, grilled burgers or anywhere else you would use mustard." This dressing keeps well in a covered container in the refrigerator for up to four weeks.

— Dean Hossack, Kelowna, British Columbia

Fresh (or frozen, thawed) raspberries	2 cups	500 mL
Red wine vinegar	1 cup	250 mL
Liquid honey	4 tsp.	20 mL
Raspberry jam	3 tbsp.	50 mL
Finely chopped shallots	2 tsp.	10 mL
Grainy Dijon mustard	2 tbsp.	30 mL
Olive oil	1/4 cup	60 mL
Salt	1 tsp.	5 mL
White pepper	1/4 tsp.	1 mL

Beat first 4 ingredients in medium bowl with hand blender. Press through sieve to remove seeds. Discard seeds.

Whisk remaining 5 ingredients into raspberry mixture. Add more salt and pepper if desired. Makes 2 cups (500 mL).

2 tbsp. (30 mL): 57 Calories; 3.7 g Total Fat; 169 mg Sodium; trace Protein; 7 g Carbohydrate; 1 g Dietary Fibre

Dress It Up

Classic combinations:

Extra-virgin olive oil with red wine or balsamic vinegar

Nut-flavoured oils with balsamic or sherry vinegars

Mild-flavoured oils with flavoured vinegars, mustards or herbs

Classic flavours to add to Basic Vinaigrette:

Herbs such as tarragon, basil, thyme, chives, garlic

Mustard (Dijon or grainy are popular), sugar, honey, lemon, lime

Dried and fresh tomatoes

Creamy Mustard Dressing

"I never buy commercially prepared salad dressings. I love to try different combinations and ingredients that many people would not consider the norm. The salads in our house are never the same twice."

— Linda Craig, Edmonton, Alberta

Salad dressing (or mayonnaise)	1/3 cup	75 mL
Prepared mustard	3 tbsp.	50 mL
Red wine vinegar	3 tbsp.	50 mL
Brown sugar, packed	3 tbsp.	50 mL

Combine all 4 ingredients in small bowl. Makes 3/4 cup (175 mL).

2 tbsp. (30 mL): 97 Calories; 6.8 g Total Fat; 178 mg Sodium; trace Protein; 9 g Carbohydrate; trace Dietary Fibre

Pictured below.

Creamy Mustard Dressing, above

Gingered Fruit in Acorn Squash

The beautiful shape of the acorn squash and the colourful fruit and squash filling complement harvest suppers or any special fall dinners.

Large acorn squash (about 1 lb., 454 g, each), cut in half lengthwise and seeded	2	2
Chopped onion	1 cup	250 mL
Hard margarine (or butter)	1 tbsp.	15 mL
Finely grated gingerroot	1 tbsp.	15 mL
Brown sugar, packed	2 tbsp.	30 mL
Chopped mixed dried fruit (such as apples, apricots, prunes, peaches and pears)	3/4 cup	175 mL
Dried cranberries	3 tbsp.	50 mL
Water	1 cup	250 mL
Apple cider vinegar	1/3 cup	75 mL
Freshly squeezed lemon juice	2 tbsp.	30 mL
Finely grated lemon zest	1 tsp.	5 mL
Salt	1 tsp.	5 mL
Ground cinnamon	1/8 tsp.	0.5 mL
Ground coriander	1/8 tsp.	0.5 mL
Cayenne pepper	1/8 tsp.	0.5 mL
Ground cloves, pinch		
Flaked hazelnuts, toasted◆	4 tsp.	20 mL

Place squash, cut side down, on greased baking sheet. Bake in 375°F (190°C) oven for about 25 minutes until tender. Let stand for 10 to 15 minutes until cool enough to handle. Leaving about 1/4 inch (6 mm) thick shell, scoop out flesh. Dice. Set aside in large bowl. Carefully cut each shell lengthwise into 2 wedges. Set aside.

Sauté onion in margarine in large frying pan on medium for 5 minutes until softened.

Stir in ginger and brown sugar. Reduce heat to low. Cook and stir for about 10 minutes until onion is browned and caramelized.

Add next 11 ingredients. Stir. Bring to a boil on medium. Cook, uncovered, for about 10 minutes, stirring several times, until fruit is plump. Add to diced squash. Stir gently until combined.

Place squash wedges on ungreased baking sheet. Mound about 1/3 cup (75 mL) squash mixture in each wedge. Sprinkle each with 1/2 tsp. (2 mL) hazelnuts. Bake in 375°F (190°C) oven for 15 to 20 minutes until heated through. Serves 8.

1 serving: 124 Calories; 1 g Total Fat; 305 mg Sodium; 2 g Protein; 30 g Carbohydrate; 4 g Dietary Fibre

Pictured above.

◆*To toast the hazelnuts, place them in an ungreased frying pan. Heat on medium, stirring often, until golden.*

Lemon Parmesan Linguine

Choose this recipe when time is of the essence. In about 30 minutes, you can serve an impressive side that tastes like you've been cooking in the kitchen for hours!

Linguine pasta	1 lb.	454 g
Boiling water	16 cups	4 L
Salt	2 tsp.	10 mL
Garlic clove, crushed	1	1
Hard margarine (or butter)	1/3 cup	75 mL
Freshly grated lemon zest	1 tbsp.	15 mL
Freshly squeezed lemon juice (about 1 medium)	1/4 cup	60 mL
Salt	1/2 tsp.	2 mL
Freshly ground pepper	1 tsp.	5 mL
Chopped fresh sweet basil	1/3 cup	75 mL
Freshly grated Parmesan cheese	1/2 cup	125 mL
Green onions, sliced	6	6
Freshly grated Parmesan cheese, sprinkle		

Cook pasta in boiling water and salt in large uncovered pot or Dutch oven for 10 to 12 minutes, stirring occasionally, until tender but firm. Drain well.

Sauté garlic in margarine in large saucepan on low for 1 minute.

Add next 4 ingredients. Simmer for 1 minute until hot. Add pasta. Toss to coat.

Add next 3 ingredients to pasta mixture. Toss. Heat for 2 to 3 minutes on low to heat through. Turn into large bowl.

Sprinkle with second amount of Parmesan cheese. Serves 8.

1 serving: 318 Calories; 10.9 g Total Fat; 370 mg Sodium; 10 g Protein; 44 g Carbohydrate; 2 g Dietary Fibre

Pictured at right.

Fried Rice with Shrimp and Ham

"I find this is a really good dish to make with leftover rice and ham, poultry or other meat— even luncheon meat. But always be careful with the shrimp. It quickly goes from tender to tough if overcooked."
— Peter Cheung, Edmonton, Alberta

Diced uncooked medium shrimp (fresh or frozen, thawed)	1/2 cup	125 mL
Cornstarch	1/4 tsp.	1 mL
Freshly ground white pepper	1/4 tsp.	1 mL
Cooking oil	1 tsp.	5 mL
Diced cooked ham	1/2 cup	125 mL
Cooking oil	2 tbsp.	30 mL
Large eggs, fork-beaten	3	3
Cooking oil	2 tbsp.	30 mL
Frozen peas and carrots, cooked and drained	1/2 cup	125 mL
Green onions, sliced	2	2
Cold cooked rice	2 cups	500 mL

SEASONING SAUCE

Light soy sauce	1 tbsp.	15 mL
Sesame oil	1/4 tsp.	1 mL
Granulated sugar	1/2 tsp.	2 mL
Salt	1/2 tsp.	2 mL
Freshly ground white pepper, sprinkle		
Water (optional)	3 tbsp.	50 mL

Combine first 3 ingredients in small bowl. Mix well.

Add first amount of cooking oil to hot wok or frying pan. Add shrimp mixture and ham. Stir-fry on medium-high for 3 minutes until shrimp turns pink. Remove to bowl. Set aside.

Add second amount of cooking oil to hot wok. Add 1/2 of beaten egg. Cook on medium for 2 minutes, without stirring, until set. Remove from wok. Chop. Set aside.

Add third amount of cooking oil to hot wok. Add vegetables and rice.

Seasoning Sauce: Combine first 5 ingredients. Add water if rice is dry. Stir-fry on medium for about 5 minutes until rice is hot. Add remaining uncooked egg. Stir-fry for about 2 minutes until egg is almost set. Add shrimp mixture and cooked egg. Stir-fry for 1 to 2 minutes until heated through. Serves 4.

1 serving: 400 Calories; 21.5 g Total Fat; 883 mg Sodium; 15 g Protein; 35 g Carbohydrate; 1 g Dietary Fibre

Lemon Parmesan Linguine, left

Bacon and Cheese Spuds

These rich-tasting, big-flavoured potatoes are almost a meal in themselves served alongside a grilled vegetable salad. But they really shine as an accompaniment to a sizzling barbecued sirloin.

Unpeeled medium potatoes	4	4
Herb-flavoured non-fat spreadable cream cheese	1/4 cup	60 mL
Milk	1 tbsp.	15 mL
Grated light sharp Cheddar cheese	1/4 cup	60 mL
Salt	1/4 tsp.	1 mL
Pepper	1/16 tsp.	0.5 mL
Bacon slices, diced	3	3
Chopped fresh mushrooms	1/2 cup	125 mL
Chopped green onion	2 tbsp.	30 mL
Grated light sharp Cheddar cheese	1/4 cup	60 mL

Wash potatoes and pierce in several places with fork. Bake in 375°F (190°C) oven for 1 1/4 hours until soft when squeezed or fork slides in easily. Cool slightly. Cut 1/4 inch (6 mm) piece lengthwise from top of each potato. Scoop out pulp into medium bowl, leaving shells 1/4 inch (6 mm) thick. Discard tops once pulp is removed. Mash pulp.

Add next 5 ingredients. Beat until smooth.

Fry bacon in frying pan for 3 to 4 minutes until crisp. Remove bacon with slotted spoon. Add to potato pulp, reserving about 1 tbsp. (15 mL) for garnish.

Drain all but 1 tsp. (5 mL) fat from frying pan. Add mushrooms and green onion. Sauté until soft. Mix with potato pulp. Stuff shells.

Arrange on ungreased baking sheet. Sprinkle with second amount of Cheddar cheese. Sprinkle with reserved bacon. Bake in 350°F (175°C) oven for 20 minutes until heated through. Makes 4 stuffed potatoes.

1 stuffed potato: 257 Calories; 5.6 g Total Fat; 357 mg Sodium; 10 g Protein; 42 g Carbohydrate; 4 g Dietary Fibre

Pictured below.

Bacon and Cheese Spuds, above

Roasted Vegetables with Aioli

Traditionally, the French like to partner aioli, a rich garlic mayonnaise, with raw vegetables. We think this creamy concoction also works very well to complement these roasted vegetables. You can make aioli a day or several hours ahead of serving time. Place in a sealable container in the refrigerator. Remove from refrigerator 30 minutes before serving.

Medium carrots, peeled, halved lengthwise and chopped into 2 inch (5 cm) lengths	6	6
Medium red onions, quartered	3	3
Medium red peppers, quartered	3	3
Olive (or cooking) oil	1 tbsp.	15 mL
Salt	1/2 tsp.	2 mL
Freshly ground pepper	1/2 tsp.	2 mL
Medium zucchini, halved lengthwise and chopped into 2 inch (5 cm) lengths	6	6
AIOLI		
Garlic cloves	6 - 8	6 - 8
Egg yolks (large)	2	2
Lemon juice	3 tbsp.	50 mL
Salt	1/4 tsp.	1 mL
Light olive oil	2 cups	500 mL

Toss first 6 ingredients on 11 x 17 inch (28 x 43 cm) baking sheet with sides. Bake in 350°F (175°C) oven for 30 minutes.

Add zucchini. Stir. Bake for about 25 minutes until vegetables are tender.

Aioli: Process first 4 ingredients in food processor until well combined. With motor running, slowly pour olive oil through feed chute. Process until mixture is thick and pale. Makes 2 cups (500 mL). Serve with roasted vegetables. Serves 8 to 10.

1 serving vegetables with aioli: 616 Calories; 60.6 g Total Fat; 252 mg Sodium; 4 g Protein; 19 g Carbohydrate; 5 g Dietary Fibre

Pictured on page 108.

Spaghetti Squash with Feta and Chili Peppers

The strands of spaghetti squash have a pleasant texture and mild flavour that team well with the vibrant-tasting combination of tangy feta and piquant chili peppers.

Spaghetti squash (about 3 lbs., 1.4 kg), cut in half lengthwise and seeded	1	1
Garlic cloves, crushed	2	2
Medium red onion, chopped	1	1
Small red chili peppers, chopped◆	2	2
Olive (or cooking) oil	2 tbsp.	30 mL
Chopped fresh sweet basil	1/3 cup	75 mL
Crumbled feta cheese	1/2 cup	125 mL
Pecan halves, toasted and chopped◆◆	1/2 cup	125 mL
Salt	1 tsp.	5 mL
Freshly ground pepper	1 tsp.	5 mL

Place squash, cut-side down, on greased baking sheet. Bake in 375°F (190°C) oven for 1 1/4 hours until flesh is soft. Let stand for 5 to 10 minutes until cool enough to handle.

Scrape flesh into large bowl, creating spaghetti-like strands. Cover to keep warm.

Sauté next 3 ingredients in olive oil in frying pan on medium for 5 minutes until onion is softened. Add to squash.

Add remaining 5 ingredients. Mix well. Makes 6 cups (1.5 L).

1 cup (250 mL): 211 Calories; 14.9 g Total Fat; 578 mg Sodium; 4 g Protein; 17 g Carbohydrate; 3 g Dietary Fibre

Pictured above.

◆Wear rubber gloves when chopping chili peppers, and avoid touching your eyes.

◆◆To toast the pecans, place them in an ungreased frying pan. Heat on medium, stirring often, until golden.

Roasted Buttercup Squash and Parsnips

Two favourite autumn vegetables are combined in this simple preparation that's also tasty with other squash varieties. Wonderful with pork or beef roasts.

Buttercup squash (about 3 lbs., 1.4 kg), cut in half lengthwise and seeded	1	1
Parsnips, peeled and cut into 1 inch (2.5 cm) pieces	1 1/2 lbs.	680 g
Cooking oil	1 tbsp.	15 mL
Hard margarine (or butter), softened	3 tbsp.	50 mL
Salt	1/2 tsp.	2 mL
Freshly ground pepper	1/8 tsp.	0.5 mL

Place squash, cut-side down, on one end of greased baking sheet.

Toss parsnips with cooking oil in medium bowl. Turn out onto opposite end of baking sheet. Bake in 375°F (190°C) oven for about 1 hour, stirring parsnips twice, until squash and parsnips are tender.

Place parsnips in food processor fitted with knife blade. Spoon out flesh from squash. Add to parsnips. Add remaining 3 ingredients. Pulse until desired consistency, either small pieces or almost smooth. Makes 4 cups (1 L). Serves 6.

1 serving: 229 Calories; 9.6 g Total Fat; 279 mg Sodium; 3 g Protein; 37 g Carbohydrate; 7 g Dietary Fibre

Variation: Add 1 tsp. (5 mL) ground cardamom to squash mixture before processing.

Variation: Stir 1/4 cup (60 mL) sliced green onion into processed squash mixture before serving.

Taco Potato Wedges with Guacamole

If you love tacos and big wedge fries, these are the potatoes for you! The spicy flavour of Tex-Mex combined with crispy oven-baked fries is great with easy-to-make guacamole—or even ketchup.

Large potatoes, with peel	2	2
Taco seasoning	2 tbsp.	30 mL
Cooking oil	I tbsp.	15 mL
GUACAMOLE		
Ripe medium avocados, peeled and pits removed	2	2
Sour cream	1/4 cup	60 mL
Lemon juice	I tbsp.	15 mL
Green onions, chopped	2	2
Chili sauce	I tbsp.	15 mL
Garlic clove, crushed	I	I
Salt, sprinkle		

Cut potatoes in half lengthwise. Cut each half lengthwise into 6 wedges. Combine potato wedges, taco seasoning and cooking oil in large bowl. Mix until potatoes are well coated. Place wedges in single layer on ungreased baking sheets. Bake in 375°F (190°C) oven for 20 minutes. Turn wedges. Cook for another 25 minutes until golden. Makes 24 wedges.

Guacamole: Mash avocados in medium bowl until smooth. Add remaining 6 ingredients. Mix until well combined. Makes 1 1/2 cups (375 mL) guacamole. Transfer to small serving bowl. Set on platter. Surround with potato wedges. Serves 6.

I serving: 266 Calories; 14.3 g Total Fat; 390 mg Sodium; 5 g Protein; 33 g Carbohydrate; 5 g Dietary Fibre

Pictured on page 60.

Wahidun's Dal

"This is a richly flavoured, highly seasoned dal that my mum loves to serve with beef. Serves six to eight as a side dish." You'll find ghee in South Asian grocery stores.

— **Naazima Ali, Edmonton, Alberta**

Yellow lentils (chana dal)	I cup	250 mL
Cold water	1 1/2 cups	375 mL
Large garlic cloves, peeled and crushed	2	2
Turmeric	1/4 tsp.	I mL
Chopped onion	3/4 cup	175 mL
Medium red chili pepper, diced◆	I	I
Salt	1/4 tsp.	I mL
Ghee (or butter)	2 tbsp.	30 mL
Chopped onion	3/4 cup	175 mL
Ground cumin	1/2 tsp.	2 mL
Black mustard seed	1/2 tsp.	2 mL
Large garlic cloves, peeled and crushed	2	2
Finely chopped fresh cilantro	2-4 tbsp.	30-60 mL

Wash lentils under cold water, rubbing between hands to remove excess skin and dirt. Rinse thoroughly. Combine lentils and cold water in medium saucepan. Bring to a boil. Skim off any foam that appears.

Add next 5 ingredients. Stir. Reduce heat to medium. Cook, uncovered, for 30 minutes, until water has reduced. Lightly crush lentils against saucepan with back of spoon. Remove from heat.

Melt ghee in small saucepan. Sauté second amount of onion on medium for 5 minutes. Add next 3 ingredients. Cook, stirring constantly, for 1 to 2 minutes until garlic is golden. Add about 1/2 cup (125 mL) of cooked lentil mixture to onion mixture. Cover to capture aroma and remove from heat. Add to lentil mixture. Stir well.

Stir in cilantro just before serving. Makes 2 1/2 cups (625 mL).

2 tbsp. (30 mL): 50 Calories; 1.3 g Total Fat; 42 mg Sodium; 3 g Protein; 7 g Carbohydrate; I g Dietary Fibre

◆*Wear gloves when chopping chili peppers, and avoid touching your eyes.*

Pumpkin Curry

"If fresh pumpkin is unavailable, my mum uses butternut, spaghetti or other squash. Canadian pumpkin tends to be sweeter than Fijian, so we sometimes add lemon juice to cut the sweetness a bit. Besides serving this with chutney and Puri (page 41), it's delicious as a side dish with roast chicken, turkey or lamb." Fenugreek is available in the spice section of large grocery stores, and curry leaves can be found in specialty spice shops.

— **Naazima Ali, Edmonton, Alberta**

Cooking oil	I tbsp.	15 mL
Fenugreek	1/2 tsp.	2 mL
Medium onion, coarsely chopped	1/2	1/2
Fresh pumpkin or squash, peeled and cubed (about 2 1/2 cups, 625 mL)◆	I lb.	454 g
Fresh curry leaves	4	4
Salt, to taste		
Medium red chili peppers, sliced in half lengthwise	2	2
Freshly squeezed lemon juice (optional)	I tbsp.	15 mL
Chopped fresh cilantro, for garnish		

Heat cooking oil in large saucepan on medium. Add fenugreek. Cook, stirring slightly, for about 30 seconds until fenugreek begins to pop. Add onion. Cook, stirring occasionally, for about 5 minutes until soft.

Add next 3 ingredients. Cook on low, stirring occasionally, for 20 minutes, adding a little water if pumpkin is overly dry. Add chili peppers. Stir. Cook for about another 10 minutes, stirring occasionally, until pumpkin is soft and aromatic. Add lemon juice if too sweet.

Place in serving bowl. Garnish with cilantro. Makes about 2 cups (500 mL).

1/2 cup (125 mL): 66 Calories; 3.6 g Total Fat; 3 mg Sodium; I g Protein; 9 g Carbohydrate; I g Dietary Fibre

Pictured on page 150.

◆*We photographed Naazima's curry with butternut squash.*

Brussels Sprouts and Green Beans in Almond Citrus Butter

Two traditional turkey accompaniments combine to make one outstanding side dish for autumn meals. Vary the nuts, if you wish, using finely chopped pecans or walnuts. Garnish with freshly grated lemon zest.

Butter (or hard margarine)	3 tbsp.	50 mL
Sliced almonds	1/2 cup	125 mL
Finely grated lemon zest	1 tsp.	5 mL
Finely grated orange zest	1 tsp.	5 mL
Freshly ground pepper	1 tsp.	5 mL
Fresh small Brussels sprouts	1 1/2 lbs.	680 g
Fresh green beans, trimmed	1 lb.	454 g
Boiling water		
Salt	1 tsp.	5 mL

Melt butter in small frying pan. Add almonds. Cook on medium-low for about 5 minutes, stirring occasionally, until almonds are golden.

Add next 3 ingredients. Stir. Set aside.

Combine remaining 4 ingredients in large pot or Dutch oven. Cover. Cook on high for 5 to 7 minutes until tender-crisp. Drain well. Place in large serving dish. Add almond mixture. Mix until well combined. Serves 8 to 10.

1 serving: 143 Calories; 9.2 g Total Fat; 70 mg Sodium; 6 g Protein; 13 g Carbohydrate; 5 g Dietary Fibre

Pictured on page 133.

Roasted Buttered Beets

Beets take on an entirely different personality when baked or roasted, as their natural sweetness is intensified. (Buy beets with their tops intact and you've got two vegetables for the price of one! Beet tops are delicious just slightly cooked, much like fresh spinach.)

Unpeeled medium beets, scrubbed and trimmed◆	8	8
Butter (or hard margarine)	2 tbsp.	30 mL
Freshly ground pepper	1/2 tsp.	2 mL

Wrap beets individually in foil. Bake directly on rack in 325°F (160°C) oven for about 2 1/2 hours until tender. Remove foil. Let stand for 5 minutes to cool slightly. Peel beets. Cut into quarters. Place in large bowl.

Toss with butter and pepper until well coated. Serves 8 to 10.

1 serving: 61 Calories; 3.1 g Total Fat; 93 mg Sodium; 1 g Protein; 8 g Carbohydrate; 2 g Dietary Fibre

Pictured below.

◆ *To prevent hands from staining, wear rubber gloves while handling beets.*

Roasted Buttered Beets, above

Asparagus with Lemon Herb Dressing

The perfect spring vegetable is made even more special with tangy dressing and an innovative presentation. Serve it warm as a side vegetable or cold as a salad—fantastic either way!

Asparagus spears	40	40
Lemon peel strings, for garnish	8	8
Boiling water		
Olive oil	1/4 cup	60 mL
Lemon juice	1/4 cup	60 mL
Garlic cloves, minced	4	4
Finely chopped fresh marjoram (or oregano) leaves	1/4 cup	60 mL
Freshly ground pepper, sprinkle		
Finely grated lemon zest, for garnish		

Steam asparagus in small amount of boiling water for 5 minutes. Drain. Secure 5 asparagus spears with lemon peel string (see Lemon Twist Ties, right). Repeat with remaining asparagus and lemon peel.

Combine next 5 ingredients in small bowl. Let stand for at least 30 minutes to allow flavours to blend. Makes 1/2 cup (125 mL) dressing.

Lemon Twist Ties

Use a citrus stripper to remove a long, narrow, continuous coil of lemon peel. If you don't have a citrus stripper, use a small sharp knife to peel the lemon like an apple (you'll end up with a long, wide, continuous strip). Cut the pith (inner white part) from the peel, then slice the peel lengthwise into strips. Twist the long lemon peel strings around small bundles of cooked vegetables and tie loosely.

Pictured below and on page 54.

Place asparagus bundles on individual plates. Drizzle 1 tbsp. (15 mL) dressing over each.

Sprinkle with lemon zest. Serves 8.

1 serving: 86 Calories; 7.4 g Total Fat; 9 mg Sodium; 2 g Protein; 4 g Carbohydrate; 1 g Dietary Fibre

Pictured below and on page 54.

Marmalade-Glazed Yams

If you're a fan of baked yams or sweet potatoes with butter and brown sugar, wait until you taste what the addition of marmalade does to this classic Thanksgiving side dish.

Yams (or sweet potatoes), peeled and cut into 2 inch (5 cm) chunks	3 lbs.	1.4 kg
Cooking oil	1 1/2 tbsp.	25 mL
Salt	1 tsp.	5 mL
Freshly ground pepper	1 tsp.	5 mL
Marmalade (your choice)	1/4 cup	60 mL
Brown sugar, packed	2 tbsp.	30 mL
Butter (or hard margarine), melted	3 tbsp.	50 mL

Combine first 4 ingredients in large bowl. Arrange in single layer on ungreased baking sheet with sides. Bake in 325°F (160°C) oven for 30 minutes.

Combine remaining 3 ingredients in small bowl. Drizzle over yam. Toss until well coated. Bake for about 15 minutes until tender. Serves 8 to 10.

1 serving: 283 Calories; 7.8 g Total Fat; 371 mg Sodium; 3 g Protein; 52 g Carbohydrate; 5 g Dietary Fibre

Pictured on page 133.

Asparagus with Lemon Herb Dressing, above

Eggplant with Tomato and Mushrooms

"My mother really likes eggplant so I created this dish especially for her. I like to use Chinese cooking wine for a little extra flavour."
— Peter Cheung, Edmonton, Alberta

Cooking oil	2 tbsp.	30 mL
Medium Japanese eggplant, cut into chunks♦	1	1
Cooking oil	1 1/2 tbsp.	25 mL
Finely chopped garlic	1/2 tsp.	2 mL
Finely grated gingerroot	1/4 tsp.	1 mL
Sliced small fresh mushrooms	1 cup	250 mL
Roma (plum) tomatoes, cut into wedges and seeded	4	4
Chinese cooking wine♦♦	1 tbsp.	15 mL

SEASONING SAUCE

Water	1/2 cup	125 mL
Light soy sauce	1 1/2 tsp.	7 mL
Granulated sugar	2 tsp.	10 mL
Salt	1/4 tsp.	1 mL
Freshly ground white pepper, pinch		
Cornstarch	1 tbsp.	15 mL

Add first amount of cooking oil to hot wok or frying pan. Add eggplant. Stir-fry for about 3 to 5 minutes on high until lightly browned. Remove to bowl. Set aside.

Add second amount of cooking oil to hot wok. Add garlic and ginger. Stir-fry for 1 minute until fragrant. Add mushrooms and tomato. Stir-fry on high until mushrooms are lightly browned.

Add cooking wine. Stir.

Seasoning Sauce: Combine first 5 ingredients in small cup. Stir in cornstarch until smooth. Add to wok. Stir in eggplant. Simmer, uncovered, for 2 to 3 minutes until thickened. Serves 4.

1 serving: 193 Calories; 13.4 g Total Fat; 295 mg Sodium; 3 g Protein; 18 g Carbohydrate; 2 g Dietary Fibre

♦*If the long Japanese eggplant isn't available, use the more common pear-shaped variety, which was used for the recipe pictured.*

♦♦*Dry (or alcohol-free) sherry can be substituted for Chinese cooking wine.*

Pictured on page 64.

The Stir-Fry Simplified

Get it all ready: Stir-frying takes very little time, so have all your ingredients chopped, sliced, measured and ready to go.

Small is beautiful: For quick cooking, slice meat thinly and brown it in small batches.

Make it sizzle: Make sure your wok or pan is very hot, then add the oil, followed immediately by the ingredient(s). Food won't stick and you'll use less oil.

The 70% rule: During the first steps of a recipe, cook items about 70% done. When you put them all together, the heat from the food and the last few minutes in the pan or wok will finish the cooking.

Hard and first: Harder vegetables such as carrots take longer to cook, so they should be added to the wok or pan before softer vegetables such as snow peas or leafy bok choy.

Make space: As the name suggests, stir-frying needs room for stirring and frying. Overcrowding your wok or pan causes the food to stew in its own juices.

Stirring suggestions: Food is best cooked over high heat for a relatively short time. Keep stirring so food cooks evenly without burning.

Quick thickener: A little cornstarch blended with water and added just as you finish cooking gives your stir-fry a glossy coating of thick sauce.

Dig in: Stir-frys are best eaten immediately after cooking. Otherwise, heat from the ingredients continues the cooking so vegetables begin to soften and meat can toughen.

Fried Chinese Broccoli with XO Sauce

"This simple vegetable dish has a wonderful blend of subtle tastes. Spicy XO sauce is commonly used in Chinese cooking. It's flavoured with dried shrimp and scallop and used with any meat or vegetable dish." XO sauce is available in Asian grocery stores, but you can substitute oyster sauce.
— Peter Cheung, Edmonton, Alberta

Water	3 tbsp.	50 mL
Cooking oil	1 tsp.	5 mL
Granulated sugar	1/2 tsp.	2 mL
Chinese broccoli, trimmed	1 lb.	454 g
Cooking oil	2 tbsp.	30 mL
Finely chopped garlic	1 tsp.	5 mL
Finely grated gingerroot	1/2 tsp.	2 mL
Chinese cooking wine♦	1 tbsp.	15 mL

SEASONING SAUCE

Water	3 tbsp.	50 mL
Salt	1/4 tsp.	1 mL
Granulated sugar	1 tsp.	5 mL
Freshly ground white pepper, sprinkle		
Cornstarch	1/2 tsp.	2 mL
XO sauce	2 tsp.	10 mL
Medium carrot, thinly sliced on diagonal	1	1
Sliced gingerroot (optional)	1 tbsp.	15 mL
XO sauce	1 tsp.	5 mL

Combine first 3 ingredients in small cup. Add to hot wok. Add broccoli. Stir-fry for about 3 to 5 minutes until tender. Remove to bowl. Set aside.

Add second amount of cooking oil to hot wok. Add garlic and ginger. Sauté for 1 minute until fragrant. Add cooking wine and broccoli. Stir-fry for one minute.

Seasoning Sauce: Combine first 4 ingredients in small bowl. Stir in cornstarch until smooth. Add to wok. Stir in first amount of XO sauce.

Add carrot and sliced ginger. Stir-fry on medium-high for 4 to 5 minutes until carrot is tender-crisp.

Stir in second amount of XO sauce. Serves 4.

1 serving: 129 Calories; 9.1 g Total Fat; 187 mg Sodium; 4 g Protein; 10 g Carbohydrate; 3 g Dietary Fibre

Pictured below.

♦*Dry (or alcohol-free) sherry can be substituted for Chinese cooking wine.*

Fried Chinese Broccoli with XO Sauce, left

Buttered Herb Noodles

It's easy to make simple buttered noodles taste special—a toss with freshly chopped herbs is the key. You can pair this recipe with many entrees but it's especially good with Coq au Vin, page 126.

Egg noodles (fettuccine style)	16 oz.	454 g
Boiling water	24 cups	6 L
Salt	2 tsp.	10 mL
Butter (or hard margarine), chopped	2/3 cup	150 g
Chopped fresh parsley	1 1/2 cups	375 mL
Chopped fresh chives	2/3 cup	150 mL
Finely chopped fresh rosemary	2 tsp.	10 mL
Salt	1 tsp.	5 mL
Freshly ground pepper	2 tsp.	10 mL

Cook noodles in boiling water and salt in large uncovered pot or Dutch oven for 10 to 12 minutes, stirring occasionally, until tender but firm. Drain well. Turn into large bowl.

Add remaining 6 ingredients. Toss until well coated. Makes 12 cups (3 L).

1 cup (250 mL): 238 Calories; 11.8 g Total Fat; 314 mg Sodium; 6 g Protein; 28 g Carbohydrate; 1 g Dietary Fibre

Pictured on page 108.

Easy Dumplings

This is the real thing—old-fashioned, rough-edged and substantial all the way 'round—the very definition of comfort food. Great with absolutely any stew.

All-purpose flour	1 cup	250 mL
Baking powder	1 1/2 tsp.	7 mL
Salt	1/2 tsp.	2 mL
Milk	1/2 cup	125 mL
Butter (or hard margarine)	2 tbsp.	30 mL

Sift first 3 ingredients into medium bowl.

Put milk and butter into medium saucepan. Heat and stir on medium-high for about 3 minutes until bubbles start to form around edge of saucepan. Add to flour mixture. Stir with fork until just moistened. Roll dough into 8 rough balls of equal size. Carefully place dumplings in single layer on gently boiling prepared stew. Cover. Simmer for about 10 minutes until dumplings are firm and cooked through. Makes 8 dumplings.

2 dumplings: 186 Calories; 6.5 g Total Fat; 512 mg Sodium; 5 g Protein; 27 g Carbohydrate; 1 g Dietary Fibre

Pictured on page 93.

Mashed Potatoes

"I cannot make enough of this to suit my boys. They'd eat these potatoes for supper every night if I let them."

— Linda Rudachyk, Weyburn, Saskatchewan

Medium red potatoes, peeled and quartered	5 lbs.	2.3 kg
Water, to cover		
Salt	2 tsp.	10 mL
Butter (or hard margarine)	1/4 cup	60 mL
Garlic cloves, crushed◆	3	3
Whipping cream	1 cup	250 mL
Parsley flakes, for garnish		

Put first 3 ingredients into large pot or Dutch oven. Bring to a boil. Cook, uncovered, on medium-high for about 20 minutes until potatoes are tender. Drain well. Return to pot. Cover to keep warm.

Melt butter in medium frying pan on medium. Add garlic. Sauté for about 3 minutes until softened. Stir in whipping cream. Heat and stir until hot.

Mash potatoes until no lumps remain. Add cream mixture. Mix until light and fluffy. Garnish with parsley. Makes about 9 1/2 cups (2.4 L).

1 cup (250 mL): 269 Calories; 13.8 g Total Fat; 80 mg Sodium; 4 g Protein; 33 g Carbohydrate; 3 g Dietary Fibre

◆Linda laces these potatoes with 6 to 8 cloves of garlic for more intense flavour.

Vegetable Skewers with Pesto Dressing

These colourful vegetable kabobs look terrific glistening on the outdoor grill and are bound to attract the attention of your guests. Make the pesto dressing ahead of time to allow flavours to develop—it's also terrific as a dip served alongside grilled pita bread and chilled shrimp.

Medium red pepper, cut into 1 inch (2.5 cm) pieces	1	1
Medium yellow pepper, cut into 1 inch (2.5 cm) pieces	1	1
Small red onion, cut into wedges	1	1
Unpeeled medium zucchini, cut into 3/4 inch (2 cm) chunks	1-2	1-2
PESTO DRESSING		
Fresh sweet basil leaves	3/4 cup	175 mL
Pine nuts, toasted◆	2 tbsp.	30 mL
Freshly grated Parmesan cheese	3 tbsp.	50 mL
Garlic clove, chopped	1	1
Salt	1/8 tsp.	0.5 mL
Freshly ground pepper	1/4 tsp.	1 mL
Italian salad dressing	1/4 cup	60 mL
10 inch (25 cm) metal skewers	6	6

Combine first 4 ingredients in large bowl.

Pesto Dressing: Process first 7 ingredients in food processor until smooth. Makes about 1/2 cup (125 mL) dressing. Add 1/2 of dressing to vegetables.

Preheat grill to medium. Alternate vegetables on skewers. Cook on lightly greased grill for 12 to 15 minutes, turning several times until vegetables are tender-crisp. Serve skewers with remaining dressing. Makes 6 skewers.

1 skewer: 122 Calories; 10 g Total Fat; 277 mg Sodium; 3 g Protein; 7 g Carbohydrate; 2 g Dietary Fibre

Pictured on pages 66 and 125.

◆To toast the pine nuts, place them in an ungreased frying pan. Heat on medium, stirring often, until golden.

Orange Rice Pilaf

Make it once and we think you'll want to pair this easy rice dish with everything from chicken and pork to fish and shellfish. Vary things a bit by substituting lemon zest for the orange or use a combination of the two fruits.
— Alviera Olson, Headingley, Manitoba

Cooking oil	1 tbsp.	15 mL
Butter (or hard margarine)	1 tbsp.	15 mL
Large onion, finely chopped	1	1
Long grain white rice	1 1/2 cups	375 mL
Prepared chicken broth	2 cups	500 mL
Water	1 cup	250 mL
Chopped fresh parsley	1/4 cup	60 mL
Finely grated orange zest	1 tbsp.	15 mL
Salt	1/2 tsp.	2 mL

Heat cooking oil and butter in large saucepan on medium-high until butter is melted. Add onion. Sauté for 5 minutes until onion is softened.

Add rice. Stir until well coated.

Stir in broth and water. Bring to a boil. Reduce heat to low. Cover. Simmer for about 15 minutes until rice is tender. Fluff with a fork.

Add remaining 3 ingredients. Mix well. Makes 6 cups (1.5 L). Serves 8.

1 serving: 166 Calories; 2.1 g Total Fat; 372 mg Sodium; 4 g Protein; 31 g Carbohydrate; 1 g Dietary Fibre

Pictured on page 135.

Peach and Almond Rice

Aromatic curry, sweet peaches and the crunch of toasted almonds make this rice dish a perfect accompaniment for chicken, fish or pork.

Reserved peach juice, plus water to equal	3 cups	750 mL
Long grain white rice, uncooked	1 1/2 cups	375 mL
Cooking oil	1 tbsp.	15 mL
Medium onion, finely chopped	1	1
Garlic cloves, crushed	2	2
Curry powder	1 tbsp.	15 mL
Finely grated gingerroot	1 tsp.	5 mL
Prepared chicken broth	1/3 cup	75 mL
Can of sliced peaches, drained, juice reserved and peaches chopped	14 oz.	398 mL
Slivered almonds, toasted♦	1/3 cup	75 mL

Pour peach juice mixture into medium saucepan. Bring to a boil on medium-high. Add rice. Stir. Reduce heat to low. Cover. Cook for 15 to 20 minutes until liquid is absorbed and rice is tender. Fluff with fork. Set aside.

Heat cooking oil in large frying pan on medium. Add next 4 ingredients. Sauté for about 5 minutes until onion is softened.

Add rice and remaining 3 ingredients. Heat and stir for 3 to 5 minutes until peach mixture is hot. Makes 7 cups (1.75 L).

1 cup (250 mL): 242 Calories; 5.3 g Total Fat; 85 mg Sodium; 5 g Protein; 44 g Carbohydrate; 2 g Dietary Fibre

Pictured below.

♦To toast the almonds, place them in an ungreased frying pan. Heat on medium, stirring often, until golden.

Thai-Style Coconut Rice

Stir-fries or Asian-style dishes, especially spiced chicken or seafood, partner perfectly with this flavourful rice. But it's so good you'll find all sorts of dishes to serve with it.

Water	2 cups	500 mL
Coconut milk♦	1 cup	250 mL
Salt	1/2 tsp.	2 mL
Jasmine rice♦♦	1 1/2 cups	375 mL

Bring first 3 ingredients to a boil in large saucepan.

Add rice. Stir. Reduce heat to very low. Cover. Simmer for 20 minutes until tender. Remove from heat. Let stand for 5 minutes. Fluff with fork. Makes 4 1/2 cups (1.1 L).

1 cup (250 mL): 342 Calories; 11.8 g Total Fat; 274 mg Sodium; 6 g Protein; 54 g Carbohydrate; 1 g Dietary Fibre

Pictured on page 128.

♦For more coconut milk ideas, see page 128.

♦♦Jasmine rice lends an authentic taste and fragrance to this dish, but the recipe is also delicious using long grain white rice.

Peach and Almond Rice, left

Clockwise from top:
Kolach, page 33
Kutia, page 185
Holubtsi, page 185
Varenyky, page 186
Zonnia's Borscht, page 199

Kutia
(Cooked Wheat)

"My family also likes this wheat dish with chopped walnuts in it. The key to good kutia is to serve it cold." Kutia, traditionally served at Ukrainian Christmas Eve dinners, symbolizes prosperity, peace and good health.

— Zonnia Ostopowich, Edmonton, Alberta

Wheat berries (unprocessed wheat kernels), such as durum or red hard wheat	2 cups	500 mL
Water, to cover		
Poppy seeds	1/2 cup	125 mL
Boiling water	3/4 cup	175 mL
Boiling water, approximately	3 cups	750 mL
Demerara sugar◆	1/3 cup	75 mL
Liquid honey	3/4 cup	175 mL
Granulated sugar	2 tsp.	10 mL
Salt	1 tsp.	5 mL
Ground cloves	1/4 tsp.	1 mL
Ground nutmeg, just a pinch		

Combine wheat and water in medium bowl. Cover. Let stand for at least 8 hours or overnight. Drain.

Combine poppy seeds and first amount of boiling water in small heat resistant bowl. Cover. Let stand for at least 8 hours or overnight. Drain. Grind seeds in clean electric coffee grinder, or with mortar and pestle, until finely ground and creamy. Return to same bowl. Cover. Set aside.

Combine wheat and second amount of boiling water in large saucepan. Bring to a boil. Reduce heat to low. Cover. Simmer for about 4 1/2 hours, or cook in slow cooker on high for about [?] hours, until most wheat kernels are cracked open and tender. To prevent wheat from sticking to saucepan, add up to 1/2 cup (125 mL) boiling water, if necessary. Do not drain. Put entire contents of saucepan into large heatproof bowl. Cool to room temperature.

Combine remaining 6 ingredients in separate medium bowl. Add to wheat. Stir. Add poppy seeds. Mix well. Chill. Serve cold. Makes 6 cups (1.5 L). Serves 12.

[?] serving: 243 Calories; 3.3 g Total Fat; 203 mg Sodium; [?] g Protein; 52 g Carbohydrate; 4 g Dietary Fibre

Pictured on page 184.

◆*Demerara sugar is a coarse-textured raw sugar. It has a distinctive caramel flavour. Brown sugar may be substituted.*

Holubtsi
(Cabbage Rolls)

"Many people prepare holubtsi without tomato sauce, but this is the way my family enjoys this dish. You have to make sure that the baking dish is well greased, or lined with greased foil or parchment paper, so that the holubtsi don't stick to the sides." You can freeze holubtsi without sauce in a casserole dish. To cook from frozen, bring the sauce ingredients to a boil, pour over the frozen holubtsi and bake according to directions.

— Zonnia Ostopowich, Edmonton, Alberta

Large head of cabbage	1	1
Boiling water		
FILLING		
Long grain white rice	3 cups	750 mL
Water	4 1/2 cups	1.1 L
Salt	1 1/2 tsp.	7 mL
Pepper	3/4 tsp.	4 mL
Hard margarine (or butter)	1 1/3 cups	325 mL
Finely chopped onion	2 cups	500 mL
Salt	1 1/2 tsp.	7 mL
Freshly ground pepper	1/2 tsp.	2 mL
SAUCE		
Tomato juice	2 cups	500 mL
Tomato sauce	1 cup	250 mL
Water	3/4 cup	175 mL
Hard margarine (or butter), chopped	1 tbsp.	15 mL

Remove core from cabbage and about 1/2 inch (12 mm) or so of surrounding leaf stems. Place cabbage in large pot or Dutch oven. Cover cabbage with boiling water. Cover. Boil on medium-high for about 5 minutes until leaves begin to soften and loosen. Use tongs to quickly peel leaves from cabbage, layer by layer, setting them aside to drain. (If leaves are too soft, run under cold water to stop cooking process.) Place leaf on cutting board. Cut down both sides of spine to remove. Cut larger leaves into 3 equal-sized pieces (see photo). Repeat with remaining leaves, keeping size of pieces uniform. Some leaves may yield 2 pieces and smaller leaves may stay whole. Place cabbage pieces in layers on baking sheet with sides. Cover. Freeze overnight. Thaw completely before using.

Filling: Combine first 4 ingredients in large saucepan. Bring to a boil. Turn off heat. Cover. Leave on burner. Let stand for 15 minutes until rice is tender but still slightly firm. Turn into large bowl.

Melt margarine in large frying pan on medium-high. Add onion. Sauté for about 5 minutes until softened. Add to rice. Add salt and pepper. Mix well. Cool. Place rounded 1 tbsp. (15 mL) filling on each cabbage piece along curved side, leaving 1/2 inch (12 mm) edge on either side. Fold in sides. Roll up to enclose filling. Arrange in layers in well-greased 16 cup (4 L) roasting pan or casserole dish.

Sauce: Combine first 3 ingredients. Pour over holubtsi.

Dot with margarine. Cover with 2 sheets of waxed paper. Cover with lid. Bake in 350°F (175°C) oven for about 2 hours until cabbage can be easily pierced with fork. Makes 6 dozen.

1 holubets: 71 Calories; 3.9 g Total Fat; 193 mg Sodium; 1 g Protein; 8 g Carbohydrate; trace Dietary Fibre

Pictured on page 184.

Varenyky
(Dumplings)

These are often referred to as pyrohy or perogies. Zonnia prepares up to 200 varenyky for her family's Christmas Eve celebration. *"I make dozens at a time, and freeze them as I make them. That way I can make sure I have enough of each type prepared in time for Christmas. They keep well—but in my house, the supply never seems to meet the demand."* To freeze the filled varenyky, layer them on a baking sheet between layers of waxed or parchment paper. Cover and freeze until solid. Hit the baking sheet on a counter to dislodge the frozen varenyky. Store them in resealable freezer bags. To cook, boil the varenyky according to directions, but increase the cooking time to four minutes after they float to the top.

— **Zonnia Ostopowich, Edmonton, Alberta**

CHEESE AND POTATO FILLING

Grated Cheddar cheese (or dry curd cottage cheese, processed until smooth)	2 cups	500 mL
Mashed potato (about 2 lbs., 900 g, potatoes, cooking water reserved)	5 cups	1.25 L
Hard margarine (or butter), softened	3 tbsp.	50 mL
Finely chopped onion	1/3 cup	75 mL
Salt, sprinkle		
Freshly ground pepper, sprinkle		

DOUGH

Warm potato water◆	1 1/2 cups	375 mL
Warm water	1 cup	250 mL
Cooking oil	1/2 cup	125 mL
All-purpose flour, sifted	4 cups	1 L
Salt	2 1/2 tsp.	12 mL
All-purpose flour, sifted	2 - 3 cups	500 - 750 mL
Hard margarine (or butter)	1 cup	250 mL
Finely chopped onion	3 cups	750 mL
Water	12 cups	3 L
Salt	2 tsp.	10 mL

Cheese and Potato Filling: Measure all 6 ingredients into large bowl. Mix until well combined. Cover. Chill until cold.

Dough: Combine first 3 ingredients in large bowl. Add first amounts of flour and salt. Mix until well combined.

Add second amount of flour, 1/2 cup (125 mL) at a time, until dough is slightly sticky. Turn out onto lightly floured surface. Knead for about 2 minutes until dough is smooth. Place in sealed container. Roll out, 1 portion at a time, to 1/8 inch (3 mm) thickness. Cut into 2 1/2 inch (6.4 cm) circles.◆◆ Place rounded tablespoonful of filling in centre of each circle, ensuring filling is about 1/4 inch (6 mm) from edge, so edges stick together when folded. Fold in half. Pinch edges together firmly to seal. (To prevent fingers from getting too sticky, dip them in flour before pinching edges.) Arrange in single layer on lightly floured tea towel-lined baking sheet. Cover with tea towel. Set aside.

Melt margarine in large frying pan on medium-high. Add onion and sauté for about 10 minutes until softened. Set aside.

Bring water and salt to a boil in large pot or Dutch oven. Working quickly, add varenyky 1 at a time, cooking no more than 24 varenyky in a batch. Bring to a boil. Reduce heat to medium. Boil gently, uncovered, stirring occasionally with a wooden spoon, until varenyky float to top. Boil about 3 minutes further until dough is cooked. Remove with slotted spoon. Drain. In large bowl, toss varenyky gently with 1/4 of the onion mixture to coat. Turn into large casserole dish. Cover. Keep warm. Repeat with remaining varenyky. Gently toss all of the varenyky in the casserole dish after each addition to ensure they don't stick together. Makes about 8 dozen.

1 cheese and potato varenyk: 81 Calories; 4.5 g Total Fat; 149 mg Sodium; 2 g Protein; 9 g Carbohydrate; trace Dietary Fibre

Pictured on page 184.

◆*Use the potato water from preparation of the filling, or substitute warm water.*

◆◆*We used an empty, clean 10 oz. (284 mL) soup can for cutting circles.*

Variations: Substitute one of these fillings for the Cheese and Potato Filling.

SAUERKRAUT FILLING

Jars of sauerkraut (17 1/2 oz., 500 mL, each), rinsed, drained well and chopped	3	3
Mashed potato (about 1 small potato)	1/2 cup	125 mL
Finely chopped onion	1 cup	250 mL
Fine dry bread crumbs	1/4 cup	60 mL
Hard margarine (or butter)	1/4 cup	60 mL
Salt	1 tsp.	5 mL
Freshly ground pepper	1/4 tsp.	1 mL

Combine all 7 ingredients in large bowl. Turn into 2 quart (2 L) casserole dish. Cover. Bake in 325°F (160°C) oven for 1 to 1 1/4 hours, stirring 2 or 3 times, until sauerkraut is softened. Cool slightly. Cover. Chill until cold.

MUSHROOM FILLING

Hard margarine (or butter)	2 tbsp.	30 mL
Finely chopped mushrooms	8 cups	2 L
Medium onion, finely chopped	1	1
Whipping cream	3 tbsp.	50 mL
Garlic powder	1 tsp.	5 mL
Salt	2 tsp.	10 mL
Freshly ground pepper	1/2 tsp.	2 mL

Melt margarine in large frying pan on medium-high. Add mushrooms and onion. Sauté for about 10 minutes until softened.

Add next 4 ingredients. Cook, uncovered, for 15 to 20 minutes until liquid from mushrooms has evaporated. Turn into bowl. Cool slightly. Cover. Chill until cold.

Variation: To make vushka (miniature varenyky) to go into Zonnia's Borscht, page 199, cut 2 inch (5 cm) circles from dough. Place 1 tsp. (5 mL) mushroom filling in centre Fold. Pinch edges together. Join 2 pointed corners together by pulling up and around straight side of the vushko to form the shape of an "ear" (translation of vushko).

Green Beans with Walnuts and Garlic, below

Saucy Winter Chicken, page 138

Sauerkraut

Sausages and schnitzel served on a bun *mit Kraut* are big sellers during Oktoberfest— perhaps because they go so well with cold beer! This tender cabbage side dish comes from Mark Bingeman, whose family emigrated to Canada from Bingen, Germany.

— **Mark Bingeman, Bingemans Inc., Kitchener, Ontario**

Jar of sauerkraut, rinsed well	35 1/4 oz.	1 L
Salt	1 tbsp.	15 mL
Caraway seeds	2 tsp.	10 mL
Hot water, to cover		
Bacon slices, diced	10	10
Medium onions, sliced	3	3
White vinegar	2 tbsp.	30 mL
Granulated sugar	2 tbsp.	30 mL

Combine first 3 ingredients in large pot or Dutch oven. Cover with hot water. Bring to a boil. Reduce heat to low. Cover. Simmer for 1 hour. Drain all but 2 tbsp. (30 mL) liquid.

Fry bacon in large frying pan on medium for 5 minutes. Add onion. Cook for 10 minutes until bacon is crisp and onion is browned.

Add bacon mixture, vinegar and sugar to sauerkraut mixture. Mix well. Makes 5 1/2 cups (1.4 L).

1/2 cup (125 mL): 73 Calories; 3.1 g Total Fat; 1159 mg Sodium; 8 g Protein; 9 g Carbohydrate; 3 g Dietary Fibre

Green Beans with Walnuts and Garlic

Here's a great way to add style to frozen green beans. Thanks to the addition of chopped walnuts and a little garlic, these beans have a lovely earthy flavour further enhanced with a spritz of fresh lemon. Quick and easy.

Water	1/2 cup	125 mL
Frozen whole green beans (about 13 oz., 370 g)	4 1/2 cups	1.1 L
Butter (or hard margarine)	2 tbsp.	30 mL
Garlic clove, crushed	1	1
Chopped walnuts	2 tbsp.	30 mL
Lemon juice	1 tbsp.	15 mL
Salt	1/4 tsp.	1 mL
Freshly ground pepper	1/2 tsp.	2 mL

Bring water to a boil in large frying pan on high. Add beans. Cover. Cook for about 5 minutes, stirring occasionally, until beans are tender. Drain. Remove beans from pan.

Melt butter in same frying pan on medium- low. Add garlic. Sauté for 1 to 2 minutes, until garlic is softened.

Add beans and remaining 4 ingredients. Toss until beans are well coated and hot. Serve immediately. Serves 4.

1 serving: 109 Calories; 8.3 g Total Fat; 211 mg Sodium; 3 g Protein; 8 g Carbohydrate; trace Dietary Fibre

Pictured above.

Glazed Carrots

Even those family members who aren't fond of vegetables will find these old-fashioned buttery carrots with a brown sugar glaze hard to resist. Also great with roast pork and beef or alongside chicken and fish entrees.

— **Bernice Anderson, Hazlet, Saskatchewan**

Carrots (about 1 lb., 454 g), peeled and cut into 1/4 inch (6 mm) thick slices	5	5
Water, to cover		
Salt	1/4 tsp.	1 mL
Brown sugar, packed	1/4 cup	60 mL
Butter (or hard margarine)	1 1/2 tbsp.	22 mL
Lemon juice	1 1/2 tsp.	7 mL
Vanilla	1/8 tsp.	0.5 mL

Put first 3 ingredients into large saucepan. Bring to a boil on medium-high. Cover. Reduce heat to medium-low. Simmer for 5 minutes. Drain. Remove carrots from saucepan.

Combine remaining 4 ingredients in same saucepan. Heat on medium for 3 to 5 minutes until bubbly. Add carrots. Boil for about 10 minutes, stirring occasionally, until carrots are tender and evenly glazed. Serves 4.

1 serving: 143 Calories; 4.6 g Total Fat; 90 mg Sodium; 1 g Protein; 26 g Carbohydrate; 3 g Dietary Fibre

Garlic Basil Asparagus

Crisp and slightly smoky, these asparagus spears are a taste of spring. Flavoured with garlic and herbs, they're excellent hot or cold.
— Margaret Kovach, Kipling, Saskatchewan

Red wine vinegar	3 tbsp.	50 mL
Garlic cloves, crushed	3	3
Finely chopped fresh sweet basil	1 tbsp.	15 mL
Italian seasoning	1 tbsp.	15 mL
Salt	1/2 tsp.	2 mL
Freshly ground pepper	1/2 tsp.	2 mL
Olive (or cooking) oil	3 tbsp.	50 mL
Fresh asparagus, trimmed of tough ends	3 lbs.	1.4 kg

Stir first 6 ingredients together in small bowl. Whisk in olive oil until combined. Cover. Chill for at least 1 hour to blend flavours.

Cook asparagus on greased grill over medium-high heat for about 5 minutes, brushing occasionally with olive oil mixture, until all mixture is used and asparagus is tender-crisp. (Cooked asparagus can be cooled, covered and refrigerated for up to 2 days.) Serves 12.

1 serving: 61 Calories; 3.7 g Total Fat; 231 mg Sodium; 3 g Protein; 6 g Carbohydrate; 2 g Dietary Fibre

Soft Polenta

If you've ever wondered why the polenta in restaurants tastes so good, follow this recipe that includes the flavourful secret ingredient—cheese! The golden colour, rich flavour and creamy texture complement a robust entree, such as our Sausage Ragout, page 111, perfectly.

Prepared chicken broth (or water)	4 1/2 cups	1.1 L
Yellow cornmeal	1 1/2 cups	375 mL
Grated sharp Cheddar (or Parmesan) cheese	1/3 cup	75 mL
Butter (or hard margarine)	1 tbsp.	15 mL
Freshly ground pepper	1/2 tsp.	2 mL
Salt, to taste		

Pour broth into large saucepan. Bring to a simmer on medium. Add cornmeal in a steady stream, whisking constantly, until all cornmeal is added. Reduce heat to medium-low. Cook for about 10 minutes, stirring constantly, until thickened and mixture pulls away from side of pan. Remove from heat.

Add remaining 4 ingredients. Stir until well combined. Serve immediately. Serves 4.

1 serving: 313 Calories; 8.8 g Total Fat; 1015 mg Sodium; 13 g Protein; 44 g Carbohydrate; 3 g Dietary Fibre

Pictured on page 111.

Greek Potatoes

Lemony potatoes are a staple in Greek restaurants. They're so versatile and easy to make at home, you'll want to serve them often.
— Jo-Anne Penston, Winnipeg, Manitoba

Large Russet potatoes (about 3/4 lb., 340 g, each), peeled and quartered	2	2
Water	1/2 cup	125 mL
Olive (or cooking) oil	2 tbsp.	30 mL
Freshly squeezed lemon juice	2 tbsp.	30 mL
Dried whole oregano	1 1/2 tsp.	7 mL
Salt	1/2 tsp.	2 mL
Freshly ground pepper	1/8 tsp.	0.5 mL
Dried whole oregano (optional)	1/4 tsp.	1 mL

Place first 7 ingredients in large bowl. Toss until potato is well coated. Arrange potato in single layer in ungreased shallow 8 x 8 inch (20 x 20 cm) baking pan. Bake, uncovered, in 500°F (260°C) oven for about 40 minutes, stirring occasionally, until liquid has evaporated and potato is tender and browned.

Sprinkle second amount of oregano over top. Serves 4.

1 serving: 199 Calories; 7.1 g Total Fat; 307 mg Sodium; 4 g Protein; 32 g Carbohydrate; 3 g Dietary Fibre

Pictured below.

Greek Potatoes, above

Warm Baby Beets with Mustard Dill Sauce

"I have always enjoyed cooking and entertaining, and have served this dish many times over the years with a barbecued meat course on a nice summer evening."
— Jo-Anne Penston, Winnipeg, Manitoba

Unpeeled baby beets, scrubbed and trimmed (about 16)◆	2 lbs.	900 g

MUSTARD DILL SAUCE

Dijon mustard	3 tbsp.	50 mL
White wine vinegar	2 tbsp.	30 mL
Granulated sugar	2 tsp.	10 mL
Chopped fresh dill	3 tbsp.	50 mL
Olive oil	3 tbsp.	50 mL
Whipping cream	2 tbsp.	30 mL
Salt, to taste		
Freshly ground pepper, to taste		

Wrap beets in foil. Place on baking sheet. Bake in 400°F (205°C) oven for about 1 hour until tender. Set aside until cool enough to handle. Remove foil. Peel beets. Cut in half lengthwise.

Mustard Dill Sauce: Whisk first 3 ingredients together in medium bowl.

Add dill. Gradually stir in olive oil and cream. Season with salt and pepper. Makes 2/3 cup (150 mL) sauce. Serve drizzled over beets. Serves 8.

1 serving: 99 Calories; 6.9 g Total Fat; 139 mg Sodium; 2 g Protein; 9 g Carbohydrate; 1 g Dietary Fibre

Pictured at right.

◆To prevent hands from staining, wear rubber gloves while handling beets.

Warm Baby Beets with Mustard Sauce, left

Gingered Baby Carrots, below

Gingered Baby Carrots

"I enjoy cooking, trying new dishes, creating and changing recipes to suit my family's tastes. This recipe got a 'delicious carrots' review from the grandchildren."
— Lydia Gray, Saskatoon, Saskatchewan

Baby carrots	2 lbs.	900 g
Water, to cover		
Salt	1 1/2 tsp.	7 mL
Granulated sugar	1 1/2 tsp.	7 mL
Butter (or hard margarine)	2 tbsp.	30 mL
Grated fresh gingerroot	2 tsp.	10 mL
Garlic cloves, crushed	2	2
Prepared chicken broth	1 cup	250 mL
Soy sauce	2 tsp.	10 mL
Freshly ground pepper	1/2 tsp.	2 mL

Combine first 4 ingredients in large saucepan. Bring to a boil. Cook on high for 5 minutes. Drain.

Melt butter in large frying pan on low. Add ginger and garlic. Cover. Cook for 5 minutes, stirring twice.

Add carrot, broth and soy sauce. Increase heat to medium-high. Boil gently, uncovered, for about 10 minutes, stirring occasionally, until sauce is reduced to a glaze. Add pepper. Stir. Serves 6 to 8.

1 serving: 110 Calories; 4.4 g Total Fat; 345 mg Sodium; 3 g Protein; 16 g Carbohydrate; 4 g Dietary Fibre

Pictured above.

Cajun Garlic Butter, page 148

Lemon Mint Butter, page 148

Barbecued Corn
below

Barbecued Corn

Corn growers across the country say they love their corn barbecued, though everyone we spoke to has a slightly different technique. Here are two versions from the Tanner family in Taber. Grilling corn with the husks on keeps the kernels moist, while grilling without the husks adds a smokier flavour.

— **Jim Tanner, Barnwell, Alberta**

With husks: Remove large outer husks, turn back inner husks and remove silk. Spread with soft butter or margarine and pull husks back over corn. Wrap each ear in heavy foil, twisting ends to seal. Roast over medium heat, either directly on coals for 10 to 15 minutes or on grill for 15 to 20 minutes, turning once. To serve, pull back husks and snip off.

Without husks: Remove husks and silk. Place each ear on heavy foil. Add 1 tbsp. (15 mL) butter or margarine and 1 tbsp. (15 mL) water, plus a pinch of herbs, if desired. Wrap securely, twisting ends to seal. Roast over medium heat, either directly on coals for 10 to 15 minutes or on grill for 15 to 20 minutes, turning once.

Here's another method from Company's Coming: Grilled corn on the cob is so easy. Turn back the husks, remove the silk and spread your choice of flavoured butter on the corn. Pull the husks back over the corn and tie the cob in two or three places with butcher's string. Grill the corn over medium heat for about 15 minutes, turning several times during cooking.

Pictured above.

Creamed Corn

"My mother always made this for us when we were kids." Now Joanne continues the tradition with her own family.

— **Joanne Komienski, Scotland, Ontario**

Butter (or hard margarine)	1 tbsp.	15 mL
All-purpose flour	1 tbsp.	15 mL
Condensed chicken broth	1/2 cup	125 mL
Milk	1/2 cup	125 mL
Fresh corn kernels (about 4 medium cobs)	2 1/2 cups	625 mL
Salt	1/2 tsp.	2 mL
Freshly ground pepper	1/2 tsp.	2 mL

Melt butter in medium saucepan. Add flour. Heat and stir on medium for 1 to 2 minutes until grainy.

Gradually stir in broth, then milk. Heat and stir for 3 to 5 minutes until boiling and thickened.

Add remaining 3 ingredients. Simmer, uncovered, for 10 minutes until corn is tender. Makes 3 cups (750 mL).

1/2 cup (125 mL): 120 Calories; 4.7 g Total Fat; 313 mg Sodium; 3 g Protein; 17 g Carbohydrate; 1 g Dietary Fibre

Pesto Pasta

The flavours of basil, garlic and toasted pine nuts make this a dish to savour and remember.

Vermicelli pasta	1 lb.	454 g
Boiling water	16 cups	4 L
Salt	2 tsp.	10 mL
Chopped pine nuts	1/4 cup	60 mL
Olive oil	2 tbsp.	30 mL
Garlic cloves, crushed	3	3
Can of condensed chicken broth	10 oz.	284 mL
Water	1/2 cup	125 mL
Cornstarch	1 tbsp.	15 mL
Fresh sweet basil leaves, cut chiffonade♦	3/4 cup	175 mL
Grated Parmesan cheese	1/3 cup	75 mL

Cook pasta in boiling water and salt in large uncovered pot or Dutch oven for about 5 minutes, stirring occasionally, until tender but firm. Drain well. Turn into large bowl.

Toast pine nuts in olive oil in frying pan for 1 to 2 minutes, stirring constantly, until starting to change colour. Stir in garlic.

Combine next 3 ingredients in small bowl until smooth. Add to pine nut mixture. Add basil. Heat and stir until boiling and slightly thickened. Remove from heat. Stir in Parmesan cheese. Makes 1 1/2 cups (375 mL) sauce. Serve over pasta. Serves 6.

1 serving: 369 Calories; 7.2 g Total Fat; 430 mg Sodium; 16 g Protein; 60 g Carbohydrate; 3 g Dietary Fibre

♦To cut chiffonade, simply stack a few basil leaves at a time and roll up tightly. Slice crosswise into very thin strips.

Potatoes on a Stick

It's so easy to make potatoes a little more special for summer barbecues and patio parties. Alternate baby white and baby red potatoes on skewers for easy grilling. Vary this recipe by substituting fresh herbs like chives or summer savory.

Unpeeled baby red potatoes	10	10
Unpeeled baby white potatoes	10	10
Water	2 cups	500 mL
Olive (or cooking) oil	2 tbsp.	30 mL
Seasoned salt	1 tsp.	5 mL
Dried sweet basil	1/2 tsp.	2 mL
Dried whole oregano	1/2 tsp.	2 mL
Ground rosemary	1/8 tsp.	0.5 mL
Freshly ground pepper, sprinkle		
Long metal skewers	4	4

Preheat grill to high. Boil potatoes in water in medium saucepan for 5 minutes. Drain well. Cool enough to handle.

Combine next 6 ingredients in small bowl.

Push potatoes, alternating red and white, onto skewers. Brush potatoes on all sides with olive oil mixture. Place skewers on greased grill. Cook for about 30 minutes, turning and basting several times, until tender. Makes 4 skewers.

1 skewer (5 potatoes): 191 Calories; 7.1 g Total Fat; 347 mg Sodium; 3 g Protein; 30 g Carbohydrate; 3 g Dietary Fibre

Pictured below.

Cuban Spaghetti for Two

"My husband and I went to Cuba on a vacation. Our vacation guide suggested a quaint Italian restaurant. It wasn't very Italian, but I developed this recipe from the experience." Garnish with grated Parmesan cheese and chopped fresh parsley.
— Carolyn Barton, Victoria, British Columbia

Olive oil	2 tbsp.	30 mL
Chili powder	1 tsp.	5 mL
Garlic clove, crushed	1	1
Salt	1/2 tsp.	2 mL
Pepper	1/2 tsp.	2 mL
Chopped fresh parsley	1 tbsp.	15 mL
Grated Parmesan cheese	1 tbsp.	15 mL
Spaghetti	4 - 6 oz.	113 - 170 g
Boiling water	6 cups	1.5 L
Salt	1 tsp.	5 mL

Combine first 7 ingredients in small bowl.

Cook pasta in boiling water and salt in large uncovered saucepan for 8 to 10 minutes, stirring occasionally, until tender but firm. Drain. Return pasta to saucepan. Add olive oil mixture. Toss to coat well. Serves 2.

1 serving: 353 Calories; 15.8 g Total Fat; 671 mg Sodium; 9 g Protein; 44 g Carbohydrate; 2 g Dietary Fibre

Potatoes on a Stick, above

Two-Toned Scalloped Potatoes

Baked layers of thinly sliced red potatoes, sweet yams and creamy Brie pair well with our Walnut-Crumbed Chicken with Mushroom and Peppercorn Sauce, page 137, for an elegant dinner. These can be made a day ahead, covered with foil and chilled. To reheat, place the covered ramekins on a baking sheet and heat in a 350°F (175°C) oven for about 30 minutes until hot.

Medium red potatoes, unpeeled, thinly sliced (about 14 oz., 395 g)	2	2
Medium yam (or sweet potato), peeled and thinly sliced (9 oz., 255 g)	1	1
Brie cheese, thinly sliced	4 1/2 oz.	125 g
Whipping cream	2/3 cup	150 mL
Ground nutmeg	1/4 tsp.	1 mL
Salt	1/2 tsp.	2 mL
Freshly ground pepper	1/2 tsp.	2 mL

Grease four 1 cup (250 mL) ramekins. Divide first 3 ingredients into 8 portions. Arrange 1 portion of potato in bottom of each ramekin. Layer with a portion of yam, then a portion of Brie. Repeat layers, finishing with Brie.

Whisk remaining 4 ingredients in liquid measure. Divide cream mixture evenly among ramekins. Place ramekins on baking sheet with sides. Bake in 350°F (175°C) oven for about 50 minutes until vegetables are soft. Garnish with Crisp Basil Leaves, right. Serves 4.

1 serving: 381 Calories; 22.4 g Total Fat; 521 mg Sodium; 11 g Protein; 36 g Carbohydrate; 4 g Dietary Fibre

Pictured on page 137.

Asparagus and Mushrooms with Garlic Mustard

"This is an excellent side dish with barbecued steaks, chops or chicken. My mother gave me the recipe years ago and to this day, I get rave reviews whenever I serve this."

— **Maria Anderson, Kamloops, British Columbia**

Water	1/2 cup	125 mL
Fresh asparagus, trimmed of tough ends	1 lb.	454 g
Butter (or hard margarine)	1/4 cup	60 mL
Sliced fresh mushrooms	2 cups	500 mL
Crushed garlic	1/2 tsp.	2 mL
Grainy mustard	2 tbsp.	30 mL
Salt	1/8 tsp.	0.5 mL
Freshly ground pepper	1/4 tsp.	1 mL

Bring water to a boil in large frying pan on medium-high. Add asparagus. Cover. Cook on medium-high for about 5 minutes until asparagus is tender-crisp. Drain. Set aside. Keep warm.

Melt butter in same frying pan on medium. Add mushrooms and garlic. Sauté for about 5 minutes until mushrooms are lightly browned and any liquid from mushrooms has evaporated.

Add remaining 3 ingredients. Stir. Add asparagus. Heat and stir for 1 minute until hot. Serves 4.

1 serving: 152 Calories; 13.2 g Total Fat; 310 mg Sodium; 4 g Protein; 8 g Carbohydrate; 2 g Dietary Fibre

Crisp Basil Leaves

Small touches make a big impression, and this crisp garnish adds lots of colour and flavour to a potato or pasta dish. It can be made a day ahead and left uncovered at room temperature.

Cooking oil	2 tbsp.	30 mL
Fresh sweet basil leaves	12	12

Heat cooking oil in small frying pan on medium. Add basil leaves. Cook for 10 to 20 seconds until bright green and crisp. Remove to paper towel to drain.

3 leaves: 61 Calories; 6.9 g Total Fat; trace Sodium; trace Protein; trace Carbohydrate; 0 g Dietary Fibre

Pictured on page 137.

Kate's Roast Potatoes

Kate made this dish once for a family gathering. It was such a hit, particularly with her young nieces and nephews, that it's become a family tradition.

— **Kate Lander, Pete's Frootique, Old City Market, Saint John, New Brunswick**

Medium potatoes (about 8), peeled	3 lbs.	1.4 kg
Butter (not margarine), melted	1/4 cup	60 mL
Salt	1 -2 tsp.	5 -10 mL
Dry bread crumbs	1/3 cup	75 mL
Freshly grated Parmesan cheese	1/3 cup	75 mL

Cut thin slices every 1/4 inch (6 mm) into potatoes almost, but not quite, cutting through. Place on greased baking sheet. Brush with butter. Sprinkle with salt and bread crumbs. Bake in 350°F (175°C) oven for 1 hour until tender.

Sprinkle with Parmesan cheese. Bake for 10 minutes until crispy. Serves 6 to 8.

1 serving: 242 Calories; 10.4 g Total Fat; 651 mg Sodium; 6 g Protein; 32 g Carbohydrate; 3 g Dietary Fibre

Pictured on page 79.

Theresa's Creamed New Potatoes and Peas, below

Theresa's Creamed New Potatoes and Peas

When summer's bounty presents Theresa with garden-fresh peas and new potatoes, she makes a dish that won first prize and rave reviews from the judges in our Summer Sides Contest. We think you'll agree after the first taste.
— Theresa Wahlstrom, Hughenden, Alberta

Red baby potatoes, halved (about 3 1/2 lbs., 1.6 kg)♦	8 cups	2 L
Water, to cover		
Salt	1 tsp.	5 mL
Bacon slices, diced	4	4
Chopped red onion	1/2 cup	125 mL
All-purpose flour	2 tbsp.	30 mL
Dill weed	3/4 tsp.	4 mL
Salt	1/2 tsp.	2 mL
Freshly ground pepper	1/2 tsp.	2 mL
Whipping cream	1 cup	250 mL
Baby peas, fresh (blanched) or frozen	1 cup	250 mL

Cook potato in water and salt in large saucepan on medium-high for 10 to 15 minutes until just tender. Drain. Place in large bowl. Cover to keep warm.

While potato is cooking, cook bacon in frying pan on medium for about 5 minutes until almost cooked. Add onion. Sauté for about 5 minutes until onion is softened. Remove from pan. Set aside. Drain all but 2 tbsp. (30 mL) drippings from pan.

Add next 4 ingredients. Heat and stir on medium for 1 minute until bubbling.

Add cream. Stir until smooth and thickened. Add peas and bacon mixture. Heat and stir for about 3 minutes until peas are hot. Pour over potato. Mix until well coated. Serve immediately. Makes about 8 cups (2 L). Serves 10 to 12.

1 serving: 220 Calories; 12.3 g Total Fat; 209 mg Sodium; 5 g Protein; 23 g Carbohydrate; 3 g Dietary Fibre

Pictured above.

♦Or use red potatoes, cut into 1 to 1 1/2 inch (2.5 to 3.8 cm) cubes.

Creamy Green Onion Mashed Potatoes

Great mashed potatoes—and no peeling. The potato skins add texture and goodness— the lashings of cream and Parmesan cheese, incredible richness. If there are any leftovers (doubtful!), shape them into little patties, then sauté them in a little butter and top with poached eggs for breakfast the next day.

Unpeeled medium red potatoes, quartered	6	6
Water, to cover		
Salt	1 1/2 tsp.	7 mL
Bacon slices, chopped	4	4
Green onions, finely chopped	6	6
Garlic cloves, crushed	3	3
Butter (or hard margarine)	3 tbsp.	50 mL
Whipping cream	1/2 cup	125 mL
Freshly grated Parmesan cheese	1/2 cup	125 mL
Freshly ground pepper	1 tsp.	5 mL

Combine first 3 ingredients in large saucepan. Bring to a boil. Cook on medium-high for about 25 minutes until potatoes are tender. Drain well. Mash until no lumps remain.

Cook bacon in frying pan on medium for about 10 minutes until crisp. Remove to paper towel to drain. Discard all but 1 tsp. (5 mL) drippings from pan. Add green onion and garlic. Sauté for about 3 minutes until green onion is soft. Add to potatoes.

Add remaining 4 ingredients. Mix until well combined and smooth. Serves 8 to 10.

1 serving: 235 Calories; 13.1 g Total Fat; 230 mg Sodium; 6 g Protein; 24 g Carbohydrate; 2 g Dietary Fibre

Cream of Carrot
Soup, below

Cream of Carrot Soup

"I've been making this soup for almost 20 years and have given this recipe to friends as far away as England and North Carolina and as near as across the street. It's very filling and warming, so I always ensure a good 'rest' before serving the main course. This soup freezes well."

— Christine Ward, Winnipeg, Manitoba

Medium onions, finely chopped	2	2
Hard margarine (or butter)	2 tbsp.	30 mL
Carrots, grated	1 1/2 lbs.	680 g
Tomato paste	1 tbsp.	15 mL
Long grain white rice, uncooked	1/4 cup	60 mL
Chicken broth	4 1/2 cups	1.1 L
Salt	1/2 tsp.	2 mL
Freshly ground pepper	1/2 tsp.	2 mL
Whipping cream	3 tbsp.	50 mL
Whipping cream	3 tbsp.	50 mL
Carrot curls, for garnish		
Chopped fresh cilantro, for garnish		
Croutons, for garnish		

Sauté onion in margarine in large saucepan on medium for 5 minutes until softened.

Add next 3 ingredients and 1/4 cup (60 mL) broth. Stir for 1 to 2 minutes until broth is absorbed. Add remaining broth. Simmer, uncovered, on medium-low for 30 minutes, stirring occasionally, until carrots and rice are tender. Cool slightly. Process, in batches, in blender or food processor until smooth. Return to saucepan.

Add next 3 ingredients. Heat on medium for about 5 minutes, stirring occasionally, until hot. Makes 6 servings of 1 cup (250 mL) each.

To serve, divide soup among individual bowls. Place about 1 1/2 tsp. (7 mL) of second amount of cream in centre of each serving. Swirl with wooden pick. Garnish with remaining 3 ingredients.

1 cup: 207 Calories; 10.2 g Total Fat; 906 mg Sodium; 7 g Protein; 23 g Carbohydrate; 4 g Dietary Fibre

Pictured above.

Photo by: Ian Grant

Curried Squash and Sweet Potato Soup

"I use very little salt in this recipe, but often add a dash of hot pepper sauce. Garnish with multi-grain croutons and a sprig of watercress."
— Therese Raso, Guelph, Ontario

Medium onion, chopped	1	1
Garlic cloves, crushed	3	3
Freshly grated gingerroot	1 tsp.	5 mL
Curry powder	1 tbsp.	15 mL
Ground coriander	1 tsp.	5 mL
Ground cumin	1 tsp.	5 mL
Olive oil	1/4 cup	60 mL
Sweet potato (or yam), peeled and chopped (about 4 cups, 1 L)	1 1/2 lbs.	680 g
Butternut squash, peeled, seeded and chopped (about 2 3/4 cups, 675 mL)	1 lb.	454 g
Can of coconut milk	14 oz.	400 mL
Soy (or regular) milk	2 cups	500 mL
Salt, to taste		
Pepper, to taste		

Sauté first 6 ingredients in olive oil in large pot or Dutch oven for about 5 minutes until onion is softened.

Add next 3 ingredients. Cover. Simmer on medium for about 20 minutes until vegetables are tender.

Stir in coconut milk and soy milk. Cool slightly. Process, in batches, in blender or food processor until smooth. Return to pot. Heat on medium, stirring occasionally, for about 5 minutes until hot.

Add salt and pepper. Makes 10 cups (2.5 L).

1 cup (250 mL): 238 Calories; 15.6 g Total Fat; 185 mg Sodium; 5 g Protein; 22 g Carbohydrate; 3 g Dietary Fibre

Callaloo Soup

"This creamy island specialty is made with the large leaves of the taro root (also known as dasheen in the southern United States). It's similar in taste and colour to spinach."
— Jennifer Cockrall-King, Edmonton, Alberta

Chopped onion (about 1 medium)	1 cup	250 mL
Garlic cloves, crushed	4	4
Chopped serrano chili (or jalapeño) pepper♦	1 tbsp.	15 mL
Finely chopped ham	2/3 cup	150 mL
Hard margarine (or butter)	2 tbsp.	30 mL
Cooking oil	2 tbsp.	30 mL
Callaloo, trimmed and chopped♦♦	1/2 lb.	225 g
Finely chopped fresh flat-leaf parsley	1/4 cup	60 mL
Finely chopped celery leaves	1/4 cup	60 mL
Chicken bouillon	4 cups	1 L
Coconut milk	1 cup	250 mL
Whipping cream	1/2 cup	125 mL
Pepper	1/4 tsp.	1 mL

Sauté first 4 ingredients in margarine and cooking oil in large uncovered pot or Dutch oven on medium for 5 minutes until onion is soft.

Add next 3 ingredients. Cook until callaloo is wilted.

Add bouillon. Cover. Simmer for 10 minutes on medium until celery is soft. Purée soup, in batches, in food processor or blender until smooth.

Return soup to pot. Add remaining 3 ingredients. Heat and stir on medium until hot. Makes 5 1/2 cups (1.4 L).

1 cup (250 mL): 306 Calories; 27.7 g Total Fat; 1453 mg Sodium; 7 g Protein; 10 g Carbohydrate; 1 g Dietary Fibre

♦*Wear gloves when chopping chili peppers, and avoid touching your eyes.*

♦♦*Callaloo is available in Asian grocery stores. If you can't find it, use 1/2 lb. (225 g) fresh spinach.*

Creamy Bread Soup

"A very smooth and creamy treat to the taste buds and the palate, but traditionally scorned by some because of its modest ingredients. Doubles well."
— **Bill Berard, Gogama, Ontario**

Small loaf of crusty Italian (or French) bread, cut into 1 inch (2.5 cm) cubes	1	1
Bacon slices, diced and cooked, drippings reserved	8	8
Reserved bacon drippings	2 tbsp.	30 mL
Finely chopped onion	1 cup	250 mL
Salt	1 tsp.	5 mL
Freshly ground pepper	1 tsp.	5 mL
Chicken broth	1 1/2 cups	375 mL
Water	5 1/2 cups	1.4 L

Fresh parsley, for garnish

Bacon, cooked crisp and crumbled, for garnish

Freshly ground pepper, for garnish

Combine first 8 ingredients in large pot or Dutch oven. Cover. Bring to a boil. Reduce heat immediately. Simmer for at least 2 1/2 hours, stirring occasionally, until desired creaminess and consistency is reached.

Garnish individual servings with remaining 3 ingredients. Makes about 5 1/2 cups (1.4 L).

1 cup (250 mL): 282 Calories; 16.6 g Total Fat; 1100 mg Sodium; 9 g Protein; 24 g Carbohydrate; 2 g Dietary Fibre

Pictured at right.

Chunky Corn Chowder

"My family loves this. They take it for lunch to school or work, or eat it as a snack. It's nutritious and delicious. I make it often."
— **Colleen Haddow, North Bay, Ontario**

Bacon slices, diced	4	4
Chopped onion	1/2 cup	125 mL
Chopped celery	1 cup	250 mL
Cubed potato (about 2 large)	2 cups	500 mL
Milk	4 cups	1 L
Frozen (or fresh) kernel corn	3 1/2 cups	875 mL
Salt	1 tsp.	5 mL
Dill weed	1/2 - 1 tsp.	2 - 5 mL
Freshly ground pepper	1/8 tsp.	0.5 mL
Hot pepper sauce	1/4 tsp.	1 mL

Fry bacon in large pot or Dutch oven on medium for about 5 minutes until just beginning to brown.

Add onion and celery. Sauté for about 5 minutes until onion is softened.

Add remaining 7 ingredients. Bring to a boil on medium. Cover. Reduce heat to low. Simmer for 15 to 20 minutes, stirring often, until potato is tender. Makes 7 cups (1.75 L).

1 cup (250 mL): 233 Calories; 8.4 g Total Fat; 529 mg Sodium; 10 g Protein; 32 g Carbohydrate; 4 g Dietary Fibre

Spicy Sausage Corn Chowder

"This recipe has undergone many changes and variations to get to this point. I have made this soup for hundreds of people over the last few years and many of them have asked for my recipe. Personally, this is my favourite soup."
— **Robb Land, Ottawa, Ontario**

Hot Italian sausage, uncooked, casings removed	6 oz.	170 g
Butter (or hard margarine)	2 tbsp.	30 mL
Diced onion	1/2 cup	125 mL
Diced red pepper	1/4 cup	60 mL
Frozen (or fresh) kernel corn	2 cups	500 mL
Diced celery	1/2 cup	125 mL
Dried crushed chilies	1/2 tsp.	2 mL
Dried sweet basil	1/4 tsp.	1 mL
Dried whole oregano	1/4 tsp.	1 mL
Dried thyme	1/4 tsp.	1 mL
Tomato paste	1/2 cup	125 mL
Salt, to taste		
All-purpose flour	2 tbsp.	30 mL
Prepared chicken (or veal) broth	3 cups	750 mL
Tomato sauce	1 cup	250 mL
Whipping cream	1 cup	250 mL

Creamy Bread Soup, this page

Great Gazpacho, below

Scramble-fry sausage in medium frying pan on medium-high until browned. Drain. Set aside.

Melt butter in large pot or Dutch oven on medium. Add onion. Sauté for about 3 minutes until onion is softened.

Add next 3 ingredients. Sauté for about 10 minutes, stirring occasionally, until vegetables are tender. Reduce heat to low.

Add next 6 ingredients. Heat and stir for 2 minutes until hot.

Sprinkle flour over vegetable mixture. Stir well. Heat and stir for 2 minutes until very thick.

Add broth, tomato sauce and sausage. Bring to a boil on medium-high, stirring occasionally. Reduce heat to medium-low. Simmer, uncovered, for 10 minutes, stirring occasionally.

Add cream. Heat and stir until hot. Makes about 7 cups (1.75 L).

cup (250 mL): 288 Calories; 20.1 g Total Fat; 961 mg Sodium; g Protein; 21 g Carbohydrate; 4 g Dietary Fibre

Great Gazpacho

"This is an amazing make-ahead cold soup for a hot day! I made this for a barbecue and, although my friends were skeptical, they enjoyed the terrific flavour."
— **Dean Netterville, Edmonton, Alberta**

Whole wheat bread slices	3	3
Water, to cover		
Can of diced tomatoes	28 oz.	796 mL
Medium red pepper, chopped	1	1
Chopped red onion	1/4 cup	60 mL
Peeled, seeded and chopped cucumber	2/3 cup	150 mL
Chopped fresh sweet basil	2 tbsp.	30 mL
Garlic cloves, minced	2	2
White (or red) wine vinegar	2 tbsp.	30 mL
Salt	1/2 tsp.	2 mL
Freshly ground pepper	1/2 tsp.	2 mL
Sour cream, for garnish		
Fresh sweet basil sprigs, for garnish		

Soak bread in water in small bowl for 5 minutes. Drain. Squeeze most of water from bread.

Process bread and tomatoes in blender until nearly smooth. Pour 3/4 of tomato mixture into large bowl.

Add next 8 ingredients to blender. Process until nearly smooth. Add to tomato mixture. Mix well. Cover. Chill at least 1 hour or overnight before serving.

Garnish individual servings with dollop of sour cream and basil sprig. Makes 5 1/2 cups (1.4 L).

1/2 cup (125 mL): 42 Calories; 0.6 g Total Fat; 267 mg Sodium; 2 g Protein; 9 g Carbohydrate; 1 g Dietary Fibre

Pictured above.

Sesame Lavash
Bread, page 37

Barbara's Borscht, below

Butter (or hard margarine)	2 tbsp.	30 mL
Italian loaf slices, 1/2 inch (1.2 cm) thick	8	8
Olive oil	2 tbsp.	30 mL
Garlic clove, halved	1	1
Ripe Roma (plum) tomatoes, peeled♦	6	6
Granulated sugar	1/2 tsp.	2 mL
Salt	1/2 tsp.	2 mL
Freshly ground pepper	1/2 tsp.	2 mL
Tomato paste	3 tbsp.	50 mL
Chopped fresh Italian (flat leaf) parsley	1/3 cup	75 mL
Chopped fresh sweet basil	1 tbsp.	15 mL
Grated fresh Parmesan cheese	1/2 cup	125 mL

Combine first 4 ingredients in large pot or Dutch oven. Cover. Bring to boil on high. Reduce heat to medium. Simmer for 20 minutes.

Sauté onion and garlic in butter in frying pan on medium for about 5 minutes until onion is soft. Set aside.

Brush both sides of bread slices with olive oil. Arrange in single layer on ungreased baking sheets. Bake in 350°F (175°C) oven for about 10 minutes, turning once during baking. Remove from oven. Rub both sides of bread slices with garlic.

Process next 5 ingredients in blender until smooth. Add to bean mixture. Add onion mixture. Stir. Cover. Heat on low for about 10 minutes until hot.

Put 1/2 of bread slices on bottom of soup tureen or large serving bowl. Spoon on 1/2 of soup. Sprinkle with 1/2 of parsley, basil and Parmesan cheese. Repeat with remaining bread, soup, parsley, basil and Parmesan cheese. Cover. Let stand for 5 minutes before serving. To serve, dip ladle deeply to ensure each serving has some bread, vegetables and broth. Makes 10 1/2 cups (2.6 L). Serves 6.

1 serving: 485 Calories; 33 g Total Fat; 1911 mg Sodium; 15 g Protein; 35 g Carbohydrate; 5 g Dietary Fibre

♦For easy peeling, plunge tomatoes into boiling water for 1 or 2 minutes, then into ice water. The skins should come off easily.

Barbara's Borscht

Health and nutrition professionals tell us vegetables that are highly coloured, like beets, are better for us. In that case, this classic cold-weather soup is a winner! Hearty and delicious.

— Barbara Farrus, Vegreville, Alberta

Medium beets, peeled and chopped♦	3	3
Medium carrot, chopped	1	1
Large potato, peeled and chopped	1	1
Small onion, chopped	1	1
Chicken broth (or water)	5 cups	1.25 L
Frozen peas	1/2 cup	125 mL
White vinegar	1 tbsp.	15 mL
Salt	1 tsp.	5 mL
Freshly ground pepper	1/2 tsp.	2 mL
Butter (or hard margarine)	1 tbsp.	15 mL
Whipping cream	1/4 cup	60 mL
All-purpose flour	1 tbsp.	15 mL
Whipping cream	3/4 cup	175 mL
Chopped fresh dill	2 tsp.	10 mL

Combine first 5 ingredients in large pot or Dutch oven. Bring to a boil. Boil, uncovered, on medium-high for 15 minutes until vegetables are tender.

Add next 5 ingredients. Heat and stir until butter is melted.

Stir first amount of whipping cream into flour in small bowl until smooth. Stir into soup. Add second amount of cream and dill. Stir. Heat on medium for about 5 minutes, stirring occasionally, until hot. Makes 8 cups (2 L).

1 cup (250 mL): 178 Calories; 12.7 g Total Fat; 877 mg Sodium; 6 g Protein; 11 g Carbohydrate; 2 g Dietary Fibre

Pictured above.

♦To prevent hands from staining, wear rubber gloves while handling beets.

Layered Green Bean and Bread Soup

"The traditional Zuppa di Fagiolini is considered one of the region's lighter soups. This is a tasty start to dinner—the basil, parsley and tomatoes suggest the flavours of courses to come. Very Italian. The beans should be fresh or frozen, not canned. We went quite heavy with the garlic."

— Kathy Murrie and Bill Sass, Edmonton, Alberta

Fresh green beans, cut into 1 inch (2.5 cm) pieces	1 lb.	454 g
Olive oil	1/2 cup	125 mL
Cans of condensed beef broth (10 oz., 284 mL, each)	4	4
Water	3 1/2 cups	875 mL
Small onion, chopped	1	1
Garlic cloves, crushed	4	4

Egyptian Lentil Soup

"I came to Canada from Egypt with my family earlier this year and want to share a dish that has been cooked since the time of the ancient Pharaohs. It is still cooked in Egypt today. It's a really good-tasting dish that's very easy to make. For a whole meal, serve it with boiled white rice on the side."
— Maha Barsoom, Toronto, Ontario

Water	4 cups	I L
Large onion, quartered	I	I
Large carrot, quartered	I	I
Large tomato, quartered	I	I
Large potato, peeled and quartered	I	I
Red split lentils, rinsed and drained	I cup	250 mL
Garlic cloves	2	2
Salt	I tbsp.	15 mL
Freshly ground pepper	I tsp.	5 mL
Ground cumin	1/2 tsp.	2 mL
Ground allspice	1/4 tsp.	I mL
Bay leaf	I	I
Ground nutmeg, pinch		
Cardamom pods	2	2
Medium onion, diced	I	I
Garlic cloves, minced	4	4
Butter (or 1/4 cup, 60 mL, cooking oil)	2 tbsp.	30 mL
Sliced green onion, for garnish		

Bring water to a boil in large pot or Dutch oven. Add next 5 ingredients. Bring to a boil.

Add next 7 ingredients. Open cardamom pods. Add seeds to lentil mixture. Discard pods. Cover. Cook lentil mixture on medium for 20 minutes until vegetables and lentils are tender. Cool slightly. Remove and discard bay leaf. Process, in batches, in blender or food processor until smooth. Return to pot.

Sauté onion and garlic in butter in frying pan for 5 minutes until golden. Add to lentil mixture. Heat on medium-low for about 5 minutes, stirring occasionally, until hot.

Sprinkle each serving with green onion. Makes 7 cups (1.75 L).

I cup (250 mL): 220 Calories; 4 g Total Fat; 1062 mg Sodium; 2 g Protein; 37 g Carbohydrate; 5 g Dietary Fibre

Pictured on page 168.

Zonnia's Borscht

Unlike borscht served throughout the year, the soup served on Ukranian Christmas Eve is meatless (vegetable stock only) and may include miniature mushroom dumplings called vushka (see Mushroom Filling, page 186). Just before serving, add cooked vushka and heat through.
— Zonnia Ostopowich, Edmonton, Alberta

Unpeeled medium beets, scrubbed and trimmed (about 2 lbs., 900 g)◆	8	8
Water, to cover		
Hot water	8 cups	2 L
Medium carrots, grated	2	2
Celery ribs, finely chopped	2	2
Chopped fresh dill	3 tbsp.	50 mL
Finely shredded cabbage	1/2 cup	125 mL
Fresh parsley	2 tbsp.	30 mL
Can of condensed tomato soup	10 oz.	284 mL
Cooking oil	3 tbsp.	50 mL
Large onion, finely chopped	I	I
Garlic clove, crushed	I	I
White vinegar (optional)	2 - 3 tbsp.	30-50 mL
Salt, to taste		
Pepper, to taste		

Put beets and water into large pot or Dutch oven. Bring to a boil. Drain. Return to pot.

Add hot water. Bring to a boil. Reduce heat to medium-high. Cook beets, uncovered, for 5 minutes. Remove from heat. Remove beets with slotted spoon, reserving liquid. Peel and julienne.◆◆ Return beets to reserved liquid in pot.

Add next 6 ingredients. Stir. Set aside.

Heat cooking oil in medium frying pan on medium-high until hot. Add onion and garlic. Sauté for 5 minutes until onion is softened. Add to beet mixture. Bring to a boil. Reduce heat to medium. Simmer, uncovered, for about 5 minutes until cabbage is tender-crisp.

Add remaining 3 ingredients. Stir. Makes about 13 cups (3.25 L). Serves 8 to 10.

I serving: 126 Calories; 6 g Total Fat; 343 mg Sodium; 3 g Protein; 17 g Carbohydrate; 3 g Dietary Fibre

◆To prevent hands from staining, wear rubber gloves while handling beets.

◆◆To julienne, cut into thin slices, then cut each slice into thin strips.

Pictured on page 184.

Corn Chowder

This creamy chowder from the Jensens' corn stand is simple and delicious. David Jensen says the secret to good corn is to keep it cool from the time it's picked until it reaches your kitchen. Then eat it as soon as possible. Try this sprinkled with chopped crispy bacon.
— Jensen Family, Taber, Alberta

Medium onions, chopped	2	2
Small green pepper, chopped	I	I
Butter (or hard margarine)	3 tbsp.	50 mL
Fresh corn kernels (about 5 medium cobs)	3 cups	750 mL
Milk	2 cups	500 mL
Chopped fresh parsley	2 tbsp.	30 mL
Dried savory leaves	1/2 tsp.	2 mL
Salt	3/4 tsp.	4 mL
Freshly ground pepper	1/4 tsp.	I mL
Half-and-half cream	I cup	250 mL
Egg yolks (large), fork-beaten	2	2
Bacon, cooked crisp and crumbled, for garnish		
Chopped fresh chives, for garnish		

Sauté onion and pepper in butter in large saucepan on medium for 5 minutes until soft.

Add next 6 ingredients. Bring to a boil. Reduce heat to low. Stir. Cover. Simmer for 7 minutes until corn is tender. Cool slightly. Process in blender until almost smooth. Return corn mixture to same saucepan. Heat and stir on medium until hot.

Pour cream into medium saucepan. Heat on medium-high for about 3 minutes until hot. Remove from heat. Whisk in egg yolks until well combined. Stir into hot corn mixture.

Garnish with bacon and chives. Makes 7 1/2 cups (1.9 L).

I cup (250 mL): 97 Calories; 3.2 g Total Fat; 380 mg Sodium; 4 g Protein; 15 g Carbohydrate; 2 g Dietary Fibre

Pictured on page 42.

Tomato, Beef and Bean Soup

This filling soup takes its inspiration from a hearty bowl of chili. Garnish with a little sour cream and finely chopped avocado, and serve with one of our delicious flatbreads (recipes on pages 34 to 37).

Lean ground beef	3/4 lb.	340 g
Cooking oil	2 tsp.	10 mL
Medium onion, chopped	1	1
Celery ribs, chopped	2	2
Carrot, chopped	1	1
Rutabaga, peeled and chopped (about 3 1/2 cups, 875 mL)	3	3
Garlic cloves, crushed	2	2
Chili powder	1 tsp.	5 mL
Ground cumin	2 tsp.	10 mL
Ground coriander	1 tsp.	5 mL
Can of diced tomatoes	28 oz.	796 mL
Tomato paste	1/4 cup	60 mL
Beef broth	6 cups	1.5 L
Can of chickpeas (garbanzo beans), rinsed and drained	19 oz.	540 mL
Chopped fresh oregano leaves	1 tbsp.	15 mL
Salt	1 tsp.	5 mL
Freshly ground pepper	1/4 tsp.	1 mL

Scramble-fry ground beef in first amount of cooking oil in large pot or Dutch oven on medium-high until no longer pink. Turn into small bowl. Set aside.

Add next 8 ingredients to same pot. Sauté on medium for 5 minutes.

Add beef and next 3 ingredients. Mix well. Bring to a boil. Reduce heat to low. Cover. Simmer for about 15 minutes until vegetables are tender.

Add remaining 4 ingredients. Stir. Heat on medium for about 5 minutes, stirring occasionally, until hot. Makes 15 cups (3.74 L).

1 cup (250 mL): 126 Calories; 4.4 g Total Fat; 663 mg Sodium; 9 g Protein; 14 g Carbohydrate; 3 g Dietary Fibre

Pictured below.

Turnip and Blue Cheese Soup

Rich and flavourful, this warming soup is an especially nice first course before roast beef or roast pork, or serve it alongside a stacked-meat sandwich. Use the dark orange variety of sweet potato for this recipe.

Medium onion, chopped	1	1
Garlic cloves, chopped	3	3
Cooking oil	1 tbsp.	15 mL
Sweet potato (or yam), peeled and chopped (about 3 3/4 cups, 925 mL)	1 lb.	454 g
Turnips, peeled and chopped (about 3 1/4 cups, 800 mL)	1 lb.	454 g
Maple syrup	3 tbsp.	50 mL
Chicken broth	6 cups	1.5 L
Salt	1/2 tsp.	2 mL
Freshly ground pepper	1 tsp.	5 mL
Half-and-half cream	1 1/2 cups	375 mL
Blue cheese (about 2 oz., 57 g), crumbled	1/3 cup	75 mL
Green onions, sliced	4	4
Hazelnuts, toasted and chopped, for garnish◆		

Sauté onion and garlic in cooking oil in large pot or Dutch oven on medium for about 5 minutes until onion is softened.

Add next 6 ingredients. Bring to a boil. Reduce heat to low. Cover. Simmer for about 15 minutes until vegetables are tender.

Add next 3 ingredients. Stir. Cool slightly. Process, in batches, in blender or food processor until smooth. Return to pot. Heat on medium for about 5 minutes, stirring occasionally, until hot. Makes about 10 cups (2.5 L).

To serve, divide soup among individual bowls. Sprinkle with hazelnuts.

1 cup: 204 Calories; 7.7 g Total Fat; 729 mg Sodium; 7 g Protein; 27 g Carbohydrate; 4 g Dietary Fibre

◆To toast the hazelnuts, place them in an ungreased frying pan. Heat on medium, stirring often, until golden.

Whole Wheat Pita Bread, page 34

Tomato, Beef and Bean Soup, above

Photo by: Ian Grant

Flatbread with Sesame Seeds
and Oregano, page 36

Roasted Parsnip and
Coconut Soup, below

Roasted Parsnip and Coconut Soup

The humble parsnip, combined with exotic ingredients from the Thai pantry, delivers a big-flavoured soup set off beautifully by a vibrant cilantro pesto. You can easily turn up the heat with a little more curry paste.

Medium parsnips, peeled and coarsely chopped (about 4 cups, 1 L)	8	8
Cooking oil	1 tbsp.	15 mL
Salt	1/2 tsp.	2 mL
Finely grated gingerroot	2 tsp.	10 mL
Garlic cloves, chopped	2	2
Small onion, chopped	1	1
Red curry paste	1-2 tbsp.	15-30 mL
Cooking oil	1 tbsp.	15 mL
Chicken broth	5 cups	1.25 L
Crunchy peanut butter	2 tbsp.	30 mL
Fish sauce	2 tsp.	10 mL
Finely grated lime zest	1 tsp.	5 mL
Freshly squeezed lime juice	1 tbsp.	15 mL
Can of coconut milk	14 oz.	398 mL
CILANTRO PESTO		
Fresh cilantro	1/2 cup	125 mL
Roasted salted peanuts	1/4 cup	60 mL
Garlic clove	1	1
Salt	1/4 tsp.	1 mL

Combine parsnip, first amount of cooking oil and salt in large bowl. Transfer to greased baking sheet with sides. Bake in 350°F (175°C) oven for 50 minutes, stirring once, until parsnip is golden.

Sauté next 4 ingredients in second amount of cooking oil in large pot or Dutch oven on medium for about 5 minutes until onion is softened.

Add parsnip and next 5 ingredients. Stir.

Reserve 1/4 cup (60 mL) coconut milk. Stir remaining coconut milk into parsnip mixture. Cool slightly. Process, in batches, in blender or food processor until smooth. Return to pot. Heat on medium for about 5 minutes, stirring occasionally, until hot. Makes 8 servings of 1 cup (250 mL) each.

Cilantro Pesto: Put first 3 ingredients into food processor. Process until well combined.

Add reserved coconut milk and salt. Process until smooth. Makes 1/2 cup (125 mL) pesto. To serve, divide soup among individual bowls. Place dollop of pesto on each serving. Swirl with wooden pick.

1 cup: 272 Calories; 19.9 g Total Fat; 898 mg Sodium; 8 g Protein; 19 g Carbohydrate; 3 g Dietary Fibre

Pictured above.

Matchli Soup
(Fish Soup)

According to the Alis, soup is not traditional in India, but is reminiscent of their Fijian heritage. *"My mum would cook fish curry one night and a fish in coconut soup the next. We had lots of variety with fish, prawns and crabs readily available at the market—or Dad would go to the sea and catch them himself. My mum serves this soup as is, or with boiled taro or cassava. You can use fresh coconut milk as well."*

— Naazima Ali, Edmonton, Alberta

Halibut steaks (about 6 oz., 170 g, each), skin removed and cut into quarters	2	2
Lime juice	1/2 cup	125 mL
Cooking oil	1 tbsp.	15 mL
Cooking oil	2 tsp.	10 mL
Medium onion, coarsely chopped	1/2	1/2
Garlic cloves, chopped	2	2
Medium red chili pepper, seeded and finely chopped◆	1	1
Bunch of baby bok choy, chopped into 1 1/2 inch (3.8 cm) pieces	1	1
Water	1 tbsp.	15 mL
Can of coconut milk	14 oz.	398 mL
Chopped fresh cilantro	1 tsp.	5 mL
Salt, to taste		

Place halibut in medium bowl. Add lime juice. Chill for 5 minutes. Rinse with cold water. Pat dry. Remove any bones. Sauté halibut in first amount of cooking oil in frying pan on medium for about 3 minutes per side until browned. Set aside.

Heat second amount of cooking oil in medium saucepan. Add next 3 ingredients. Cook on medium for about 3 minutes, stirring constantly, until onion is soft.

Add bok choy and water. Stir. Cover. Cook for 2 minutes until tender-crisp. Stir in coconut milk and cilantro. Add halibut. Gently stir. Bring to a gentle boil. Remove from heat. Add salt. Stir. Makes 3 cups (750 mL). Serves 4.

1 serving: 355 Calories; 28.1 g Total Fat; 72 mg Sodium; 21 g Protein; 9 g Carbohydrate; 1 g Dietary Fibre

◆*Wear gloves when chopping chili peppers, and avoid touching your eyes.*

Homemade Mushroom Soup

"If I tell my boys that we're having homemade mushroom soup for lunch, I know I have to double the recipe. My daughter will also sneak in some friends from school for lunch. If you're lucky enough to have leftover soup, thicken it slightly for a great sauce or gravy for meat, chicken or potatoes."

— Linda Rudachyk, Weyburn, Saskatchewan

Butter (or hard margarine)	1/4 cup	60 mL
Large onion, finely chopped	1	1
Sliced fresh mushrooms (about 2 lbs., 900 g)	12 cups	3 L
Dried thyme	1 tsp.	5 mL
Salt	1 tsp.	5 mL
Freshly ground pepper	1/4 tsp.	1 mL
All-purpose flour	1/4 cup	60 mL
Prepared chicken broth	4 cups	1 L
Half-and-half cream	3 cups	750 mL

Melt butter in large pot or Dutch oven on medium. Add onion. Sauté for about 5 minutes, stirring occasionally, until softened.

Add next 4 ingredients. Increase heat to medium-high. Sauté for about 10 minutes, stirring occasionally, until mushrooms are softened. Reduce heat to medium.

Add flour. Heat and stir for 1 to 2 minutes until thickened.

Add broth. Heat and stir for 5 minutes until slightly thickened. Stir in cream. Heat and stir for about 5 minutes until heated through. Makes 11 cups (2.75 L).

1 cup (250 mL): 173 Calories; 12.3 g Total Fat; 598 mg Sodium; 6 g Protein; 11 g Carbohydrate; 1 g Dietary Fibre

Coconut and Crab Corn Chowder

As good as standard corn chowder can be, this version provides an interesting Asian twist. Lime, coconut and fresh ginger highlight the naturally sweet flavours of crab and corn.

Fine coconut	1/2 cup	125 mL
Cooking oil	2 tbsp.	30 mL
Chopped shallots	1 cup	250 mL
Diced red pepper	1/2 cup	125 mL
Sambal oelek (chili paste)	1 tsp.	5 mL
Salt	1/2 tsp.	2 mL
All-purpose flour	2 tbsp.	30 mL
Freshly squeezed lime juice (about 2 medium limes)	1/4 cup	60 mL
Prepared vegetable broth	2 cups	500 mL
Water	1 cup	250 mL
Cubed potato (about 2 large)	2 cups	500 mL
Frozen (or fresh) kernel corn	2 cups	500 mL
Can of cream-style corn	14 oz.	398 mL
Cans of crabmeat (5 oz., 142 g, each), with liquid, cartilage removed	2	2
Can of light coconut milk	14 oz.	398 mL
Freshly grated gingerroot	1 tbsp.	15 mL
Chopped green onion	1/4 cup	60 mL

Toast coconut in large pot or Dutch oven on medium, stirring constantly, until lightly browned. Remove from pot. Set aside.

Heat cooking oil in same pot on medium. Add next 4 ingredients. Sauté for about 10 minutes, stirring occasionally, until shallots are softened.

Add flour. Heat and stir for 1 minute until bubbly. Gradually stir in next 3 ingredients Heat and stir on medium until boiling.

Add next 3 ingredients. Mix well. Bring to a boil. Reduce heat to medium-low. Simmer, uncovered, for 20 to 25 minutes, stirring occasionally, until potato is tender.

Add remaining 4 ingredients. Heat and stir on medium until just beginning to boil. Spoon into individual serving bowls. Sprinkle with toasted coconut. Makes 11 cups (2.75 L).

1 cup (250 mL): 203 Calories; 9.4 g Total Fat; 551 mg Sodium; 8 g Protein; 25 g Carbohydrate; 3 g Dietary Fibre

Pictured on page 203.

Smoky Corn Chowder with Black Beans

"Low-fat with lots of veggies—my children between the ages of four and 14 and my husband give this recipe a thumbs-up! To make the chowder even better, I roast fresh corn on the cob under the broiler, then cut the kernels off."
— **Margaret Steele, North Vancouver, British Columbia**

Tomatoes (about 9 small), stems removed	2 lbs.	900 g
Olive (or cooking) oil	1 tbsp.	15 mL
Chopped onion	1 cup	250 mL
Prepared chicken broth	3 cups	750 mL
Frozen (or fresh) kernel corn	2 cups	500 mL
Can of black beans, drained and rinsed	19 oz.	540 mL
Ground cumin	2 tsp.	10 mL
Salt	1 tsp.	5 mL
Dried whole oregano	1 tsp.	5 mL
Cayenne pepper, just a pinch		
Chopped fresh cilantro	1/4 cup	60 mL
Sour cream, for garnish		

Arrange tomatoes in single layer on baking sheet with sides. Broil about 5 inches (12.5 cm) from heat for 10 to 15 minutes, turning once or twice, until skin is evenly blistered and blackened. Let stand until cool enough to handle. Remove and discard skins. Coarsely chop tomatoes, reserving juice.

Heat olive oil in large pot or Dutch oven on medium. Add onion. Sauté for about 5 minutes until softened. Add tomato with juice. Stir.

Add next 7 ingredients. Stir. Bring to a boil on medium-high. Reduce heat to medium-low. Cover. Simmer for 20 minutes, stirring occasionally.

Add cilantro. Stir. Spoon into individual serving bowls.

Add a dollop of sour cream to each serving. Makes about 10 cups (2.5 L).

1 cup (250 mL): 120 Calories; 2.9 g Total Fat; 581 mg Sodium; 6 g Protein; 19 g Carbohydrate; 4 g Dietary Fibre

Pictured at right.

Smoky Corn Chowder with Black Beans, left

Coconut and Crab Corn Chowder, page 202

Corn Chowder with Sweet Potato

"When I think of preparing corn chowder, I remember the story my friend Jane relayed to me. My seven-year-old son Justin was staying with her for a few days. One evening Jane was preparing to make fries and burgers for supper (just the type of food most seven-year-olds thrive on), when Justin piped up he wanted corn chowder instead. This is an old traditional family recipe with the addition of a little sweet potato. I like it because it's quick and easy." We used the dark orange variety of sweet potatoes.

— Bonny Cross, Tancook Island, Nova Scotia

Chopped onion	1 cup	250 mL
Dried summer savory	1/4 tsp.	1 mL
Italian seasoning	1/4 tsp.	1 mL
Water	2 cups	500 mL
Diced potato (about 4 large)	4 cups	1 L
Diced sweet potato (or yam)	1 1/2 cups	375 mL
Can of kernel corn, with liquid	12 oz.	341 mL
Can of cream-style corn	19 oz.	540 mL
Butter (or hard margarine)	1/3 cup	75 mL
Whipping cream (or half-and-half)	1 cup	250 mL
Salt, sprinkle		
Pepper, sprinkle		

Put first 6 ingredients into large pot or Dutch oven. Bring to a boil on medium-high. Reduce heat to medium-low. Cover. Simmer for about 10 minutes, stirring occasionally, until potatoes are tender.

Add remaining 6 ingredients. Heat and stir until hot. Makes 10 cups (2.5 L).

1 cup (250 mL): 277 Calories; 15.1 g Total Fat; 342 mg Sodium; 4 g Protein; 35 g Carbohydrate; 3 g Dietary Fibre

Fragrant Duck Soup

Chinese cooks have long extolled the flavours of duck, especially when used to good advantage in soups such as this one.

Whole duck◆ (approximately 5 lbs., 2.3 kg)	1	1
Water	8 cups	2 L
Medium carrot, chopped	1	1
Celery rib, chopped	1	1
Medium onion, chopped	1	1
Cooking oil	2 tsp.	10 mL
Julienned gingerroot◆◆	1 tbsp.	15 mL
Garlic cloves, crushed	2	2
Stalk of lemon grass (white part only), cut in half crosswise (optional)	1	1
Soy sauce	2 tbsp.	30 mL
Sherry (or alcohol-free sherry)	1 tbsp.	15 mL
Medium carrot, cut julienne◆◆	1	1
Salt	1 tsp.	5 mL
Fresh bean sprouts	1/2 cup	125 mL
Fresh cilantro	1/4 cup	60 mL

If using fresh duck, remove and discard neck and giblets from cavity of duck. Rinse duck. Pat dry inside and out with paper towels. Place breast-side up on wire rack in roasting pan. Prick skin all over with metal skewer, being careful not to pierce through to flesh. Roast in 300°F (150°C) oven for 3 hours. Meat thermometer inserted into breast (or thickest part) should register 180°F (82°C). Remove and discard skin. Remove duck meat from bones. Reserve bones. Shred duck meat. Place in small bowl. Cover. Chill.

Combine reserved duck bones and next 4 ingredients in large pot or Dutch oven on high. Bring to a boil. Reduce heat to medium-low. Simmer, uncovered, for 1 hour, skimming and discarding any foam from surface. Strain duck stock into medium bowl. Discard solids.

Heat cooking oil in large pot or Dutch oven on medium-high. Add ginger, garlic and lemon grass. Sauté for 1 minute until fragrant.

Add duck stock. Stir. Add next 4 ingredients. Stir. Cover. Heat on medium-high for 5 minutes. Remove lemon grass. Add duck meat. Heat and stir until heated through.

Ladle into serving bowls. Garnish with bean sprouts and cilantro. Serves 6.

1 serving: 239 Calories; 13.1 g Total Fat; 808 mg Sodium; 24 g Protein; 5 g Carbohydrate; trace Dietary Fibre

◆*If you'd like, buy barbecued duck from an Asian market, remove and discard skin, then proceed with the recipe.*

◆◆*To julienne, cut into thin slices, then cut each slice into thin strips.*

Bean Soup

"My kids have always loved this soup. It's a family favourite that I usually make after a big dinner, like Easter, when I can use the leftover bone and ham bits. I like it chunky so I use a potato masher—a blender makes it too fine."

— Rose Dennis, Regina, Saskatchewan

Dried navy beans (about 2 1/3 cups, 575 mL)	1 lb.	454 g
Water, to cover		
Water	4 cups	1 L
Can of diced tomatoes, with juice	28 oz.	796 mL
Ham bone◆ (about 1 1/2 lbs., 680 g), trimmed of fat	1	1
Freshly ground pepper	1 tsp.	5 mL
Cooking oil	1 tbsp.	15 mL
Chopped onion	1 cup	250 mL
Chopped celery	1 cup	250 mL
Worcestershire sauce	2 tbsp.	30 mL
Salt	1 - 2 tsp.	5 - 10 mL
Grated medium Cheddar cheese, for garnish		

Soak beans in water in large bowl overnight. Drain. Put into large pot or Dutch oven.

Add next 4 ingredients. Stir. Bring to a boil on medium-high. Reduce heat to medium-low. Cover. Simmer for about 2 1/2 hours, stirring occasionally, until beans are softened. Remove from heat. Remove ham bone. Set aside. Mash beans with potato masher until thick, chunky texture. Remove meat from ham bone. Chop. Add to bean mixture. Discard bone.

Heat cooking oil in large frying pan on medium. Add onion and celery. Sauté for about 10 minutes, stirring occasionally, until onion is softened. Add to bean mixture.

Add Worcestershire sauce and salt to bean mixture. Bring to a boil on medium-high. Reduce heat to medium-low. Simmer, uncovered, for 10 minutes, stirring occasionally.

Sprinkle individual servings with cheese. Makes about 11 cups (2.75 L).

1 cup (250 mL): 203 Calories; 3.3 g Total Fat; 394 mg Sodium; 14 g Protein; 30 g Carbohydrate; 8 g Dietary Fibre

◆*If you don't have a leftover ham bone, buy one from your butcher or use a smoked pork hock instead.*

Strawberry Shortcake

"This recipe is from my mom, Florence Stuyvesant, who lives in Madison, Tennessee. Okanagan strawberries are small and sweet, like homegrown. For the best shortcake, grow berries in your own garden or in strawberry pots right outside your door." Serve with a dollop of whipped cream.

— Heather Page, Kelowna, British Columbia

All-purpose flour	2 cups	500 mL
Granulated sugar	2 tbsp.	30 mL
Baking powder	1 tbsp.	15 mL
Salt	1 tsp.	5 mL
Hard margarine (or butter)♦	1/3 cup	75 mL
Milk	1 cup	250 mL
Sliced fresh strawberries	4 cups	1 L
Granulated sugar	1/2 cup	125 mL

Combine first 4 ingredients in medium bowl. Cut in margarine until crumbly. Stir in milk. Mix well. Spoon into greased and floured 8 inch (21 cm) round cake pan. Spread evenly. Bake in 450°F (230°C) oven for 15 to 20 minutes until lightly browned. Wooden pick inserted in centre should come out clean. Remove from pan to wire rack.

Combine strawberries and sugar. Slice cake in half horizontally. Place top layer of cake, rounded side down, on serving plate. Spoon about 1/2 of strawberries over top. Place second cake layer, cut side down, on top. Spoon remaining strawberries over all. Serves 8.

1 serving: 305 Calories; 10 g Total Fat; 361 mg Sodium; 5 g Protein; 49 g Carbohydrate; 3 g Dietary Fibre

Pictured above.

♦*Heather's original recipe used shortening. We tested it with hard margarine and it was great. You also have the option of using butter.*

Variation: For individual shortcake biscuits, drop dough by large spoonfuls onto greased baking sheet. Bake in 450°F (230°C) oven for 15 minutes until lightly browned. Cool. Slice in half horizontally. Fill with strawberries. Makes 8.

Funny Cake

"This is a dessert my mother-in-law made often and we all enjoyed. We still make it and always remember her when we do. The Butterscotch Sauce sinks through the cake and creates a layer on the pastry bottom. The top retains some sauce and gets golden and yummy! Great with vanilla ice cream."
— **Shirley Minogue, Edmonton, Alberta**

Pastry for a 9 inch
(22 cm) deep dish
pie shell, your own
or a mix

BUTTERSCOTCH SAUCE

Hard margarine (or butter)	1/4 cup	60 mL
Brown sugar, packed	1/2 cup	125 mL
Golden corn syrup	2 tbsp.	30 mL
Water	3 tbsp.	50 mL
Vanilla	1/2 tsp.	2 mL

CAKE

Hard margarine (or butter), softened	1/4 cup	60 mL
Granulated sugar	3/4 cup	175 mL
Large egg	1	1
Milk	1/2 cup	125 mL
Vanilla	1 tsp.	5 mL
All-purpose flour	1 1/4 cups	300 mL
Baking powder	1 tsp.	5 mL
Salt	1/2 tsp.	2 mL
Finely chopped pecans (or medium coconut)	1/4 cup	60 mL

Line 9 inch (22 cm) deep-dish pie plate with pastry, and make high fluted edge.

Butterscotch Sauce: Melt margarine in small saucepan. Add brown sugar and corn syrup. Stir until sugar is dissolved. Bring to a boil. Gradually add water. Return to a boil. Boil for 2 minutes. Remove from heat. Stir in vanilla. Cool.

Cake: Cream margarine and granulated sugar together in medium bowl. Beat in egg. Stir in milk and vanilla.

Combine next 3 ingredients in small bowl. Add to milk mixture. Stir until smooth. Pour into pastry shell. Sprinkle with pecans. Carefully pour sauce over batter. Bake in 350°F (175°C) oven for 50 to 55 minutes until top is golden brown. Wooden pick inserted in centre should come out clean. Serves 8.

1 serving: 463 Calories; 21.7 g Total Fat; 397 mg Sodium; 5 g Protein; 63 g Carbohydrate; 1 g Dietary Fibre

Pictured above.

Granny Fern's Date and Orange Cake

"A tasty, high-energy food, concocted and passed on to me by my mother. I always marvelled at the way she could pull a recipe out of her head, never failing to please her 11 children. This was always a favourite with us, as well as with our lumberjack father."
— Fernande Berard, Gogama, Ontario

Hard margarine (or butter), softened	1/2 cup	125 mL
Granulated sugar	1 cup	250 mL
Sour milk, room temperature♦	1 cup	250 mL
Freshly grated orange zest	1 tbsp.	15 mL
All-purpose flour	2 cups	500 mL
Baking powder	1 tsp.	5 mL
Chopped pecans	1/2 cup	125 mL
Chopped dates	1 cup	250 mL
Baking soda	1 tsp.	5 mL
Warm water	1/4 cup	60 mL
TOPPING		
Granulated sugar	1/2 cup	125 mL
Freshly squeezed orange juice (about 1 medium)	1/4 cup	60 mL

Cream margarine and sugar in medium bowl until light and fluffy.

Add sour milk and orange zest. Mix well.

Add next 4 ingredients. Mix well.

Dissolve baking soda in warm water in small bowl. Add to batter. Mix well. Pour into greased 9 x 13 inch (22 x 33 cm) pan. Bake in 350°F (175°C) oven for 35 to 40 minutes until golden. Poke about 12 holes in cake with skewer.

Topping: Beat sugar and orange juice in small bowl for 5 minutes until sugar is dissolved. Pour over hot cake. Cuts into 18 pieces.

1 piece: 229 Calories; 8 g Total Fat; 163 mg Sodium; 3 g Protein; 38 g Carbohydrate; 2 g Dietary Fibre

♦To make sour milk, add 1 tbsp. (15 mL) white vinegar to milk to equal 1 cup (250 mL).

Lemon Cake

"We raised our five children on the farm and they always had big appetites. This dessert was one of their favourites."
— Sophia Campbell, Kindersley, Saskatchewan

Hard margarine (or butter), softened	1/2 cup	125 mL
Granulated sugar	1 cup	250 mL
Egg yolks (large), fork-beaten	3	3
Baking powder	1 tbsp.	15 mL
All-purpose flour	1 1/2 cups	375 mL
Milk	1 cup	250 mL
FILLING		
Freshly squeezed lemon juice	2/3 cup	150 mL
Granulated sugar	1 cup	250 mL
Cornstarch	1 tbsp.	15 mL
Large eggs, fork-beaten	2	2
Hard margarine (or butter)	1/2 cup	125 mL
TOPPING		
Medium coconut	1/2 cup	125 mL
Egg whites (large), room temperature	3	3
Granulated sugar	1/4 cup	60 mL
Medium coconut	1/2 cup	125 mL

Cream margarine and sugar in medium bowl until light and fluffy. Beat in egg yolks.

Combine baking powder and flour in small bowl. Add to egg mixture in 3 additions, alternating with milk. Pour into greased 9 x 13 inch (22 x 33 cm) pan. Bake in 350°F (175°C) oven for 25 minutes.

Filling: Combine all 5 ingredients in double boiler or heavy saucepan. Heat and stir for 5 minutes until thickened. Pour onto slightly cooled cake.

Topping: Sprinkle first amount of coconut over top of filling.

Beat egg whites in medium bowl until soft peaks form. Gradually beat in sugar until dissolved. Spread over coconut.

Sprinkle second amount of coconut over top. Bake in oven for 10 to 12 minutes until coconut and egg white are lightly browned. Refrigerate for at least 1 hour. Cuts into 12 pieces.

1 piece: 456 Calories; 23.7 g Total Fat; 322 mg Sodium; 6 g Protein; 58 g Carbohydrate; 1 g Dietary Fibre

Pictured below.

Lemon Cake, above

Swirl Ice Cream with Grilled
Cake and Berries, below

Swirl Ice Cream with Grilled Cake and Berries

Make simple pound cake and vanilla ice cream spectacular. Flavour the one with orange and ginger, the other with chocolate and almond. Grill one, freeze the other. When you serve it with mixed berries in liqueur, you won't believe the compliments.

Vanilla ice cream, softened	2 cups	500 mL
Toasted flaked almonds♦	1/3 cup	75 mL
Chocolate fudge sauce	1/2 cup	125 mL

GRILLED CAKE

Grated orange zest	1 tsp.	5 mL
Freshly squeezed orange juice	1/2 cup	125 mL
Brown sugar, packed	2 tbsp.	30 mL
Hard margarine (or butter), melted	1/4 cup	60 mL
Ground ginger	3/4 tsp.	4 mL
Frozen pound cake, thawed	10 1/2 oz.	298 g

BERRIES

Frozen mixed berries, thawed, with juice	3 cups	750 mL
Icing (confectioner's) sugar	1/4 cup	60 mL
Orange-flavoured liqueur	3 tbsp.	50 mL

Place ice cream in medium bowl. Add almonds. Stir. Swirl chocolate sauce through ice cream. Freeze for 2 to 3 hours until firm. Makes 2 1/2 cups (625 mL) ice cream.

Grilled Cake: Combine first 5 ingredients in small bowl.

Preheat grill to medium. Peel or cut top crusts off cake. Cut into 6 slices crosswise. Cut each slice in half diagonally. Brush liberally with orange juice mixture until all is used. Cook on well greased grill for 3 minutes per side until browned.

Berries: Combine all 3 ingredients in medium bowl. Makes 2 1/3 cups (575 mL) berries. To serve, place 1 scoop of ice cream on each serving plate. Add 2 slices of cake and 1/2 cup (125 mL) of berries. Serves 6.

1 serving: 701 Calories; 31.4 g Total Fat; 374 mg Sodium; 8 g Protein; 100 g Carbohydrate; 4 g Dietary Fibre

Pictured above.

♦To toast the almonds, place them in an ungreased frying pan. Heat on medium, stirring often, until golden.

Egg Yolk Sponge Cake

Egg yolks add up if you're making macaroons or meringues. Add them to scrambled eggs or hollandaise sauce for a richer texture, or try this simple recipe.

Hard margarine (or butter), softened	6 tbsp.	100 mL
Granulated sugar	3/4 cup	175 mL
Egg yolks (large)	4	4
Vanilla	3/4 tsp.	4 mL
Milk	3/4 cup	175 mL
All-purpose flour	1 1/2 cups	375 mL
Baking powder	1 1/2 tsp.	7 mL
Salt	1/4 tsp.	1 mL

Cream first 3 ingredients together in large bowl until light and fluffy.

Add vanilla and milk. Beat until well combined. Mixture may look curdled.

Sift remaining 3 ingredients into medium bowl. Fold into butter mixture. Turn into greased 9 x 9 inch (22 x 22 cm) pan. Bake in 350°F (175°C) oven for about 25 minutes until wooden pick inserted in centre comes out clean. Let stand in pan for 10 minutes. Turn out onto wire rack to cool completely. Cuts into 9 pieces.

1 piece: 254 Calories; 10.4 g Total Fat; 233 mg Sodium; 4 g Protein; 36 g Carbohydrate; 1 g Dietary Fibre.

Zuccotto

"There's no other name for this dessert than what the Tuscans call it! We suggest you go easy on the alcohol (follow the amounts listed) or it can overpower the nutty undertones of the filling. If you like, add a drizzle of melted chocolate, accents of shaved semi-sweet chocolate or fresh berries as a finishing touch just before serving."

— Leslie Maze and David Holehouse, Edmonton, Alberta

Dried cranberries, chopped	1/3 cup	75 mL
Brandy	2 tbsp.	30 mL
Cherry-flavoured liqueur	1/4 cup	60 mL
Orange-flavoured liqueur	1/4 cup	60 mL
Frozen pound cakes, thawed (10 1/2 oz., 298 g, each)	2	2
Envelope of unflavoured gelatin	1/4 oz.	7 g
Cold water	1/4 cup	60 mL
Whipping cream	2 1/2 cups	625 mL
Icing (confectioner's) sugar	2/3 cup	150 mL
Cocoa, sifted	3 tbsp.	50 mL
Grated milk chocolate (not baking squares)	1/2 cup	125 mL
Slivered almonds, toasted and chopped♦	1/2 cup	125 mL
Sliced hazelnuts, toasted and chopped♦	1/3 cup	75 mL

Combine first 4 ingredients in small bowl. Cover. Let stand for 15 minutes. Drain, reserving liquid.

Line 18 cup (4.5 L) round-bottomed, dome-shaped glass bowl with plastic wrap. Peel or cut top crusts off cakes. Cut each cake lengthwise into 1/2 inch (12 mm) thick slices. Cut each slice in half diagonally (see diagram 1). Brush both sides of cake with reserved liqueur mixture. Line inside of bowl with cake, narrow ends meeting in centre in bottom of bowl and wide ends extending above rim of bowl, crust side against cut side, until bowl is completely lined (see diagram 2). You will have cake and liqueur mixture left over to cover top. Cover with plastic wrap to keep moist while making filling.

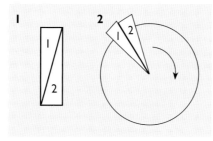

Sprinkle gelatin over cold water in small saucepan. Let stand for 3 to 5 minutes until softened. Heat and stir on low for 1 to 2 minutes until gelatin is dissolved. Cool.

Beat cream until soft peaks form.

Fold in icing sugar and gelatin mixture. Divide mixture equally between 2 medium bowls. Fold cocoa and chocolate into first bowl. Spread chocolate filling mixture over bottom and up sides of cake 1 inch (2.5 cm) thick and to within 1 1/2 inches (3.8 cm) of top edge of bowl.

Fold cranberries, almonds and hazelnuts into second bowl. Spoon into cavity to same level as chocolate filling. Trim cake pieces to 1/2 inch (12 mm) above level of filling. Brush remaining cake slices with liqueur mixture. Cover filling with trimmed cake pieces and remaining cake slices. Cover. Chill for 8 hours or overnight. Remove cover. Invert onto serving plate. Carefully remove plastic wrap. Cut into wedges. Serves 8.

1 serving: 757 Calories; 50.6 g Total Fat; 338 mg Sodium; 9 g Protein; 62 g Carbohydrate; 3 g Dietary Fibre

♦To toast the almonds and hazelnuts, place them in an ungreased frying pan. Heat on medium, stirring often, until golden.

No-Egg Chocolate Cake

When Ottawa's Martha Murphy discovered her future daughter-in-law had an egg allergy, she asked Jean Paré for a cake recipe without eggs. Chocolate cake lovers of all sorts will ask for seconds.

All-purpose flour	3 cups	750 mL
Granulated sugar	2 cups	500 mL
Cocoa	1/2 cup	125 mL
Baking soda	2 tsp.	10 mL
Salt	1 tsp.	5 mL
Cooking oil	3/4 cup	175 mL
Vinegar	2 tsp.	10 mL
Vanilla	2 tsp.	10 mL
Water	2 cups	500 mL
Icing sugar, sprinkle		

Measure first 5 ingredients into large bowl. Stir. Make a well in centre.

Add next 4 ingredients to well. Mix until smooth. Pour into greased 9 x 13 inch (22 x 33 cm) pan. Bake in 350°F (175°C) oven for 35 to 40 minutes until wooden pick inserted in centre comes out clean. Cool.

Sprinkle with icing sugar. Cuts into 24 pieces.

1 piece: 198 Calories; 7.6 g Total Fat; 207 mg Sodium; 2 g Protein; 31 g Carbohydrate; 1 g Dietary Fibre

Chocolate Cake

"Often Mom would have this cake, still warm from the oven, waiting for us when we climbed off the school bus and got home. We were treated to a slice with fresh cream. My children ask for this cake for their birthdays. Grandma taught our daughter how to bake this cake and she won first prize at the local agriculture fair."

— Brenda Fraser, Morinville, Alberta

All-purpose flour	1 1/2 cups	375 mL
Granulated sugar	1 1/4 cups	300 mL
Cocoa	3 tbsp.	50 mL
Salt	1 tsp.	5 mL
Baking soda	1 tsp.	5 mL
Cream of tartar	1/4 tsp.	1 mL
Milk	1 cup	250 mL
Large eggs, fork-beaten	2	2
Vanilla	1 tsp.	5 mL
Hard margarine (or butter), melted	1/2 cup	125 mL

Sift first 6 ingredients into large bowl. Stir.

Add remaining 4 ingredients. Stir well until smooth. Pour batter into greased 9 x 9 inch (22 x 22 cm) pan. Bake in 350°F (175°C) oven for about 35 minutes. Wooden pick inserted in centre of cake should come out clean. Cool. Cuts into 9 pieces.

1 serving: 324 Calories; 12.6 g Total Fat; 562 mg Sodium; 5 g Protein; 49 g Carbohydrate; 1 g Dietary Fibre

Cran-Blueberry Cake

"I've made this cake for years and it's just awesome." The original blueberry cake came from an old church cookbook from Antigonish, Nova Scotia. Adding cranberries gives this colourful cake its sweet/tart taste. It's delicious as is, but if you'd like to dress it up, we think it would be especially good with your favourite lemon icing.

— Claire Doyle, Isle Madame, Nova Scotia

Butter (or hard margarine), softened	1 cup	250 mL
Granulated sugar	1 1/2 cups	375 mL
Salt	1/2 tsp.	2 mL
Vanilla	2 tsp.	10 mL
Egg yolks (large)	4	4
All-purpose flour	3 cups	750 mL
Baking powder	2 tsp.	10 mL
Milk	2/3 cup	150 mL
Egg whites (large)	4	4
Granulated sugar	1/2 cup	125 mL
Fresh (or frozen) blueberries	3 cups	750 mL
Fresh (or frozen) cranberries, coarsely chopped	2 cups	500 mL
All-purpose flour	1 tbsp.	15 mL
Granulated sugar	2 tsp.	10 mL

Beat first 4 ingredients in large bowl until light and creamy. Add egg yolks. Beat until well combined.

Sift first amount of flour and baking powder in medium bowl. Add to butter mixture in 2 additions, alternating with milk.

Beat egg whites in medium bowl until soft peaks form. Fold in second amount of sugar. Fold into batter.

Toss blueberries and cranberries in second amount of flour in large bowl. Stir into batter. Pour into greased 9 x 13 inch (22 x 33 cm) pan.

Sprinkle with last amount of sugar. Bake in 350°F (175°C) oven for about 1 hour until wooden pick inserted in centre comes out clean. Cuts into 18 pieces.

1 piece: 313 Calories; 12.4 g Total Fat; 238 mg Sodium; 4 g Protein; 47 g Carbohydrate; 2 g Dietary Fibre

Pictured below.

Cranberry Gingerbread Cake

As her husband Hubert can attest, Claire is a big ginger fan! Dried cranberries add a chewy texture and extra flavour to this fragrant traditional cake.

— Claire Doyle, Isle Madame, Nova Scotia

Butter (or hard margarine), softened	3/4 cup	175 mL
Brown sugar, packed	1 cup	250 mL
Large eggs	2	2
Fancy (mild) molasses	1 cup	250 mL
Hot water	1 cup	250 mL
All-purpose flour	3 cups	750 mL
Baking soda	1 tbsp.	15 mL
Salt	1 tsp.	5 mL
Ground ginger	2 tsp.	10 mL
Ground cinnamon	1 tsp.	5 mL
Dried cranberries, chopped	2 cups	500 mL

Beat butter and brown sugar together in large bowl until light and creamy. Add eggs. Beat until well combined.

Combine molasses and hot water in small bowl.

Sift next 5 ingredients into medium bowl. Add cranberries. Stir. Add flour mixture to butter mixture in 2 additions, alternating with molasses mixture. Stir until well combined. Pour into greased and floured 9 x 13 inch (22 x 33 cm) pan. Bake in 350°F (175°C) oven for 35 to 40 minutes until wooden pick inserted in centre comes out clean. Cuts into 18 pieces.

1 piece: 283 Calories; 9.9 g Total Fat; 366 mg Sodium; 3 g Protein; 46 g Carbohydrate; 2 g Dietary Fibre

Cran-Blueberry Cake, above

Jelly Roll, below

Photo by: Ian Grant

Jelly Roll

Classic jelly rolls are always best eaten on the day they're made. (Somehow we don't think that will pose a problem with this delightful sweet.) You can vary the recipe by using lemon curd or apricot jam in place of the berry jam.

All-purpose flour	1 cup	250 mL
Baking powder	2 tsp.	10 mL
Egg whites (large)	4	4
Berry sugar	1/2 cup	125 mL
Egg yolks (large)	4	4
Hot milk	1/4 cup	60 mL
Berry sugar	2 tbsp.	30 mL
Raspberry jam (or strawberry) heated	1 cup	250 mL

Sift flour and baking powder into medium bowl. Using seond medium bowl, sift flour and baking powder 2 additional times.

Beat egg whites in large bowl on high until soft peaks form. Add first amount of sugar, 1 tbsp. at a time, beating well after each addition. Beat in egg yolks, 1 at a time, until pale and thickened. Fold in flour mixture and hot milk. Spread mixture into greased and parchment paper-lined jelly roll pan. Bake in 350°F (175°C) oven for about 8 to 10 minutes until cake is golden and springs back when lightly pressed.

Sprinkle second amount of sugar onto parchment or waxed paper. Turn warm cake onto sugared paper. Trim crisp edge from long sides. Spread jam evenly over cake. Using paper as a guide, roll up, starting from short side. Cool. Cuts into 10 slices.

1 slice: 219 Calories; 2.3 g Total Fat; 118 mg Sodium; 4 g Protein; 47 g Carbohydrate; 1 g Dietary Fibre

Pictured above.

Apple Coffee Cake

This cake isn't overly sweet and is wonderful when served warm.

Hard margarine (or butter), softened	3/4 cup	175 mL
Granulated sugar	2/3 cup	150 mL
Large eggs	3	3
All-purpose flour	1 1/2 cups	375 mL
Baking powder	2 tsp.	10 mL
Milk	1/3 cup	75 mL
Medium tart cooking apples (such as Granny Smith), peeled, cored and thinly sliced	2	2
Apricot jam, heated and sieved	3 tbsp.	50 mL

Cream margarine and sugar together in large bowl. Beat in eggs, 1 at a time, beating well after each addition.

Sift flour and baking powder into medium bowl. Add to margarine mixture alternately with milk. Mix well. Turn into greased 8 inch (20 cm) springform pan.

Arrange apples, slightly overlapping, on top. Bake in 350°F (175°C) oven for about 1 hour until wooden pick inserted in centre comes out clean. Let stand in pan for 5 minutes. Remove side of pan. Brush jam over cake while still warm. Cuts into 8 pieces.

1 piece: 384 Calories; 20.5 g Total Fat; 337 mg Sodium; 6 g Protein; 46 g Carbohydrate; 1 g Dietary Fibre

Haunted Castle Cake

An abandoned castle with broken-down shutters, jumbled tombstones, gnarly trees and a murky moat—what a spooktacular centrepiece for a Halloween party! Your young ghosties and ghoulies will have a howling good time creating this eerie dessert made of cake mix, icing and a whole loot bag full of treats. A monstrously good way to have your cake—and eat it too!

SUPPORT BASE
You will need: 21 x 17 inch (52.5 x 42.5 cm) piece of foam board; 1 large sheet of brown or green construction paper; tape or glue; aluminum foil

Cover one side of the foam board with construction paper. Secure with tape or glue. Cut a sheet of foil into a 12 x 14 inch (30 x 35 cm) rectangle. Secure the foil with tape or glue to the centre of the foam board,

leaving a 1/2 inch (12 mm) edge all around. Fold up the edges of the foil to form sides. Pinch the corners to form right angles.

CAKE
Boxes of golden cake mix (2 layer size)	3	3

ICING
Icing sugar	7 1/2 cups	1.9 L
Hard margarine (or butter), melted	3/4 cup	175 mL
Milk	1/2 cup	125 mL
Black paste food colouring◆		

Cake: Prepare cakes according to package directions, using 9 x 13 inch (22 x 33 cm) pan for each. Cool cakes completely. Cut 2 inches (5 cm) from one short side of each cake, creating three 9 x 11 inch (22 x 28 cm) cakes. Cut trimmed ends into 1 1/2 inch (3.8 cm) cubes.◆◆

Icing: Combine first 3 ingredients in large bowl. Beat on medium speed with electric mixer until smooth. Add food colouring, a bit at a time, until icing is a dark grey colour. Place one cake in centre of foil on board. Spread icing over top of cake with spatula. Place second cake on top. Spread icing over top. Place third cake on top. Spread icing over top and sides of entire cake. You will have icing left over for decorating (for decorating ideas, see Delicious Decorating, page 213). Serves 36.

1 serving of cake with icing (no decorations): 422 Calories; 16.8 g Total Fat; 364 g Sodium; 4 g Protein; 65 g Carbohydrate; 0 g Dietary Fibre

Pictured above and on page 213.

◆*Paste food colouring is available at craft or cake decorating stores.*

◆◆*For easier icing, put the cakes and cake cubes into the freezer for 2 hours until firm. This prevents cake crumbs from getting into the icing during spreading.*

Delicious Decorating

Here's a list of items and ideas that we used to create our Haunted Castle Cake, but have fun exploring the candy aisle and coming up with your own creative touches.

Turrets: Ice cream cones covered with icing, and licorice string coiled at the base.

Parapet around top of castle: Iced cubes of cake and licorice nibs.

Roof and bridge texture: Poppy seeds.

Windows: Licorice ribbons cut into triangles.

Castle corners: Licorice rectangles.

Castle door, tombstones and bridge: Fruit leather cut with scissors.

Ghosts, bats and letters: Soft candy centres and layers from all-sorts, rolled flat and cut into shapes.

Goblins: Gumdrops in various shapes.

Cobblestone roadway: Brown and dark green jellybeans.

Outer wall of moat: Toasted coconut marshmallows and nut fudge clusters.

Border around support base: Licorice discs cut in half.

"Glue" to hold everything together: Icing.

Stone pattern: Use a wooden skewer to mark the sides of the iced cake. Don't worry if the lines are a little uneven (or even if the cake is a bit lumpy or broken); it makes the castle more dilapidated and scary!

Moat water: Prepare separate batches of blue and black-coloured fruit-flavoured gelatin in shallow pans. When set, scoop out spoonfuls and arrange on the foil around the outside of the castle to suggest water.

Chocolate trees: Microwave chocolate melting wafers in a resealable freezer bag on medium-high for about 1 1/2 minutes, squishing every 20 seconds or so, until just melted. Snip a small hole in one corner of the bag, drizzle twisted tree shapes with branches onto waxed paper, making sure the base of the trunk is thicker. Let the trees harden, then use icing to "plant" them next to the castle. The melted chocolate was also used to pipe lines on the castle door.

Dark Fruitcake

A touch of tradition is part of the appeal of Christmas, and for many, the taste of a moist, dense slice of fruitcake combines aromatic flavours with fond memories of holidays past. In our version, we've kept the basic fruitcake ingredients and method, but with two variations: the whisky-steeped fruit mixture is boiled before the dry ingredients are added, and only one dousing with spirits is needed before storage. For convenience, you can make this moist, dark fruitcake at least a month in advance; for taste, you'll be glad you did.

Dates, chopped	1 1/2 cups	375 mL
Dark raisins	2 cups	500 mL
Sultana raisins	1 1/2 cups	375 mL
Currants	1 cup	250 mL
Mixed peel	1/2 cup	125 mL
Glazed pineapple, chopped	1/2 cup	125 mL
Glazed cherries, halved	1/2 cup	125 mL
Glazed ginger, chopped (optional)	1/3 cup	75 mL
Scotch whisky	2/3 cup	150 mL
Water	1 cup	250 mL
Hard margarine (or butter), cut up	1 cup	250 mL
Can of sweetened condensed milk	14 oz.	398 mL
White vinegar	1 tsp.	5 mL
All-purpose flour	2 cups	500 mL
Baking soda	1 tsp.	5 mL
Baking powder	1 tsp.	5 mL
Pumpkin pie spice	2 tsp.	10 mL
Blanched almonds	2 tbsp.	30 mL
Glazed cherries, halved	1/4 cup	60 mL
Scotch whisky	1/4 cup	60 mL

Combine first 9 ingredients in large bowl. Cover. Let stand at room temperature for 6 hours or overnight, or longer if desired. This mixture can be prepared up to 4 weeks ahead and stored in an airtight container. Line bottom and sides of 3 inch (7.5 cm) deep 8 x 8 inch (20 x 20 cm) cake pan with 2 layers of brown paper and 1 layer of parchment paper, ensuring layers come 2 inches (5 cm) above sides of pan.

Combine fruit mixture, water and margarine in large pot or Dutch oven. Bring to a boil. Reduce heat to medium-high. Boil gently for 3 minutes. Transfer to large bowl. Cool for 15 minutes, stirring several times.

Add condensed milk and vinegar to fruit mixture. Mix well.

Sift next 4 ingredients together in medium bowl. Add to fruit mixture. Mix well.

Spoon cake batter into prepared cake pan. Spread with spatula to ensure even surface. Knock pan on solid surface 3 or 4 times to remove air bubbles. Decorate top with almonds and second amount of cherries. Bake in 300°F (150°C) oven for 3 to 3 1/4 hours until top is firm to touch and a thin-bladed knife gently inserted in thickest part of the fruitcake comes out clean, but sticky from the fruit.

Drizzle second amount of whisky over hot fruitcake. Cover fruitcake loosely with foil. Cool completely before turning out of pan. Wrap cake in plastic wrap and then foil. To store at room temperature, place wrapped cake in an airtight container. Let stand for at least 1 week. Stored properly, fruitcake will keep for up to 6 months in a cool, dark place. To freeze, place wrapped cakes in resealable freezer bags. Freeze for up to 12 months. To serve, cut into 1 inch (2.5 cm) slices and then cut each slice into 4 pieces, for a total of 32 pieces.

1 piece: 277 Calories; 8 g Total Fat; 146 mg Sodium; 3 g Protein; 47 g Carbohydrate; 2 g Dietary Fibre

Pictured below.

Nutty About Fruitcake

- Soak the fruit the night before, or longer if time permits.

- Have the cake pan and all the ingredients ready before you start.

- Sift the dry ingredients so they can be thoroughly incorporated throughout the fruit mixture.

- Fruitcake bakes for a significantly longer time than most cakes; lining the pan with several layers of brown and parchment paper ensures that the cake cooks evenly without forming a hard, thick crust.

- Grease between the paper layers so they stick to each other and stay in place.

- Bake fruitcake slowly in a low-temperature oven; if it's too hot, the cake will crack and form a hard crust.

- The longer the fruitcake sits, the richer the flavour.

Orange, Yogurt and Poppy Seed Cake

By using whole oranges—make sure you choose juicy, sweet ones—this cake emerges beautifully moist with an intense orange flavour. Ground almonds and poppy seeds add a nice crunch. Serve with a little lightly sweetened whipped cream.

Large oranges	2	2
Hot water, to cover		
Whole blanched almonds, toasted✦	2 cups	500 mL
Large eggs	6	6
Granulated sugar	1 cup	250 mL
Plain yogurt	2/3 cup	150 mL
Poppy seeds	1/4 cup	60 mL
All-purpose flour	1 1/2 cups	375 mL
Baking powder	1 tbsp.	15 mL
ORANGE DECORATION AND SYRUP		
Large oranges	2	2
Water	1 cup	250 mL
Granulated sugar	1 cup	250 mL

Place oranges in large pot or Dutch oven. Add enough hot water to cover oranges. Cover. Bring to a boil. Reduce heat to medium-low. Simmer for 2 hours, adding more hot water as needed to keep oranges covered. Drain. Cool. Cut into quarters. Remove any seeds.

Process almonds in food processor until finely chopped. Remove to small bowl. Process orange quarters in same food processor until smooth. Set aside.

Beat eggs and sugar together in large bowl until thick and pale. Fold in yogurt, poppy seeds, processed orange and almonds.

Sift flour and baking powder into medium bowl. Stir. Fold into orange mixture. Grease and flour 10 inch (25 cm) springform pan. Spoon mixture into pan. Smooth top. Bake in 350°F (175°C) oven for about 1 hour until wooden pick inserted in centre comes out clean. Cool in pan for 10 minutes. Remove cake to wire rack. Cover to keep warm.

Orange Decoration and Syrup: Use vegetable peeler to peel oranges from top to bottom into 2 1/2 to 3 inch (6.4 to 7.5 cm) lengths. Cut away any pith from peel (see photo). Cut peel into thin strips.

Combine water and sugar in medium saucepan. Heat and stir on low until sugar is dissolved. Add orange strips. Simmer, uncovered, on medium, without stirring, for about 15 minutes until orange strips are translucent. Remove orange strips with slotted spoon to foil or parchment paper to cool. Brush warm cake with 2 tbsp. (30 mL) syrup. Arrange orange strips over top of cake. Serves 8 to 10.

1 serving: 626 Calories; 25.2 g Total Fat; 208 mg Sodium; 16 g Protein; 90 g Carbohydrate; 7 g Dietary Fibre

Pictured above.

✦To toast the almonds, place in single layer in ungreased shallow pan. Bake in 350°F (175°C) oven for 5 to 10 minutes, stirring or shaking often, until desired doneness.

Almond Torte with Raspberry Sauce

Moist and ultra-rich, this is the sort of chocolate dessert featured in upscale restaurants. Serve in smaller pieces than regular chocolate cake—though you may want more than one piece! (Keep this dessert in mind when you're looking for a flourless cake.)

Semi-sweet chocolate, chopped	5 oz.	140 g
Butter (or hard margarine), cut up	1/2 cup	125 mL
Granulated sugar	2/3 cup	150 mL
Ground almonds	3/4 cup	175 mL
Prepared strong coffee	2 tbsp.	30 mL
Egg yolks (large)	3	3
Egg whites (large)	3	3
RASPBERRY SAUCE		
Packages of frozen raspberries in syrup (10 oz., 300 g, each), about 4 cups (1 L)	2	2
Icing sugar	1/2 cup	125 mL
Finely grated orange zest	1 tbsp.	15 mL

Whipped cream, optional

Combine chocolate and butter in small saucepan. Heat and stir on medium for about 3 minutes until melted. Transfer to large bowl.

Add next 4 ingredients. Stir until well combined.

Beat egg whites in medium bowl until soft peaks form. Fold into chocolate mixture in 2 batches. Pour into greased and parchment paper-lined 8 inch (20 cm) springform pan. Bake in 350°F (175°C) oven for about 35 minutes until set. Cool in pan. Cover. Chill for at least 6 hours or overnight.

Raspberry Sauce: Combine all 3 ingredients in large saucepan. Heat and stir on medium for about 10 minutes until raspberries are thawed and mixture is slightly thickened. Press raspberry mixture through sieve into 2 cup (500 mL) liquid measure. Discard solids. Chill for 2 hours. Makes about 1 2/3 cups (400 mL) raspberry sauce.

To serve, spread 3 tbsp. (50 mL) raspberry sauce onto each of 8 serving plates. Remove side from cake pan. Cut cake into 8 pieces with hot wet knife. Carefully place 1 piece of cake in centre of raspberry sauce. Place a dollop of whipped cream on cake. Repeat for remaining servings. Serves 8.

1 serving: 435 Calories; 25.2 g Total Fat; 155 mg Sodium; 5 g Protein; 52 g Carbohydrate; 3 g Dietary Fibre

Pictured below.

Saucy Hearts and a Filigree Flower

For a professional finish, encircle each torte slice with creamy hearts etched in raspberry sauce. The chocolate filigree flower is the final touch. To make this dessert absolutely stunning, serve it on a dinner plate.

For the hearts: Combine 3 tbsp. (50 mL) of sour cream and 1 tbsp. (15 mL) of water in a small bowl (this makes enough to go with eight slices of torte). After spreading the raspberry sauce onto the plate, carefully spoon seven or eight dots of cream at even intervals about 1/2 inch (12 mm) in from the edge of the sauce. Allow about 1/8 tsp. (0.5 mL) of cream for each dot. To avoid accidental spilling, we recommend spooning individual per-dot portions rather than pouring seven or eight times from a full teaspoonful. (An eyedropper works really well.)

Once you've spooned out the sour cream mixture for all the servings, you're ready to connect the dots into hearts. Position a wooden pick in the raspberry sauce between two dots but closest to the one you're going to start with. Draw the wooden pick through the centre of the first dot and continue around, without stopping, until you've gone through all of the circles, creating hearts as you go.

Pictured at left and on page 147.

For the flower: Follow the directions for the Heart Token filigree, page 242— just change the pattern. For eight 3 inch (7.5 cm) diameter chocolate flowers, you'll need about 3 1/2 oz (100 g) of milk or dark chocolate. After piping the flower, add a chocolate-covered coffee bean in the centre of each. Chill the filigree until the chocolate is set. Just before serving, place on top of the dollop of whipped cream.

Pictured at left.

Chilled Chocolate and Pecan Cheesecake

If you're a fan of chocolate pecan pie, you know just how great these two ingredients are together—but wait until you taste them in combination with classic cheesecake ingredients. Decorate with chocolate curls, piped whipped cream and chocolate-covered pecan halves for a simply irresistible dessert.

CRUST

Chocolate wafer crumbs	1 1/2 cups	375 mL
Pecan halves	1/2 cup	125 mL
Butter (not margarine), melted	1/4 cup	60 mL

FILLING

Envelope of unflavoured gelatin	1/4 oz.	7 g
Cold water	1/4 cup	60 mL
Cream cheese, softened	12 oz.	375 g
Ricotta cheese	1 cup	250 mL
Vanilla	1 tsp.	5 mL
Granulated sugar	1/4 cup	60 mL
Milk chocolate chunks	8 oz.	225 g
Mars candy bars (1 3/4 oz., 50 g, each), chopped	3	3

Crust: Process wafer crumbs and pecans in food processor until finely ground and mixed well. Place in medium bowl. Add butter. Stir until well combined. Press mixture in bottom and up side of ungreased 9 inch (22 cm) springform pan. Chill for 1 hour.

Filling: Sprinkle gelatin over cold water in small saucepan. Let stand for 3 to 5 minutes until softened. Heat and stir on low until gelatin is dissolved. Cool.

Beat next 4 ingredients in large bowl until smooth.

Melt milk chocolate and chocolate bars in large heavy saucepan on low, stirring constantly. Do not overheat. Stir into cream cheese mixture. Stir in gelatin until well combined. Spoon mixture into crust. Cover. Chill for 6 hours or overnight.

Cuts into 12 wedges.

1 wedge: 446 Calories; 31.7 g Total Fat; 236 mg Sodium; 8 g Protein; 36 g Carbohydrate; 1 g Dietary Fibre

Pictured at right.

Banana Cheesecake with Caramel Sauce

This creamy banana cheesecake with its butterscotch-like sauce is the perfect finale to a special meal. The final accent of whipped cream and banana slices is especially attractive.

CRUST

All-purpose flour	1 1/4 cups	300 mL
Icing (confectioner's) sugar	1/4 cup	60 mL
Cold butter (not margarine)	1/3 cup	75 mL
Egg yolks (large)	3	3
Cold water, approximately	1 tbsp.	15 mL

BANANA FILLING

Cream cheese, softened	16 oz.	500 g
Granulated sugar	1/2 cup	125 mL
Mashed banana (about 3 medium)	1 1/2 cups	375 mL
Large eggs	3	3
Vanilla	2 tsp.	10 mL
Dark rum (or 1 tsp., 5 mL, rum flavouring)	1 1/2 tbsp.	25 mL

CARAMEL SAUCE

Whipping cream	1/2 cup	125 mL
Brown sugar, packed	1/2 cup	125 mL
Butter (not margarine), cut up	1/2 cup	125 mL
Whipped cream	2 cups	500 mL
Medium banana, sliced	1	1

Crust: Sift flour and icing sugar into large bowl. Cut in butter until mixture is crumbly.

Stir in egg yolks and enough cold water until mixture forms a soft dough. Turn out onto lightly floured surface. Knead for 1 minute until smooth. Cover with plastic wrap. Chill for 30 minutes. Press pastry in bottom and up side of greased 9 inch (22 cm) springform pan using a lightly floured straight-sided glass until pastry is 1/2 inch (12 mm) from the top. Refrigerate for 30 minutes. Cover pastry with parchment paper. Gently push down on bottom. Sprinkle about 1 cup (250 mL) dried beans or rice over waxed paper. Bake in 375°F (190°C) oven for 10 minutes. Remove beans or rice and waxed paper. Bake for another 10 minutes until lightly browned. Cool.

Banana Filling: Beat cream cheese and sugar in large bowl until smooth.

Add remaining 4 ingredients. Beat until well combined. Pour filling into crust. Bake in 350°F (175°C) oven for about 45 minutes until just set. Turn off oven. Run a knife around edge of pan. Cool in oven with door ajar for 2 hours. Chill for 6 hours or overnight.

Caramel Sauce: Combine first 3 ingredients in medium saucepan. Heat and stir on low until butter is melted. Simmer, uncovered, for 1 minute. Makes about 1 cup (250 mL) sauce.

Top cheesecake with whipped cream and banana slices. Serve sauce warm over individual slices. Cuts into 12 wedges.

1 wedge: 567 Calories; 41 g Total Fat; 294 mg Sodium; 8 g Protein; 43 g Carbohydrate; 1 g Dietary Fibre

Chilled Chocolate and Pecan Cheesecake, left

Almond and Raspberry Cheesecake, belov

Almond and Raspberry Cheesecake

This magnificent baked cheesecake features a soft, creamy texture, the citrus kick of lemon and the irresistible temptation of fresh raspberries. It's a perfect party piece to delight friends and family.

CRUST

Vanilla wafers (or 3/4 cup, 175 mL, wafer crumbs)	1 cup	250 mL
Ground almonds	3/4 cup	175 mL
Butter (not margarine), melted	1/4 cup	60 mL

FILLING

Cream cheese, softened	8 oz.	250 g
Ricotta cheese	1 cup	250 mL
Granulated sugar	1 cup	250 mL
Large eggs	4	4
Egg yolk (large)	1	1
Sour cream	1 cup	250 mL
All-purpose flour	3 tbsp.	50 mL
Finely grated lemon zest	1 tbsp.	15 mL
Fresh raspberries	1 1/4 cup	300 mL
Flaked (sliced) almonds	1/3 cup	75 mL
Fresh raspberries, for garnish		

Crust: Process wafers in food processor into fine crumbs. Combine wafer crumbs, almonds and butter in medium bowl. Press mixture in bottom of greased 9 inch (22 cm) springform pan using flat bottomed glass. Chill for 1 hour.

Filling: Beat first 3 ingredients in large bowl until smooth.

Add next 5 ingredients. Mix well. Pour mixture onto crust.

Sprinkle top of filling evenly with raspberries and almonds. Bake in 350°F (175°C) oven for about 1 hour until centre is almost set. Turn of oven. Run a knife around edge of pan. Cool in oven with door ajar for 2 hours. Chill for 6 hours or overnight.

Garnish with raspberries. Cuts into 12 wedges

1 wedge: 363 Calories; 24 g Total Fat; 174 mg Sodium; 9 g Protein; 30 g Carbohydrate; 1 g Dietary Fibre

Pictured above.

Orange, Yogurt and Poppy Seed Cheesecake

Orange and poppy seeds are commonly used in many European cakes. We've combined these traditional partners with yogurt to make a light-tasting, thoroughly delicious cheesecake.

CRUST

Graham cracker crumbs	2 cups	500 mL
Butter (not margarine), melted	1/2 cup	125 mL

FILLING

Envelopes of unflavoured gelatin (1/4 oz., 7 g, each)	2	2
Cold water	1/3 cup	75 mL
Cream cheese, softened	16 oz.	500 g
Plain yogurt	1 cup	250 mL
Granulated sugar	3/4 cup	175 mL
Finely grated orange zest	2 tbsp.	30 mL
Freshly squeezed orange juice	1/4 cup	60 mL
Poppy seeds	3 tbsp.	50 mL

TOPPING

Prepared orange juice	3/4 cup	175 mL
Cornstarch	1 1/2 tbsp.	25 mL
Granulated sugar	1 tbsp.	15 mL
Orange-flavoured liqueur (optional)	1 tbsp.	15 mL
Orange slices, for garnish		

Crust: Combine graham crumbs and butter in medium bowl until well mixed. Press firmly in bottom and up side of 9 inch (22 cm) ungreased springform pan. Chill for 1 hour.

Filling: Sprinkle gelatin over cold water in small saucepan. Let stand for 3 to 5 minutes until softened. Heat and stir on low until gelatin is dissolved. Cool.

Beat next 5 ingredients in large bowl until smooth.

Stir in gelatin mixture and poppy seeds. Spoon into crust. Cover. Chill for about 3 hours until set.

Topping: Combine first 3 ingredients in medium saucepan until smooth. Heat and stir on medium-high until mixture is boiling and thickened.

Stir in liqueur. Cool for 1 minute. Gently spread topping over cheesecake. Chill until topping is set.

Garnish with orange slices. Cuts into 12 wedges.

1 wedge: 379 Calories; 25.5 g Total Fat; 314 mg Sodium; 7 g Protein; 32 g Carbohydrate; 1 g Dietary Fibre

Pictured below.

Just the Facts on Cheesecake Cracks

Too hot an oven: Cheesecakes should bake slowly, otherwise the outside of the cake sets before the inside has had time to expand and settle. The best temperature is 325 to 350°F (160 to 175°C).

Over-baking: Time matters as much as temperature. With cheese, eggs and sugar as the main ingredients, cheesecakes are more affected by baking time than flour-based cakes.

Over-beating: When too much air is incorporated into the cheesecake batter, it rises, then collapses and splits. Beat in the eggs, one at a time, on low until just blended.

Temperature change: Instead of moving the cheesecake directly from a hot oven onto the counter to cool (where even drafts can affect it), turn the oven off, leave the cheesecake in the oven with the door ajar and let it gradually cool.

Sticking to the pan: Run a knife between the pan and the side of the cheesecake so that as the cake cools, it can pull away from the pan (instead of sticking and causing the filling to crack or become uneven).

Cracks Still Attack?

Camouflage is the answer: Top the cheesecake with whipped topping! It'll taste just as wonderful and be gone just as fast.

Sweets & Treats: Cookies & Other Hand-Held Delights

Clockwise from top:
Mini Coconut Cake, page 229
Macadamia Crescents, page 221
Shortbread Stars, page 221
White Chocolate Cherry
Fudge, page 229

Shortbread Stars

Shortbread—in any shape or form—never fails to please. These star-shaped shortbreads will be enjoyed by everyone in your home, and they make great holiday gifts.

Butter (not margarine), softened	1 1/3 cups	325 mL
Icing sugar	1 1/4 cups	310 mL
All-purpose flour	2 1/4 cups	560 mL
Rice flour	1/3 cup	75 mL
Silver dragées, for decoration◆	1/2 - 1 tbsp.	7 - 15 mL

Beat butter and icing sugar in medium bowl until smooth.

With beater on low, gradually add both flours. Beat until dough comes together. Turn out onto lightly floured surface. Knead for about 1 minute until smooth. Return to bowl. Cover with plastic wrap. Chill for 30 minutes. Turn out onto lightly floured surface. Roll out to 1/4 inch (6 mm) thickness. Cut star shapes from dough using 2 inch (5 cm) cookie cutter. Arrange stars 1 inch (2.5 cm) apart on ungreased cookie sheets.

Lightly press dragées into stars. Bake in 300°F (150°C) oven for about 25 minutes until just firm. Do not brown. Cool on cookie sheets for 5 minutes. Remove to wire racks to cool completely. Makes about 48 cookies.

1 cookie: 96 Calories; 5.5 g Total Fat; 55 mg Sodium; 1 g Protein; 10 g Carbohydrate; trace Dietary Fibre

◆*Dragées are small edible silver balls available specialty shops and in the cake decorating section of some grocery stores.*

Pictured on page 220.

Sugar Cookies

These are easy-to-make, all-time favourites. They freeze well if you want to make them ahead of time.

Hard margarine (or butter), softened	3/4 cup	175 mL
Granulated sugar	3/4 cup	175 mL
Large egg	1	1
Vanilla	1 tsp.	5 mL
All-purpose flour	2 cups	500 mL
Baking soda	1 tsp.	5 mL
Cream of tartar	1 tsp.	5 mL
Ground cardamom (optional)	1/4 tsp.	1 mL
Salt	1/4 tsp.	1 mL
Sugar sprinkles, for decoration		

Beat margarine and sugar in large bowl until light and fluffy. Add egg and vanilla. Beat until well combined.

Sift next 5 ingredients into medium bowl. Stir into margarine mixture. Turn out onto lightly floured surface. Roll out to 1/8 inch (3 mm) thickness. Cut with cookie cutters into desired shapes.

Decorate with sugar sprinkles. Arrange 1 inch (2.5 cm) apart on greased cookie sheets. Bake in 350°F (175°C) oven for about 10 minutes until firm. Cool on cookie sheets for 5 minutes. Remove to wire racks to cool completely. Makes about 7 dozen cookies.

1 cookie: 35 Calories; 1.8 g Total Fat; 41 mg Sodium; trace Protein; 4 g Carbohydrate; trace Dietary Fibre

Pictured below.

Tray Chic

- Nestle sweets, especially crumb-topped or gooey ones, in decorative baking cups to keep trays and fingers neat and clean. The cups are also a handy way to have extras ready to replenish trays. Patterned and foil versions are available in cake decorating stores or in the baking section of some grocery stores.

- Varied shapes—square, triangular, round, cut out—make for a more visually interesting sweet tray, but keep the pieces about the same size.

- Design on the diagonal when setting out rows of sweets on trays, and choose different shapes for each row. You'll be amazed at what a difference it makes in eye-appeal.

Macadamia Crescents

This is a traditional Christmas cookie recipe that uses macadamia nuts to great effect in place of the usual almonds or walnuts.

Butter (not margarine), softened	1 cup	250 mL
Icing sugar	1/2 cup	125 mL
Vanilla	1 tsp.	5 mL
All-purpose flour	2 1/4 cups	550 mL
Macadamia nuts, finely chopped	2/3 cup	150 mL
Icing sugar, approximately	1/2 cup	125 mL

Beat butter in medium bowl until light and fluffy. Add first amount of icing sugar and vanilla. Beat until well combined.

Gradually stir in flour, 1 cup (250 mL) at a time, until all flour is incorporated. Stir in nuts. Using 1 tbsp. (15 mL) dough, roll into cigar shapes with pointed ends. Bend into crescent shapes. Arrange 1 inch (2.5 cm) apart on ungreased baking sheets. Bake in 350°F (175°C) oven for 15 minutes until just firm. Do not brown. Cool on baking sheets for 5 minutes. Transfer to wire racks to cool completely.

Dredge crescents in second amount of icing sugar, ensuring thick, even coating. Makes 40 crescents.

1 crescent: 99 Calories; 6.7 g Total Fat; 50 mg Sodium; 1 g Protein; 9 g Carbohydrate; trace Dietary Fibre

Pictured on page 220.

Sugar Cookies, above

Cookie Cut-Outs

Kids will love customizing these colourful cookies with fun designs piped in bright icing. Just follow the step-by-step piping instructions at right.

Hard margarine (or butter), softened	1/3 cup	75 mL
Package of flavoured gelatin (jelly powder), any flavour or colour	3 oz.	85 g
Large egg	1	1
All-purpose flour	1 1/4 cups	300 mL
Baking powder	3/4 tsp.	4 mL
Salt	1/4 tsp.	1 mL

ICING

Icing (confectioner's) sugar	2 cups	500 mL
Milk	1 tbsp.	15 mL
Hard margarine (or butter), melted	2 tsp.	10 mL

Sprinkles or coloured sugar (optional)

Beat first 3 ingredients in medium bowl with electric mixer on medium until smooth.

Add next 3 ingredients. Beat on low until well combined. Separate dough into 2 portions. Shape each portion into slightly flattened ball. Wrap in plastic wrap. Chill for 1 hour. Roll out on lightly floured surface, 1 portion at a time, to 1 inch (3 mm) thickness. Cut out shapes with cookie cutters. Arrange 2 inches (5 cm) apart on greased cookie sheets. Bake in 350°F (175°C) in oven for 10 to 12 minutes until edges start to brown. Remove to wire racks. Let stand for 5 minutes. Remove cookies to sheet of waxed paper to cool completely. Makes 2 dozen cookies.

Icing: Combine all 3 ingredients in separate medium bowl. If necessary, add more milk, 1 tsp. (5 mL) at a time, until icing is smooth and creamy. Makes 1 cup (250 mL) icing.

Spread icing on cookies. Decorate with sprinkles or coloured sugar. Let icing harden on cookies before storing between layers of waxed paper.

1 cookie: 115 Calories; 3.3 g Total Fat; 84 mg Sodium; 1 g Protein; 20 g Carbohydrate; trace Dietary Fibre

Pictured at right.

Step-by-Step Piping

Divide uncoloured icing into four bowls and add a small amount of different food colouring into each. Use separate spoons to mix well, adding colouring bit by bit until you get the tint you want (see photo 1).

Place a freezer bag into the glass and roll the open edges over the rim. Use a spatula to pour the icing from 1 bowl into the bag-lined glass (see photo 2).

Close up the bag. Squeeze the icing down and secure with an elastic band. Repeat with the other bowls of icing. Use the scissors to cut a very small hole in one corner of each bag, just big enough to squeeze out icing in a thin line (see photo 3).

Gently squeeze the bag to pipe desired words or designs onto the cookies (see photo 4).

Flour Power

Keep the rolling pin, cookie cutters and working surface lightly floured so the dough doesn't stick.

De-Icing

If the icing becomes too stiff to pipe, warm it in the microwave for about 15 seconds or massage the bag in your hands.

Gingerbread Men and Ladies

"Sometimes my children have given knickers, bow ties and buttons to the men, and curly hair and frilly aprons to the ladies. Some years we've also poked a hole at the top of each cookie with a straw, threaded a pretty ribbon and hung them on the tree. This year, we have a little grandchild joining our Christmas gingerbread baking fun for the first time."

— **Maria Henderson, Edmonton, Alberta**

Butter (or hard margarine), softened	1 cup	250 mL
Boiling water	1/2 cup	125 mL
Large eggs	2	2
Fancy (mild) molasses	1 cup	250 mL
Demerara sugar, packed◆	1 cup	250 mL
All-purpose flour	6 cups	1.5 L
Baking soda	2 tsp.	10 mL
Ground cinnamon	2 tsp.	10 mL
Ground ginger	2 tsp.	10 mL
Ground cloves	1/2 tsp.	2 mL
Salt	1 tsp.	5 mL

DECORATOR'S ROYAL ICING

Icing sugar, sifted	1 lb.	454 g
Meringue powder◆◆	1/4 cup	60 mL
Warm water	1/2 cup	125 mL
Liquid (or paste) food colouring		

Using heavy-duty mixer, beat butter and boiling water in large bowl on medium speed until well mixed.◆◆◆

Add next 3 ingredients. Beat until well combined.

Sift next 6 ingredients into large bowl. Gradually add to butter mixture. Beat on medium until well combined. Separate dough into 4 portions. Flatten out each portion to approximately 1 inch (2.5 cm) thickness. Cover with plastic wrap. Chill for 2 to 3 hours. Roll out, 1 portion at a time, to 1/4 inch (6 mm) thickness. Cut out gingerbread men and ladies with 5 inch (12.5 cm) long cookie cutters. Arrange 1 inch (2.5 cm) apart on greased cookie sheets. Bake in 375°F (190°C) oven for 8 to 10 minutes until gingerbread springs back when lightly pressed. For crisper cookies, cook 2 to 3 minutes longer. Cool on cookie sheets for 5 minutes. Remove to wire racks to cool completely. Makes about 38 cookies.

Decorator's Royal Icing: Beat first 3 ingredients in clean, large bowl on low for 5 to 7 minutes until very thick. Based on number of desired colours, divide icing into small bowls. Add food colouring to each portion until desired shade is reached. Mix well. Cover with damp cloth to prevent hardening. Makes about 1 1/2 cups (375 mL) icing. Place icing in small piping bags fitted with narrow nozzle. Pipe onto gingerbread.

1 cookie without icing: 195 Calories; 5.6 g Total Fat; 193 mg Sodium; 3 g Protein; 34 g Carbohydrate; 1 g Dietary Fibre

Pictured above.

◆*Demerara sugar is a coarse-textured raw sugar with a distinctive caramel flavour. Brown sugar may be substituted.*

◆◆*Available at kitchen stores or cake decorating suppliers.*

◆◆◆*This is a large recipe and the dough is quite stiff. Based on her experience, Maria recommends using a heavy-duty electric mixer; we agree. You need that kind of power to get the job done.*

Surprise Carrot Cookies

"My wife used to make these when she worked at the Vancouver Sun *cafeteria before we were married."*
— **Larry Shearer, Prince George, British Columbia**

Large egg	1	1
Cooking oil	1/3 cup	75 mL
Granulated sugar	1/3 cup	75 mL
All-purpose flour	3/4 cup	175 mL
Baking powder	1 tsp.	5 mL
Salt	1/4 tsp.	1 mL
Mashed cooked carrot	1/3 cup	75 mL
Finely grated lemon zest	1 tsp.	5 mL
Lemon juice	1 tsp.	5 mL
Finely grated orange zest	2 tsp.	10 mL
Raisins	1/4 cup	60 mL
Chopped walnuts	1/4 cup	60 mL

Beat first 3 ingredients together until smooth.

Combine next 3 ingredients in medium bowl. Add to egg mixture.

Add remaining 6 ingredients. Mix well. Drop by heaping tablespoonfuls, 2 inches (5 cm) apart, onto greased baking sheets. Bake in 350°F (175°C) oven for about 12 minutes until golden brown. Makes 18 cookies.

1 cookie: 97 Calories; 5.7 g Total Fat; 60 mg Sodium; 1 g Protein; 11 g Carbohydrate; 1 g Dietary Fibre

Pictured on page 225.

Cranberry and White Chocolate Cookies

Dried cranberries do a great imitation of candy as far as kids' taste buds are concerned, but provide a neat, delicious bit of nutrition to cookies like these.

Large eggs	2	2
Brown sugar, packed	1 3/4 cups	425 mL
Vanilla	1 tsp.	5 mL
All-purpose flour	1 3/4 cups	425 mL
Baking powder	1 tsp.	5 mL
Baking soda	1/2 tsp.	2 mL
Cooking oil	1/2 cup	125 mL
Dried cranberries	1 cup	250 mL
White chocolate chips	1 cup	250 mL

Beat first 3 ingredients together in medium bowl for 2 to 3 minutes until mixture changes colour.

Combine next 3 ingredients in large bowl. Add egg mixture and remaining 3 ingredients. Mix well. Cover. Chill for 1 hour. Shape into 1 tbsp. (15 mL) balls. Arrange 2 inches (5 cm) apart on greased baking sheets. Bake in 375°F (190°C) oven for about 10 minutes until golden. Cool on baking sheets for 10 minutes before removing cookies to wire rack to cool completely. Makes about 45 cookies.

1 cookie: 105 Calories; 4.1 g Total Fat; 33 mg Sodium; 1 g Protein; 17 g Carbohydrate; 1 g Dietary Fibre

Pictured below.

The World's Easiest Peanut Butter Cookies

Could there be a quicker, easier peanut butter cookie recipe? Made for the young bakers in your house, this recipe has only three ingredients. Great for lunch or recess—or after school with a glass of cold milk and a ripe banana.

Crunchy peanut butter	1 cup	250 mL
Granulated sugar	1 cup	250 mL
Large egg, fork-beaten	1	1

Combine all 3 ingredients in medium bowl. Chill for 5 minutes. Shape into 1 tbsp. (15 mL) balls. Arrange 2 inches (5 cm) apart on greased baking sheets. Bake in 350°F (175°C) oven for 12 to 14 minutes until golden. Cool on baking sheets for 5 minutes before removing cookies to wire rack to cool completely. Makes 24 cookies.

1 cookie: 104 Calories; 5.9 g Total Fat; 58 mg Sodium; 3 g Protein; 11 g Carbohydrate; 1 g Dietary Fibre

Pictured below.

The World's Easiest Peanut Butter Cookies, above

Cranberry and White Chocolate Cookies, above

Mo's Date-Filled Cookies, below

Surprise Carrot Cookies, page 224

Chocolate Chippers, below

Chocolate Chippers

This is one of Jean Paré's favourite chocolate chip cookie recipes. The trick to their wonderfully soft texture is the quantities of brown sugar and cornstarch. And don't overbake them!

Hard margarine (or butter), softened	1 cup	250 mL
Brown sugar, packed	1 1/2 cups	375 mL
Large eggs	2	2
Vanilla	1 tsp.	5 mL
All-purpose flour	2 cups	500 mL
Cornstarch	1/4 cup	60 mL
Salt	3/4 tsp.	4 mL
Baking soda	1 tsp.	5 mL
Semi-sweet chocolate chips	2 cups	500 mL
Chopped walnuts (optional)	1 cup	250 mL

Cream margarine and brown sugar together in large bowl. Beat in eggs, one at a time. Add vanilla. Mix well.

Sift next 4 ingredients into medium bowl. Stir. Add to margarine mixture. Stir in chocolate chips and walnuts. Drop by tablespoonfuls onto greased cookie sheet. Bake in 350°F (175°C) oven for 10 to 12 minutes until golden. Do not overbake. Makes 5 1/2 dozen.

1 cookie: 91 Calories; 4.7 g Total Fat; 85 mg Sodium; 1 g Protein; 12 g Carbohydrate; trace Dietary Fibre

Pictured above.

Mo's Date-Filled Cookies

"I remember these cookies from the thirties, and was thrilled when my sister unearthed the recipe from the cookbook of Maud Black (1872-1948). Mrs. Black was my grandmother and she lived at Rochfort Bridge, Alberta. The cookies are as good today as I remember them being back then."
— **Ruby Bauer, Victoria, British Columbia**

FILLING

Granulated sugar	1/2 cup	125 mL
Dates, chopped	1 cup	250 mL
Water	1/2 cup	125 mL
Vanilla	1/4 tsp.	1 mL
All-purpose flour	1 1/2 cups	375 mL
Quick-cooking rolled oats (not instant)	1 1/2 cups	375 mL
Brown sugar, packed	1 cup	250 mL
Baking powder	2 tsp.	10 mL
Baking soda	1 tsp.	5 mL
Hard margarine (or butter)	3/4 cup	175 mL
Milk	1/4 cup	60 mL

Filling: Combine first 3 ingredients in medium saucepan. Heat and stir on medium until sugar is dissolved. Heat, uncovered, on medium for 5 to 7 minutes, stirring occasionally, until mixture is thickened. Cool. Stir in vanilla.

Combine next 5 ingredients in large bowl. Cut in margarine until crumbly. Gradually stir in milk until stiff dough forms. Roll out 1/3 of dough onto lightly floured surface to 1/8 inch (3 mm) thick. Cut into 2 1/2 inch (6.4 cm) circles. Place 1 1/2 tsp. (7 mL) filling in centre of 1/2 of circles. Spread to within 1/2 inch (12 mm) of edge. Top with remaining circles. Pinch edges together to seal. Place 3 inches (7.5 cm) apart on greased baking sheets. Repeat with remaining dough and filling. Bake in 350°F (175°C) oven for 15 minutes until golden. Makes 24 cookies.

1 cookie: 186 Calories; 6.6 g Total Fat; 161 mg Sodium; 2 g Protein; 31 g Carbohydrate; 2 g Dietary Fibre

Pictured above.

Pecan Truffles

Dark chocolate, pecans and coffee-flavoured liqueur in a milk chocolate shell—what a sinfully delicious way to end a festive meal! You can use these and the Apricot Brandy Truffles on this page for our Truffle Tree Centrepiece, page 227.

Whipping cream	1/4 cup	60 mL
Butter (not margarine)	2 tbsp.	30 mL
Good-quality dark chocolate bars, finely chopped	10 1/2 oz.	300 g
Pecans, finely chopped	3/4 cup	175 mL
Coffee-flavoured liqueur (or strong dark coffee)	1 tbsp.	15 mL
Cocoa, sifted	1/4 cup	60 mL
Milk chocolate melting wafers, melted	6 1/4 oz.	175 g
Dark chocolate sprinkles	2/3 cup	150 mL

Combine cream and butter in small heavy saucepan. Heat and stir on high until butter is melted. Bring to a boil. Remove from heat. Add dark chocolate. Stir until chocolate is melted. Transfer to medium bowl.

Add pecans and liqueur. Stir until well combined. Chill, uncovered, for about 50 minutes, stirring twice, until firm enough to roll into balls but not set. For variety and tapered effect on tree, make 2 different sized balls with 2 different coatings. Shape 1/3 of mixture into 1 1/2 tsp. (7 mL) balls. Shape remaining 2/3 portion into 1 tsp. (5 mL) balls. Chill for 30 minutes.

Roll 1/2 of both sizes of balls in cocoa to coat. Place on foil or waxed paper-lined baking sheet.

Dip remaining balls into milk chocolate, allowing excess to drip back into bowl. Roll in sprinkles before chocolate sets completely. Place on same baking sheet. Chill for 30 minutes until set. Makes about 45 truffles.

1 small-sized cocoa-covered truffle: 94 Calories; 6.8 g Total Fat; 12 mg Sodium; 1 g Protein; 9 g Carbohydrate; 1 g Dietary Fibre

Pictured on page 227.

Apricot Brandy Truffles

Stylish black-and-white chocolate exteriors hold a white chocolate filling studded with apricots and laced with brandy. An eye-catching addition to a sweets tray or our Truffle Tree Centrepiece, page 227.

Whipping cream	1/4 cup	60 mL
Butter (not margarine)	2 tbsp.	30 mL
Good-quality white chocolate bars, finely chopped	10 1/2 oz.	300 g
Dried apricots, finely chopped	3/4 cup	175 mL
Brandy (or brandy flavouring)	1 tbsp.	15 mL
White chocolate melting wafers, melted	6 1/4 oz.	175 g
Medium coconut	1/4 cup	60 mL
Dark chocolate melting wafers, melted	6 1/4 oz.	175 g

Combine cream and butter in small heavy saucepan. Heat and stir on high until butter is melted. Bring to a boil. Remove from heat. Add first amount of white chocolate. Stir until chocolate is melted. Tranfer to medium bowl.

Add apricots and brandy. Stir until well combined. Chill, uncovered, for about 50 minutes, stirring twice, until firm enough to roll into balls but not set. For variety and tapered effect on tree, make 2 different sized balls with 2 different coatings. Shape 1/3 of mixture into 1 1/2 tsp. (7 mL) balls. Shape remaining 2/3 portion into 1 tsp. (5 mL) balls. Chill for 30 minutes.

Dip 1/2 of both sizes of balls into second amount of white chocolate, allowing excess to drip back into bowl. Roll in coconut before chocolate sets completely! Place on foil or waxed paper-lined baking sheet.

Dip remaining balls into dark chocolate, allowing excess to drip back into bowl. Place on same baking sheet. Chill for 30 minutes until set. Makes about 45 truffles.

1 small-sized coconut-covered truffle: 103 Calories; 6.4 g Total Fat; 18 mg Sodium; 1 g Protein; 11 g Carbohydrate; trace Dietary Fibre

Pictured on page 227.

Tree Tips

- Work around the cone, building up rows.

- There's no right or wrong pattern when it comes to which colour or texture of truffle goes where (though you probably don't want to put all of one type together!). Bear in mind that the white-coated varieties tend to stand out the most visually, but other than that, follow your own good instincts and your personal sense of style to create a one-of-a-kind tree.

- To ensure cocoa-coated balls don't leave flecks on other truffles, hold a small piece of plastic wrap around each ball as you place it on the toothpick. You can gently remove the plastic as you go or when the tree is done.

- Look at the tree from all sides to see how it's shaping up, and don't be afraid to reposition a truffle or two if need be.

Melting Chocolate

Making tempting truffles starts with handling the chocolate properly. For smooth melting, heat the chocolate in a double boiler or in a stainless steel or glass bowl over a small saucepan of simmering water, until almost completely melted, stirring occasionally. Don't rush things by using higher heat—boiling water in the bottom pan creates too much steam, which could overheat the upper container and cause the chocolate to burn.

To microwave, heat the chocolate in a small uncovered microwave-safe bowl on medium-high, (70%), for 30 seconds, then stir. Repeat until chocolate is smooth.

Chocolate continues melting after it's removed from the heat—stir it to a smooth, glossy finish off the heat.

Never put a lid on melting chocolate—with a cover comes condensation and even the tiniest drop of water will cause the chocolate to seize.

To give your truffles a smooth coating, use a fork to dip them, one at a time, into the melted chocolate.

Truffle Tree Centrepiece

Materials needed *(most are available from a craft or wedding supply store)*

- 1 foam craft cone, 3 7/8 x 9 inches high (9.75 x 22 cm)
- gold foil to cover cone
- clear adhesive tape
- 1 round decorative plate, 9 inches (23 cm) in diameter
- 1 tbsp. (15 mL) melted chocolate (we used melting wafers)
- approximately 85 round wooden toothpicks
- approximately 85 truffles (recipes on page 226)
- 10 - 12 gold baubles, 1/2 - 3/4 inch (1.2 - 2 cm) in diameter
- 8 gold leaves
- 8 gold ribbon buds (1/4 inch, 60 mm, wide wire ribbon rolled into a tiny rosette shape)

Cover the cone firmly and smoothly with gold foil. Secure the foil with adhesive tape. Spoon the melted chocolate onto the centre of your plate. Centre the cone over the plate and secure it in position by pressing the base onto the melted chocolate (see photo 1). Let stand for 10 minutes until the chocolate is set.

Start building the truffle tree from the bottom of the cone. Insert a toothpick about 1/2 inch (1.2 cm) up from the bottom (so the truffle will clear the plate), leaving about 1/2 inch (1.2 cm) protruding. Push one of the large truffles onto the toothpick. Repeat the process with the remaining toothpicks and truffles, using large truffles around the bottom, graduating truffle sizes as you move up the cone and ending with small truffles at the top. Arrange truffles in a brick-like pattern rather than one immediately above the other (see photo 2). You may need to cut the toothpicks in half as you come to the narrower top of the cone so they don't poke through to the other side. Arrange gold baubles, leaves and ribbon buds in the small spaces between truffles.

Taco Cheese-Flavoured
Popcorn, page 229

School Trail Mix, page 229

Taco Cheese-Flavoured Popcorn

A salty treat and so good to eat. You can pack pouches of this seasoned popcorn into lunch boxes for kids to enjoy at recess or on the way home from school. Get them to make it the night before—after the supper dishes are done, of course! This will keep for up to a week in a sealed container.

Popped corn (about 1/2 cup, 125 mL, unpopped)	12 cups	3 L
Hard margarine (or butter), melted	1/4 cup	60 mL
Envelope taco seasoning mix	1 1/4 oz.	35 g
Powdered cheddar cheese product, sifted	1/3 cup	75 mL
Salt	1/2 tsp.	2 mL

Place popped corn in large bowl. Drizzle with margarine. Toss until well coated.

Combine remaining 3 ingredients in small bowl. Sprinkle over popcorn. Toss until well coated. Store in large resealable plastic bags or airtight containers. Makes 12 cups (3 L).

1 cup (250 mL): 85 Calories; 6.2 g Total Fat; 542 mg Sodium; 1 g Protein; 6 g Carbohydrate; trace Dietary Fibre

Pictured on page 228.

School Trail Mix

As popular with kids as it is with parents, a good trail mix can provide a solid bit of satisfaction for a growling tummy. Our version is packed with flavour and eye-catching colour. For a variation, add cashews, candied ginger or pineapple, or dried figs. This will keep for up to two weeks in a sealed container.

Sunflower seeds	1/2 cup	125 mL
Pumpkin seeds	1 cup	250 mL
Dried apricots, halved	1 cup	250 mL
Golden raisins	1 cup	250 mL
Dried cranberries	1 cup	250 mL
Whole wheat squares cereal	2 cups	500 mL
Pecans	1 cup	250 mL
Sweetened flake coconut	1/2 cup	125 mL
Mini candy-coated chocolate (such as mini M&M's)	1 cup	250 mL

Combine all 9 ingredients in large bowl. Store in airtight containers. Makes 8 cups (2 L).

1/2 cup (125 mL): 125 Calories; 17.6 g Total Fat; 68 mg Sodium; 9 g Protein; 37 g Carbohydrate; 7 g Dietary Fibre

Pictured on page 228.

Mini-Coconut Cakes

For best results, make sure all the ingredients for these delightful mini-cakes are at room temperature. Wonderful recipe for holiday bake sales.

Butter (or hard margarine), softened	1/2 cup	125 mL
Granulated sugar	1 cup	250 mL
Large eggs	2	2
All-purpose flour	1 1/2 cups	375 mL
Baking powder	1 tbsp.	15 mL
Medium coconut	1/2 cup	125 mL
Sour cream	1 cup	250 mL
Milk	1/3 cup	75 mL

COCONUT ICING

Icing sugar	2 cups	500 mL
Butter (or hard margarine), melted	3 tbsp.	50 mL
Milk	2 tbsp.	30 mL
Coconut extract	1/2 tsp.	2 mL

DECORATIONS
Ribbon coconut
Silver dragées♦
Sugar cubes, coarsely crushed

Silver foil cup cake holders (measuring 1 1/4 inch across the bottom)	45	45

Beat butter and sugar in large bowl until light and fluffy. Add eggs, one at a time, beating well after each addition.

Sift flour and baking powder into medium bowl. Add to butter mixture. Add coconut. Stir. Fold in sour cream and milk. Fill greased mini-muffin cups 3/4 full. Bake in 350°F (175°C) oven for about 20 minutes until wooden pick inserted in centre of cakes comes out clean. Cool in pan for 10 minutes. Turn out onto wire rack to cool completely.

Coconut Icing: Combine all ingredients in medium bowl. Makes about 1 cup (250 mL). Ice tops of each cake with 1 tsp. (5 mL) icing.

Decorations: Top iced cakes with coconut, dragées or sugar as desired.

To serve, place in silver foil cupcake holders. Makes about 45 cakes.

1 iced cake topped with coconut: 109 Calories; 5.1 g Total Fat; 62 mg Sodium; 1 g Protein; 15 g Carbohydrate; trace Dietary Fibre

Pictured on page 220.

♦Dragées are small edible silver balls available in specialty shops and in the cake decorating section of some grocery stores.

White Chocolate Cherry Fudge

Quick and easy to prepare, this fudge is also delicious with other fruit and nut combinations, such as pecans and dried apricots or almonds and dried mango.

Homogenized milk	3/4 cup	175 mL
Granulated sugar	1 1/2 cups	375 mL
Butter (not margarine), cut up	2/3 cup	150 mL
Package of white chocolate chips	8 oz.	225 g
Vanilla	1 tsp.	5 mL
Unsalted cashews, coarsely chopped	1/2 cup	125 mL
Dried cherries, coarsely chopped	1/2 cup	125 mL

Combine first 3 ingredients in large saucepan. Heat and stir on medium for about 5 minutes until sugar is dissolved and butter is melted. Bring to a boil. Boil vigorously on medium-high for about 5 minutes, without stirring, until slightly thickened. Remove from heat.

Add chocolate chips and vanilla. Stir until chocolate chips are melted.

Add cashews and cherries. Mix until well combined. Spread in foil-lined 8 x 8 inch (20 x 20 cm) pan. Smooth top. Chill for at least 4 hours or overnight. Cut into 1 x 1 1/2 inch (2.5 x 3.8 cm) pieces.♦ Makes 40 pieces.

1 piece: 109 Calories; 5.8 g Total Fat; 41 mg Sodium; 1 g Protein; 14 g Carbohydrate; trace Dietary Fibre

Pictured on page 220.

♦For easy cutting, extend the foil above the top of the pan and use as handles to remove fudge from pan to cutting board. Heat your knife under hot water before cutting.

Cranberry White Chocolate Almond Bark

Hand-made white chocolate bark studded with red berries and golden almonds—what a splendid treat to offer guests or tuck into gift boxes.

Good-quality white chocolate, melted (see Melting Chocolate, page 226)	1 lb. 2 oz	500 g
Natural almonds	1 1/2 cups	375 mL
Dried cranberries	1 cup	250 mL

Combine all 3 ingredients in large bowl. Mix well. Pour mixture into 11 x 17 inch (28 x 43 cm) waxed paper-lined baking sheet with sides. Spread mixture to 1/4 inch (6 mm) thickness. Chill until set. Break into approximately 1 1/2 x 2 inch (3.8 x 5 cm) pieces. Makes about 56 pieces.

1 piece: 77 Calories; 4.9 g Total Fat; 9 mg Sodium; 1 g Protein; 7 g Carbohydrate; 1 g Dietary Fibre

Pictured below.

Chocolate-Dipped Orange Peel

Enjoy these pretty little holiday treats just as they are, or use them to dress up simple desserts like pound cake, ice cream or custard and fruit. Boxed and ribboned, they also make a lovely hostess gift.

Large oranges	2	2
Hot water	1 1/2 cups	375 mL
Good-quality milk chocolate, chopped	1/3 lb.	150 g

Use vegetable peeler to peel oranges from top to bottom into 2 1/2 to 3 inch (6.4 to 7.5 cm) lengths approximately 1 inch (2.5 cm) wide. Cut each length into 1/4 inch (6 mm) wide strips. Place in large saucepan. Add hot water. Bring to a boil. Reduce heat to medium-low. Cover. Simmer for 5 to 8 minutes until tender. Remove orange strips with slotted spoon to paper towels to cool and dry.

Heat chocolate in medium stainless steel or glass bowl over a small saucepan of simmering water, stirring occasionally, until almost completely melted. Remove from heat. Stir until smooth. (Or microwave, uncovered, in small microwave-safe bowl on medium-high, 70%, for 30 seconds. Stir. Repeat until chocolate is smooth.) Dip orange strips into chocolate, allowing excess to drip back into bowl. Place on foil or waxed paper-lined baking sheet. Chill until set. Makes about 65 strips.

5 strips: 64 Calories; 3.6 g Total Fat; 10 mg Sodium; 1 g Protein; 8 g Carbohydrate; 1 g Dietary Fibre

Cranberry White Chocolate Almond Bark, this page

Vanilla Coconut Ice Cream

Here's a refreshing, cool treat to enjoy on a warm day or following a spicy main course. Set out small dishes of chopped peanuts, sliced banana or mango and freshly chopped mint as toppings. Quick to prepare, but make a day ahead to let it freeze overnight.

Cans of coconut milk (14 oz., 400 mL, each)	2	2
Milk	1 cup	250 mL
Vanilla extract	1/2 tsp.	2 mL
Egg yolks (large)♦	10	10
Granulated sugar	1 1/2 cups	375 mL
Sweetened flake coconut, toasted♦♦	1/3 cup	75 mL

Heat first 3 ingredients in large saucepan until very hot, but not boiling. Remove from heat.

Beat egg yolks and sugar in large bowl. Gradually whisk in hot milk mixture. Return mixture to saucepan. Heat and stir on medium until mixture thickens slightly and coats back of metal spoon. Strain. Place mixture in large container. Cover. Freeze until set. Remove from freezer. Process in blender or food processor until smooth. Return mixture to same container. Cover. Freeze until set.

Scoop ice cream into tall serving glasses or individual bowls. Sprinkle with coconut. Makes 6 cups (1.5 L).

1/2 cup (125 mL): 297 Calories; 18.8 g Total Fat; 31 mg Sodium; 4 g Protein; 31 g Carbohydrate; trace Dietary Fibre

Pictured at right.

♦Egg whites can be frozen for later use, such as the Spring Tulips, page 244.

♦♦To toast the coconut, place it in an ungreased frying pan. Heat on medium, stirring often, until golden.

Ginger Sorbet
with Grilled
Mangoes, below

Ginger Sorbet with Grilled Mangoes

This is an inspired dessert that's a refreshing end to any barbecue party. The warm, cinnamon-flavoured mango and chilled, sweet gingery sorbet are a scrumptious combo. Try this recipe using grilled fresh peaches, pineapple or firm bananas in place of, or in combination with, the mangoes.

GINGER SORBET		
Granulated sugar	1 1/2 cups	375 mL
Water	2 cups	500 mL
Finely grated gingerroot	1 tbsp.	15 mL
Egg white (large)	1	1
GRILLED MANGOES		
Medium mangoes	3	3
Butter (not margarine), melted	2 tbsp.	30 mL
Brown sugar, packed	1/2 tbsp.	7 mL
Ground cinnamon	1/2 tsp.	2 mL

Ginger Sorbet: Combine granulated sugar and water in large saucepan. Heat and stir on low until sugar is dissolved. Bring to a boil. Remove from heat. Add ginger. Pour mixture into large shallow dish. Freeze for about 3 hours until set.

Spoon mixture into food processor. Add egg white. Process until smooth. Makes about 3 cups (750 mL) sorbet. Return mixture to same dish. Freeze until set.

Grilled Mangoes: Preheat grill to medium. Slice through flat side of 1 mango near centre, carving around curve of pit. Repeat down other side (see photo 1). Using small sharp knife, score flesh in small diamonds until tip of knife hits skin but does not go through. Repeat with remaining mangoes.

Combine remaining 3 ingredients in small bowl. Brush mango flesh with butter mixture. Grill, skin side up, for 6 to 8 minutes until soft and lightly browned. Remove from grill. Brush mango flesh with remaining butter mixture. Using hands, press on skin side with thumbs, turning each section inside out and spreading the diamonds apart (see photo 2). Serve with Ginger Sorbet. Serves 6.

1 serving: 316 Calories; 4.4 g Total Fat; 54 mg Sodium; 1 g Protein; 72 g Carbohydrate; 2 g Dietary Fibre

Pictured above.

Peach Cobbler

"Family recipes are a special tradition and this is one from my mom. I hope you'll enjoy making memories for your family with this peach cobbler."
— Heather Page, Kelowna, British Columbia

Sliced, peeled ripe peaches (5 - 6 medium)	5 cups	1.25 L
Granulated sugar	1/2 cup	125 mL
Cornstarch	2 tbsp.	30 mL
Granulated sugar	2 tbsp.	30 mL
TOPPING		
All-purpose flour	1 cup	250 mL
Granulated sugar	2 tbsp.	30 mL
Baking powder	1 1/2 tsp.	7 mL
Salt	1/2 tsp.	2 mL
Hard margarine (or butter)♦	1/3 cup	75 mL
Milk	3 tbsp.	50 mL
Large egg	1	1

Ice cream (or whipped cream), optional

Combine peaches and first amount of sugar in medium bowl. Let stand for about 30 minutes until juices are released. Strain and reserve 3/4 cup (175 mL) juice.♦♦

Stir cornstarch into second amount of sugar in small cup. Whisk into reserved peach juice until dissolved and no lumps remain. Pour over peaches. Stir. Place in ungreased 3 quart (3 L) casserole.

Topping: Combine first 4 ingredients in medium bowl. Cut in margarine until crumbly.

Whisk milk and egg together in small bowl. Stir into flour mixture. Drop by rounded tablespoonfuls onto peaches. Bake in 375°F (190°C) oven for about 25 minutes until golden brown.

Serve warm with ice cream. Serves 6.

1 serving: 329 Calories; 11.9 g Total Fat; 431 mg Sodium; 4 g Protein; 53 g Carbohydrate; 2 g Dietary Fibre

♦*Heather's original recipe used shortening. We tested it with hard margarine, but you also have the option of using butter.*

♦♦*If peaches don't release enough juice to make 3/4 cup (175 mL), add apple or orange juice to make up the difference.*

Ginger Allspice Oranges

One of the best ways to enjoy these highly flavoured spiced oranges is to team them with something creamy like mascarpone cheese, thick cream or rich vanilla ice cream.

Large oranges	4	4
Sweet white (or alcohol-free) wine♦	1 cup	250 mL
Piece of gingerroot (1 inch, 2.5 cm, length), cut into 8 slices	1	1
Ground allspice	1 tsp.	5 mL
Granulated sugar	1 cup	250 mL
Water	1 cup	250 mL

Cut both ends from each orange. Place oranges cut-side down on cutting board. Remove peel with sharp knife, cutting down and around orange (see photo 1), leaving as little pith as possible on orange. Over small bowl, cut on either side of membranes to release segments (see photo 2).

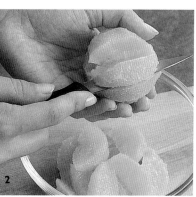

Combine remaining 5 ingredients in large saucepan. Heat and stir on low until sugar is dissolved. Bring to a boil. Reduce heat to medium. Simmer, uncovered, for about 10 minutes. Add orange. Simmer, uncovered, for 10 minutes further, until sauce is slightly syrupy. Sauce will thicken as it cools. Transfer to large bowl. Cover. Chill for 3 hours or overnight, stirring several times. Serves 4.

1 serving: 313 Calories; 0.2 g Total Fat; 5 mg Sodium; 1 g Protein; 70 g Carbohydrate; 3 g Dietary Fibre

♦A Moselle or Riesling wine would be a good choice to accompany this dish.

Poached Peaches in Raspberry Sauce

Gloriously colourful, this no-fuss dessert makes the most of fresh peaches when in season, though canned peaches can be used, too. Ideal for those lazy late-summer days.

Fresh firm peaches	8	8
Boiling water	9 cups	2.25 L
RASPBERRY SAUCE		
Fresh (or frozen, thawed) raspberries	14 oz.	400 g
Icing (confectioner's) sugar	1/4 cup	60 mL
Raspberry or orange-flavoured liqueur (or raspberry or orange flavouring)	1/4 cup	60 mL
Sliced almonds, toasted♦	1/3 cup	75 mL

Add peaches to boiling water in large saucepan. Simmer for 5 minutes. Remove to bowl of cold water. Let stand for 10 minutes. Peel skin, leaving peaches whole.

Raspberry Sauce: Process all 3 ingredients in food processor until almost smooth. Press mixture through sieve, discarding solids. Makes 1 2/3 cups (400 mL) sauce.

Place peaches in individual serving bowls or glasses. Drizzle with raspberry sauce. Sprinkle with almonds. Serves 8.

1 serving: 144 Calories; 3.4 g Total Fat; 1 mg Sodium; 2 g Protein; 24 g Carbohydrate; 4 g Dietary Fibre

♦To toast the almonds, place them in an ungreased frying pan. Heat on medium, stirring often, until golden.

Mango Mousse

"I really love this mousse in chocolate cups with raspberry sauce drizzled on top." It's light and airy—also wonderful simply garnished with fresh mint leaves. Very refreshing!
— Patricia Gibb, St. Albert, Alberta

Large mangoes, peeled and cut up	2	2
Lime juice	2 tbsp.	30 mL
Egg white (large)	1	1
Salt, just a pinch		
Granulated sugar	3 tbsp.	50 mL
Whipping cream	1/4 cup	60 mL

Process mango and lime juice in food processor until smooth. Transfer mixture to large bowl.

Beat egg white and salt until soft peaks form. Gradually beat in sugar until dissolved.

Whip cream in small bowl until stiff peaks form. Fold whipped cream into egg white mixture. Fold mixture into mango purée. Spoon into individual dessert bowls or glasses. Chill for at least 3 hours. Serves 4.

1 serving: 158 Calories; 5.4 g Total Fat; 22 mg Sodium; 2 g Protein; 28 g Carbohydrate; 2 g Dietary Fibre

Pictured below.

Mango Mousse, above

Apfelstrudel

Before the advent of commercial phyllo, and before Oktoberfest crowds numbered in the thousands, the women of Kitchener's venerable Concordia Club would make and stretch the dough for this classic dessert by hand.
— **Concordia Club, Kitchener, Ontario**

FILLING

Peeled and sliced tart cooking apples (such as Granny Smith), about 4 - 5 medium	4 cups	1 L
Dark raisins (optional)	2 tbsp.	30 mL
Finely grated orange or lemon zest (optional)	1/2 tsp.	2 mL
Granulated sugar	1/4 cup	60 mL
Ground cinnamon	1 1/2 tsp.	7 mL
Fine dry bread crumbs	1/2 cup	125 mL
Phyllo pastry sheets	6	6
Butter, melted	1/4 cup	60 mL
Half-and-half cream (or milk)	1/2 tbsp.	7 mL
Granulated sugar	1 tbsp.	15 mL
Ground cinnamon, sprinkle		

Filling: Combine first 6 ingredients in large bowl. Mix well. Set aside.

Lay tea towel on work surface, short side closest to you. Starting at closest side, place 1 phyllo sheet on towel. Place second phyllo sheet above first sheet on towel, overlapping 1 inch (2.5 cm) in middle. Working quickly, brush both sheets (now 1 long sheet) with butter. Place 2 phyllo sheets on top in same manner. Brush with butter. Repeat with remaining phyllo sheets and butter.

Mound filling on phyllo 6 inches (15 cm) from side closest to you. Fold bottom end of phyllo up and over filling. Using towel as a guide, tightly roll up to enclose filling. Rolling tightly is important or juices will leak. Pack any loose apple back into roll. Do not tuck in sides.

Transfer to greased baking sheet. Brush with cream. Sprinkle with second amount of sugar. Bake in 350°F (175°C) oven for 45 minutes until crisp and deep golden brown. Cut into 2 inch (5 cm) slices to serve.

Sprinkle with cinnamon. Serves 6.

1 serving: 256 Calories; 10.2 g Total Fat; 258 mg Sodium; 3 g Protein; 40 g Carbohydrate; 2 g Dietary Fibre

Pictured above.

Plums in Red Wine Syrup

As delicious as fresh plums are, lightly cooking them releases even more of their natural flavour and juice. Especially good with ice cream, yogurt or custard.

Red (or alcohol-free) wine	2 cups	500 mL
Granulated sugar	1/2 cup	125 mL
Freshly ground pepper	1/2 tsp.	2 mL
Ripe red plums, quartered and pitted	8	8

Pour wine into medium saucepan. Bring to a boil. Boil, uncovered, for 5 minutes. Reduce heat to medium-low. Add sugar and pepper. Heat and stir until sugar is dissolved. Increase heat to medium-high. Boil, uncovered, without stirring, for 8 to 10 minutes until slightly thickened. Strain. Cool.

Place plums in large glass bowl. Pour wine mixture over plums. Chill for at least 1 hour before serving. Serves 6 to 8.

1 serving: 177 Calories; 0.6 g Total Fat; 4 mg Sodium; 1 g Protein; 31 g Carbohydrate; 1 g Dietary Fibre

The Phyllo File

Here are three super-easy, creative ways to use up those last few sheets of phyllo left in the package after you've made phyllo-wrapped entrees or the Apfelstrudel on the opposite page.

Bundle Up: Layer three buttered phyllo sheets, then cut them into 12 rectangles. Place a 1/2 inch (1.25 cm) cube of cheese and a dab of jelly in the centre of each rectangle. Gather the edges together to form a bundle around the filling. These are meltingly delicious when the phyllo has baked to a golden brown. Try Stilton with mango chutney, Brie with cranberry sauce or aged Cheddar with blackberry jam.

Pictured at right.

Quick Cups: For bite-sized appetizers or individual desserts, cut three layers of buttered phyllo into six rectangles and press them into greased muffin tins. Baked until golden, then cooled, these crispy cups are ready for your choice of sweet or savoury filling: custard and fruit, ice cream and chocolate sauce, chicken à la king or creamy seafood. Cut the sheets into 12 rectangles if you want to use a mini muffin tin as your mould.

Pictured at right.

Sail Away: After layering three sheets of buttered phyllo, brush warm liquid honey over the top and sprinkle with ground cardamom. Cut the phyllo into 12 rectangles, then cut each rectangle diagonally. Bake the "sails" on a well-greased pan until golden, making sure to remove them carefully from the pan while they're still warm. Looks lovely set atop a scoop of ice cream.

Pictured below.

Bundle Up, left

Quick Cups, left

Sail Away, above

More Phyllo Facts

Lay on more flavour: Instead of butter, brush phyllo sheets with herb-flavoured olive oil. For extra flavour, grate some Parmesan cheese over each layer. Sweet pastries have added crunch with a sprinkle of sugar or ground nuts between buttered sheets.

Check the package: Once your leftover solution has taken shape, bake according to package directions.

Hold on: If you don't want to make these right away, you can wrap left-over thawed phyllo tightly in plastic wrap and refrigerate it for two to three days.

Speak out: From the Greek word for "leaf" comes phyllo, also spelled filo, often called FI-loh but rightly pronounced FEE-loh.

Baked Marmalade Apples with Cinnamon Custard

Serve comforting old-fashioned baked apples in a pool of custard, and sprinkle with cinnamon.

Butter (not margarine), softened	1/4 cup	60 mL
Orange marmalade	3 tbsp.	50 mL
Dates, finely chopped	1/4 cup	60 mL
Dried apricots, finely chopped	1/4 cup	60 mL
Slivered almonds, toasted and chopped♦	3 tbsp.	50 mL
Large Granny Smith apples	6	6
CINNAMON CUSTARD		
Whole milk	2 cups	500 mL
Cinnamon stick (3 inch, 7.5 cm, length)	1	1
Egg yolks (large)	4	4
Granulated sugar	1/2 cup	125 mL

Beat butter in medium bowl until creamy. Add marmalade. Beat until well combined.

Add next 3 ingredients to butter mixture. Mix well.

Remove core from each apple (see photo 1).♦♦ Cut 1/4 inch (6 mm) off bottom of each core. Press back into base of each apple (see photo 2). Score apple skin in several places to prevent skin from shrinking when cooked (see photo 3). Fill apple cavities with 1 1/2 tbsp. (25 mL) butter mixture. Place apples in greased baking dish. Bake, uncovered, in 350°F (175°C) oven for about 50 minutes, brushing apples with pan juices 2 or 3 times during baking, until apples are tender. Makes 6 baked apples.

Cinnamon Custard: Combine milk and cinnamon stick in small saucepan. Bring mixture just to a boil. Remove from heat. Let stand for 10 minutes. Remove cinnamon stick. Beat egg yolks and sugar on high in medium stainless steel or glass bowl for 30 to 45 seconds until thick and creamy. Place bowl over small saucepan of simmering water. Gradually whisk in milk mixture. Heat and stir for 15 to 20 minutes until all milk is added and custard is thickened. Makes 3 1/2 cups (875 mL). Serve with baked apples. Serves 6.

1 serving: 583 Calories; 25.8 g Total Fat; 205 mg Sodium; 9 g Protein; 86 g Carbohydrate; 6 g Dietary Fibre

Pictured below.

♦To toast the almonds, place them in an ungreased frying pan. Heat on medium, stirring often, until golden.

♦♦An apple corer works best, but a paring knife may also be used.

Layered Citrus Meringue Dessert

All sweetness and light, this sumptuous dessert is as refreshingly delicious as it is pretty. Perfect for an end-of-summer special occasion.

Orange juice	1 cup	250 mL
Lemon spread	1 cup	250 mL
CITRUS FILLING		
Orange juice	1/2 cup	125 mL
Lemon juice	3 tbsp.	50 mL
Blocks of cream cheese (8 oz., 250 g, each), softened	3	3
Icing (confectioner's) sugar	1/2 cup	125 mL
Whipping cream	1 cup	250 mL
Packages of ladyfingers (5 1/3 oz., 150 g, each)	2	2
MERINGUE TOPPING		
Egg whites (large)	3	3
Berry sugar	3/4 cup	175 mL

Combine orange juice and lemon spread in small saucepan. Heat and stir on medium-low until smooth. Cool.

Citrus Filling: Beat first 4 ingredients in medium bowl until smooth.

Beat cream in small bowl until soft peaks form. Fold whipped cream into cream cheese mixture.

Dip 1/2 of ladyfingers into 1/2 of the orange juice mixture. Arrange in single layer in ungreased shallow 10 cup (2.5 L) baking dish. Spread 1/2 of Citrus Filling over ladyfingers. Repeat with remaining ladyfingers, orange juice mixture and Citrus Filling. Cover. Chill for 6 hours or overnight.

Meringue Topping: Beat egg whites in medium bowl until soft peaks form. Gradually beat in berry sugar until dissolved. Spread over filling. Make peaks in meringue. Place 3 to 4 inches (7.5 to 10 cm) under heated broiler for about 1 minute until golden. Serves 12.

1 serving: 558 Calories; 33.1 g Total Fat; 304 mg Sodium; 11 g Protein; 56 g Carbohydrate; trace Dietary Fibre

Preparing an Apple for Baking

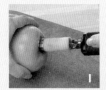 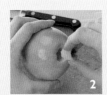 

Baked Marmalade Apples with Cinnamon Custard, above

Lemon White Chocolate Cream with Fresh Berries

Creamy-smooth lemon custard flavoured with white chocolate is absolutely scrumptious with fresh berries. For a more filling variation, add a slice of pound cake or a piece of nutty biscotti alongside each serving.

Granulated sugar	1/3 cup	75 mL
All-purpose flour	1/4 cup	60 mL
Salt	1/4 tsp.	1 mL
Half-and-half cream	2 cups	500 mL
White chocolate baking squares (1 oz., 28 g, each), cut up	2	2
Egg yolks (large), fork-beaten	4	4
Vanilla	1 tsp.	5 mL
Whipping cream	1/3 cup	75 mL
Lemon spread	1 cup	250 mL
Finely grated lemon zest	1 tbsp.	15 mL
Freshly squeezed lemon juice	1 tbsp.	15 mL
Yellow food colouring (optional)		
Assorted fresh berries	4 cups	1 L

Combine first 3 ingredients in medium heavy saucepan. Gradually stir in cream and chocolate. Heat and stir on medium until boiling and thickened.

Gradually stir 1/2 of cream mixture into egg yolks in small bowl. Add egg yolk mixture to remaining cream mixture. Bring to a gentle boil. Reduce heat. Cook for 2 minutes. Remove from heat.

Stir in vanilla. Turn into large bowl. Cover with plastic wrap. Chill for 30 minutes, stirring twice.

Beat whipping cream in separate small bowl until soft peaks form.

Beat in next 4 ingredients Fold into cream mixture. Cover with plastic wrap directly on surface. Chill until cool.

To serve, place 1/4 cup (60 mL) berries in each of 8 small dessert bowls. Spoon 1/2 cup (125 mL) custard onto berries. Top with 1/4 cup (60 mL) berries. Serves 8.

1 serving: 294 Calories; 14.8 g Total Fat; 131 mg Sodium; 5 g Protein; 37 g Carbohydrate; 3 g Dietary Fibre

Rhubarb Dessert

"I got this recipe from a friend. It's become a favourite family dessert and my daughter's #1 choice for any occasion. It's best made with fresh rhubarb. For a change of taste, I add strawberries when they're available."
— **Stella Bray, Edmonton, Alberta**

BASE

All-purpose flour	2 cups	500 mL
Granulated sugar	2 tbsp.	30 mL
Hard margarine (or butter), cut up	1 cup	250 mL

MIDDLE LAYER

Sliced fresh rhubarb (or frozen, thawed and drained)	5 cups	1.25 L
Egg yolks (large)	6	6
Granulated sugar	1 3/4 cups	425 mL
Sour cream	1 cup	250 mL
All-purpose flour	1/4 cup	60 mL
Salt, just a pinch		

TOPPING

Egg whites (large), room temperature	6	6
Berry sugar	3/4 cup	175 mL
Vanilla	2 tsp.	10 mL
Unsweetened fine coconut	1/2 cup	125 mL

Base: Combine flour and sugar in small bowl. Cut in margarine until crumbly. Press into greased foil-lined 9 x 13 inch (22 x 33 cm) pan. Bake in 350°F (175°C) oven for 15 minutes until lightly browned. Cool.

Middle Layer: Combine all 6 ingredients in large bowl. Spread evenly on base. Bake for 55 minutes until almost set.

Topping: Beat egg whites in medium bowl until soft peaks form. Gradually beat in berry sugar. Add vanilla and coconut. Spread on cake. Bake in 375°F (190°C) oven for 10 minutes until golden. Cuts into 15 pieces.

1 piece: 401 Calories; 19.4 g Total Fat; 186 mg Sodium; 6 g Protein; 52 g Carbohydrate; 2 g Dietary Fibre

Variation: Decrease rhubarb to 4 cups (1 L). Add 1 cup (250 mL) fresh, sliced strawberries.

Death by Maple Dessert, below

Death by Maple Dessert

David says serving maple syrup on pancakes doesn't allow for full and proper appreciation of this pure, sweet nectar. So he concocted this delicious dessert, guaranteed to create a maple memory.
— **David Forestell, Slocum & Ferris, Old City Market, Saint John, New Brunswick**

Chopped pecans	2 tbsp.	30 mL
Chopped slivered almonds	2 tbsp.	30 mL
Maple syrup	1 tbsp.	15 mL
Butter (not margarine)	1 tbsp.	15 mL
Brown sugar, packed	2 tbsp.	30 mL
Lemon juice	1 tsp.	5 mL
Vanilla ice cream (about 4 scoops)	1 cup	250 mL
Maple syrup	2 tbsp.	30 mL

Combine first 6 ingredients in small frying pan. Heat and stir for about 5 minutes until nuts start to brown.

Place scoops of ice cream in 2 tall serving glasses. Drizzle with second amount of maple syrup. Sprinkle 2 tbsp. (30 mL) nut mixture on each. Serves 2.

1 serving: 412 Calories; 22.1 g Total Fat; 124 mg Sodium; 4 g Protein; 53 g Carbohydrate; 1 g Dietary Fibre

Pictured above.

Apricot Pecan Crème Brûlée

The secret to making crème brûlée (krehm broo-LAY), a rich, cold custard with a hard sugar crust, is the *bain-marie* (water bath) process. Follow our easy steps for a creamy, satisfying result.

Dried apricots, finely chopped	2/3 cup	150 mL
Orange-flavoured liqueur	1/2 cup	125 mL
Water	3/4 cup	175 mL
Granulated sugar	1/3 cup	75 mL
Water	1 tbsp.	15 mL
Pecan halves	1/4 cup	60 mL
Large egg	1	1
Egg yolks (large)♦	5	5
Granulated sugar	1/2 cup	125 mL
Whipping cream	3 cups	750 mL
Vanilla bean (or 1 tsp., 5 mL vanilla extract)	1	1
Boiling water, approximately	4 cups	1 L

Combine first 3 ingredients in small saucepan. Bring to a boil. Reduce heat to medium-low. Cook, uncovered, for 35 minutes, stirring occasionally, until apricots are softened and mixture is thickened. Divide among eight 1/2 cup (125 mL) ramekins.

Combine first amount of sugar and second amount of water in medium saucepan. Heat and stir on low until sugar is dissolved. Increase heat to medium-high. Boil gently for 5 to 7 minutes until mixture is caramel-coloured.

Arrange pecans on greased baking sheet. Drizzle sugar mixture over pecans. Cool completely. Break into pieces. Process in blender or food processor until finely chopped.

Beat next 3 ingredients on medium-high in medium glass or stainless steel bowl until pale and thickened (see photo 1).

Pour cream into small saucepan. Split vanilla bean down centre and scrape seeds into saucepan (see photo 2). Reserve pod for another use.♦♦ Bring to a boil. Remove from heat. (If using vanilla extract, add at this point.)

Gradually whisk hot cream mixture into egg mixture. Mixture should coat back of spoon (see photo 3). Strain.

Place ramekins in shallow 4 quart (4 L) casserole (or baking pan). Pour cream mixture into ramekins. Carefully pour boiling water into pan until water comes halfway up sides of ramekins (see photo 4). Bake in 300°F (150°C) oven for about 1 hour until mixture is just set. Mixture may wobble a little in middle but will continue to set as it cools. Remove ramekins from pan. Cover. Chill for at least 6 hours or overnight. Just before serving, sprinkle each with pecan mixture (see photo 5). Place ramekins on baking sheet. Broil 3 inches (7.5 cm) from heat for 2 to 3 minutes until bubbling and lightly browned. Topping will harden quickly as it cools. Serve within 5 minutes of crust forming. Serves 8.

1 serving: 536 Calories; 36.7 g Total Fat; 49 mg Sodium; 5 g Protein; 40 g Carbohydrate; 1 g Dietary Fibre

Pictured above.

♦*Egg whites can be frozen for another use, such as the Spring Tulips, page 244.*

♦♦*Instead of discarding the vanilla pod, add it to a container of sugar or a mug of steamed milk for flavour.*

Glazed Pears with Panna Cotta

Velvety rich, milk-white custard, perfectly complemented with sweet/spicy, wine-glazed winter pears and crisp wafer cookies, makes a spectacular ending to a meal.

PANNA COTTA

Unflavoured gelatin	2 tsp.	10 mL
Milk	1/4 cup	60 mL
Milk	1/2 cup	125 mL
Whipping cream	1 1/4 cups	300 mL
Granulated sugar	1/2 cup	125 mL
Vanilla	1 1/2 tsp.	7 mL

GLAZED PEARS

Red (or alcohol-free) wine	1 cup	250 mL
Granulated sugar	1 cup	250 mL
Water	1/3 cup	75 mL
Freshly ground pepper	1/4 tsp.	1 mL
Firm medium pears, peeled and quartered	2	2
Crispy rolled store-bought cookies (or cookies of your choice)	8	8

Panna Cotta: Sprinkle gelatin over first amount of milk in small bowl. Let stand for 3 to 5 minutes until softened.

Combine next 4 ingredients in large saucepan. Heat and stir on medium until sugar is dissolved and mixture is hot. Remove from heat. Add gelatin mixture. Mix well. Strain into liquid measure. Pour into 4 lightly greased 3/4 cup (175 mL) moulds or ramekins. Cover. Chill overnight until set.

Glazed Pears: Combine first 4 ingredients in large pot or Dutch oven. Heat and stir on medium until sugar is dissolved.

Add pear. Bring to a boil. Reduce heat to medium-low. Simmer, uncovered, for 20 to 25 minutes, turning several times, until syrup is thickened and pear is glazed. Place in medium bowl. Cover. Chill overnight, stirring occasionally.

To serve, turn Panna Cotta onto 4 individual serving plates. Place 2 pieces of pear on each plate. Drizzle pears with syrup. Place 2 cookies on each plate. Serves 4.

1 serving: 677 Calories; 27 g Total Fat; 86 mg Sodium; 5 g Protein; 97 g Carbohydrate; 2 g Dietary Fibre

Pictured below.

Chocolate Chip Cookie
Dessert, below

Lemon Delight

"This is a wonderful light dessert that's great after a huge steak barbecue."
— Olga Cunningham, Lashburn, Saskatchewan

Can of evaporated milk	13 1/2 oz.	385 mL
Graham cracker crumbs	3 cups	750 mL
Brown sugar, packed	1/3 cup	75 mL
Hard margarine (or butter), melted	1/2 cup	125 mL
Package of lemon-flavoured gelatin (jelly powder)	3 oz.	85 g
Boiling water	1 1/4 cups	300 mL
Freshly squeezed lemon juice	1/4 cup	60 mL
Granulated sugar	1/2 cup	125 mL

Pour evaporated milk into medium bowl. Cover and place in freezer.

Combine next 3 ingredients in separate medium bowl. Mix well. Reserve 1/2 cup (125 mL). Press remaining crumb mixture in bottom of greased 9 x 13 inch (22 x 33 cm) pan.

Stir remaining 4 ingredients in small bowl until dissolved. Chill for about 1 1/4 hours, stirring twice, until partially set. Beat evaporated milk for about 5 minutes until soft peaks form. Fold in lemon mixture until smooth. Pour over crust. Sprinkle with reserved crumb mixture. Chill overnight. Cuts into 12 pieces.

1 piece: 299 Calories; 13 g Total Fat; 285 mg Sodium; 5 g Protein; 42 g Carbohydrate; 1 g Dietary Fibre

Chocolate Chip Cookie Dessert

Two great tastes—coffee and chocolate—come together in this scrumptious, two-tone, double-layered delight. Make it ahead of time for added convenience. *"Keeps well in fridge for about four days, if need be."*
— **Marjorie Hall**, Edmonton, Alberta

Whipping cream	2 cups	500 mL
Icing (confectioner's) sugar	1/3 cup	75 mL
Vanilla	1 tsp.	5 mL
Packages of chocolate chip cookies (12 1/2 oz., 350 g, each)	2	2
Milk	3/4 cup	175 mL
Coffee-flavoured liqueur	1/2 cup	125 mL
Grated chocolate	1/3 cup	75 mL

Beat cream in medium bowl until soft peaks form. Fold in icing sugar and vanilla.

Quickly dip 1/2 of cookies into 1/2 of milk. Arrange in single layer in ungreased, straight-sided 9 x 13 inch (22 x 33 cm) pan. Drizzle on 1/2 of liqueur. Spread 1/2 of cream mixture over cookies. Repeat layering with remaining cookies, milk, liqueur and cream mixture.

Sprinkle with chocolate. Cover. Chill for 6 hours or overnight. Cuts into 18 pieces.

1 piece: 292 Calories; 15.3 g Total Fat; 145 mg Sodium; 3 g Protein; 33 g Carbohydrate; trace Dietary Fibre

Pictured above.

Cherry Pear Clafoutis

Classic French clafoutis (kla-FOO-tee) is a cross between a cake and a pudding. This delightful sweet is easy to put together and can be made with a variety of fresh or canned fruit. Add a dusting of icing sugar just before serving with ice cream or whipped cream.

Cans of pitted Bing cherries, drained (14 oz., 398 mL, each)	3	3
Medium firm pears, peeled and chopped	3	3
Large eggs	8	8
Granulated sugar	1 cup	250 mL
Vanilla	2 tsp.	10 mL
Milk	1 cup	250 mL
Whipping cream	1 cup	250 mL
All-purpose flour	1 1/3 cups	325 mL
Baking powder	1 1/2 tsp.	7 mL

Combine cherries and pear in greased 9 x 13 inch (22 x 33 cm) casserole dish (16 cup, 4 L, capacity).

Beat next 3 ingredients in large bowl until pale.

Add remaining 4 ingredients. Stir. Pour over fruit mixture. Bake in 375°F (190°C) oven for about 50 minutes until lightly browned and set. Serve warm. Serves 8 to 10.

1 serving: 458 Calories; 15.9 g Total Fat; 163 mg Sodium; 12 g Protein; 70 g Carbohydrate; 3 g Dietary Fibre

Pictured below.

Sweet Almond and Cardamom Couscous Dessert

Just as rice can be used in sweet dishes, so too can couscous. Fresh fruit, such as sliced pears, is a nice accompaniment to this dessert.

Can of evaporated milk	13 1/2 oz.	385 mL
Sweetened condensed milk	1/4 cup	60 mL
Cardamom pods, bruised♦	6	6
Brown sugar, packed	3 tbsp.	50 mL
Ground ginger	1/4 tsp.	1 mL
Salt	1/4 tsp.	1 mL
Couscous	1 3/4 cups	425 mL
Slivered almonds, toasted♦♦	3/4 cup	175 mL

Combine first 3 ingredients in large saucepan. Bring to a boil. Remove from heat. Cover. Let stand for 10 minutes. Remove and discard cardamom pods.

Add next 3 ingredients. Heat and stir on medium-low until brown sugar is dissolved. Bring to a boil. Remove from heat. Add couscous. Stir. Cover. Let stand for 5 minutes.

Add almonds. Fluff with fork. Serve immediately. Serves 6 to 8.

1 serving: 458 Calories; 14.2 g Total Fat; 198 mg Sodium; 16 g Protein; 68 g Carbohydrate; 4 g Dietary Fibre

Pictured on page 247.

♦To bruise cardamom pods, press with flat side of knife blade until flattened slightly.

♦♦To toast the almonds, place them in an ungreased frying pan. Heat on medium, stirring often, until golden.

Cherry Pear Clafoutis, above

Chocolate Pots

This is what happens to chocolate pudding when it grows up! Make this rich, luscious and deceptively simple dessert in almost no time at all. The longer it chills, the better the flavour—so whip it together a day or two in advance.

Whipping cream	1 2/3 cups	400 mL
Semi-sweet chocolate, chopped	10 1/2 oz.	300 g
Egg yolks (large)	3	3
Brandy	2 tbsp.	30 mL
Butter (not margarine)	3 tbsp.	50 mL
Whipping cream	6 tbsp.	100 mL
Cocoa, for dusting		
Crispy rolled store-bought cookies	12	12

Heat cream in medium saucepan until bubbles form around edge. Remove from heat. Add chocolate. Whisk until chocolate is melted and mixture is well combined.

Add egg yolks and brandy. Whisk until well combined.

Add butter, 1 tbsp. (15 mL) at a time, to chocolate mixture, whisking after each addition until well combined. Makes about 3 cups (750 mL). Divide chocolate mixture among 6 small cups or ramekins. Cover. Chill for at least 8 hours or overnight.

Beat second amount of cream until soft peaks form. To serve, place dollop of whipped cream on each chocolate pot. Dust with cocoa. Add 2 cookies. Serves 6.

1 serving: 670 Calories; 52.7 g Total Fat; 132 mg Sodium; 8 g Protein; 47 g Carbohydrate; 3 g Dietary Fibre

Pictured at left and on back cover.

Heart Tokens

These can easily become heart-broken, so treat them gently.

If you don't want to create your chocolate heart-and-squiggle filigree freehand, draw several patterns on a sheet of paper (our filigree are about 3 1/2 inches, 9 cm tall). Line a baking sheet with parchment paper. Lay the pattern paper under the parchment paper at one end.

You'll need about 2 oz. (56 g) of semi-sweet chocolate to make 12 filigree. Chop up the chocolate, then heat and stir it in a small non-reactive or glass bowl set over a small saucepan of simmering water. You want the chocolate just melted, which should take two to three minutes.

Put the chocolate into a small piping bag fitted with a narrow tip. Pipe 12 filigree onto the parchment paper. If you're using a pattern, trace the design in chocolate, then reuse the pattern sheet by carefully sliding it to a new position under the parchment paper. Make the stem of your filifgree thicker than the heart, for extra stability. Chill the filigree until the chocolate sets. Just before serving, decorate each dessert with two of your creations.

Pictured above.

Caramel and Chocolate Brownie Tart

Brownie, butter tart and chocolate lovers are bound to swoon over this delightful dessert based on a nutty pastry. A bit of unsweetened whipped cream on the side is also a nice touch.

PROCESSOR PECAN PASTRY		
All-purpose flour	1 cup	250 mL
Icing sugar	1/4 cup	60 mL
Cold butter (or hard margarine), cut up	1/2 cup	125 mL
Finely chopped pecans	1/2 cup	125 mL
Egg yolks (large)	2	2
Cold water	1 tbsp.	15 mL
CARAMEL FILLING		
Butter (or hard margarine)	1/3 cup	75 mL
Can of sweetened condensed milk	11 oz.	300 mL
Brown sugar, packed	2 tbsp.	30 mL
Whipping cream	3 tbsp.	50 mL
BROWNIE TOPPING		
Butter (or hard margarine)	1/3 cup	75 mL
Granulated sugar	1/2 cup	125 mL
Semi-sweet chocolate, chopped	3 oz.	85 g
Large egg	1	1
All-purpose flour	1/3 cup	75 mL
Cocoa, sifted	2 tbsp.	30 mL

Icing sugar, for dusting

Processor Pecan Pastry: Process first 3 ingredients in food processor until mixture is crumbly.

Add pecans. Pulse with on/off motion 2 to 3 times to combine. Add egg yolks and cold water. Process until dough forms a ball. Shape into flattened ball. Cover with plastic wrap. Chill for 30 minutes. Roll out on lightly floured surface to fit 10 inch (25 cm) tart pan with removable bottom. Line tart pan with pastry. Cover with plastic wrap. Chill for 30 minutes. Remove plastic wrap and place tart pan on baking sheet with sides. Lay 18 inch (45 cm) circle of parchment paper on top of pastry in tart pan. Press into tart pan. Fill with dried beans, rice or pastry weights. Tuck edge of paper under tart pan. Bake in 375°F (190°C) oven for 10 minutes. Carefully lift and remove parchment paper and dried beans. Bake for 10 minutes further until pastry crust is lightly browned around edge. Cool in tart pan.

Caramel Filling: Combine all 4 ingredients in large saucepan. Heat and stir on medium for

Sweet Designing

Sometimes it's not what you do, but how you do it. Fancy up the dusting of icing sugar by creating a pattern on the surface of the tart.

Cut 12 strips, 1/2 inch (12 mm) wide and 10 inches (25 cm) long, from thick paper. Arrange six paper strips, 1 inch (2.5 cm) apart, across the tart in one direction and the remaining six strips across the tart in the opposite direction, to form diamond shapes. Then dust with icing sugar. Carefully remove the paper strips.

Pictured above.

about 10 minutes until mixture is pale caramel colour and thick enough to ribbon.♦ Cool slightly until thick enough to spread. Spoon into baked pastry crust. Spread evenly. Let stand for about 30 minutes until set.

Brownie Topping: Put butter and sugar into medium saucepan. Heat and stir on medium low, without boiling, until butter is melted and mixture is hot. Remove from heat.

Add chocolate. Stir until melted. Add next 3 ingredients. Mix well. Spread over caramel filling. Bake in 350°F (175°C) oven for 25 to

30 minutes until just set. Cool in tart pan. Cover. Chill for at least 2 hours or overnight.

Remove from tart pan. Dust with icing sugar. Serve at room temperature. Serves 10.

1 serving: 570 Calories; 36.1 g Total Fat; 292 mg Sodium; 7 g Protein; 58 g Carbohydrate; 2 g Dietary Fibre

Pictured above.

♦ The caramel is the right consistency when you lift it with a spoon and, as it falls back into the saucepan, it makes and holds a ribbon-like shape on the surface for a few seconds.

Spring Tulips

Celebrate spring with this gorgeous dessert. The sorbet needs freezing time, so be sure to make it the day before. Prepare everything in advance for quick assembly just before serving. The biscuits become fragile when cool, so make a few extras. Any broken pieces can be used to decorate the sorbet.

TULIP BISCUITS

Icing sugar	2/3 cup	150 mL
All-purpose flour	1/2 cup	125 mL
Ground cinnamon	1 tsp.	5 mL
Egg whites, about 4 large	1/2 cup	125 mL
Butter (not margarine), melted and cooled slightly	1/4 cup	60 mL
Vanilla	1 tsp.	5 mL

RHUBARB SORBET

Chopped fresh rhubarb (or frozen, thawed)	2 lbs.	900 g
Water	1/2 cup	125 mL
Granulated sugar	2 cups	500 mL
Freshly squeezed orange juice	1/2 cup	125 mL
Freshly squeezed lemon juice	1 tbsp.	15 mL
Grenadine syrup, for colour (optional)	1 tbsp.	15 mL
Chopped candied ginger (about 3 oz., 85 g)	1/2 cup	125 mL

STRAWBERRIES IN ORANGE LIQUEUR

Sliced fresh strawberries (or frozen, thawed)	3 cups	750 mL
Granulated sugar	1/4 cup	60 mL
Orange-flavoured liqueur	1/4 cup	60 mL
Low-fat vanilla yogurt	1 cup	250 mL

Tulip Biscuits: Sift first 3 ingredients into medium bowl. Add egg whites. Mix until smooth.

Gradually stir in butter until well combined. Add vanilla. Stir. On well-greased baking sheet, spread 1 1/2 tbsp. (25 mL) batter into circle, approximately 7 inches (18 cm) in diameter (see photo 1). Bake in 375°F (190°C) oven for 5 to 6 minutes until edge is lightly browned. Immediately place biscuit on small inverted jar or glass (see photo 2). Gently press tea cup over biscuit (see photo 3). Leave on for 1 minute.♦ Remove tulip biscuit and store upright in airtight container. (Baked biscuits can be stored at room temperature for up to 1 week. If biscuits lose their crispness, heat in 375°F (190°C) oven for 3 minutes.) Makes about 18 tulip biscuits.

Rhubarb Sorbet: Combine first 3 ingredients in large saucepan. Bring to a boil on medium-high. Reduce heat to medium-low. Simmer, uncovered, for 45 minutes until rhubarb is mushy.

Add next 3 ingredients. Mix well. Pour mixture into 3 quart (3 L) shallow dish. Freeze for about 5 hours until set.

Put ginger into food processor. Pulse with on/off motion until very finely chopped. Add 1/2 of frozen rhubarb mixture. Process until smooth. Transfer to 2 quart (2 L) container. Repeat with remaining rhubarb mizture. Stir to combine batches. Cover. Freeze for at least 8 hours. (Sorbet can be kept in the freezer for up to 1 month.) Makes 7 cups (1.75 L).

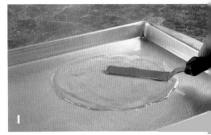

Strawberries in Orange Liqueur: Combine all 3 ingredients in medium non-reactive bowl. Stir. Cover. Chill for at least 2 hours, stirring occasionally, to blend flavours. (Strawberries can be prepared up to 1 day in advance.) Makes about 3 cups (750 mL).

On each of 12 dessert plates, assemble as follows:

1. Place 1/2 tsp. (2 mL) yogurt in centre of dessert plate to prevent Tulip Biscuit from slipping. Set biscuit on top.

2. Place 2 medium scoops of Rhubarb Sorbet into each biscuit.

3. Top with 3 tbsp. (50 mL) Strawberries in Orange Liqueur.

4. Decorate top with 1 tbsp. (15 mL) yogurt.

Repeat for 12 desserts. Break remaining biscuits into pieces to top each dessert. Serve immediately. Makes 12 desserts.

1 dessert: 338 Calories; 4.9 g Total Fat; 84 mg Sodium; 4 g Protein; 69 g Carbohydrate; 1 g Dietary Fibre

Pictured at left.

♦*Once comfortable with this technique, you can bake 2 biscuits at a time, but work quickly. The second biscuit needs to be hot when it goes onto the jar; if it cools too quickly on the pan, return it to the oven for 1 minute to soften.*

Banana Macadamia Sundaes

Kids will call it a great sundae; adults will think of it as a wonderfully decadent dessert. But everyone will agree that the combination of caramel, chocolate and banana is simply outstanding. Once the sauces are made, it's quick to assemble the layers of flavours.

CARAMEL SAUCE

Brown sugar, packed	1/2 cup	125 mL
Butter (not margarine), cut up	1/3 cup	75 mL
Whipping cream	1/3 cup	75 mL
Vanilla	1/2 tsp.	2 mL

CHOCOLATE FUDGE SAUCE

Whipping cream	1/2 cup	125 mL
Semi-sweet chocolate, chopped	3 1/2 oz.	100 g
Large marshmallows, chopped	6	6
Chocolate ice cream, approximately	3 cups	750 mL
Ripe medium bananas	6	6
Whipped cream	1 1/2 cups	375 mL
Macadamia nuts, toasted,♦ coarsely chopped	3/4 cup	175 mL

Caramel Sauce: Combine all 4 ingredients in medium saucepan. Heat and stir on medium until sugar is dissolved and butter is melted.

Bring to a boil on medium. Boil gently, without stirring, for 5 minutes. Remove from heat. Makes about 2/3 cup (150 mL) caramel sauce. Serve slightly warm.

Chocolate Fudge Sauce: Combine whipping cream, chocolate and marshmallows in medium saucepan. Heat and stir on medium until mixture is smooth. Makes about 1 cup (250 mL) fudge sauce. Serve slightly warm.

In each of six 1 1/2 cup (375 mL) capacity serving glasses, such as parfait or large wine glasses, layer as follows:

1. 1 scoop of ice cream (about 1/4 cup, 60 mL)
2. 1/2 banana, sliced
3. 1 1/2 tbsp. (25 mL) Caramel Sauce
4. 2 tbsp. (30 mL) whipped cream
5. 1 tbsp. (15 mL) macadamia nuts
6. 1 scoop of ice cream (about 1/4 cup, 60 mL)
7. 1/2 banana, sliced
8. 2 1/2 tbsp. (37 mL) Chocolate Fudge Sauce
9. 2 tbsp. (30 mL) whipped cream
10. 1 tbsp. (15 mL) macadamia nuts

Makes 6 sundaes.

1 sundae: 854 Calories; 58.4 g Total Fat; 202 mg Sodium; 8 g Protein; 86 g Carbohydrate; 5 g Dietary Fibre

Pictured below.

♦To toast the macadamia nuts, place them in an ungreased frying pan. Heat on medium, stirring often, until golden.

Chocolate Dips

Chocolate-covered banana chips are a pretty way to top off these sundaes. Plan on three chips per sundae.

Line a baking sheet with parchment paper. For 18 banana chips, chop up 2 oz. (56 g) of semi-sweet chocolate. Heat and stir the chocolate in a small non-reactive or glass bowl set over a small saucepan of simmering water until just melted (two to three minutes). Dip half of each banana chip in chocolate, allowing the excess to drip back into the bowl. Place the dipped chips on the parchment paper, then chill until the chocolate is set.

Pictured at right.

Apricot and Marmalade Pudding

This bread pudding is lighter in fat but still packs lots of flavour into every satisfying spoonful.

Dried apricots, finely chopped	1/3 cup	75 mL
Boiling water, to cover		
Baguette loaf, cut into 1/3 inch (1 cm) slices	1/2	1/2
Orange marmalade	1/3 cup	75 mL
Milk	4 cups	1 L
Large eggs	4	4
Granulated sugar	2/3 cup	150 mL

Put apricots into small heatproof bowl. Cover with boiling water. Let stand for 10 minutes. Drain well. Cool slightly. Gently squeeze apricots to remove excess water.

Spread one side of each baguette slice with marmalade. Arrange, marmalade-side up and slightly overlapping, in greased shallow 2 quart (2 L) baking dish. Sprinkle apricots over top.

Whisk next 3 ingredients together in large bowl or 8 cup (2 L) liquid measure. Carefully pour 1/2 over baguette slices. Let stand for 10 minutes. Stir remaining milk mixture. Carefully pour over baguette slices. Place dish in larger baking pan. Slowly pour boiling water into pan until water comes halfway up sides of dish. Bake, uncovered, in 325°F (160°C) oven for 1 1/2 to 1 3/4 hours until set and knife inserted in centre comes out clean. Remove dish from pan. Let stand for 20 minutes before serving. Serves 6 to 8.

1 serving: 328 Calories; 5.8 g Total Fat; 255 mg Sodium; 12 g Protein; 58 g Carbohydrate; 2 g Dietary Fibre

Pictured below.

Apricot and Marmalade Pudding, above

Special Bread Pudding

Smooth rum sauce and meringue topping elevate the humble bread pudding to a dessert fit for fine winter dining. For a change, try our Caramel Sauce, page 249, in place of the Rum Sauce.

— Connie Petherbridge, Whispering Hills, Alberta

White bread slices, with crusts, broken into small pieces	9	9
Granulated sugar	1 cup	250 mL
Can of 2% evaporated milk	13 1/2 oz.	385 mL
Milk	2 cups	500 mL
Vanilla	1 tsp.	5 mL
Egg yolks (large)	4	4
Butter (or hard margarine), melted	1/3 cup	75 mL
MERINGUE		
Egg whites (large), room temperature	4	4
Granulated sugar	1/4 cup	60 mL
RUM SAUCE		
Butter (or hard margarine), softened	1/2 cup	125 mL
Granulated sugar	1 cup	250 mL
Rum	1/4 cup	60 mL

Scatter bread pieces in greased shallow 2 quart (2 L) baking dish.

Whisk next 6 ingredients together in large bowl or 8 cup (2 L) liquid measure until well combined. Carefully pour over bread pieces. Let stand for 10 minutes. Bake, uncovered, in 350°F (175°C) oven for about 45 minutes until set and knife inserted in centre comes out clean.

Meringue: Beat egg whites in medium bowl until soft peaks form. Gradually add sugar, beating until stiff, glossy peaks form. Spread meringue over bread pudding. Bake for 5 to 7 minutes until lightly browned. Let stand for 20 minutes before serving.

Rum Sauce: Cream butter and sugar together in medium saucepan until light and fluffy. Bring to a boil on medium-high. Add rum. Boil for 2 minutes, stirring frequently. Makes 1 cup (250 mL) sauce. Serve immediately over bread pudding. Serves 8 to 10.

1 serving: 615 Calories; 25.5 g Total Fat; 479 mg Sodium; 12 g Protein; 83 g Carbohydrate; 1 g Dietary Fibre

Creamy Rice Pudding,
page 249

Hot Cross Bun
Pudding, below

Sweet Almond and
Cardamom Couscous
Dessert, page 241

Hot Cross Bun Pudding

We think this is as good for breakfast as it is
served for dessert. And keep it in mind come
Easter—what a great way to use up leftover hot
cross buns!

Hot cross buns, cut into 1 inch (2.5 cm) pieces	4 cups	1 L
Half-and-half cream	1 2/3 cups	400 mL
Plain yogurt	1/3 cup	75 mL
Large eggs	2	2
Brown sugar, packed	3 tbsp.	50 mL
Liquid honey, warmed	2 tbsp.	30 mL
Vanilla	1 tsp.	5 mL
Slivered almonds	1/4 cup	60 mL
Ground nutmeg, sprinkle		

Scatter bun pieces in greased shallow 2 quart
(2 L) baking dish.

Whisk next 6 ingredients together in medium
bowl or 4 cup (1 L) liquid measure until well
combined. Carefully pour 1/2 over bun pieces.
Let stand for 10 minutes.

Stir remaining cream mixture. Carefully pour
over bun pieces. Sprinkle almonds and nutmeg
over top. Place dish in larger baking pan. Slowly
pour boiling water into pan until water comes
halfway up sides of dish. Bake, uncovered, in
325°F (160°C) oven for 1 to 1 1/2 hours until
set and knife inserted in centre comes out
clean. Remove dish from pan. Let stand for
20 minutes before serving. Serves 6.

1 serving: 277 Calories; 13.2 g Total Fat; 171 mg Sodium;
8 g Protein; 32 g Carbohydrate; 1 g Dietary Fibre

Pictured above.

Shallow Recommendation

Slow, gentle, even baking is the key
to custard-like bread puddings. For
best results, use a shallow baking
dish that's 2 to 2 1/2 inches (5 to
6.4 cm) deep.

Apple Croissant Pudding

Dried apples and apple jelly are perfect in this brandy-flavoured pudding that makes good use of day-old croissants.

Chopped dried apple	2/3 cup	150 mL
Medium croissants	4	4
Apple jelly	1/3 cup	75 mL
Milk	2 cups	500 mL
Whipping cream	2 cups	500 mL
Large eggs	4	4
Granulated sugar	2/3 cup	150 mL
Brandy (or 2 tsp., 10 mL, brandy flavouring)	3 tbsp.	50 mL

Ground cinnamon, sprinkle

Icing sugar, optional

Scatter apple in greased shallow 2 quart (2 L) baking dish.

Cut croissants in 1/2 horizontally. Spread jelly on cut sides. Leave as is or cut each 1/2 into 3 equal pieces. Arrange, jelly-side up and slightly overlapping, over apple.

Whisk next 5 ingredients together in large bowl or 8 cup (2 L) liquid measure. Carefully pour 1/2 over croissant pieces. Let stand for 10 minutes.

Stir remaining cream mixture. Carefully pour over croissant pieces. Sprinkle cinnamon over top. Place dish in larger baking pan. Slowly pour boiling water into pan until water comes halfway up sides of dish. Bake, uncovered, in 325°F (160°C) oven for 1 1/2 to 1 3/4 hours until set and knife inserted in centre comes out clean. Remove dish from pan. Let stand for 20 minutes before serving.

Dust icing sugar over individual servings. Serves 8.

1 serving: 490 Calories; 28.7 g Total Fat; 286 mg Sodium; 9 g Protein; 49 g Carbohydrate; 2 g Dietary Fibre

Pictured above.

Cinnamon Bun Pudding with Caramel Sauce

This wonderfully rich bread pudding is complemented—and made even richer!—by the accompanying caramel sauce. Delish!

Large un-iced cinnamon buns, cut into 1 inch (2.5 cm) pieces (about 3 cups, 750 mL)	2	2
Milk	2 1/2 cups	625 mL
Large eggs	3	3
Brown sugar, packed	1/4 cup	60 mL
Pecans, chopped	1/3 cup	75 mL
CARAMEL SAUCE		
Brown sugar, packed	1/2 cup	125 mL
Butter (or hard margarine), cut up	1/2 cup	125 mL
Whipping cream	1/2 cup	125 mL

Scatter bun pieces in greased shallow 2 quart (2 L) baking dish.

Whisk next 3 ingredients together in medium bowl or 4 cup (1 L) liquid measure until well combined. Carefully pour over bun pieces. Sprinkle pecans over top. Let stand for 10 minutes. Bake, uncovered, in 350°F (175°C) oven for 40 to 45 minutes until set and knife inserted in centre comes out clean. Let stand for 20 minutes before serving.

Caramel Sauce: Combine all 3 ingredients in medium saucepan. Heat and stir on medium until brown sugar is dissolved and butter is melted. Bring to a boil. Reduce heat to medium-low. Simmer, without stirring, for 5 minutes. Makes 1 cup (250 mL) sauce. Serve warm over pudding. Serves 6.

1 serving: 593 Calories; 37.7 g Total Fat; 423 mg Sodium; 11 g Protein; 56 g Carbohydrate; 1 g Dietary Fibre

Pictured below.

Creamy Rice Pudding

"This recipe, which I have modified, was given to me in a Grade 5 cooking class (40 years ago)."
— Lise Mailloux, Vaudreuil-Dorion, Quebec

Basmati rice	1/2 cup	125 mL
Milk♦	5 cups	1.25 L
Granulated sugar	1/4 cup	60 mL
Large eggs, fork-beaten	2	2
Vanilla	1 tsp.	5 mL
Salt	1/2 tsp.	2 mL

Combine first 3 ingredients in large saucepan. Bring to a boil. Cover. Reduce heat to low. Cook for 25 to 30 minutes until rice is tender.

Combine next 3 ingredients in small bowl. Add 1 tbsp. (15 mL) rice mixture to egg mixture. Stir. Add egg mixture to rice mixture. Mix well. Cook, uncovered, on medium-low for about 40 minutes, stirring occasionally, until thickened. Serve warm or cold. Serves 6.

1 serving: 211 Calories; 4.1 g Total Fat; 327 mg Sodium; 10 g Protein; 32 g Carbohydrate; trace Dietary Fibre

♦*Note: Although Lise makes this recipe with skim milk, we tested it with 1%.*

Pictured on page 247.

Cinnamon Bun Pudding with Caramel Sauce, above

Peanut Butter Pie

You'll love every rich, creamy bite of this pie. It's the most delicious combination of chocolate and peanut butter—and more peanut butter.

— Colleen Mackin, Renfrew, Ontario

Hard margarine (or butter), melted	1/3 cup	75 mL
Graham cracker crumbs	1 1/3 cups	325 mL
Granulated sugar	1/4 cup	60 mL

FIRST LAYER

Box of instant chocolate pudding powder (4 serving size)	1	1
Milk	1 1/2 cups	375 mL
Peanut butter cups, chopped	4	4

SECOND LAYER

Whipping cream	1 cup	250 mL
Cream cheese, softened	8 oz.	250 g
Smooth peanut butter	1/2 cup	125 mL
Icing (confectioner's) sugar	1 cup	250 mL
Vanilla	1 tsp.	5 mL
Peanut butter cups, chopped	3	3

TOPPING

Whipping cream	1 cup	250 mL
Peanut butter cups, chopped	2	2

Combine first 3 ingredients in medium bowl. Press mixture into 9 inch (22 cm) pie plate. Bake in 375°F (190°C) oven for 8 minutes. Cool.

First Layer: Combine pudding powder and milk in medium bowl. Beat for 2 minutes until thickened. Spread in pie crust. Top with peanut butter cups.

Second Layer: Beat cream in medium bowl until soft peaks form.

Beat next 4 ingredients together in large bowl until smooth. Fold in peanut butter cups and whipped cream. Spread over peanut butter cups in pie plate.

Topping: Beat whipping cream in medium bowl until soft peaks form. Spread over second layer. Sprinkle with peanut butter cups. Chill for at least 3 hours or overnight. Serves 8.

1 serving: 685 Calories; 47.6 g Total Fat; 621 mg Sodium; 12 g Protein; 58 g Carbohydrate; 2 g Dietary Fibre

Pictured above.

Banana Coconut Ice Cream Pie

Take a few minutes—literally!—out of a busy morning to make this delightful treat and it's ready to serve after dinner. Chocolate curls and drizzles of extra caramel sauce make it even more impressive.

Caramel sauce	1/3 cup	75 mL
Prepared graham cracker crust	1	1
Thinly sliced bananas (about 2 medium)	1 2/3 cups	400 mL
Vanilla ice cream, softened	2 3/4 cups	675 mL
Medium coconut, toasted◆	1/3 cup	75 mL
Caramel sauce	2/3 cup	150 mL

Spread first amount of caramel sauce over graham crust. Arrange banana over top.

Combine remaining 3 ingredients in medium bowl. Mix well. Spread over bananas. Cover. Freeze for 6 hours or overnight. Serves 8.

1 wedge: 425 Calories; 15.6 g Total Fat; 362 mg Sodium; 4 g Protein; 72 g Carbohydrate; 1 g Dietary Fibre

◆To toast the coconut, place it in an ungreased frying pan. Heat on medium, stirring often, until golden.

Old-Fashioned Two-Crust Lemon Pie

"This is a beautiful pie that I have often made over the past 50 years." The homemade lemony filling is soft and smooth, and the top crust bakes to a golden brown.

— Olive Roy, Halifax, Nova Scotia

Pastry for a 2 crust 9 inch (22 cm) pie, your own or a mix	1	1
Cornstarch	1/4 cup	60 mL
Water	1/4 cup	60 mL
Boiling water	1 1/2 cups	375 mL
Granulated sugar	1 1/2 cups	375 mL
Hard margarine (or butter)	1 tbsp.	15 mL

Large eggs, fork-beaten	2	2
Finely grated lemon zest	2 tbsp.	30 mL
Freshly squeezed lemon juice	1/4 cup	60 mL
Brown sugar, packed	1 tsp.	5 mL
Water, approximately	1/2 tsp.	2 mL

Roll out 1/2 of pastry on lightly floured surface to 13 inch (33 cm) circle. Lay in 9 inch (22 cm) greased pie plate.

Combine cornstarch and first amount of water in small saucepan until smooth. Stir in boiling water. Heat and stir on medium until boiling and thickened. Remove from heat.

Stir in granulated sugar and margarine. Cool.

Stir in next 3 ingredients until well combined. Pour into pie shell. Roll out remaining pastry on lightly floured surface to about 10 inch (25 cm) circle. Place on top of lemon mixture. Pinch to flute edge. Cut slits in top.

Mix brown sugar with enough water to make spreadable consistency. Brush on top of pastry. Bake in 375°F (190°C) oven for about 30 minutes until crust is golden. Cuts into 8 wedges.

1 wedge: 434 Calories; 17.6 g Total Fat; 268 mg Sodium; 4 g Protein; 66 g Carbohydrate; trace Dietary Fibre

Variation: Substitute envelope of lemon pie filling (4 oz., 113 g, size), prepared according to package directions, for the filling.

Lemon Lore

Grating: Large, rough lemons are best used for grating. Choose lemons that are firm and heavy for their size, with bright, unblemished skin. Lemons will keep at room temperature for about one week. To keep longer, they should be stored in the refrigerator.

When a recipe calls for grated zest (yellow part of the peel) and juice, it's easier to grate the lemon first, then juice it. When grating, only grate in the same spot on the lemon three times, whether using the fine or medium grate. Any more than that and you'll remove the pith (white part of the peel), which is bitter and best avoided.

Freezing: Lemon juice, peel and zest all freeze well. Freeze the juice in an ice cube tray or small plastic containers so you only have to defrost as much as you need. Store the peel or zest in a resealable plastic freezer bag.

When fresh lemons are at their best in appearance and price, why not pick a peck of perfect lemons and stock your freezer!

Quebec Sugar Pie

You can't go anywhere in Quebec without finding this traditional *tarte au sucré,* and every home cook has her own recipe. Anne Jewett-Pagé always uses Canada #1 Extra Light maple syrup, whether she's cooking sweet or savoury dishes.

— **Anne Jewett-Pagé, Knowlton, Quebec**

All-purpose flour	6 tbsp.	100 mL
Brown sugar, packed	1 1/2 cups	375 mL
Butter (or hard margarine), melted	1/4 cup	60 mL
Salt, just a pinch		
Large eggs, fork-beaten	3	3
Maple syrup	1 1/2 cups	375 mL
Vanilla	1 1/2 tsp.	7 mL
Unbaked 9 inch (22 cm) pie shell	1	1

Combine flour and brown sugar in large bowl.

Stir in next 5 ingredients, in order given. Combine well after each addition.

Pour into pie shell. Bake in 350°F (175°C) oven for about 1 hour until top is browned and knife inserted in centre comes out clean. Let stand at room temperature to cool completely before slicing. Serves 8 to 10.

1 **serving:** 515 Calories; 13.4 g Total Fat; 211 mg Sodium; 4 g Protein; 97 g Carbohydrate; trace Dietary Fibre

Pictured above.

Yuba County Peach Pie

"This recipe has travelled north from California's Yuba County. Now made with Okanagan peaches, home is where the peach pie is!"

— **Marion Dendy, Kelowna, British Columbia**

Pastry for 1 crust 9 inch (22 cm) pie, your own or a mix		
Sliced, peeled ripe peaches (2-3 large)	3 1/2 cups	875 mL
Granulated sugar	1/2 cup	125 mL
All-purpose flour	2 tbsp.	30 mL
Salt, sprinkle		
Ground nutmeg	1/2 tsp.	2 mL
Half-and-half cream	1/2 cup	125 mL
Vanilla	1/2 tsp.	2 mL

Roll pastry out to 9 inch (22 cm) circle. Line ungreased pie plate. Arrange peaches in single layer, slightly overlapping, in bottom of pie shell in spiral pattern.

Combine remaining 6 ingredients in small bowl. Pour over peaches. Bake in 450°F (230°C) for 10 minutes. Reduce oven to 350°F (175°C). Bake for about 40 minutes until peaches are tender and crust is golden brown. If crust darkens too quickly, cover with foil. Cool until set. Serves 8.

1 **serving:** 194 Calories; 6.9 g Total Fat; 109 mg Sodium; 2 g Protein; 32 g Carbohydrate; 2 g Dietary Fibre

Elgin Pie

"This is a scrumptious pie and because it's rich, a little goes a long way. It's a real favourite among family and friends."
— Linda Rudachyk, Weyburn, Saskatchewan

Large egg	1	1
Vanilla	1/2 tsp.	2 mL
All-purpose flour	1/4 cup	60 mL
Granulated sugar	1/4 cup	60 mL
Brown sugar, packed	1/4 cup	60 mL
Butter (or hard margarine), melted	1/2 cup	125 mL
Chocolate chips	1/2 cup	125 mL
Chopped pecans, toasted♦	1/2 cup	125 mL
Butterscotch chips	1/4 cup	60 mL
Unbaked 9 inch (22 cm) pie shell	1	1
Whipped cream (optional)		

Beat egg in medium bowl until foamy. Add next 4 ingredients. Beat until well combined.

Add butter. Stir. Add chocolate chips, pecans and butterscotch chips. Stir until well combined.

Pour filling into pie shell. Bake in 325°F (160°C) oven for 30 to 35 minutes until filling is set and top is browned. Cool.

Serve with a dollop of whipped cream. Serves 8.

1 serving: 395 Calories; 26.7 g Total Fat; 266 mg Sodium; 3 g Protein; 37 g Carbohydrate; 1 g Dietary Fibre

♦*To toast the pecans, place them in an ungreased frying pan. Heat on medium, stirring often, until golden.*

ELGIN TARTS: Place 12 unbaked 3 inch (7.5 cm) tart shells on baking sheet with sides. Divide filling evenly among tart shells. Bake in 325°F (160°C) oven for 25 to 30 minutes until tops are browned. Cool. Makes 12 tarts.

Lime Meringue Pie

"One version of Caribbean lime pie has a custard-style filling made with condensed milk. This recipe is more typical of the lemon meringue pie familiar to Canadian cooks."
— Jennifer Cockrall-King, Edmonton, Alberta

All-purpose flour	1 cup	250 mL
Cold butter (not margarine), cut up	1/2 cup	125 mL
Egg yolks (large)	2	2
Cold water	1 tbsp.	15 mL
FILLING		
Granulated sugar	1 1/2 cups	375 mL
Cornstarch	1/2 cup	125 mL
Water	1/2 cup	125 mL
Freshly squeezed lime juice	1/2 cup	125 mL
Egg yolks (large)	3	3
Butter (not margarine), softened	2 tbsp.	30 mL
Boiling water	1 1/2 cups	375 mL
Finely grated lime zest	1 tsp.	5 mL
Green food colouring (optional)		
MERINGUE		
Egg whites (large), room temperature	5	5
Berry sugar	1 1/4 cups	300 mL

Measure flour into medium bowl. Cut in butter until crumbly. Mix in egg yolks and enough cold water to make smooth dough. Wrap in plastic wrap. Chill for 15 minutes. Roll out pastry on lightly floured surface to fit 9 inch (22 cm) pie plate. Line pie shell with parchment paper. Fill 1/2 full of dry beans or uncooked rice. Bake in 400°F (205°C) oven for 10 minutes. Remove beans and paper. Bake for 5 to 7 minutes until browned. Cool.

Filling: Combine first 4 ingredients in medium saucepan. Whisk until smooth.

Stir in egg yolks and butter until well combined.

Gradually add boiling water. Bring mixture to a boil. Reduce heat. Simmer, uncovered, for 1 minute. Remove from heat. Add lime zest and food colouring. Mix well. Turn into cooled pie shell.

Meringue: Beat egg whites until stiff peaks form. Gradually beat in sugar until dissolved. Spoon or pipe meringue onto filling. Bake in 350°F (175°C) oven for 10 to 15 minutes until lightly browned. Cuts into 8 wedges.

1 wedge: 744 Calories; 24.5 g Total Fat; 260 mg Sodium; 8 g Protein; 126 g Carbohydrate; 1 g Dietary Fibre

Pictured below.

Lime Meringue Pie, above

Deluxe Raspberry Pie with Butter Pastry

Everyone will save room for a slice of this lovely fresh raspberry pie. Make it a day or two ahead of your picnic and store well wrapped in the refrigerator. Allow it to lose its chill before serving for maximum flavour.

All-purpose flour	2 cups	500 mL
Icing (confectioner's) sugar	1/2 cup	125 mL
Butter (or hard margarine), cut up	3/4 cup	175 mL
Egg yolks (large)	2	2
Cold water, approximately	1/4 cup	60 mL

RASPBERRY FILLING

Fresh raspberries	6 cups	1.5 L
Granulated sugar	2/3 cup	150 mL
Cornstarch	1/4 cup	60 mL
Finely grated lemon zest	1 tsp.	5 mL
Freshly squeezed lemon juice	1 tbsp.	15 mL
Ground cinnamon	3/4 tsp.	4 mL

| Egg yolk (large), fork-beaten | 1 | 1 |
| Granulated sugar | 2 tsp. | 10 mL |

Process first 3 ingredients in food processor until mixture is crumbly.♦

With motor running, add first amount of egg yolks and enough cold water to just form a ball. Divide into 2 equal portions. Cover with plastic wrap. Chill for 30 minutes. Roll out 1 portion on lightly floured surface to 1/8 inch (3 mm) thickness. Line ungreased 9 inch (22 cm) pie plate with pastry. Cover with plastic wrap. Chill for 15 minutes. Roll out second portion of dough to 1/8 inch (3 mm) thickness for top crust. Cover.

Raspberry Filling: Combine first 6 ingredients in medium bowl. Let stand for 5 minutes.

Spoon filling into shell. Dampen edge of bottom crust with water. Cover with top crust. Trim and crimp edges to seal. Cover. Chill for 15 minutes. Cut slits in crust. Brush pastry with egg yolk. Sprinkle with granulated sugar. Bake in 375°F (190°C) oven for 40 to 45 minutes until pastry is golden brown. Cool completely in pie plate on wire rack. Serves 8.

1 serving: 478 Calories; 21.1 g Total Fat; 191 mg Sodium; 6 g Protein; 69 g Carbohydrate; 6 g Dietary Fibre

Pictured on page 130.

♦*Note: If you don't have a food processor, combine flour and icing sugar in medium bowl. Cut in butter until crumbly. Stir in egg yolks and water with fork.*

Mini-Pumpkin Pies

These small pie tarts remind us of the individual dessert pies served in the best restaurants. (They team beautifully with the Maple Orange Whipped Cream, page 255).

Pastry for 2 crust 9 inch (22 cm) pie, your own or a mix		
Large eggs	2	2
Can of pure pumpkin (not pie filling)	14 oz.	398 mL
Evaporated milk	1 1/3 cups	325 mL
Granulated sugar	1/2 cup	125 mL
Brown sugar, packed	1/4 cup	60 mL
Ground cinnamon	1 tsp.	5 mL
Ground ginger	1/2 tsp.	2 mL
Ground cloves	1/4 tsp.	1 mL

Roll out pastry to 1/8 inch (3 mm) thickness. Cut sixteen 4 inch (10 cm) circles from pastry. Line ungreased muffin cups with pastry circles. Cover with plastic wrap. Chill for 30 minutes.

Whisk eggs in large bowl for about 2 minutes until frothy.

Add remaining 7 ingredients. Beat until smooth. Divide pumpkin mixture among pastry shells. Bake in 375°F (190°C) oven for about 40 minutes until wooden pick inserted in centre comes out clean. Cool in pan for 10 minutes. Remove to wire rack. Makes 16 individual pies.

1 pie: 160 Calories; 6 g Total Fat; 144 mg Sodium; 4 g Protein; 23 g Carbohydrate; 1 g Dietary Fibre

Pictured at left.

Mini-Pumpkin Pies, right, with Maple Orange Whipped Cream, page 255

Mum's Apple Pie with Rich Shortcrust Pastry, below, with Maple Orange Whipped Cream, below

Mum's Apple Pie with Rich Shortcrust Pastry

A recipe that's come from quite a distance. *"This has always been a favourite of mine that my mum makes back home in Australia. She makes her own pastry, but for convenience you can use a pie crust mix; the end result is just as delicious. Mum always uses Granny Smith apples as their tart firmness is perfect for this apple pie. And butter—can't beat the flavour of butter, she says."* Make sure to serve it with our Maple Orange Whipped Cream, at right.

— Lovoni Walker, Edmonton, Alberta

All-purpose flour	1 3/4 cups	425 mL
Granulated sugar	1 tbsp.	15 mL
Cold butter (or hard margarine), cut up	3/4 cup	175 mL
Egg yolk (large)	1	1
Cold water	2 - 3 tbsp.	30 - 50 mL
Brown sugar, packed	1 cup	250 mL
All-purpose flour	1/2 cup	125 mL
Ground cinnamon	1/2 tsp.	2 mL
Ground nutmeg	1/2 tsp.	2 mL
Ground allspice	1/2 tsp.	2 mL
Ground cloves	1/4 tsp.	1 mL
Butter (or hard margarine), cut up	1/2 cup	125 mL
Medium tart cooking apples (such as Granny Smith)	7	7

Combine flour and sugar in large bowl. Cut in butter until mixture is crumbly. Stir in egg yolk. Add water, 1 tbsp. (15 mL) at a time, stirring after each addition, until soft dough forms. Shape into flattened ball. Cover with plastic wrap. Chill for 30 minutes. Roll out on lightly floured surface to fit 9 inch (22 cm) deep dish pie plate. Line pie plate. Cover with plastic wrap. Chill for 30 minutes.

Combine next 6 ingredients in large bowl. Cut in butter until mixture is crumbly. Sprinkle 1/3 of mixture over pastry.

Peel and core apples. Cut each apple into 8 slices. Arrange over brown sugar layer. Sprinkle remaining brown sugar mixture over apples. Bake in 425°F (220°C) oven for 45 to 50 minutes until golden. Serves 8 to 10.

1 serving: 593 Calories; 31.9 g Total Fat; 324 mg Sodium; 5 g Protein; 75 g Carbohydrate; 3 g Dietary Fibre

Pictured above.

Maple Orange Whipped Cream

Don't even think of serving regular whipped cream with your Thanksgiving desserts when this simply delicious recipe is sure to win raves from everyone. This makes enough to serve with Mum's Apple Pie with Rich Shortcrust Pastry, and with the Mini-Pumpkin Pies, page 254.

Whipping cream	2 cups	500 mL
Maple syrup	1/4 cup	60 mL
Orange-flavoured liqueur	3 tbsp.	50 mL

Beat all 3 ingredients together on medium-high in large bowl until soft peaks form. Makes 4 cups (1 L).

1/4 cup (60 mL): 121 Calories; 10.1 g Total Fat; 12 mg Sodium; 1 g Protein; 6 g Carbohydrate; 0 g Dietary Fibre

Pictured above and on page 254.

Sweet Treats: *Squares*

Cherry Chocolate Nanaimo
Bars, page 257

Cappuccino Nanaimo
Bars, right

Cherry Chocolate Nanaimo
Bars, page 257

Peppermint Nanaimo
Bars, page 257

Cappuccino Nanaimo Bars

Nanaimo Bars are only about a half century old, but they're so much a part of our culture that folks could be forgiven for thinking they've been around since Confederation! The original recipe is an all-time familiar classic, but you might like to add these tasty variations to your collection.

BASE

Hard margarine (or butter)	1/2 cup	125 mL
Granulated sugar	1/4 cup	60 mL
Cocoa	1/3 cup	75 mL
Large egg, fork-beaten	1	1
Graham cracker crumbs	1 3/4 cups	425 mL
Fine (or medium) coconut	3/4 cup	175 mL
Finely chopped walnuts	1/2 cup	125 mL

CAPPUCCINO LAYER
(or try one of the filling variations on page 257)

Instant coffee granules	1 tsp.	5 mL
Hot water	3 tbsp.	50 mL
Hard margarine (or butter), softened	1/3 cup	75 mL
Vanilla	1 tsp.	5 mL
Icing (confectioner's) sugar	2 cups	500 mL

TOPPING

Semisweet chocolate baking squares (1 oz., 28 g, each)	4	4
Hard margarine (or butter)	2 tbsp.	30 mL

Base: Heat first 3 ingredients in top of double boiler or in heavy saucepan on low until margarine is melted.

Add egg. Heat and stir until boiling and thickened. Remove from heat.

Stir in next 3 ingredients. Press firmly into ungreased foil-lined 9 x 9 inch (22 x 22 cm) pan.

Cappuccino Layer: Stir coffee granules into hot water in small dish until dissolved. Cool.

Beat margarine, vanilla and cooled coffee in medium bowl until combined. Gradually beat in icing sugar until smooth. Spoon onto first layer. Spread evenly. Let stand for 10 minutes. Pat smooth.

Topping: Melt chocolate and margarine in double boiler or heavy saucepan on low. Cool until still runny. Spread on second layer. Chill. Cuts into 36 squares.

1 square: 156 Calories; 10.3 g Total Fat; 110 mg Sodium; 2 g Protein; 16 g Carbohydrate; 1 g Dietary Fibre

Pictured on page 256.

Variations: Substitute one of these fillings for the Cappuccino Layer in the Cappuccino Nanaimo Bars.

CHERRY CHOCOLATE LAYER

Hard margarine (or butter), softened	1/4 cup	60 mL
Maraschino cherry juice	2 tbsp.	30 mL
Almond flavouring	1 tsp.	5 mL
Icing (confectioner's) sugar	2 cups	500 mL
Chopped maraschino cherries	1/3 cup	75 mL

Beat first 4 ingredients together in medium bowl on low until icing sugar is combined. Beat on high until well combined.

Drain cherries on paper towel. Stir into icing sugar mixture. Drop dabs randomly onto first layer. Spread evenly. Let stand for 10 minutes. Pat smooth.

Pictured on page 256.

PEPPERMINT LAYER

Hard margarine (or butter), softened	1/3 cup	75 mL
Milk	3 tbsp.	50 mL
Peppermint flavouring	1 tsp.	5 mL
Icing (confectioner's) sugar	2 cups	500 mL
Green food colouring		

Beat first 4 ingredients together in medium bowl. Add enough food colouring to reach desired colour. Drop dabs randomly onto first layer. Spread evenly. Let stand for 10 minutes. Pat smooth.

Pictured on page 256.

Pineapple Squares, below

Pineapple Squares

"This was a favourite Sunday dessert when my children were young. I don't get a chance to make this very much now that they are all grown up."
— Natalie Karbashewski, Edmonton, Alberta

All-purpose flour	1 3/4 cups	425 mL
Granulated sugar	1/2 cup	125 mL
Baking powder	1 tsp.	5 mL
Hard margarine (or butter)	1/2 cup	125 mL
Granulated sugar	1/4 cup	60 mL
All-purpose flour	2 tbsp.	30 mL
Can of crushed pineapple, with juice	14 oz.	398 mL
Large eggs	2	2
Granulated sugar	1/4 cup	60 mL
Medium coconut	1 1/2 cups	375 mL
Hard margarine (or butter), melted	1 tbsp.	15 mL

Combine first 3 ingredients in large bowl. Cut in margarine until crumbly. Press mixture in bottom of greased 9 x 13 inch (22 x 33 cm) pan.

Combine second amounts of sugar and flour in small saucepan. Stir in pineapple. Heat on medium until boiling and thickened. Cool slightly. Carefully spread mixture over base.

Beat eggs and third amount of sugar until thick and creamy. Stir in coconut and margarine. Spread over pineapple mixture. Bake in 350°F (175°C) oven for 30 to 35 minutes until golden. Cuts into 54 squares.

1 square: 74 Calories; 3.9 g Total Fat; 34 mg Sodium; 1 g Protein; 9 g Carbohydrate; Trace Dietary Fibre

Pictured above.

Fudge Brownies, page 259

Double Chocolate Peanut
Squares, page 259

Fudge Brownies

Thoroughly chocolate inside and out, these
are the fudgiest brownies ever—a chocolate
lover's fantasy!

Hard margarine (or butter)	3/4 cup	175 mL
Unsweetened chocolate baking squares (1 oz., 28 g, each), chopped	4	4
Large eggs	3	3
Granulated sugar	1 1/2 cups	375 mL
Vanilla	1 1/2 tsp.	7 mL
Salt	1/2 tsp.	2 mL
All-purpose flour	1 1/4 cups	300 mL
Chopped walnuts (or pecans), optional	1/2 cup	125 mL

Melt margarine and chocolate in small heavy
saucepan on low. Let cool to room temperature.

Beat next 4 ingredients together in medium
bowl. Add chocolate mixture and flour. Beat
until well combined. Spread evenly in greased
foil-lined 9 x 9 inch (22 x 22 cm) pan. Bake
in centre of 350°F (175°C) oven for 35 to
40 minutes. Wooden pick inserted in centre
should come out clean. Remove from oven.

Sprinkle walnuts over top. Cuts into 36 squares.

1 square: 110 Calories; 6.2 g Total Fat; 86 mg Sodium;
1 g Protein; 13 g Carbohydrate; 1 g Dietary Fibre

Pictured on page 258.

Double Chocolate Peanut Squares

Creating a tasty treat can be as simple as
opening a few packages. *"This is similar to
(the old chocolate bar) Cuban Lunch, but with
more peanuts!"*
— Lucy Rosenberger, Edmonton, Alberta

Package of semisweet chocolate chips	10 1/2 oz.	300 g
Package of peanut butter chips	10 1/2 oz.	300 g
Unsalted Spanish peanuts	2 1/2 cups	625 mL
Crushed ripple potato chips	2 1/2 cups	625 mL
White chocolate baking square, chopped	1 oz.	28 g

Melt chocolate chips and peanut butter chips
in small heavy saucepan on low. Add peanuts
and potato chips. Press into greased foil-lined
9 x 13 inch (22 x 33 cm) pan. Chill.

Melt white chocolate in small heavy saucepan
on low. Drizzle over top. Cut into squares with
hot knife. Cuts into 48 squares.

1 square: 130 Calories; 9 g Total Fat; 36 mg Sodium;
4 g Protein; 11 g Carbohydrate; 1 g Dietary Fibre

Pictured on page 258.

Coffee Apple Squares

Even better than your favourite coffee cake. These fragrant squares are topped with a luscious Caramel Icing that complements the flavours of apples and coffee.

Golden raisins	1/2 cup	125 mL
Instant coffee granules	1 tbsp.	15 mL
Water	1/2 cup	125 mL
Hard margarine (or butter)	1/2 cup	125 mL
Brown sugar, packed	1 cup	250 mL
Large egg	1	1
All-purpose flour	1 1/2 cups	375 mL
Baking powder	1 tsp.	5 mL
Baking soda	1 tsp.	5 mL
Ground cinnamon	1/2 tsp.	2 mL
Medium tart cooking apple (such as Granny Smith), peeled and grated	1	1

CARAMEL ICING

Hard margarine (or butter)	1/4 cup	60 mL
Brown sugar, packed	1/4 cup	60 mL
Milk	3 tbsp.	50 mL
Icing (confectioner's) sugar	1 2/3 cups	400 mL
Chopped walnuts	1/2 cup	125 mL

Combine first 3 ingredients in small saucepan. Bring to a boil. Remove from heat. Cool.

Cream margarine and brown sugar together in large bowl until light and fluffy. Beat in egg until smooth. Add raisin mixture. Stir. Turn into large bowl.

Sift next 4 ingredients together in separate small bowl. Add to raisin mixture. Stir.

Add apple. Stir well. Spread evenly in greased foil-lined 9 x 13 inch (22 x 33 cm) pan. Bake in 350°F (175°C) oven for about 25 minutes. Wooden pick inserted in centre should come out clean.

Caramel Icing: Heat margarine and brown sugar in small saucepan on medium until margarine is melted and sugar is dissolved. Add milk. Heat and stir until smooth. Remove from heat.

Gradually stir in icing sugar. Ice squares.

Sprinkle with walnuts. Cuts into 48 squares.

1 square: 76 Calories; 3.2 g Total Fat; 65 mg Sodium; 1 g Protein; 11 g Carbohydrate; trace Dietary Fibre

Pictured below

Frieda's Number 89

Folks are always asking Jean Paré how this recipe got its name. Here's the story, direct from Jean: *"Each tray of squares being photographed for my first cookbook, 150 Delicious Squares, was tagged with its name and a number for quick identification. When it came time to photograph #89, the name of the recipe was nowhere to be found. My daughter-in-law, Frieda, searched in vain. We finally decided to just shoot the photo and the unidentified squares have been Frieda's Number 89 ever since."*

Hard margarine (or butter), softened	1/4 cup	60 mL
Brown sugar, packed	1/2 cup	125 mL
Granulated sugar	1/2 cup	125 mL
Large egg	1	1
Vanilla	1 tsp.	5 mL
Sour cream	1/4 cup	60 mL
All-purpose flour	1 cup	250 mL
Baking powder	1 tsp.	5 mL
Salt	1/4 tsp.	1 mL
Ground cinnamon	1/4 tsp.	1 mL
Coarsely chopped cranberries, fresh or frozen	1/2 cup	125 mL
Chopped walnuts	1/2 cup	125 mL
Peeled, cored and coarsely chopped apple	1/2 cup	125 mL

TOPPING

Granulated sugar	1 tbsp.	15 mL
Ground cinnamon	1/2 tsp.	2 mL

Cream first 4 ingredients together in medium bowl until light and fluffy. Beat in vanilla and sour cream until combined.

Stir in next 4 ingredients.

Add next 3 ingredients. Mix well. Spread evenly in greased foil-lined 9 x 9 inch (22 x 22 cm) pan.

Topping: Combine granulated sugar and cinnamon in small bowl. Sprinkle over batter. Bake in 350°F (175°C) oven for 30 minutes. Wooden pick inserted in centre should come out clean. Cuts into 36 squares.

1 square: 69 Calories; 2.8 g Total Fat; 47 mg Sodium; 1 g Protein; 10 g Carbohydrate; trace Dietary Fibre

Pictured below.

Coffee Apple Squares, above

Frieda's Number 89, above

Orange and Almond
Squares, below

Orange and Almond Squares

Fruit and nuts were never better together than in these elegant squares that feature the flavours of orange, ground almonds and apricot jam. Stylish enough for company or as a hostess gift.

CRUST

Hard margarine (or butter), softened	1/2 cup	125 mL
Berry sugar	1/4 cup	60 mL
All-purpose flour	1 cup	250 mL
Hard margarine (or butter), softened	1/3 cup	75 mL
Berry sugar	1/3 cup	75 mL
Finely grated orange zest	1 tbsp.	15 mL
Large eggs	2	2
Ground almonds	1 1/2 cups	375 mL
Sliced almonds	1/2 cup	125 mL
Apricot jam, warmed and sieved	1/4 cup	60 mL

Crust: Cream first amounts of margarine and sugar together in small bowl until light and fluffy. Stir in flour in 2 batches. Spread evenly in greased foil-lined 9 x 13 inch (22 x 33 cm) pan.

Cream next 3 ingredients in small bowl until just combined. Add eggs. Stir until just combined. Stir in ground almonds. Press onto crust. Sprinkle with sliced almonds. Bake in 350°F (175°C) oven for about 25 minutes. Wooden pick inserted in centre should come out clean.

Brush with jam. Let cool in pan before cutting. Cuts into 48 squares.

1 square: 85 Calories; 6.1 g Total Fat; 44 mg Sodium; 2 g Protein; 7 g Carbohydrate; 1 g Dietary Fibre

Pictured above.

Mint Squares

"Here's a great recipe. I add food colouring to the icing for special occasions."
— Deborah Wainwright, Edmonton, Alberta

Semi-sweet chocolate chips	1 cup	250 mL
Half-and-half cream	1/2 cup	125 mL
Vanilla	1/2 tsp.	2 mL
Graham cracker crumbs	2 cups	500 mL
Icing (confectioner's) sugar	1/2 cup	125 mL
Chopped nuts	1/2 cup	125 mL
MINT ICING		
Hard margarine (or butter)	1/4 cup	60 mL
Icing (confectioner's) sugar	2 cups	500 mL
Milk	2 tbsp.	30 mL
Peppermint flavouring	1 tsp.	5 mL
Semi-sweet chocolate chips	1/4 cup	60 mL
Water	1 tbsp.	15 mL

Combine chocolate chips and cream in small saucepan. Cook on low for about 6 minutes, stirring often, until chocolate is melted. Stir in vanilla.

Combine next 3 ingredients in medium bowl. Add chocolate mixture. Press into greased 9 x 9 inch (22 x 22 cm) pan. Chill.

Mint Icing: Beat first 4 ingredients together in medium bowl. Spread over base.

Combine chocolate chips and water in small saucepan. Cook on low for about 4 minutes, stirring often, until chocolate is melted. Drizzle over frosting. Chill for 1 hour until firm. Cuts into 36 squares.

1 square: 113 Calories; 5.1 g Total Fat; 48 mg Sodium; 1 g Protein; 17 g Carbohydrate; 1 g Dietary Fibre

The Cutting Edge

To get the perfect square cut, choose the right knife.

For most squares, including those with a nut topping, use a long, sharp knife. Position your knife and just press down from the tip to the handle in one motion.

When your squares have a top layer of chocolate, heat your knife in hot water, dry it quickly with a paper towel (before it has a chance to cool) and press down slowly. The hot knife blade will help to soften the chocolate as the squares are being cut. Wipe the knife blade clean and repeat for each cut.

Use a hot, wet knife when cutting sticky squares such as caramel, wiping the blade clean between cuts. A long serrated knife and a sawing motion are best for cutting cake-like squares that tend to crumble easily.

Getting Squared Away

Bake the squares in a greased foil-lined pan, making sure there's about a 2 inch (5 cm) overhang of foil on each of the four sides.

Once the squares have been baked and cooled, or thoroughly chilled (depending on the recipe), take hold of the edges of the foil and lift the squares out of the pan onto a cutting surface. Carefully push the foil away from the squares so that it doesn't interfere with the cutting.

Trim about 1/4 inch (6 mm) from each side so you have a neat, uniform square. (Your family will be happy to eat the trimmings!) Decide on the total number of pieces you want, then start cutting.

Rich Chocolate
Brownies, below

Lumber Camp Squares, right

Rich Chocolate Brownies

Pecans and chocolate chips add great texture to these moist, rich, sumptuous brownies. Tofu adds valuable nutrients to this sweet treat.

All-purpose flour	1 cup	250 mL
Cocoa	1/2 cup	125 mL
Granulated sugar	2 cups	500 mL
Chopped pecans	1 cup	250 mL
Semisweet chocolate chips	1 cup	250 mL
Package of silken tofu (12.3 oz., 349 g), drained	1/2	1/2
Cooking oil	1/4 cup	60 mL
Large eggs	3	3
CHOCOLATE ICING		
Silken tofu, blended smooth	3 tbsp.	50 mL
Icing (confectioner's) sugar	1 cup	250 mL
Cocoa	1/4 cup	60 mL
Milk◆	1/2 tbsp.	7 mL
Chopped pecans	3 tbsp.	50 mL

Sift flour and cocoa into large bowl. Stir. Stir in next 3 ingredients.

Process next 3 ingredients in blender until smooth. Add to flour mixture. Mix well. Pour into lightly greased foil-lined 9 x 13 inch (22 x 33 cm) pan. Bake in 350°F (175°C) oven for about 35 minutes until set. Brownies will still be soft inside. Cool in pan. Cover. Chill for 2 to 3 hours until firm. Remove from pan.

Chocolate Icing: Combine first 4 ingredients in small bowl until smooth. Makes 1/2 cup (125 mL) icing. Spread over brownies.

Sprinkle with pecans. Cut into 32 pieces.

1 piece: 172 Calories; 7.7 g Total Fat; 8 mg Sodium; 3 g Protein; 26 g Carbohydrate; 2 g Dietary Fibre

Pictured above.

◆*For a dairy-free alternative, substitute soy milk for regular milk.*

Lumber Camp Squares

Adapted from an old Isle Madame church cookbook, Claire's fruit-filled version is a Doyle family favourite. *"We always serve these over the holidays. Friends and relatives love them."*
— **Claire Doyle, Isle Madame, Nova Scotia**

Peeled and finely chopped cooking apples (such as McIntosh)	1 cup	250 mL
Finely chopped dates	1 cup	250 mL
Finely chopped dried cranberries	1 cup	250 mL
Finely grated orange zest	1/2 tsp.	2 mL
Freshly squeezed orange juice	1/4 cup	60 mL
Boiling water	3/4 cup	175 mL
Baking soda	1 tsp.	5 mL
Butter (or hard margarine), softened	1/2 cup	125 mL
Granulated sugar	1 cup	250 mL
Large egg	1	1
Vanilla	1 tsp.	5 mL
All-purpose flour	1 1/2 cups	375 mL
Salt	1/2 tsp.	2 mL
TOPPING		
Butter (or hard margarine)	1/4 cup	60 mL
Brown sugar, packed	1/2 cup	125 mL
Flake coconut	1 cup	250 mL
Milk	1/4 cup	60 mL

Combine first 7 ingredients in large heatproof bowl. Cool.

Beat butter and sugar in medium bowl until light and creamy. Add egg and vanilla. Beat until well combined.

Sift flour and salt in medium bowl. Add to butter mixture in 2 additions, alternating with apple mixture. Pour into greased 9 x 13 inch (22 x 33 cm) pan. Bake in 350°F (175°C) oven for 35 to 40 minutes until wooden pick inserted in centre comes out clean.

Topping: Combine all 4 ingredients in medium saucepan. Heat and stir on low for about 3 minutes until butter is melted and sugar is dissolved. Spread topping over hot squares. Bake in 350°F (175°C) for about 10 minutes until topping is golden. Cool in pan. Cuts into 18 pieces.

Pictured on this page.

1 piece: 255 Calories; 10.1 g Total Fat; 240 mg Sodium; 2 g Protein; 41 g Carbohydrate; 3 g Dietary Fibre

Editorial Index

Contributor Index